HISTORY

OF THE

GREAT CIVIL WAR

1642–1649

BY

SAMUEL R. GARDINER, D.C.L., LL.D.

LATE FELLOW OF MERTON COLLEGE, OXFORD

IN FOUR VOLUMES

VOLUME I. — 1642 – 1644

THE
WINDRUSH
PRESS
LONDON

History of the Great Civil War
was first published by
Longmans, Green and Co.

This edition first published by
The Windrush Press
50 Edithna Street
London SW9 9JP
in 1987

Introduction © Christopher Hill 1987

ISBN 0 900075 10 4 (cased)
ISBN 0 900075 00 7 (paperback)

British Library Cataloguing in Publication Data

Gardiner, Samuel Rawson
  History of the Great Civil War.
  Vol. 1: 1642–1644
  1. Great Britain—History—Charles I,
  1625–1649 2. Great Britain—History
  —Commonwealth and protectorate, 1649–
  1660
  I. Title
  942.06'2   DA405

ISBN 0 900075 10 4
ISBN 0 900075 00 7 Pbk

Printed and bound in Great Britain by
Biddles Ltd, Guildford and King's Lynn

PREFACE.

THE present edition is substantially the same as the first, but a few slight alterations have been made in consequence of suggestions made by reviewers and friends. The authorities which I have consulted may be ascertained by the references given in the notes. The names of pamphlets in the British Museum Library are followed by the letters or numbers signifying the press mark. Of the inner life of the House of Commons we unfortunately know less during the Civil War than during the first year and a half of the Long Parliament. D'Ewes, dissatisfied with the course of events, grows much more reticent than he had formerly been, and two other diaries, those of Whitacre and Yonge, which I have used, I believe, for the first time, do not fully supply his place. Whitacre reports no speeches, and Yonge does so only occasionally. As Yonge wrote chiefly in symbols—particular marks being employed to represent all the commoner words—it requires a certain amount of preparation to read him, though, as an explanation of these symbols is prefixed to each of his four volumes, there is no real difficulty in the matter.

It is fortunate that since the publication of Warburton's '*Memoirs of Rupert and the Cavaliers*,' a considerable part of the MSS. which he used has been acquired by the Museum Library, not merely because there are letters in the collection of which he made no use, but because he neglected to take the trouble to read ciphered letters, even when the materials for doing so were to be found at the distance of a few pages. It will be seen that a part of a despatch of Digby's, written on the morning of the second battle of Newbury, yields interesting information of which no word appears in Warburton's transcript, though it must be acknowledged that he did not fail to indicate the fact that he had not printed the whole letter. Mr. C. H. Firth has also been kind enough to lend me his volumes of transcripts of Rupert's correspondence, containing many letters of which the originals cannot at present be found. The collection of the books of the Committee of Both Kingdoms in the Record Office is too well known to require special recognition. Unfortunately only two volumes of the letters received by the Committee—in many respects the most important of the series—have been preserved. Even better known than these are the Thomason Tracts in the Museum Library, that unequalled collection of pamphlets and newspapers which makes a residence in or near London absolutely essential to any historian of the Civil War ; whilst frequent visits to Oxford are rendered necessary by the existence of the Carte MSS. in the Bodleian Library, in which so much of Irish history lies concealed, and of the Tanner and Clarendon collections, in the latter of which are to be found increasingly as the war draws to a close the materials for setting forth the policy of the Royalist party.

Of the value of newspapers as a subsidiary source of knowledge, much of a very divergent character has been said. *Mercurius Aulicus*, the Oxford organ, remains untrustworthy to the end. Birkenhead, its writer, composes his attacks on the enemy under no sense of responsibility, and with the sole end of making Puritans and Parliamentarians ridiculous, though even in his work are sometimes included reports or despatches of Royalist commanders which add something to our knowledge. The Parliamentary newspapers begin hardly better. For some time they invent freely ; but either on account of the character of the readers for whom they catered, or on account of the competition to which they were subjected—fifteen or twenty weekly newspapers being published in London for one at Oxford—they mend their ways before many months are past.

A reader has, no doubt, to be on his guard against stories of
Cavalier outrages, especially upon women, which are probably
for the most part as imaginary as are, I hope, the stories which
were told in Ireland of both sides as habitually carrying babies
on the ends of pikes ; but when this sort of thing is set aside
as a common formula, there remains to the credit of the
London newspapers an evident wish to ascertain the facts, and
a constant habit of warning readers not to accept as certain
news which has just come to hand.

No one who writes about Montrose's campaigns will under-
estimate the value of Napier's *Memorials* and *Memoirs* of
Montrose. His industry has made it almost impossible to
discover any facts unnoticed by him. It is only in his description of battles that one hesitates to follow him, as there are no
signs of his having visited the localities, and it is certain that
Wishart and probable that Patrick Gordon, the authors on whom
he mainly relies, did not. Wishart especially is sometimes be
trayed into palpable error by his topographical ignorance, and
the knowledge that this is the case has made me doubt
whether I have arrived at anything like accuracy when I have
had to build on his evidence, even when I have been able to
correct it by the use of my own eyes.

In my inquiries on the spot into the topography of
Montrose's six great victories, I have had much valuable local
assistance, and I feel bound to express my hearty thanks to
those whose knowledge of the ground proved helpful—to Mr.
George Bain, the editor of the *Nairnshire Telegraph*, who conducted me over the field of Auldearn ; to Mr. R. F. O.
Farquharson, of Hoghton, on whose property is the site of the
battle of Alford ; to the Rev. Dr. Milne, of Fyvie, for his explanation of Montrose's position at Fyvie Castle ; and to Mr
A. M. Munro, of the City Chamberlain's office at Aberdeen, without whose antiquarian knowledge of the locality in which the
battle of Aberdeen was fought I should have been entirely at
fault, as the ground is now covered with streets.

I have also to thank the Earl of Leicester for his kindness

in allowing his copy of *Rinuccini's Memoirs* to lie at the British Museum for some time, thereby enabling me to use them in a leisurely fashion. These Memoirs were compiled by a priest from Rinuccini's papers after his death, and afford a good deal of information not to be found in the despatches printed in the *Nunziatura*, and contains a considerable number of unpublished documents. A description of the MS. is given by Mr. J. T. Gilbert in the Ninth Report of the Historical MSS. Commission, Appendix II., page 340. Mr. Gilbert has also printed in his *History of the Irish Confederation*, and his *Contemporary History of Affairs in Ireland*, a large amount of hitherto unused material.

Of the papers at Kingston Lacy, which Mr. Bankes was good enough to allow me to examine, the most important is the book of the Parliamentary Committee for Dorset, and some letters from Digby to Jermyn, which are shown by the marks on them to have belonged originally to the papers taken from Digby at Sherburn, most of which are in the Record Office.

No writer of the history of the Civil War can avoid the difficult task of forming a judgment on the character and aims of Cromwell. If this is to be done with even an approximation to success, it is absolutely necessary to take Carlyle's monumental work as a starting point. Every satisfactory effort to understand the character of a man must be based on his own spoken and written words, though it is always possible to throw in further light and shade from other sources.

To one seeking further knowledge two lines of inquiry present themselves—first, the examination of new evidence, and secondly the critical sifting of evidence which has long been before the world. With respect to the material falling under the first head, pre-eminent importance belongs to *The Clarke Papers*, of which the first volume has recently been edited by my friend, Mr. C. H. Firth, for the Camden Society. Mr. Firth has obligingly lent me the copies which he had made for a second volume, which will probably appear at no distant date. These copies have been quoted by me as *Clarke MSS.* to distinguish them from the printed volume. A third set of papers, bound in a folio volume, contain notes of the trials of Hamilton, Capel, and others involved in the second civil war, and have been quoted by me as *Clarke Trials*. I desire to express my obligations to the authorities of Worcester College, in whose possession the originals are, for permission to make use of this latter MS., which is still uncopied. Unfortunately, the reports of the trials were so badly taken as to be in many places unintelligible, but a good deal of matter of considerable interest may nevertheless be extracted from them. Taken altogether, these *Clarke Papers* bring strongly out the conservative and hesitating side of Cromwell's character, whilst they also bring us, as we have never been brought before, into the very heart of that army, in the midst of which Cromwell lived and moved, and enable us to trace the movements of political thought which afterwards developed themselves in the constitutional experiments of the Commonwealth.

Mr. Firth's discovery of the *Clarke Papers* throws every other accession of material into the shade, but valuable information is to be gained from the despatches of the French ambassadors and agents. Many of them have been copied from our Record Office. Montreuil's letters to Mazarin, however, are still only to be found in the Archives of the French Foreign Office. Another valuable source of information is contained in copies lately sent from Rome to the Public Record Office under the title of 'Newsletters,' and quoted by me as the *Roman Newsletters*. This title, however, fails to convey a true idea of their value. The writer was, as appears from internal evidence, a Tuscan priest residing in England, who, in the summer of 1647 was employed by Bellièvre to convey messages between him and the army leaders, and who therefore speaks, especially during the time of his employment, with an authority not usually enjoyed by a writer of newsletters.

In the second place arises the necessity of criticising the often-quoted pamphlets written at the time by Cromwell's enemies, which present a consensus of opinion to the last degree unfavourable to his uprightness of character. Subjecting these writings to the first rule of criticism, a large number of them may be peremptorily set aside, either as merely containing vague charges, or as produced by men who had no means whatever of knowing the truth. It would be sheer partisanship to treat in the same way the accusations brought by men of transparent honesty such as Lilburne and Wildman, both of whom had considerable means of becoming acquainted with the external facts of Cromwell's life. Yet these accusations stand in such startling contrast with all that we know of Cromwell from his own written and spoken words that, at the first blush, a conscientious inquirer is fairly puzzled.

Here, however, as in so many other knotty matters, the thread leading out of the maze is to be found by a strict adherence to chronology. It was with no little surprise that I found one charge after another melt away as I was able to fix a date to the words or actions which had given rise to hostile comments. Thus tested, the Cromwell of Lilburne and Wildman shows himself the same man as the Cromwell of the letters and the *Clarke Papers*—no divinely inspired hero, indeed, or faultless monster, but a brave, honourable man, striving, according to his lights, to lead his countrymen into the paths of peace and godliness. The investigation which I have thus conducted is the more conclusive because, whilst it shows that Cromwell was not a hypocrite, it also shows that it was the most natural thing in the world that other men should think him to be one.

An eighteenth century copy of a lost account of the siege of Colchester, which is quoted as 'Mr. Round's MS.,' was lent me by Mr. James Round, whose cousin, Mr. J. H. Round kindly accompanied me in my investigation of the sites connected with the siege, and placed at my disposal his store of local knowledge. As far as the social history of the period is concerned, I have been allowed by Sir Harry Verney to make use of the vast collection of private letters preserved at Claydon House. I have attempted in dealing with them to confine myself for the most part to such as throw light directly or indirectly on public affairs. Those of my readers who wish to continue their acquaintance with Sir Ralph Verney and his family have an opportunity of doing so in Lady Verney's *Memoirs of the Verney Family during the Civil War.*

Since the Hamilton Papers were published by me for the Camden Society I have been able again to examine, by the permission of Sir W. Fraser, K.C.B., who at that time had this valuable collection in his charge, the letters written in the early part of 1648 by agents of the Hamilton party. Several of these letters are in undeciphered cipher, and were consequently omitted in my volume, and they also find no place in Sir W. Fraser's report to the Historical Commission. On my second visit, however, I found that the ciphers used could be interpreted with the help of decipers interlined in other letters, and I was therefore enabled without much difficulty to make out almost every one of them. They are here quoted as *Hamilton Papers, Addenda*, and they will, I hope, be printed in the next volume of the Camden Society's Miscellany.

I ought to say a few words about the maps inserted in these volumes. Of the coloured maps, those which give the relative positions of the two English parties at certain dates have been constructed with the help of contemporary newspapers and letters. There must always, however, have been a certain number of private houses holding out for the King or for the Parliament which have escaped my researches, some of which indeed could hardly have been included in a map on so small a scale. The map of Ireland, as far as Ulster and Connaught are concerned, has been constructed in the same way, and is liable to the same drawbacks. The line separating the two parties in Leinster and Munster is distinctly marked in the text of the Treaty of Cessation, though even there fortified posts in possession of either party at the date of the treaty were to remain in the hands of those who held them. As to the other two provinces, the treaty merely states that each party shall hold its own. Consequently, unless where a post is of sufficient importance to be named in some contemporary letter, it would not come under my notice. The divisions of the clan territories in the map of the Highlands of Scotland are copied from those in the map in General Stewart's *Sketches of the Highlands*, but the colouring showing the side taken by each clan is taken from the statements of contemporary writers, though in one or two cases I have had considerable doubt about its accuracy.

Of the smaller maps, those of battle-fields have given me considerable difficulty. There are in existence modern maps of the principal battles in which the numbers and position of the combatants are laid down with great minuteness. It has frequently happened that I have been unable to satisfy myself as to the accuracy of these details, and I have preferred to allow my maps to be less full than to fill up the gaps in my knowledge by conjecture.

The two maps of the battles of Newbury are founded on 'A Map of the County of Berks . . . by the late J. Rocque,' in eighteen sheets, published in 1762, and therefore having spaces open which are now enclosed. To Mr. A. M. Munro I owe an indication of Milne's plan of Aberdeen, published from a survey taken in 1789, and therefore before modern buildings had sprung up, on which my plan of the battle is founded. The map of the siege of Bristol is taken, with some slight omissions, with the permission of the Rev. W. Hunt, from his work on *Bristol* in the series of 'Historic Towns.'

I wish it were possible for me to give adequate expression to my sense of the obligation under which I am to Mr. Firth. He has generously allowed me to draw on his vast stores of knowledge concerning the men and things of this period, and has been always ready to discuss with me every point of importance as it arose, often very considerably modifying the opinion at which I had originally arrived.

CONTENTS

OF

THE FIRST VOLUME.

————◦✧◦————

CHAPTER I.

CAVALIERS AND ROUNDHEADS.

CHAPTER II.

POWICK BRIDGE AND EDGEHILL.

CHAPTER III.

TURNHAM GREEN.

CHAPTER IV.

THE CRY FOR PEACE.

CHAPTER V.

THE TREATY OF OXFORD.

CHAPTER VI.

IRISH CATHOLICS AND SCOTCH PRESBYTERIANS

CHAPTER VII.

READING AND STRATTON.

CHAPTER VIII.

THE ROYALIST VICTORIES.

CHAPTER IX.

BRISTOL AND GAINSBOROUGH.

CHAPTER X.

GLOUCESTER AND NEWBURY.

CHAPTER XI.

THE IRISH CESSATION AND THE SOLEMN LEAGUE AND COVENANT.

CHAPTER XII.

WINCEBY AND ARUNDEL.

CHAPTER XIII.

PRESBYTERIANS AND INDEPENDENTS.

CHAPTER XIV.

LIBERTY OF CONSCIENCE.

CHAPTER XV.

THE COMMITTEE OF BOTH KINGDOMS.

CHAPTER XVI.

NEWARK, CHERITON, AND SELBY.

CHAPTER XVII.

THE PARTING OF ESSEX AND WALLER.

CHAPTER XVIII

MARSTON MOOR.

MAPS.

INTRODUCTION

Samuel Rawson Gardiner lived from 1829 to 1902. He was educated at Oxford, but his membership of the Irvingite sect precluded him from obtaining an academic post in that university: it no doubt contributed to his understanding of seventeenth-century Puritanism. He maintained himself by teaching in London; from 1872 onwards he was first Lecturer, then Professor at King's College, London University. His whole life was dedicated to the study of the English Revolution, starting with ten volumes running from the accession of James I in 1603 to the outbreak of civil war in 1642. The first two volumes of this vast work, published in 1863, were a flop, and had to be pulped. Undeterred, he proceeded with the next two volumes(1869), which sold 500 copies; and very slowly he won his way to recognition. He edited a dozen volumes for the Camden Society, and a volume of *Constitutional Documents* for the period 1625–60, which became a standard work. From 1891–1901 he was Editor of the *English Historical Review*. He published many other books and articles on his chosen period.

What distinguished Gardiner's work from that of his predecessors was his objectivity (within the limits of the assumptions of his age), his prodigious learning and his meticulous attention to detail. He ransacked the archives of the European countries with which England had diplomatic relations in the seventeenth century. He cycled round the civil war battlefields in England, Scotland and Ireland. All later historians of the period stand on his shoulders. He established the basic narrative for what he called the Puritan Revolution.

He was absorbed in getting the facts right, and rightly

arranged. A legend says that he refused to look at a new source casting light on 1654 until he had finished dealing with 1653. He eschewed generalisation, though he noted everything of importance; he often tucked away in footnotes points which seemed of greater significance to his successors; but he missed nothing. He had a flair for degutting a book or a pamphlet: often when I have found what I thought a revealing quotation from a seventeenth-century text, I have discovered that Gardiner had spotted that one sentence a century before me.

But although Gardiner did not indulge in the big generalisations, he had his assumptions, some those of his age, of which he was probably no more conscious than we are of our assumptions. Gardiner was descended from Oliver Cromwell's eldest daughter. A nonconformist himself, he invented or at least popularised the concept of 'the Puritan Revolution', a concept which now seems old-fashioned. And he thought of Parliament as representing 'the nation', and struggling for 'liberty'. Some of his successors pointed out that Parliament represented only about ten per cent of the adult males in the seventeenth century; they might have added that fifty per cent of the population were debarred from voting because of their sex. I would wish to ask 'liberty for whom to do what?' rather than speaking of liberty in the abstract: freedom for landowners might mean eviction for copyholders. But Gardiner's idea is still alive today in the USA and in other parts of 'the free world'.

Gardiner's assumptions were those of a liberal-minded middle-class Victorian Englishman. He thought Oliver Cromwell was 'the greatest because the most typical Englishman of all time'; 'the national hero of the nineteenth century'. In a watered-down form his interpretation of seventeenth-century history established itself as orthodoxy from his own day till the nineteen-thirties. Then a generation which had absorbed the ideas of Marx, Weber and Tawney became sceptical about the self-sufficiency of religion as a motive force, and replaced this orthodoxy by a new one. Now this Tawneyite orthodoxy is coming under challenge from 'revolutionists', and it is possible to look back more objectively to Gardiner. We are in no danger – I hope – of returning to what we may call 'vulgar Gardinerisations', so we can appreciate the many shrewd insights which he often failed fully to develop.

It will surprise some of Gardiner's detractors that at the very beginning of the first volume of his *History* he spoke of 'the laws by which the progress of human society is governed'. These laws, he said, 'work not irrespective of human agency, but by the influence of surrounding conditions upon human wills, whereby the activity of those wills is roused to react upon the conditions'.[1] I find that an agreeably dialectical way of stating that history is not just a chapter of accidents, not just one damn thing after another, but that events have long-term causes and consequences of which the actors are not always conscious. There is a certain dry sarcasm in Gardiner's description of the origins of political convictions: 'as often happens, an opinion based on political convenience took shape in men's minds as a conviction of absolute justice'.[2] Such remarks are thrown out by the way as he proceeds with his narrative.

I wish to quote at length two remarkable passages in which he discusses Scottish Presbyterianism. It was thanks to Presbyterianism that 'the Scottish middle class received its political education. Men learned to act together in the church courts, where they were not over-shadowed, as they were in their single House of Parliament, by great lords and ministers of state. It was not an education which would encourage variety of character. The established principles of morality and religion were taken for granted in every discussion. But if the system bred no leaders of thought, it bound man to man in an indissoluble bond'.[3]

'Every new social class as it rises into power needs, in proportion to its previous ignorance, a strictness of discipline which becomes unnecessary as soon as it has learned to bear lightly the responsibilities of its new position. That discipline in England was afforded to the middle classes by the rule, grasping, unscrupulous and immoral as it was, of Henry VIII. In Scotland it was by the Presbyterian clergy that the middle classes were organised, and the organisation thus given enabled them to throw

---

[1] *History of England, 1603–1642* (1883–4), I, p. 9.

[2] *History of the Commonwealth and Protectorate* (1894–1901), IV, pp. 203–4.

[3] *1603–1642*, VIII, pp. 308–9.

off the yoke of the feudal nobles and ultimately to assert their own predominance.

'It was with little thought of the political result of their rule that the clergy strove to maintain themselves in the position to which they had been elevated. . . . They strove by means of church discipline, enforced in the most inquisitorial manner, to bring a whole population under the yoke of the moral law. . . . The Scottish system . . . was not a rule for those alone who sought counsels of perfection, whilst the mass of mankind was left to content themselves with a lower standard of morality. In Scotland there was to be a parity of moral law as there was to be a parity of ministerial office. The fierce ruffians who in the sixteenth century had reddened the country with the feuds of noble houses, the rude peasants who wallowed in impurity, were made to feel the compulsion of a never-resting, ever-abiding power, which pried into their lives and called them to account for their deeds as no lay government, however arbitrary, could venture to do. Therefore the Scottish people has rightly venerated as its saviours those to whom it is mainly owing that, even in that race after material wealth which set in amongst a people whose soil was poor and whose climate was ungenial, it has ever kept in honour the laws of righteousness.

'The Scottish clergy were likely to be the last to perceive that what was possible in Scotland was impossible in England, or that a nation whose middle classes had been disciplined under the Tudor monarchy, and had already ceased to feel alarm at the pretensions of the nobility, would never place itself under the Presbyterian system. . . . Their superior social organisation would make them intolerant of a masterful ecclesiastical rule'.[1]

I have quoted at such length because, allowing for the slightly old-fashioned language, that seems to me a superb piece of sociological analysis and political evaluation. Gardiner, anticipating later researchers, saw witch persecution as an integral part of the discipline being imposed. Or take this analysis of the Laudian régime's opposition to the Feoffees for Impropriations, who collected funds in order to buy up church livings to which they presented Puritan ministers: 'of all modes of supporting a clergy

[1] *1642–1649* I, pp. 226–8.

yet invented, their maintenance by a body of capitalists living for the most part at a distance from the scene of their ministrations is, in all probability, the worst'. Nevertheless, he added, 'there are . . . times when the most irregular manifestations of life are welcome'; Laud was 'setting aside the life and energy of individual initiative in favour of the cold hard pressure of official interference'.[1] And of Laud's revival of the pre-reformation metropolitical visitation in 1634: 'like the levy of Ship Money, Laud's claim rested on precedents of undoubted antiquity. Like Ship Money, too, it contained the germs of a great revolution'.[2]

As opposed to our present 'revisionists', Gardiner did believe that there were analysable long-term causes of the English Revolution, although it was immediately provoked by 'a short-sighted conservatism . . . in both parties'.[3] His awareness of social and economic factors as well as religious is often forgotten. In his account of the 'line-up for civil war in 1642 he stresses social divisions.[4] Of the second civil war he said: 'the question of the supremacy of King or Parliament was giving way to a strife of classes'.[5] He noted that 'how to get the best soldiers was the problem which made Cromwell tolerant', a tolerance built on 'a material foundation'. Cromwell 'remained always the practical man, asking not so much what the thing is as how it can be done'.[6]

Readers will find for themselves many examples of such penetrating comments.

Gardiner anticipated the conclusions of research published long after his death, such as Valerie Pearl's *London and the Outbreak of the Puritan Revolution* (Oxford U.P., 1961);[7] Brian Manning's emphasis on the role of the London populace in bringing about the execution of the Earl of Strafford in *The English People and the English Revolution*;[8] and Caroline Hibbard's *Charles I and the Popish*

[1] *1603–1642*, VIII, p. 259.
[2] *Ibid.*, VIII, p. 107.
[3] *Ibid.*, X, p. 182.
[4] *Ibid.*, X, *passim; 1642–1649*, I, *passim.*
[5] *1642–1649*, IV, p. 192.
[6] *Ibid.*, I, p. 312.
[7] Cf. *1642–1649*, III, 8, 11, 22.
[8] *1603–1642*, IX, p. 361.

Plot (North Carolina U.P., 1983).[1] Unlike Professor Kishlansky and more wisely in my view, Gardiner stresses the financial reorganisation which accompanied the establishment of the New Model Army, and its effectiveness.[2] Unlike Professor Davis, who believes that the Ranters are a figment of historians' imaginations, and that for Gardiner they 'were a phenomenon which could be passed over in silence', Gardiner certainly did not miss them (he missed nothing) and he has a useful passage on their persecution and suppression.[3] Gardiner is as nearly infallible as a historian can be. I was once criticised for saying that the troops which were sent to the West Indies on Oliver Cromwell's Western Design of 1655 were those whom their regimental commanders wished to get rid of. I was able to silence my critic by quoting Gardiner's opinion.[4]

I have cited mainly passages in Gardiner's writings which have a bearing on present controversies about the nature of the English Revolution. Gardiner cannot be claimed by either side. He did not believe in the 'accident' theory of history, and he did believe in long-term causes. He wrote too early to have assimilated the sociological insights of Marx and Weber, but he was more aware that religion had a social function than is always appreciated. One of Gardiner's – to me – admirable qualities is his awareness of and use of English literature, anticipating Tawney in this. Gardiner's essay on 'The Political Element in Massinger' of 1876 was the first and is still I think the best piece of writing by a historian on the relations of Jacobean drama to the society for which it was written. It is characteristic of Gardiner that, though he is a great historian of Parliament, and edited many volumes of Parliamentary debates, he never supposed that politics consisted of the doings of kings and Parliaments only. The great writers and the poorest citizens were also part of the age which he studied so carefully and depicted with such insight and imagination.

[1] *1603–1642*, IX, pp. 222, 251, 265, and *passim; 1642–1649*, I, p. 246.

[2] M. Kishlansky, *The Rise of the New Model Army* (Cambridge U.P., 1979); *1642–1649*, II, p. 117.

[3] J. C. Davis, *Fear, Myth and History* (Cambridge U.P., 1986), p. 4; *1642–1649*, II, pp. 3–4.

[4] My *People and Ideas in 17th-century England* (Brighton, 1986), p. 172.

He knew his subject so intimately, he had such a knack of finding the right quotation to clinch an argument, such a grasp of individuality, that he made it impossible for his successors not to feel overshadowed by him.

It is possible to criticise him for his failure to synthesize, for his tireless empiricism and his intense religious involvement; others may regard these as virtues. His style never scintillates; there are no dazzling epigrams; like Bunyan's snail, he

> 'goes but softly, but he goeth sure . . .
> And certainly they that do travel so
> The prize they do aim at they do procure'.

Gardiner has in the recent past been more often criticised than read. But even those who disagree with him cannot ignore his pioneering labours, least of all in the present crisis in interpretation of the English Revolution. The Windrush Press has rendered a great service in republishing these four of his eighteen volumes. Perhaps one day . . . ?

Christopher Hill
1987

THE GREAT CIVIL WAR.

CHAPTER I.

CAVALIERS AND ROUNDHEADS.

THE CIVIL WAR, the outbreak of which was announced by the floating of Charles's standard on the hill at Nottingham, was

1642.
Aug. 22.
The Civil
War.
rendered inevitable by the inadequacy of the intellectual methods of the day to effect a reconciliation between opposing moral and social forces which derived their strength from the past development of the nation. The personal characters of the leaders might do much to shorten or prolong the time of open warfare, but no permanent restoration of harmony would be possible till some compromise, which would give security alike to the disciples of Hooker and to the disciples of Calvin, had been not only thought out by the few, but generally accepted by the many.

On both sides the religious difficulty was complicated by a political difficulty ; and, amongst the King's followers at all

The war
party at
Nottingham.
events, it was from those who were least under the influence of religious motives that the loudest cry for war was heard. Men who had served in armies abroad, and who were familiar with the licence of camps ; Cavaliers who had stood by Charles on the day of baffled hopes when he had swooped down in vain upon the five members at Westminster, combined in that cry with many a gentleman of high temper and generous instincts, who might be indifferent to the character of the theology which was inculcated from the

pulpits, but whose moral irregularities gave him good reason to
dread the stern pressure of Puritan austerity.[1]

Such men soon discovered a leader in Charles's nephew,
Rupert, who, with the true instinct of a soldier, had come,
Prince   bringing his younger brother, Maurice, with him, to
Rupert.   place his sword at his uncle's disposal almost at the
moment when his elder brother, the Elector Palatine, was
slinking away from England to avoid the necessity of making a
choice between two parties, either of which might one day be
useful to him in supporting his pretensions in Germany. Of
Rupert, it was truly said that he was first and last a soldier.[2]
Coming at the age of twenty-three to that England which he
had only seen as a visitor, it was not likely that he would
interest himself in the deeper side of the controversy in which
he lightly engaged. It was enough for him that he had rebels
to contend against. Unfortunately for the cause to which he
attached himself, he came from a land in which the soldier
was everything and the civilian nothing. He despised courtiers
and politicians as heartily as he despised rebels. If he wisely
regarded as unintelligible the scruples of those who thought it
possible to make war in a legal and constitutional way, he also,
with less wisdom, set his face against those who thought it
possible to bring the war to an end otherwise than by complete
victory.

If Rupert had been as fit to meet all the exigencies of war
as he was to lead a charge of cavalry, it would have gone hard
with the King's enemies. As it was, he knew how to inspire
his followers with his own dashing energy and untiring courage ;
but though he was as capable of planning a campaign as he
was of conducting a charge, he was apt to lose his head in the
heat of battle ; and to despise his enemies too much to take
into account the full strength of their resistance. Charles at

[1] At Kidderminster, to take an instance from a lower grade, Baxter
found himself and his friends reviled by ' every drunken sot ; ' but ' when
the wars began, almost all these drunkards went into the King's army,
and were quickly killed, so that scarce a man of them came home again.'
Reliquiæ Baxterianæ, 42.

[2] Warwick, *Memoirs*, 227.

once appointed him General of the Horse. From one point
of view no better selection could be made. There was no fear
Rupert General of the Horse. now that the royal cavalry would turn their backs upon
the enemy as, three years before, they had turned their
backs, under Holland's command, upon the Scots at
Kelso. From another point of view the appointment was disastrous. Rupert demanded and obtained the privilege of taking
Lindsey Commander-in-chief. orders from the King alone.[1] The Earl of Lindsey,
devoted to the Royalist cause, and trained in the
severe school of the Dutch wars, had been named
Commander-in-chief, but was now informed that the cavalry
was not within his sphere of action. By this strange arrange-
Conditions under which he holds the command. ment, Charles repeated in the field the mistaken
tactics of his Cabinet. He wished to be himself
supreme in war as he had wished to be supreme in
government, and, as Strafford and Laud had found to their
cost, his only notion of the way in which supremacy was to be
secured was never to give his entire confidence to any single
person.

In his joyous and abounding self-confidence, and in his
contemptuous hatred of rebels, Rupert found himself in accord
The Cava-liers at Nottingham. with a feeling which prevailed even among the more
sober Royalists. That rebellion was an unpardonable
crime, was a maxim which had been inculcated upon
three generations of Englishmen. It had grown up at a time
when almost blind obedience to the sovereign had alone gua-
ranteed the nation—first against feudal anarchy at home, and
afterwards against spiritual and military aggression from abroad.
Such an opinion was certain to retain its hold upon Englishmen long after the cause which had brought it into existence
had passed away ; and there were not a few round Charles at
Nottingham in whose minds the political creed which they had
received from their fathers had been rekindled by the adverse
gusts of Puritanism.

Of the strength of this purely Royalist feeling over coarser
natures, something may be gathered from its hold upon men

---

[1] *Clarendon,* vi. 78.

who had nothing in common with gay riders like Rupert or with debauchees like Goring. Sir Edmund Verney, to whom the King had entrusted the care of the standard, had been in Charles's service from his boyhood, and had held the office of Knight Marshal for many years. A pure-minded and thoroughly religious man, his dislike of the Laudian practices had led both him and his eldest son, Sir Ralph, to vote steadily as members of the House of Commons in opposition to Charles's wishes.[1] Yet he could not endure to desert his master in his hour of peril. Finding his way to York, he explained to Hyde the motives by which he had been influenced. "You," he said, "have satisfaction in your conscience that you are in the right that the King ought not to grant what is required of him, . . . but, for my part, I do not like the quarrel, and do heartily wish that the King would yield and consent to what they desire, so that my conscience is only concerned in honour and in gratitude to follow my master. I have eaten his bread, and served him near thirty years, and will not do so base a thing as to forsake him ; and choose rather to lose my life—which I am sure to do—to preserve and defend those things which are against my conscience to preserve and defend : for I will deal freely with you—I have no reverence for bishops, for whom this quarrel subsists."[2]

Sir Edmund Verney.

[1] This appears from an allusion in a letter from Henry Verney, one of Sir Edmund's younger sons, who was at this time in the Dutch army. Henry was told that he could not expect promotion because Wycombe and Aylesbury were against him. These were the boroughs for which Sir Edmund and his eldest son sat. The allusion would have been unintelligible unless both had voted against the Court. Another son writes thus to Sir Ralph, "The opinion, I see, of the great ones most at the Court is that my father and you are all for the Parliament, and not for the King." E. Verney to Sir R. Verney. Aug. 12. *Verney MSS.*

[2] Clarendon's *Life*, ii. 66. That the religious question was at the bottom of the quarrel is here plainly asserted. D'Ewes more diffusely says the same thing when he writes thus :—" Above all, his Majesty's infelicity was that he had too vehemently and obstinately stuck to the wicked prelates and other like looser and corrupter sort of the clergy of this kingdom, who doubtless had a design, by the assistance of the Jesuits and the Papists here at home and in foreign parts, to have extirpated all the power and purity of religion and to have overwhelmed us in ignorance,

Less personal was the tie which bound Edmund Verney, a younger son of the Knight Marshal, to the Royal cause.

Edmund Verney the younger.

High-minded and chivalrous, as few of his companions were, he submitted his life to the stern duties imposed upon him by a religion firmly held and, in its essence, hardly distinguishable from Puritanism. Yet his warmth of character, combined with his military training—he had served first under the Dutch, and afterwards in the ill-fated Northern Army—fixed him on the side of Charles.

His letter to his brother.

"Brother," he wrote to Sir Ralph, who remained constant to the Parliamentary cause, "what I feared is proved too true, which is your being against the King. Give me leave to tell you, in mine opinion 'tis most unhandsomely done, and it grieves my heart to think that my father already, and I, who so dearly love and esteem you, should be bound in consequence—because in duty to our King—to be your enemy. I hear it is a great grief to my father.[1] I beseech you consider that Majesty is sacred. God saith, 'Touch not mine anointed.' It troubled David that he cut but off the lap of Saul's garment. I believe ye will all say ye intend not to hurt the King, but can any of ye warrant any one shot to say it shall not endanger his very person? I am so much troubled to think of your being of the side you are, that I can write no more ; only I shall pray for peace with all my heart ; but if superstition, and idolatry, which was doubtless the main cause that put the two Houses, with the help of the City of London and other parts of the kingdom, to enter upon this great, high, and dangerous design, that so they might the more easily compass and bring about a full and perfect reformation in the Church, which they evidently foresaw that it could not possibly be otherwise effected." D'Ewes's Diary, *Harl. MSS.* 163, fol. 324b. *The Memoirs of a Cavalier* cannot be quoted as genuine contemporary evidence, but they proceed from a shrewd writer in the next generation who had access to traditional information, and his account of the matter corresponds with that of D'Ewes and Verney. "My old comrades," the fictitious cavalier is supposed to write, "were some with us, some against us, as their opinions happened to differ in religion." Many of the contemporary pamphlets take a similar view of the situation.

[1] There is a touch of human nature in this. The father is displeased with his eldest son for doing precisely what he had only refrained from doing because of his own personal obligations to Charles.

God grant not that, yet that He will be pleased to turn your heart that you may so express your duty to your King that your father may still have cause to rejoice in you."[1]   There was but little worldly wisdom in this letter, and it cost the writer a brother's affection, till common misfortune brought together again the hearts which had been rudely severed ; but its warmth and impetuosity renders it the more instructive to those whose duty it is to trace the causes which gave to Charles some of the most faithful of his supporters.   Not the Puritans alone found in the writings of the Old Testament, composed under Eastern skies, an infallible guide amidst the political controversies of the Western world, especially when the language of those writings favoured conduct of which the reader happened to approve.

With all the fervour of an honest heart, young Edmund Verney might pray for peace, but there was nothing in his conception of the situation which was likely to hasten it.

The moderate Royalists.

More was to be expected from the little group which gathered round Falkland, and which included Spencer, Southampton, and Carnarvon.   It is true that such men as these had not much more reverence for bishops than the Knight Marshal had, but dread of a Puritan domination was common to them all.   They did not, indeed, wage war against it in the spirit of a convocation of divines.   What they disliked was the mental narrowness of its teachers.   Theirs was the rebellion of the modern world, with its intellectual inquisitiveness and its distrust of authoritative assertion, against the strict formulas of the Calvinistic creed, and the rigid insistence of its holders upon the due payment of the anise and cummin of human duty.   Their political ideas grew out of their intellectual principles.   Something, too, was due to their dread of social changes.   A great landowner, accustomed to an assured position in the world, would be hardly likely to welcome the claim of artisans and tradesmen to be heard on the questions of the day.   He naturally leant to the maintenance of authority, though he wished to see authority tempered and restrained

---

[1] E. Verney to Sir R. Verney.   Sept. 14.   *Verney MSS.*

by the opinion of the upper classes assembled in Parliament.
Yet, bitterly as these men were opposed to the rule of the
Calvinist preacher, they were no less bitterly opposed to the
rule of the soldier.   Their intellectual position combined with
their social position to bring them into sharp antagonism with
the military party, and they did their utmost to urge Charles
to reopen the negotiations with his Parliament, against which
he seemed to have firmly closed the door.

If Falkland and his friends had but little influence upon
the immediate course of affairs, it was not because their
opinions were moderate.   Nothing can be more falla-
cious than the popular belief that in times of revolution violent counsels prevail merely because they are
violent.   In reality they prevail because those who advance
them have a keen though limited perception of the conditions
under which they are called upon to act.   To be moderate, in
any real sense of the word, requires the highest powers of the
imagination.   He who would reconcile adverse parties must
possess something more than a love of peace and a contempt
of extreme doctrines.   He must have a clear and sympathetic perception of that which is best and noblest on either
side ; and it was the perception of anything good or noble in
Puritanism that Falkland and his associates were entirely
lacking.

Causes of their weakness.

The gay soldier, the modest country gentleman, the medi-
tative reasoner, do not complete the tale of Royalism.   One
figure is still lacking.   Edmund Waller remained
at Westminster, preferring the dishonourable post
of a spy on Charles's behalf to active service in the field.[1]
Rich, witty, and licentious,[2] the writer of smooth verses,
addressed sometimes to the Queen, whose favour he courted
as assiduously as he afterwards courted that of the Lord
Protector, or of Charles II., he regarded war and Puritanism
with equal aversion.   If occasionally, for fashion's sake, he
gave utterance to patriotic sentiments, in his heart he preferred

Edmund Waller.

[1] *Clarendon,* vii. 55.

[2] The testimony of D'Ewes to Waller's immorality has been printed
by Mr. Gosse.   *From Shakspere to Pope,* 89.

the sunny days spent at court to the clash of civil debate. There was no high imagination in his art or in his life, and when the war broke out he merely sought to make the best of an awkward situation.

It is easy to pass by a career such as Waller's with a sneer at the folly of poetical dreamers who engage in the hard reali-

Waller's literary position.

ties of political life. For those who wish to pene trate to the springs of human action it is difficult to find a more instructive personage in the whole course of the century in which he lived. It is little that, at the Court of Henrietta Maria, he threw himself ardently into the literary movement which substituted in poetry the balanced fall of that rhymed verse which reached its highest perfection in the hands of Pope for the chastened irregularity of the Elizabethan poets. What is important is that the causes which made him one of the most striking of the literary precursors of that style which is usually known as that of the Restoration, made him also a precursor of Restoration morals and of Restoration politics.

Something, no doubt, of that great law of reaction by which the courses of humanity are governed is visible in the adoption, by one whose own life was so dissolute as to cast off all moral restraints, of a scheme of poetry of which the chief characteristic is the subordination of independent thought and fancy to the severest artificial laws of style. Yet, even in this respect, Waller was floating on a tide which ran with a greater sweep than could be accounted for by the peculiarities of his individual character. The wild exuberance of the Elizabethan literature, wasting itself away in pretty emptinesses and frigid conceits, called aloud for writers who would place a curb upon its extravagances, if it were only the curb of form.

Elizabethan moral effort needed the curb as much as its poetry, and in men of lower aims the form imposed would

Waller's pure Royalism.

necessarily have but little connection with the spiritual realities of life. Not to forsake the pursuit of sensual pleasure but to combine it with social politeness became a second nature to Waller and his like. To honour the King, because he exercised no minute supervision over the conduct of his admirers, became the keynote of their simple politics, whilst peace was an object of desire, merely because it made it easier to pursue a career of self-indulgence. The pure Royalism of the Restoration already appeared in Waller in all its native offensiveness.

Yet, offensive as it was, it was of a piece with the other strivings of the time. Everywhere was to be seen the pursuit, not of liberty, but of a limiting order. The Royal au-

Its relations to other movements.

thority, the Book of Common Prayer, the Laudian ceremonies, were dear to many minds as stays to the weaknesses of their individual natures. Above all, it was Puritanism which gave to those whose energies were most self-centred the power which always follows upon submission to law. Puritanism not only formed the strength of the opposition to Charles, but the strength of England itself. Parliamentary liberties, and even Parliamentary control, were worth contending

Possibility of compromise.

for ; but on these points it would not have been difficult to discover some working compromise sufficient, if not to satisfy Charles, at least to satisfy his more reasonable supporters. On the other hand, the Parliamentary leaders had not yet committed themselves to the adoption of the complete Presbyterian system, which, with its apparatus of Church courts and its rigid orthodoxy, was almost as terrible in the eyes of those who looked hopefully to the free play of cultivated intelligence as it was to those who merely wished to give the rein to their animal passions. Yet even this Presbyterianism covered something greater than itself. The laws by which the progress of human society is governed work not ir-

The strength of Puritanism.

respective of human agency, but by the influence of surrounding conditions upon human wills, whereby the activity of those wills is roused to react upon the conditions. Therefore, it is not enough that the intellect be cultivated, or that forms of government or of worship be established to nourish the social feelings. Knowledge may cover the earth as the waters cover the sea, order may be secured, and reverence may be shown where reverence is due, but unless the resolute will be there to struggle onwards and upwards towards an ideal higher still, the gift will have been bestowed in vain.

It is the glory of Puritanism that it found its highest work
in the strengthening of the will.   To be abased in the abiding
presence of the Divine Sufferer, and strengthened in the assurance of help from the risen Saviour, was the path which led
the Puritan to victory over the temptations which so easily
beset him.   Then, as ever, it was not in the lap of ease and
luxury that fortitude and endurance were most readily fostered,
nor was it by culture and intelligence that the strongest
natures were hardened.   The spiritual and mental struggle
through which the Puritan entered on his career of Divine
service was more likely to be real with those who were already
inured to a hard struggle with the physical conditions of the
world, and whose minds were not distracted by too comprehensive knowledge of many-sided nature.   The flame which
flickered upwards burnt all the purer where the literature of
the world, with its wisdom and its folly, found no entrance.
It is not in the measured cadences of Milton, but in the
homely allegory of the tinker of Elstow, that the Puritan
gospel is most clearly revealed.

England, it has been said by one who, in our own days,
has exhibited the old Puritan virtues to a world which had
well-nigh forgotten them, has been saved by its adventurers—
that is to say, by the men who, careless whether their ways
are like the ways of others, or whether there may not be
some larger interpretation of the laws by which the world
is governed than any which they have themselves been
able to conceive, have set their hearts on realising, first in
themselves and then in others, their ideal of that which is
best and holiest.   Such adventurers the noblest of the Puritans
were.   Many things existed not dreamed of in their theology,
many things which they misconceived, or did not even conceive at all ; but they were brave and resolute, feeding their
minds upon the bread of heaven, and determined within themselves to be servants of no man and of no human system.   It
was with such as these that Falkland failed to count ; and to
fail to count with them was to neglect that very quality of self-
denying and therefore masterful purpose, the presence of which
saves Parliamentary majorities from dwindling into a mere

expression of predominant indolence, and the accumulation of knowledge from ministering to the satisfaction of learned drones.

Thus it came about that, whilst the noblest elements on the King's side were favourable to peace, the noblest elements on Militant Puritanism. the side of the Parliament were favourable to war. That it was so was not merely owing to the bitter memories which had been branded on the mind of the Puritan by long oppression. The man of intellect necessarily looks forward to a gradual process of amelioration which can but be checked by the interposition of violence. The man of strong moral purpose is no less prompt to think that the evil of the world can be removed or at least diminished by the intervention of power ; and in this particular case he had to dread, if Charles regained his authority, not merely the absence of power in his own hands, but its active exercise against himself.

If war there was to be, it was well that it should not be waged entirely on social or political grounds, and, above all, The war not a war of classes. that it should not degenerate, like the troubles of the French Revolution, into a war of classes. It is true that, on the whole, the nobility and gentry took the side of the King, whilst the townsmen and the yeomanry took the side of the Parliament. Yet there were enough of Puritan nobles and gentlemen, and enough of townsmen and yeomen who were not Puritans, to prevent the religious cleft from accurately coinciding with the social cleft.

Of the two parties, the Parliamentary was the more prompt to throw off the delusion that peace was still attainable. Six days before the Royal Standard was unfurled, the Houses had taken care Aug. 16. Pennington, Lord Mayor. to secure their position in London. On August 16, Isaac Pennington, a vigorous and determined Puritan, was chosen Lord Mayor in Gurney's room,[1] and the organisation of the City was thus secured for Parliament in spite of the notorious Royalism of the leading merchants. Every effort was made to hinder the transmission of arms and ammunition to the North. The newly raised soldiers, unused

[1] *L.J.* v. 297.

to the trammels of discipline, broke into the houses of
Search for
arms and
ammunition. suspected persons, rifled them of their contents,
Plundering
of the
soldiers. and often sold their booty for the merest trifle. As
might have been expected, the Catholics bore the
brunt of this violence; but they did not suffer alone.
Two members of Parliament had to complain that they had
been plundered by soldiers.[1] At Colchester, the mob, hearing
Aug. 22.
Disturb-
ances at
Colchester. that Sir John Lucas had collected arms and horses,
and was about to start with them for the North,
broke open his doors, sacked his house, and seized
upon his person. At the house of Lady Rivers, who, as a
Catholic, was specially obnoxious, property valued at 40,000*l.*
was destroyed or carried off. The House of Commons at
once despatched two of its members to restore order in Colchester; but, though no further acts of violence were committed, very little of the plunder was recovered.[2]

In Essex Royalists were few. In Kent opinion was more
divided. The means taken to secure the county for Parliament
Aug. 21.
Surprise of
Dover
Castle. were prompt and efficacious. Dover Castle was surprised on the 21st.[3] During the next few days a small
force visited the places where resistance was most
Kent
brought
under sub-
jection. likely to be made, imprisoning suspected Royalists,
and carrying off money and arms. The houses of
William Boteler and Sir Edward Dering were plundered. At Canterbury, arms and gunpowder were found stored
The soldiers
in Canter-
bury Cathe-
dral. in the deanery. The soldiers broke into the cathedral, battered down the organ, pulled up the com-
munion rails, and carried the table into the centre of
the choir. A representation of the Saviour embroidered on a
piece of tapestry they hacked out with their knives, and another
carved in stone and placed over the south gate was made a
mark for their bullets.[4]

[1] D'Ewes's Diary, *Harl. MSS.* 163, fol. 295b; *A relation of the
exploits of the London soldiers,* E. 114, 13.

[2] *C.J.* ii. 734; D'Ewes's Diary, *Harl. MSS.* 163, fol. 297b; *A message sent to Parliament,* E. 114, 30.

[3] *A relation of a brave exploit,* E. 115, 8.

[4] *Letter of Dr. Paske,* E. 116, 22. The Lords summoned Dr. Paske

The Houses did what they could to restrain the violence of the soldiers, and threatened them with the penalties of the law.[1]

The Houses try to restrain plundering.

In the immediate neighbourhood of London their efforts met with success, but they failed to secure obedience from troops scattered in country quarters. As it fared with the Parliament, it fared with the King. He,

The King's efforts in the same direction.

too, was never remiss in giving orders to his followers to abstain from plundering, but the troopers who were scouring the Midlands to collect arms in his name were no more likely to spare the goods of a notorious Roundhead than the Parliamentary soldiers were likely to spare the goods of a notorious Cavalier.

Charles's own mind mirrored alternately the views of the two parties which were disputing the mastery at his Court.

Charles asked to negotiate.

Scarcely had his standard been raised when he was besieged with entreaties to open negotiations. His ear was easily gained. He was not a man of blood, and his own position was well-nigh desperate. His followers were but few, and even if he were able to raise an army, he had as yet no means of supplying it with weapons. It is certain that he

Aug. 25. Negotiations to be opened.

was then and always sincerely anxious to make peace, if it could be made on his own terms, and it is not unlikely that he was glad, in view of the probable rejection of his overtures, to place his opponents in the wrong, or even to gain time to prepare for war.[2] A defeat of his troops in a skirmish near Coventry came opportunely to strengthen the party of peace, and on the 25th he despatched Southampton and Culpepper to Westminster to ask that commissioners might be appointed to treat for peace, and to declare his own determi-

before them to justify his statements. As he could not name the authors of the outrages, they ordered the Mayor of Canterbury to inquire whether any of the townsmen had participated in them. *L.J.* v. 360.

[1] *Id.* v. 327.

[2] This view of the case, which is thoroughly consonant with Charles's character, would reconcile Clarendon's statement that he wanted to test his opponents with Spencer's, who assured his wife that ' the King, when he sent those messages, did heartily desire ' an accommodation. Spencer to Lady Spencer. *Sidney Papers*, ii. 607.

nation 'to advance the true Protestant religion,' and 'to secure
the law of the land.'

The Lords, though they compelled Southampton to deliver
his message at the bar, threw no further obstacles in his way.

Aug. 27.
Southampton and Culpepper at Westminster.
In the Commons, a strong party wished to refuse
permission to Culpepper to address the House at all.
Strode asked that the question of expelling the messenger from his seat might first be taken into consideration, and when Pym, wiser than his more violent supporters, rose to oppose the ill-timed motion, an attempt was
made to hoot down the great leader of the party of resistance.
At last Culpepper was called to the bar. There the representative of the King, 'looking more like a culprit than a Privy
Councillor,' silently delivered his message in writing. A reply

Rejection of the proposed negotiation.
was almost immediately returned by both Houses, to
the effect that until the King had taken down his
standard, and recalled his denunciation of treason
against their members, they could not treat.[1]

The Houses, as well as Charles, had their own constitutional
scheme, the abandonment of which they regarded as worse than
war itself, and it was most improbable that any negotiation
would produce that responsible ministry and that Puritan settlement of the Church on which their hearts were set. Yet it can
hardly be doubted that their chief motive in rejecting the proposal made was their personal distrust of Charles. Their knowledge of his past intrigues led them to conclude that the present overture merely concealed an intention to gain time to
injure them.[2]

At all events, if the Houses rejected Charles's offer, it was
not because they underestimated the gravity of their situation.

Sept. 2.
Ordinance against stage-plays.
"Whereas," they declared on September 2, "public
sports do not well agree with public calamities, nor
public stage-plays with the seasons of humiliation,
this being an exercise of sad and pious solemnity, and the other

[1] *Rushw.* iv. 784; *L.J.* v. 326; D'Ewes's Diary, *Harl. MSS.* 163,
fol. 303b.

[2] This is the explanation of the Venetian ambassador, who was by no
means inclined to invent excuses for the Parliament.

being spectacles of pleasure too commonly expressing lascivious mirth and levity, it is therefore thought fit that while these sad causes and set times of humiliation do continue, public stage-plays shall cease and be forborne.' Prynne had his way at last, though the terms of the announcement were hardly such as to give him complete satisfaction.

Sad as the outlook appeared, there was no expectation at Westminster of a prolonged war. No one there believed that,

The war expected to be short.

if prompt measures were taken, there would be any difficulty in reducing the King to submission. They were quite sure that moral right was on their side. The seizure of arms and the plunder of suspected houses which, when it was the work of Parliamentary officers, was at worst an irregularity, was an intolerable crime in a Royalist commander. The nickname 'Prince Robber' was soon affixed

'Prince Robber.'

to Rupert. The imputation did him less than justice. Though the licence which Rupert allowed his soldiers surprised and shocked a generation which had never seen the face of war,[1] he did not enrich himself by plunder. It is strange that he had not contracted more of the vices of that evil school in which he had been trained.

At York, the Parliamentarians and not the Royalists were held to be the plunderers ; but there was no difference of opinion

The King's military weakness.

on the relative military strength of the two parties. " I know," wrote a Royalist lady in the North to a friend whose husband was a member of Parliament who still

Letter of a Royalist lady.

remained at Westminster, "he has chosen the strongest part, but I cannot think the best ; but am confident he does believe 't is the best, and for that he chose it ; but truly, my heart, it staggers me that he should not see clearly all their ways, being 't is so apparent ; for how 't is for the liberty of the subject to take all from them that are not of their mind, and to pull down their houses and to imprison them, and leave them

---

[1] *Rushw.* v. 1. "If the soldiers," wrote Rupert in answer to a charge of cruelty to prisoners, " did, as the law of arms allows them, strip some of their captains " (i.e. officers captured), " was I engaged either to prohibit them the making the best of their prisoners ?" *Prince Rupert, his reply,* 8122, d.

to the mercy of the unruly multitude, I cannot find that this is
the liberty of the subject ; nor do I find that it is in God's law to
take arms against their lawful King to depose him ; for sure they
have not made his person known to all those that they have
employed in this war to spare him and not to kill him ; [1] but I
trust God will protect him ; and, my dear, if any of my friends
fall in this quarrel, I trust their souls will be happy ; for sure
't is lawful to fight for one's lawful King. I did believe that they
would receive the King's message as they have done, when it
was sent ; for surely 't is not peace which they desire. Sure
they trust in that mighty host." [2]

Rupert was doing his best to give to his uncle some chance
of being able to resist 'that mighty host.' On September 6 he

Sept. 6.
Rupert at
Leicester.

Sept. 8.

appeared before Leicester, and summoned the town
to lend the King 2,000*l.* The citizens paid 500*l.*
and appealed to Charles for redress. Charles at
once disavowed his nephew, declaring that he ab-
horred the very thought of compelling men to lend him money
against their wills.[3]

Charles, it would seem, was still anxious to stretch constitutional formulas even against himself. Yet when he

Sept. 5.
Falkland
sent with
a second
message of
peace.

forbore the exaction of so large a sum of money
from a Puritan town, he must have known that war
was absolutely unavoidable except on terms which
he could not bring himself to grant. On the 5th he
had despatched a second overture to the Houses, and this
time he had entrusted its delivery to Spencer and Falkland,
the two men who, of all around him, were most anxious to
bring the negotiation to a successful issue. Charles's present
offer was that both the Parliament and himself should withdraw the accusations of treason which each had brought against
the followers of the other, and that he would then take down
his standard. Thus much upon their arrival Spencer and

---

[1] This is exactly the same language as that of Edmund Verney (*see*
p. 5), yet one letter was written from Ireland and the other from York.

[2] Lady Sydenham to Lady Verney, Sept. 2.   *Verney MSS.*

[3] Rupert to the Mayor of Leicester, Sept. 6 ; the King to the Mayor
of Leicester, Sept. 8 ; Warburton's *Rupert and the Cavaliers*, i. 393.

Falkland publicly said.[1] Privately, the Parliamentary leaders were informed by Falkland that the King was now ready to 'consent to a thorough reformation of religion,' as well as to anything else that they 'could reasonably desire.'[2]

Sept. 6.
A secret
message.

That Pym and his adherents should distrust Charles's sincerity was unhappily only too intelligible ; but only the violence of party spirit can explain the mode in which the Royal offer was rejected. The Houses declared that they would never lay down arms until his Majesty should withdraw his protection from all persons who had been or might hereafter be voted to be delinquents, 'to the end that both this and succeeding generations may take warning with what danger they incur the like heinous crimes ; and also to the end that those great charges and damages wherewith all the Commonwealth hath been burdened . . . since his Majesty's departure from the Parliament, may be borne by the delinquents and other malignant and disaffected persons ; and that all his Majesty's good and well-affected subjects who, by the loan of moneys or otherwise at their charge, have assisted the Commonwealth, or shall in like manner hereafter assist the Commonwealth in time of extreme danger, may be repaid all sums of money by them lent for those purposes, and be satisfied their charges so sustained out of the estates of

Declaration
of the
Houses re-
jecting the
King's offer.

Delinquents
to bear the
expenses of
the war.

---

[1] *L.J.* v. 338 ; *C.J.* ii. 752.

[2] This rests on D'Ewes's evidence. Writing on March 6, 1643, he says that the King ' at Nottingham, in August last past, during his distressed condition a little after the defeat of his troops near Coventry . . . did secretly intimate that he would consent to a thorough reformation in religion besides what else we could reasonably desire ; but then nothing would be accepted but that his Majesty must desert all those that had come to his assistance, and leave them to those men to dispose of their lives.' The date given would seem to refer the offer to the time of Culpepper's mission, but the last clause attaches it to that of Falkland. I have no doubt that the latter explanation is correct. It is most improbable that, if this offer had been rejected in August, Charles would have sent another mission in September. D'Ewes's Diary, *Harl. MSS.* 164. fol. 314b.

the said delinquents, and of the malignant and disaffected party in this kingdom.' [1]

Such a declaration could only be justified even by the authors of it on the ground on which, to say the truth, they

Character of the Declaration of Parliament.

always claimed to act, that they represented the nation, and that the King's followers were a mere handful of delinquents acting traitorously to the nation, and therefore liable to those penalties of death and confiscation of property which had been meted out by kings to all who had traitorously levied war against themselves. On any larger consideration it was as impolitic as it was unjustifiable. It was a sentence of confiscation suspended over the heads of all who had resisted the pretensions of Parliament. It completed the division of England into two opposite camps, and threatened to lengthen out the Civil War beyond all possible calculation. Up to this moment there had been nothing but hesitation at Nottingham.[2] There would be no hesitation now. Those who had been eager for peace would never accept it on such terms. Those who had been eager for war would no longer fear lest the King should abandon them to the vengeance of their enemies.[3] The threat of confiscation con-

Effect of this Declaration at Nottingham.

verted many a lukewarm supporter into an enthusiastic partisan. During the week which followed the reception of the Parliament's answer, recruits poured in from all quarters, and before many days Charles found himself at the head of an army of 10,000 men.

Parliament had given to Charles a numerous and loyal following, but it could not give him more. It was for himself to convert his resistance into a national movement. If he

---

[1] *L. J.* v. 341.

[2] Giustinian to the Doge, Sept. $\frac{8}{18}$. *Venetian Transcripts, R. O.*

[3] Both Clarendon and D'Ewes take the same view of the effect of the reply of Parliament. The latter (*Harl. MSS.* 163, fol. 318b) writes that by it the Houses ' made not only particular persons of the nobility and others, but some whole counties quite desperate . . . by which means without a special providence of God, they were likely to help the King in his distressed condition with those considerable forces which he was never else likely to obtain.'

could proclaim aloud what he had authorised Falkland to whisper in secret, he would have gone far to disarm opposition. Unhappily for himself, this was what he could not do. His proposal represented, at the most, but a passing mood. Having failed to do his work it was flung aside, with the sole result of increasing the suspicions of those to whom it had been made, when they saw concessions so distinctly held out and so recklessly abandoned.

The adoption by the Houses of a policy of confiscation was followed by a high bid for the assistance of the Scots.

Sept. 7. Episcopacy to be abolished. The General Assembly had lately suggested that unity of religion would prove the soundest basis of a political alliance. On September 7, the Commons, without a dissentient voice, approved of a letter in which the

Sept. 10. Scots were assured that episcopacy should be abolished, and this letter was ratified by the Lords.[1] It is true that the promise which it contained had no legal force, but it marked the time at which those who now posed as the nation set themselves to reorganise the institutions of the Church, not upon mature consideration of the whole conditions of the problem, but according to the exigencies of warfare.

Such pretensions could only be made good by overwhelming force, and at this time Parliament had every reason to

The military position. believe that such a force was at its disposal. On the 7th Portsmouth capitulated to Sir William

Sept. 7. Surrender of Portsmouth. Waller,[2] and, with the exception of Sherborne Castle, where Hertford still held out, all the South of England acknowledged the authority of the Houses. In the East and in the South, as well as in the Eastern Midlands, there was no sign of reluctance, and in those days the South and East of England contained by far the greater part of the

The Parliamentary army. wealth and population of the country. The principal army, with which it was intended to strike the decisive blow, was quartered about Coventry and Northampton, and reinforcements were daily being forwarded to it to increase

[1] *C.J.* ii. 754 ; *L.J.* v. 348.
[2] *A declaration of all the passages at the taking of Portsmouth*, E. 117, 10.

that numerical superiority over the King's army which it still possessed.

The Parliamentary army had all the weakness of new-levied troops, and it had special weaknesses of its own. Some Its want of of the soldiers of whom it was composed anticipated discipline. the stern Puritanism of the New Model, but there were others who were attracted by the prospects of a holiday, the expenses of which were not to fall upon themselves. On their way from London they broke into churches, burnt Communion rails, and tore up Prayer-books and surplices. A clergyman found wearing a surplice was held to be a fair mark for insult and outrage. Royalist houses were plundered, and fat bucks in Royalist parks shot down. Such men as these were hard to control. At one time a body of them broke into mutiny, demanding increase of pay. At another time a number of foot-soldiers were attacked and robbed by their comrades of the cavalry.[1]

Essex had too long delayed his departure for the army under his command. For some days he had been disputing Essex with the Parliamentary leaders on the title which he wishes to be was to assume. He wished to have the powers of a Lord High Constable. Lord High Constable, with full authority to negotiate terms of peace with the King.[2] The Houses naturally feared lest, by granting his request, they might give themselves a master, and probably the knowledge that in a recent debate Essex had expressed himself in opposition to the proposal to abolish episcopacy,[3] made them more decided in their refusal to give way to his wishes. It speaks much for the loyalty of Essex's nature that the refusal did not turn him aside from the Sept. 9. path of duty, though it was observed that when, on He takes September 9, he took leave of the Houses, his leave of the Houses. manner was less gracious than was to be expected even from a man so reserved as himself. Of the presence

---

[1] Wharton to Willingham, Sept. 3, 7; *Archæologia*, xxxv. 310.

[2] Giustinian to the Doge, Sept. $\frac{8}{18}$. *Venetian Transcripts, R.O.*

[3] Forster to Chavigny, Sept. $\frac{15}{25}$. *Arch. des. Aff. Etrangères*, xlix. fol. 157.

of the Commons on that occasion he took no notice whatever. "My Lords," he briefly said, "you have employed me
about a service which I am willing to undertake, and therefore I
desire to know what you will please to command me." He then
withdrew without waiting for an answer. Some little time afterwards, a large number of the members of the House of
Commons came to look for him, hoping to obtain some word
of recognition. They found him smoking in the Court of
Wards. He stood up and gravely saluted them in silence,
with his hat in one hand and his pipe in the other. That
afternoon he rode off towards Northampton, carrying with him
his coffin and his winding-sheet, together with the scutcheon

*Sept. 10.
Essex at
Northamp-
ton.* which would be needed at his funeral. This was
his reply to any who might doubt his fidelity.
When he arrived at Northampton he found himself
*Confidence
of his army.* at the head of 20,000 men. Scarcely anyone in
London doubted that he would make short work
with the King and his supporters.[1] If the gossip of the

---

[1] D'Ewes's remarks bring vividly before us the feeling of the time.
He had himself refrained from appearing at the leave-taking of the
General, not wishing to see him set off 'against his distressed Sovereign, being now reduced to the greatest calamity of any person living,
for he had sent twice to the two Houses within this fortnight several submissive messages to crave peace, which were rejected with infinite scorn
and contempt. His Majesty in person—having nothing but the name and
shadow of majesty left—was now at Nottingham, or near thereabouts,
and had wanted money for about a week's space to pay any of his soldiers,
horse and foot, who daily slipped from him ; and those who stuck to him
. . . were merely left to slaughter and destruction if they fought it out, to
punishment if they were taken, or to an ignoble flight if they would save
themselves. And, for such noblemen and gentlemen as had been drawn
to him by his own letters, and to whom he had given his promise to protect and defend them from violence, they were everywhere pursued, taken,
and made captives, and like to be utterly ruined in their fortunes, because
the two Houses of Parliament had already declared that the Commonwealth should be satisfied all the charges of this war out of their estates,
and that was likely to grow to an immense sum ; for we were now at
above 30,000*l.* charge weekly for the maintenance of the forces under the
command of the said Earl of Essex and his officers ; and great also was
the calamity everywhere of those counties in which his Majesty's forces or
ours came, neither side abstaining from rapine and pillage ; and, besides,

Royalists is to be believed, the conversation of his officers ran upon the ease with which Charles might be captured in his own quarters.[1]

the rude multitude in divers counties took advantage of those civil and intestine broils to plunder and pillage the houses of the nobility, gentry, and others, who were either known Papists, or being Protestants, had sent or provided horses, money, or plate to send to the King, or such as being rich they would make malignants.'—D'Ewes's Diary, *Harl. MSS.* 163, fol. 324b.

[1] The Queen to the King, Sept. 29. *Letters of Henrietta Maria,* 22.

CHAPTER II.

POWICK BRIDGE AND EDGEHILL.

WHEN Essex arrived at Northampton his intention was to march straight upon Nottingham. Charles, who, though he
1642.
Essex in-
tends to
march on
Notting-
ham.
Charles's
plans.
was no longer in danger of a surprise, as Essex still believed him to be, was not yet strong enough to accept a battle, resolved to march westwards in search of reinforcements. A body of 5,000 Welshmen were only awaiting his arrival to join him, and Shropshire and Cheshire had a sufficiently large Cavalier element to furnish him with a contingent.[1] Chester was the port of transit for Ireland, offering possibilities of future aid from that quarter.

On the 13th, Charles left Nottingham. If the gentry of Nottinghamshire and the neighbouring shires were mainly on
Sept. 13.
Charles
leaves
Notting-
ham.
his side, the opinion of the townsmen and the freeholders was against him. He therefore disarmed the trained bands, and distributed their pikes and muskets amongst his followers. On his way he sought to bind more closely to his cause all who now bore arms in his defence, by reiterating the assurances, which he had frequently given of late, that he had no intention of returning to the system of Laud and Strafford. On the 19th,
Sept. 19.
His mani-
festo to his
army.
on the road between Stafford and Wellington, he called his army round him : "Your consciences and your loyalty," he said, " have brought you hither, to fight for your religion, your King, and the laws of the land.

---

[1] Nicholas to Roe, Sept. 13; Nicholas to Boswell, Sept. 15. *S.P. Dom.* ccccxcii. 13, 14. *Special Passages*, E. 118, 10.

You shall meet with no enemies but traitors, most of them
Brownists, Anabaptists, and Atheists ; such who desire to
destroy both Church and State, and who have already condemned you to ruin for being loyal to us." He would promise
that, if God gave him the victory, he would 'defend and main-

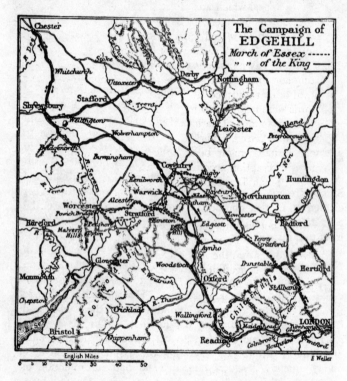

tain the true Reformed Protestant religion established in the
Church of England ;' he would 'govern according to the
known laws of the land, maintain the just privileges and
freedom of Parliament,' and 'observe inviolably the laws' to
which he had given his consent in the existing Parliament.
He hoped that if, in waging war, he was compelled temporarily
to violate the law, the mischief which would ensue might be

laid at the door of those who were the real authors of the war.[1]

The effect of this manifesto was all that Charles could wish. Those who heard him, and thousands more who subsequently read his words, enthusiastically responded to an appeal which was directed to one of the strongest of the permanent instincts of human nature: its desire to be guarded by the law and customs to which it has long been habituated. Charles's partisans, at least, did not care to remind him that it was mockery to ask those who believed that the existing law consecrated injustice to be content to wait for the removal of that injustice till the King and a complete House of Lords were ready to attend to their complaints.

Its effect.

Yet, even among Charles's own followers, voices of dissatisfaction were raised. Those who could think of no way in which Puritans might be conciliated were disgusted at the favourable reception accorded by Charles to Catholics. "How much I am unsatisfied with the proceedings here," wrote Spencer to his wife, "I have at large expressed in several letters. Neither is there wanting daily handsome occasion to retire, were it not for grinning honour. For let occasion be never so handsome, unless a man were resolved to fight on the Parliament side, which, for my part, I had rather be hanged, it will be said without doubt that a man is afraid to fight. If there could be an expedient found to salve the punctilio of honour, I would not continue here an hour. The discontent that I and many other honest men receive daily is beyond expression."[2]

Sept. 21.
Spencer's
letter.

Into this desire for peace, fear of the enemy no longer entered. On the 20th, Charles occupied Shrewsbury; on the 23rd he made himself master of Chester. The neighbouring gentry flocked in to fight for him, as they had flocked in at Nottingham. Exaggerated rumours of the mutinous state of the Parliamentary army were rife in the royal quarters. It was generally believed that Essex's men deserted as fast as they came in, and that

Sept. 20.
Charles at
Shrewsbury;
Sept. 23.
And at
Chester.

[1] *L.J.* v. 376.
[2] Spencer to Lady Spencer, Sept. 21. *Sidney Papers,* ii. 667.

those who remained with the colours were entirely beyond
Rumours of the mutinous state of Essex's army. control. Some of them, it was said, had jeeringly
refused to obey orders by calling out to the officers
who gave them, "We are all fellow-traitors here." [1]
Such men, it was thought, would either run away, or
desert to the King in the first engagement.

Such rumours were not entirely baseless. The city apprentices and country labourers, of whom Essex's army was
Condition of the Parliamentary troops. in great part composed, were as yet unaccustomed
to the control of military discipline. With large
numbers of them the old feeling, that it was a sin as
well as a crime to resist the King, had not yet died out. The
doctrine that they were summoned to fight for King and
Parliament was, indeed, no merely hypocritical pretext. Those
who announced it deduced from that constitutional doctrine
which Pym had enunciated in his assault upon Strafford—the
doctrine that the King is weakened and endangered by separating himself from Parliament—the principle that whoever
fought for Parliament was in reality fighting for the King as
well. Whatever might be said in its favour, it was, at least,
wanting in the directness which alone commends a principle
to ordinary minds. Men who had been trained up under
teachers who had assured them that rebellion was the worst
of impieties could not help feeling uncomfortable when they
were called on to march in battle array against the King in
person.

Whether, if the King had obtained the upper hand, the Parliamentary liberties of the country would have been safe in the
hands of the Spencers and the Southamptons is a question
which may be answered in various ways by different persons,
but there can be no doubt whatever that Puritanism would not
have been safe. To thousands of Englishmen, Puritanism was
the very Gospel itself, the voice of God speaking to a careless
Militant Puritanism. generation. Those who believed this were ready to
die rather than allow God's voice upon earth to be
silenced. If the existing law was against it, let the law be

---

[1] Nicholas to Boswell, Sept. 15. *S.P. Dom.* ccccxcii. 14.

broken. If Parliamentary majorities were against it, let them be
silenced. It was this feeling, entirely ignored by the Royalists,
which was already leavening Essex's army, and which was
ultimately to permeate the army of Fairfax and Cromwell.
Such a feeling demands something more than respectful recognition from those whose lot has fallen in days when strength of
conviction has no need to assert its rights by the sword, because it is allowed free space to win its way by the tongue and
the pen. It is to the pressure of determined minorities,
weighing, in the full light of freedom, upon lukewarm or hostile
majorities, that all worthy reforms are still owing. That the
use of force only renders the object aimed at more difficult of
attainment was precisely the fact which Charles and Hyde
were unable to perceive, and which, it must in fairness be
acknowledged, their Puritan opponents were also unable to
perceive.

If Charles could not understand the religious strength of
the army opposed to him, still less could he understand the
offence given by the rough and ready ways by which Rupert
was collecting supplies. The two motives for resistance were
significantly joined together in some letters from Nehemiah
Wharton, a subaltern in Essex's army. "Wednesday morning," he wrote, "we had tidings that Prince Rupert, that
diabolical cavalier, had surrounded Leicester and demanded
2,000*l.* or else threatened to plunder the town ; whereupon
our soldiery were even mad to be at them. . . . Friday morning, worthy Mr. Obadiah Sedgwick gave us a worthy sermon,
and my company in particular marched to hear him in
rank and file. Mr. John Sedgwick was appointed to preach
in the afternoon, but we had news that Prince Rupert had
plundered Marlborough and fired some adjacent towns, and
our regiment was immediately drawn into the field. . . . Sabbath-day morning, Mr. Marshall, that worthy champion of
Christ, preached unto us ; afternoon, Mr. Ash. These, with
their sermons, have already subdued and satisfied more
malignant spirits amongst us than a thousand armed men
could have done." [1]

[1] Wharton to Willingham, Sept. 13. *Archæol.* xxxv. 322.

The indignation with which Rupert was regarded was none the less genuine because many of the Parliamentary soldiers had been guilty of plundering innocent householders, or of shooting deer in the parks of the Royalist gentry. The time was now coming when the military ardour of the soldiers would be put to the test. On September 14, the day after the King quitted Nottingham, Essex reviewed his army at Northampton. He saw enough to convince him that there was no hope of maintaining order unless his troops were punctually paid. On the 15th he wrote to request the Houses to send him 100,000*l.* He was still confident that with that sum, and 'with God's blessing,' he should be able 'to bring these unhappy distractions to an end suddenly.'[1] The Houses, as usual, appealed to the City, and before long the new Lord Mayor was able to report that the collection of the money was going vigorously on. Voluntary in name, this contribution was not easy to evade. "The whole City," as the soldiers tersely put it, "were now either real or constrained Roundheads."[2]

Sept. 14. Essex reviews his army.

Sept. 15. And sends to London for money.

Sept. 17. Which is provided by the City.

As Essex looked to London, the King had no less naturally turned to Oxford for support. As early as July 11, the University and several of the colleges sent money and plate to the King. On August 13, an order was given for a view of arms. Graduates and undergraduates eagerly responded to the appeal. Books were flung away, and day after day some three or four hundred members of the University diligently practised their drill. On the 28th, Sir John Byron appeared with a body of the King's horse. An attempt was made to fortify the city. Bows and arrows were purchased to serve in the defence. Oxford, however, was, as yet, too far from the King's quarters to hold its own. The townsmen, for the most part, were favourable to the Parliament, and on September 10 Byron rode off, taking with him about one

July 11. Money sent to the King from Oxford.

Aug. 13. Drilling of the scholars.

Aug. 28. Arrival of Sir J. Byron.

---

[1] 'Suddenly' means 'soon.'

[2] *C.J.* ii. 772. *The Parliament's instructions.* E. 118, 11. *Common Council Journal Book*, Sept. 15, xi. fol. 38.

hundred armed scholars as volunteers, and what money he
Sept. 10. had been able to collect.   On the 12th, Colonel
Byron leaves Goodwin arrived at the head of a Parliamentary
Oxford.
Sept. 12. force, and on the 14th he was followed by Lord Say,
Oxford occu- who had come as the Parliamentary Lord Lieutenant
pied for
Parliament. of the county, to trample out the disaffection of
the University.

Say's conduct was as conciliatory as could be expected.
There was a bonfire in the street of 'Papist' books and
pictures, and the soldiers scoffed at the idolatrous
Sept. 14.
Say at windows in the Cathedral, and fired shots at the
Oxford. images of the Virgin with the infant Saviour in her
arms, over the gates of St. Mary's and All Souls. Say, however,
was lenient with the University itself. The Christ Church plate
he found hidden behind a wainscot, and this, with other concealed property, he adjudged to be lawful prize, but he told
the Fellows that as long as they kept their plate 'in places fit
for plate, the treasury or buttery,' it 'should remain untouched.'
Most of the colleges promised to comply with Say's require-
ment, receiving from him in return an assurance that there
should be no attempt to injure the liberties and privileges of
the University.[1]

Whilst Say was doing his best to establish the authority of
the Parliament in Oxford, Byron was making his way towards
Sept. 19. Worcester, which he entered on the 16th.   The
Byron at news quickened the movements of Essex, who broke
Worcester.
up from Northampton on the 19th, moving westwards
in a direction parallel with the King's march on Shrewsbury.
The next day he was told that Rupert was fortifying Worcester.
On the 22nd there was the rumour, which ultimately proved
false, to the effect that a battle was already raging before the
Sept. 22 city between Byron and a Parliamentary detachment
The march sent under Nathaniel Fiennes in advance of the
to Wor-
cester. main army.   Shouts of "To Worcester! to Worcester!" were heard along the ranks, and one regiment at

[1] Compare Wood's *Hist. of the Univ. of Oxford*, ed. Gutch, ii. 438,
with the dedication of Cheynell's *Rise, Growth, and Danger of Socinianism.* E. 103, 14.

least pressed on for two miles at a running pace. The next

Sept. 23.

day there was equal eagerness. The army was now but four miles from Worcester, and the soldiers were clamouring to be led to battle.[1]

The day did not pass without fighting. Worcester was no place to be defended against a superior force. Its walls were in ruin, and Byron had made up his mind to retreat. Rupert had arrived to cover his march ; but Rupert was not content

Rupert at Worcester.

with the simple fulfilment of so humble a task. Whilst Byron was preparing to march off with his treasure, the Prince rode out to the south with a small body of horse. Finding no enemy, the party dismounted to rest upon the grass. Suddenly Rupert espied a body of well-armed cavalry making its way towards him along a narrow lane. They were Fiennes' horse, who had been induced to leave

The fight at Powick Bridge.

their strong position behind the Teme at Powick Bridge by the news which reached them from Worcester that Byron was on the move. Flinging himself on horseback, Rupert called upon his followers to charge. In an instant the two bodies were in collision. The Royalists were without defensive armour, but they had the advantage, always so great with raw troops, of being the attacking force. The Parliamentarians were driven back in confusion as they attempted to struggle out of the lane. After a short resistance they broke and fled. For nine miles they did not draw rein, long after the enemy had ceased to follow them. At last, crossing the Severn at Upton, they came up at Pershore with Essex's body-guard of a hundred picked men, many of whom afterwards occupied high posts in that Cromwellian army where cowardice was never tolerated They were as yet new to war, and they too galloped in hot haste away from a foe who was many miles distant, and who had wheeled round as soon as victory was secured.[2]

[1] Wharton to Willingham, Sept. 26. *Archæol.* xxxv. 324.

[2] I have taken my account from Clarendon and the contemporary pamphlets. Compare Baxter's *Rel. Baxterianæ*, 42 ; Ludlow's *Memoirs*, 19. Wharton's letters of Sept. 26, 30 (*Archæol.* xxxv. 324), are especially interesting. It was the belief in the Parliamentary army that the

A successful skirmish could not save Worcester for the King, and on the 24th, having been evacuated by Rupert and Byron, it was occupied by Essex. On the ground that Worcester remained in the possession of the Parliamentary army, the London press, never weary of claiming victory in battles which had never been fought, declared that the King had been worsted at Powick Bridge. The Royalists, with better reason, asserted that the Roundheads had been defeated. They saw in their own success the certain assurance of a victory far more decisive.[1]

Worcester evacuated.

Sept. 24. Essex at Worcester.

The prisoners, wrote Falkland, were most of them raw soldiers, who acknowledged themselves to be 'tailors or embroiderers, or the like.' One of the officers, who had died of his wound, had with his last breath asked pardon of God and man for engaging in rebellion. Such men, Falkland thought, could not long resist the well-mounted and loyal gentlemen who followed the Royal standard.[2]

Sept. 27. Prediction of Falkland.

The view taken in this letter was that which was prevalent at Shrewsbury. When Charles returned from Chester he found his whole camp full of confidence. To a demand made by Essex that he would listen to a petition from Parliament in which he was asked to return to Westminster, leaving to their merited punishment the wicked persons by whom he had been misled, he replied that he would receive nothing at the hands of one who was a proclaimed traitor.

The King returns to Shrewsbury.

Sept. 28. And refuses to receive a petition.

man who induced Fiennes to move forward by reporting that Byron was going to leave was purposely employed to lead them into an ambush. Rupert's letter (*Rushw.* v. 24) seems, however, clearly to show that this was a mistake. The fight is described with much local knowledge in Webb's *Civil War in Herefordshire,* i. 144.

[1] Falkland to Cumberland, Sept. 27. E. 121, 122.

[2] *Letter of Falkland to Cumberland,* Oct. 7. E. 121, 22. A controversy sprang up as to the alleged confession of Sandys, the officer referred to. Whatever the truth may have been, the important fact is that Royalists should have thought it quite natural that those who fought on the other side should feel themselves guilty, as soon as their sin was brought home to them by sickness.

If it had been in his power he would have taken the field at once ; but, in spite of Rupert's efforts, he was still ill-provided with arms.   He had money enough to pay his infantry,

Plundering on both sides. but the horsemen had to forage for themselves, or, in other words, to plunder those whom they suspected of opposition to the King.[1]   It was a saying among the soldiers, that all rich men were Roundheads.[2]   In spite of all that Essex could do, the Royalist gentry in the neighbourhood of Worcester shared the fate of their opponents round Shrewsbury.   Essex assured the Houses that he and his officers had done their best to restrain these malpractices, but that he could not wonder at the misconduct of his men, 'seeing freedom of plunder was permitted on the other side.'[3]

Whilst the main armies were confronting one another, a series of local struggles had been going on in different parts of

Local struggles. England, and the result had, on the whole, been favourable to the Parliament.   A force detached by Essex had occupied Hereford.   Hertford had at last abandoned Sherborne Castle, and, crossing the Bristol Channel

Hertford in Wales. from Minehead, was doing his best to organise resistance to the Houses in South Wales.   For the present, however, the King had no partisans in arms in the West except Sir Ralph Hopton, who, with a small body of

Hopton in Cornwall. horse and a few of his friends, quitted Hertford at Minehead, and made his way to Cornwall.   Pendennis Castle [4] was in trusty hands and might serve him as a refuge if his call to Cornishmen to rise for the King met with no response.   Hopton was a man of singular force of character, and of no despicable skill as a commander ; but, as yet, his possession of these qualities was unsuspected, and no appre-

---

[1] " The horse have not been paid, but live upon the country." Spencer to Lady Spencer. *Sidney Papers*, ii. 667. This disposes of Clarendon's statement to the contrary.

[2] *A continuation of the late proceedings.* E. 121, 38.

[3] D'Ewes's Diary. *Harl. MSS.* 163, fol. 412.

[4] *The latest remarkable truths.* E. 240, 23. Hopton's Narrative, *Clarendon MSS.* 1738 (1). This document, which was for some time missing, has been recovered by Mr. Macray.

hension was felt at Westminster in consequence of his proceedings.

In the North, opinion was less in favour of Parliament than in the South. Yet even there the towns were mostly on its side. Manchester, the London of the North, as from its noted Puritanism it was scornfully termed by the neighbouring cavaliers, had been for some time besieged by Lord Strange, who now became Earl of Derby upon his father's death. On October 2, the new Earl was compelled to abandon the hope of taking Manchester.[1] In Yorkshire opinion was divided, and the gentry on either side agreed to hold their county neutral in the struggle which had already commenced elsewhere.[2]

Oct. 2.
The siege of Manchester raised.

Sept. 29.
Pacification of Yorkshire.

Whether it be true or not that Lord Fairfax only agreed to the pacification on condition of its obtaining the sanction of Parliament,[3] it was inevitable that the Houses would refuse their assent to an arrangement which would only serve to increase the forces of the King. If the Yorkshire gentry were freed from danger at home, they would place their services at Charles's disposal elsewhere, whilst it was unlikely that the citizens of Leeds or Bradford would leave their looms to take service under Essex at Worcester. Even in Yorkshire the pacification was not everywhere accepted. The Hothams were already disinclined to acknowledge the supremacy of the Fairfaxes, and the fact that Lord Fairfax had agreed to suspend operations served as a spur to the younger Hotham to distinguish himself by a military exploit. On October 4 he swooped down on Cawood Castle, which had been fortified by Archbishop Williams. Williams fled in terror, making no attempt at a

Oct. 4.
Hotham takes Cawood Castle.

---

[1] *A true and exact relation of the siege of Manchester.* E. 121, 45.

[2] *Fourteen articles of peace.* E. 121, 29.

[3] The protest of Fairfax is mentioned by Rushworth (iv. 686). But unless we knew the authority on which this statement was based, it would be impossible to say what value is to be attached to it. Nothing of the kind is to be found in Fairfax's own letter, nor does D'Ewes allude to it in any way.

defence.   A few days afterwards letters arrived from the
Houses, setting aside the pacification, and Hotham
was able to regard himself as the true interpreter of
the wishes of Parliament.[1]

The pacification broken.

In this way England was divided by an undulating line,
which left only the less wealthy and the less thickly populated
districts of the North and West to Charles.   Yet it
would be a mistake to estimate his strength solely
by geographical considerations.   Some of the counties, such as Worcestershire and Herefordshire, were strongly
Royalist in feeling, though they were for the present obliged
to dissemble their sentiments.   In many others the majority
of the gentry were either already gathered round Charles at
Shrewsbury, or were ready to support him at home if a favourable opportunity occurred.   A victory in the field might be
followed by serious consequences.   If the Royalist gentry
should, at any time, succeed in getting the upper hand, it
would be difficult to overthrow them.   They were accustomed
to take the lead in county business, and the smaller towns
would be too isolated to hold out long against them.   If
Parliament was to win, it must either gain a decisive victory at
the opening of the campaign, or it must substitute a new and
stronger organisation for that to which the country districts had
long been accustomed.   For the present the hopes of all men
were fixed upon the main armies.   One battle, it was generally
believed, would decide everything.

Respective strength of the combatants.

Now that it had become evident to all at Westminster that
the difficulties of the task had been underrated, increasing
anxiety was shown by Parliament to give a legal colour
to its undertaking.   In spite of opposition from the
plain-spoken Marten, the Commons ordered that
pamphlets containing attacks upon the King's per-
son should be publicly burnt.[2]   It was easier to do this than
to carry on war against the King without encroaching on the
King's authority.   For a time the demand for voluntary contri-

The Houses order the burning of disloyal pamphlets.

---

[1] *L.J.* v. 385.   *Special Passages.*   E. 121, 31.   *A declaration of Capt.
Hotham,* E. 121, 32.

[2] D'Ewes's Diary.   *Harl. MSS.* 163, fol. 417b.

butions had been liberally responded to, but that source of

Their need of taxation. revenue was already nearly exhausted. Nothing short of regular taxation would supply the require-

Which they are not yet ready to impose. ments of the army, and from regular taxation the Houses shrank. They continued to ask for volun-tary gifts or loans, but, like the benevolences de-manded by former kings, those voluntary payments were as like enforced taxation as possible.

It was unlikely that such a course would remain long unchallenged. A lawyer named Fountain refused to reply to

Oct. 5.
Imprison-ment of Fountain. a request for a voluntary gift, and appealed to the Petition of Right. The Petition of Right, said Marten bluntly, was intended to restrain kings, not to restrain Parliaments. Fountain was finally sent to prison for contempt in refusing to answer. A committee was ap-pointed to prepare a declaration, asserting that the Houses were legally entitled to require a contribution, and that those who refused payment were to be marked as malignants and disaffected persons.[1]

Charles was in even greater straits for money. He obtained 6,000*l.* by the sale of a peerage to Sir Richard Newport, a wealthy

Sale of a peerage. Shropshire knight.[2] Enthusiastic Royalists offered their stores of plate to be melted into coin, and no scruple was felt in compelling those who were not enthusiastic Royalists to make a similar sacrifice.[3] Amongst those who were most forward in offering assistance were the Catholic gentry. Their loyalty was never doubtful. Wherever the Parliament held

The Catho-lics support Charles. sway they were liable to outrage and plunder, whilst from time to time they heard that one or other of the priests whom they reverenced had been butchered according to law. Before Charles left Chester, he called on the numerous Catholics of Lancashire to provide themselves with arms, and he now invited all the Catholics of his kingdom to

---

[1] *C.J.* ii. 804, 805. D'Ewes's Diary. *Harl. MSS.* 164, fol. 146.

[2] *Clarendon*, vi. 67. His son is the supposed writer of the *Memoirs of a Cavalier.*

[3] Giustinian to the Doge. *Venetian Transcripts, R.O.* Oct. $\frac{14}{24}$.

assist him with their purses as well as with their swords.[1] " This
is to tell you," he had written to Newcastle, after his return to
Shrewsbury, "that this rebellion is grown to that height, that I
must not look of[2] what opinion men are who at this time are
willing and able to serve me.   Therefore I do not only permit
but command you to make use of all my loving subjects' services,
without examining their consciences—more than their loyalty
to me—as you shall find most to conduce to the upholding of
my just legal power."[3]   No doubt he in this way obtained support which he could ill spare, but, in so doing, he raised a fresh
barrier between himself and the hearts of his Protestant subjects.

It was not the Queen's fault that plentiful supplies had not
flowed in from beyond the seas.   No sooner had she arrived in
Holland, than she threw herself with characteristic
ardour into the task of raising money with which to
purchase arms, and of inducing officers and soldiers
of English birth to forsake the Dutch service for that of their
native Prince.   She had jewels to pawn,[4] and she had in her
favour the powerful assistance of the Prince of Orange ; but,
on the other hand, the commercial oligarchy, which filled the
Assembly of the States of Holland, was jealous of the Prince
and of his royal alliance.   The populace, usually in favour of
the House of Orange, was excited against his Catholic guest.
The English Parliament sent over an able diplomatist, Walter
Strickland, to plead its cause.   Even after Henrietta Maria had
succeeded in bearing down opposition in Holland, fresh disappointment was in store for her.   A vessel which she contrived
to despatch was driven by stress of weather into Yarmouth,
where it was seized by order of Parliament.   Two
ships of war, the sole remains of the Royal Navy,
which were intended to escort across the North Sea a little

The Queen's activity in Holland.

Oct. 4.

---

[1] The King to Gerard and others, Sept. 27.   *Rushw.* v. 50.   *Clarendon,* vi. 65.

[2] The word ' of ' is not in the original.

[3] The King to Newcastle, Sept. 23.   *Ellis,* Ser. I. iii. 291.

[4] These were not identical with the magnificent service of plate on
which Buckingham had attempted to raise money.

fleet laden with munitions of war, were surrendered to Parliament by their own sailors. The States of Holland put an embargo on the transport of warlike stores to the King. Though the Queen succeeded in sending 200 men over in small boats, she was unable to despatch the arms which were so much needed at Shrewsbury. She had at one time hoped to be able soon to rejoin her husband in England. She now lamented that she could do but little for him, and talked of seeking a refuge in France till his fate had been decided in the field.[1]

Ill equipped as the Royal army was, it was at last able to move. On October 12 Charles set out from Shrewsbury on

Oct. 12. The King leaves Shrewsbury. the march which, as he fondly hoped, would conduct him back to Whitehall. Amongst his adversaries at Westminster there was no flinching. On the 15th a Bill, which had already passed the Commons, for calling that

Oct. 15. Bill for an Assembly of Divines. Assembly of Divines which was expected to remodel the Church in a manner which could not fail to give offence to Charles, was read for the first time in the House of Lords, and was hurried on to a third reading only

Oct. 19. four days later. The Lords then proceeded to give their assent to several resolutions of the Lower House.

Oct. 15. Arrest of persons. All who refused to contribute to the charge of the Commonwealth were to be imprisoned and disarmed.

Sequestration of estates and of the King's revenue. The revenues of bishops, deans, and chapters, and of all notorious delinquents who had taken up arms for the King, were to be sequestered for the use of the Commonwealth ; and though Charles's own revenue was still to be paid into the proper offices of receipt, it was not to be disbursed without the formal authorisation of Parliament.

Such measures required a strong force to back them. Orders were accordingly given to call out the trained bands of the

[1] *A true and perfect relation.* E. 121, 21. *A continuation of certain special passages.* E. 121, 9. Zon to the Doge, Sept. $\frac{7}{17}$, $\frac{14}{24}$, $\frac{\text{Sept. 21}}{\text{Oct. 1}}$. *Venetian Transcripts, R.O.* Rossetti to Barberini, Sept. $\frac{11}{21}$, $\frac{18}{28}$. *Roman Transcripts, R.O.* The Queen to the King, $\frac{\text{Sept. 26, 27}}{\text{Oct. 6, 7}}$. *Letters of Henrietta Maria*, 124, 129.

counties through which the King's army was likely to pass. Yet
it was felt to be not impossible that, in spite of all resistance, Charles might reach London, and it was certain that if he occupied London he would be master
of the kingdom. London, long unused to war, was an
unfortified city, and there was no time now to fortify it. All
that could be done was to stretch chains across the streets, in
order to throw difficulties in the way of a charge of
cavalry.[1] London's strength lay in the vigour of its
citizens. On the 16th the captains of the trained
bands of the City renewed, in the name of the 8,000
men whom they commanded, their resolution to live
and die with the Parliament, and the great majority of the men
declared themselves ready to follow their leaders in
the service of the City even beyond the City precincts.[2]
The Royalists of the City, on the other hand, were growing
every day more confident that they would soon see Charles
enter London in triumph. They formed a not insignificant
minority, having amongst them many of the wealthy
merchants. They openly wore red ribbons in their
hats as a token of their opinions, and they were strong
enough to drive out a mob which broke into St. Paul's to pull
down the organ.[3]

The trained bands called out.

Measures for the defence of London.

Oct. 16.

Oct. 17.

The City Royalists hopeful.

Not only from Charles's army was danger apprehended at
Westminster. It was now known that the greater part of Cornwall had declared for the King, and that the Earl of Newcastle
had collected a force of 8,000 men in the North. The belief
that Charles was merely the instrument of a vast
Catholic conspiracy gained fresh strength from the
admission, in pursuance of the King's orders, of Catholic officers and soldiers to that which was now ordi-
narily spoken of as the Northern Papist Army. No wonder
that, in presence of the irritation thus caused, those who sighed
for peace were in despair. "No neutrality," wrote Roe, who

Oct. 18. Dangers from Corn- wall and the North.

---

[1] *L.J.* v. 402, 406.

[2] *England's memorable accidents.* E. 240, 45. *Certain propositions.*
E. 123, 24.

[3] Giustinian to the Doge, Oct. $\frac{14}{24}$. *Venetian Transcripts, R.O.*

had lately returned from his embassy, "is admitted. . . . Both
Neutrality
impossible. parties resolve that those who are not with them
are against them. London prepares for defence in
all events, and the voluntary contributions daily increase, and
all who will not are as corn between two millstones."[1]

On the 20th a fresh danger was discovered. It was known
in London that Charles was once more looking to foreign
The King
sends to
Denmark for
help, powers for aid. Two Scots—Henderson and
Cochrane—had been commissioned to visit the
King of Denmark, to urge him to send arms for
12,000 men, 24 cannon, 100,000*l.*, a fleet of ships of war,
3,000 German infantry, and 1,000 horse.[2]

At the same time it was known that Charles had arrived
within four miles of Coventry, and that he had absolutely
and refuses
to receive a
petition
from Essex. refused to receive the petition of the Houses from
the hands of Essex.[3] The challenge thus given
was promptly taken up by Pym. 'With great
vehemence and passion' he told the House that they must
Oct. 20.
Pym pro-
poses an
Association. now all perceive 'what the councillors were' who
were 'about his Majesty, seeing that he had refused
the petition of both Houses from a person of so
great honour as the Earl of Essex was, and that, therefore, they
should now resolve of some new way of linking' themselves
'together in a more firm bond and union than formerly, and
to that end he desired that a Committee might be appointed
to draw a new Covenant, or association, which all might enter
into, and that a new oath might be framed for the observing
of the said association, which all might take, and such as refused it . . . might be cast out of the House,' in order to distinguish both amongst themselves 'and in the kingdom' those
who were on their side from those who were against them.[4]

---

[1] D'Ewes's Diary. *Harl. MSS.* 164, fol. 38. Roe to the Elector
Palatine, Oct. 18. *Harl. MSS.* 1901, fol. 48b. See *Hist. of England*,
1603–1642, ix. 348.

[2] *L.J.* v. 411. Compare Fridericia, *Danmark's ydre politishe historie*,
1635–1645, p. 314.

[3] Dorset to Essex, Oct. 16. *L.J.* v. 412.

[4] D'Ewes's Diary. *Harl. MSS.* 164, fol. 40. *L.J.* v. 411, 412, 418.

It is evident that the example of the success of the Scottish Covenant had blinded Pym to the danger of dividing by yet harsher lines the already divided kingdom. For the present his proposal came to nothing. It was accepted in principle

Oct. 22.

by both Houses, and a declaration calling on all well-meaning persons to associate themselves together was put in circulation. Nothing was further done in the matter till the absolute need of Scottish succour revived the ill-considered proposition.

It was not by oaths, but by pikes and muskets in the hands of men who needed no oaths to bind them, that London was

Oct. 21.

A new army to be levied under Warwick

Oct. 22.

to be defended. On the 21st it was decided that a new army of 16,000 men should be raised to act in conjunction with the City trained bands, and that the whole of this force should be placed under the command of the Earl of Warwick. Horses were to be taken from their owners wherever they could be found in the London stables. A garrison was to be sent to occupy Windsor.[1]

Vigorous as these measures were, there was one man in the Parliamentary army by whom they were not considered adequate. Cromwell, as soon as the war threatened to break out,

Cromwell's prognostication.

had accepted a commission under Essex as a captain in a regiment of cavalry.[2] If he had none of Falkland's visionary anticipation of the intellectual charities of the future, he was second to none in grasping the needs of the present. " Your troops," he said to his cousin Hampden, in speaking of the disparity between the cavalry of the two armies,[3]

---

[1] *L.J.* v. 414, 416.

[2] Peacock's *Army Lists of the Roundheads and Cavaliers*, 56. That Cromwell was ever a captain of foot, as Carlyle thought, is a mistake. In a document in Mr. Webster's possession, printed in *N. and Q.* 2nd ser. xii. 285, he is described as captain of a troop of arquebusiers. Infantry were always in companies, not troops, and arquebusiers are described as light cavalry in Turner's *Pallas Armata*, p. 231.

[3] Carlyle's *Cromwell*, Speech XI. It is useless to attempt to fix the date of the conversation precisely, but the reference to the raising of new regiments seems to connect it with the raising of those forces under Warwick. After Edgehill there would probably have been something said of the troops which were not beaten there. At all events, Cromwell

perhaps with some thought in his mind of the headlong flight at Powick Bridge, "are most of them old decayed serving men and tapsters, and such kind of fellows, and their troops are gentlemen's sons and persons of quality. Do you think that the spirits of such base and mean fellows will ever be able to encounter gentlemen that have honour, and courage, and resolution in them? . . . . You must get men of a spirit, and take it not ill what I say—I know you will not—of a spirit that is likely to go on as far as gentlemen will go, or else you will be beaten still." Cromwell's idea seemed impracticable to Hampden. It would not be long, however, before the principles which he had enunciated would be brought to the test. Cromwell's own troopers, picked men from the Fens, were as sternly Puritan as himself.

In the meanwhile Charles was steadily pressing on, avoiding Parliamentary strongholds such as Warwick and Coventry,
and evidently eager to reach London as soon as possible. On the 21st he slept at Southam. On the following morning the powerful spell cast by Royalty over those who had no vehement opinions was illustrated by Charles's meeting with a country gentleman who cared so little for the mortal strife which was dividing his country as to be starting for the hunting field when armies were on the march. "Who is that," asked the King, "that hunts so merrily when I am going to fight for my crown and dignity?" Richard Shuckburgh, for so the gentleman was named, was summoned to Charles's presence, and left it resolved to embark heart and soul in his sovereign's cause. He gathered his tenants together, put arms into their hands, and on the following day was knighted on a field of battle.[1]

Oct. 21.
The King at Southam.

Oct. 22.
Meeting of Charles with Richard Shuckburgh.

Charles had no thought of fighting immediately when on the evening of the 22nd he arrived at Edgcott. The next day was a Sunday, and he intended, after sending on a detachment to capture Banbury, to give a day's rest to the remainder

was talking of cavalry only, as his description would not suit the Royalist infantry.

[1] Dugdale's *Antiquities of Worcestershire*, ed. Thomas, i. 309.

of his army. In the night Rupert sent him word that Essex
was on his track, and had already reached Kineton, some

Charles
hears that
he is fol-
lowed by
Essex.

seven miles to the west of the scattered positions
occupied by the Royal army. It was plainly hazard-
ous for Charles to push on without fighting, and at
Rupert's suggestion he ordered his troops to occupy
on the f .lowing morning the brow of the steep descent which
under the name of Edgehill rises high over the undulating
plain of Warwickshire.[1]

No position could have been better chosen if Charles intended to await the attack of the enemy. Yet there were no

Oct. 23.
Charles at
Edgehill.

signs that Essex would attempt such a foolhardy
enterprise as to scale the heights as long as they
were guarded by an army at least as numerous as
his own, and, in consequence of its superiority in cavalry, decidedly stronger. He had been obliged to leave garrisons in
Worcester and elsewhere, whilst Hampden with two regiments,
in charge of the greater part of the artillery, was a day's march
in the rear. The forces ready on both sides to take part in
the battle were about 14,000.[2] When Essex drew up his
troops at some little distance from the foot of the hill, the
Royal army had no choice but to descend. It was in the
midst of a hostile population, and with Banbury fortified in its
rear and the Parliamentary army in front, it would hardly
escape starvation.

Whether these considerations presented themselves to
Charles is more than doubtful. In his camp victory was re-

Confidence
of the
Royalists.

garded as a certainty. It was fully believed that
Essex had but a turbulent mob under his orders, and
that most of his soldiers and many of his officers
would refuse to fight against the King now that they knew that
he had taken the field in person.[3]

---

[1] The King to Rupert, Oct. 23. Warburton's *Memoirs of Rupert,*
ii. 12.

[2] See Col. Ross's note on the battle of Edgehill in the *Hist. Review*
for July 1887.

[3] *Clarendon,* vi. 77. Giustinian to the Doge, Oct. $\frac{21}{31}$. *Venetian
MSS.*

Full of spirit as the Royalists were, they had to contend against one fatal disadvantage. Charles had himself under-

Rupert's position in the army.

taken the direction of the campaign. Rupert was almost the Buckingham of the hour, carrying his irresolute uncle with him by his fire and energy. The young Prince had not been many days in England before he took offence at some expressions used by Digby,[1] and, by refusing to receive instructions from Charles through a secretary, had drawn down on himself a well-merited reproof from Falkland. "In neglecting me," said Falkland, "you neglect the King." Worst of all was the disastrous arrangement by which Rupert was exempted from taking the orders of the Earl of Lindsey, the General of the army, whose tried fidelity was beyond

Lindsey's career.

dispute. His career in Charles's service had been one of patient submission to conditions which could only result in failure. He had commanded the fleet which, in 1626, was baffled by storms in the Bay of Biscay, the fleet which, in 1628, had attempted in vain, after Buckingham's death, to carry succour to Rochelle, and the fleet which, in 1635, having been fitted out with the proceeds of the first levy of ship-money, sailed up and down the Channel exposed to universal mockery. Such a man was not likely to take umbrage readily. Yet even Lindsey shrank from the task of commanding an army in which he was to have no control over the cavalry, and he assured his friends that he could not regard himself as its general, and that when the day of battle arrived he would place himself at the head of his own regiment, and there would find his death.

Charles accepted Lindsey's reluctance to bear the name without the authority of a commander, and directed that his

Forth appointed to command.

place should be filled on the day of battle by the old Scotchman who had defended Edinburgh Castle, and who had recently exchanged the title of Lord Ruthven for that of Earl of Forth. He would not give to the new commander the authority which he had dashed out of Lindsey's hands.[2]

---

[1] Digby to Rupert, Sept. 10. *Warburton*, i. 368.
[2] *Clarendon*, vi. 78, 90. Bulstrode's *Memoirs*, 79. I understand the

The whole of the forenoon was taken up in collecting
Charles's army from its scattered quarters. About one o'clock

Descent of
the King's
army.

it was brought down the steep face of the hill and
established in the plain, an operation which could
safely be performed under cover of the artillery
above. If Essex had pushed forward to the foot of the slope
he would have been as surely exposed to disaster as Conway
had been, two years before, at Newburn.

BATTLE OF EDGE HILL OCT. 23rd 1642.

Scale of Miles

F.S.Weller, F.R.G.S.

There were old soldiers in the King's army who knew that
the work before it was not quite as easy as was anticipated by

Sir Jacob
Astley's
prayer.

the gay gentlemen who now for the first time saw
shots fired in earnest. The veteran Sir Jacob Astley
breathed a simple prayer with uplifted eyes. "O
Lord !" he said, " Thou knowest how busy I must be this day.
If I forget Thee, do not Thou forget me." Then he gave the
word of command, " March on, boys !" [1]

As usual, the foot was, on both sides, drawn up in the
centre, with cavalry on either wing ; but on the side of the

story about Falkland and Rupert to refer to an incident some weeks
before the battle.

[1] Warwick's *Memoirs*, 229.

Royalists the main body of horse was with Rupert on the right, whilst a smaller force, amongst which Forth had placed himself, was commanded by Wilmot on the left. In front of Wilmot, on the Parliamentary side, were three incomplete cavalry regiments, two of them under Sir Philip Stapleton and Sir William Balfour, the Scotsman who had been the gaoler of Strafford in the Tower ; whilst a third, under Lord Feilding, acted as a reserve.

Arrange-
ments of
the armies.

After a few cannon shots had been exchanged Rupert charged. Sweeping round, he fell upon the flank of the enemy's cavalry. He knew that there was treason in their midst. Sir Faithful Fortescue, who had been brought over from Ireland with his troop, had no heart in the Parliamentary cause, and had promised to desert it on the day of battle. At Rupert's approach he and his men wheeled round and joined in the attack upon their former comrades. Shaken by the unexpected desertion, the whole of the Parliamentary cavalry on that side turned and fled. Hurling themselves in wild confusion upon the line of their own infantry, they broke up four whole regiments of foot, of which only a few scattered groups of resolute men rallied to take part in that day's fight. Leaving the runaways on foot, as a prize of little worth, to scatter as best they might, Rupert and his followers dashed in hot pursuit after the flying horse, cutting down the fugitives, and even slaughtering some of Fortescue's men who had neglected to strip off the orange scarfs which marked them as the soldiers of Essex. Little recked Rupert how the battle fared behind him. It is possible that his men, unaccustomed to the discipline of war, were now out of hand, and that he could not have checked them even if he had wished to do so ; [1] but there is no reason to suppose that he made any attempt to bring them to a halt. When Kineton was reached they found the streets blocked by the carts and carriages of Essex and his staff. Many of them fell to plundering, riding over the men and women who were standing in the street. Others continued

Rupert's
charge.

---

[1] This is the view taken in the account printed in Carte's *Original Letters*, i. 10.

the pursuit till they were stopped by Hampden's two regiments
advancing along the road.

The unchecked race of Rupert's horse was not the only
error of the Royalist commanders. Wilmot's men gained the
Wilmot
follows
Rupert's
example. advantage on the left, driving Feilding's regiment
before them, and, like their comrades on the right,
started in headlong pursuit.[1] So little were the
ordinary duties of generalship attended to, that even the King's
As does the
reserve of
horse. reserve of horse galloped off after Rupert. In this
reserve was Charles's own bodyguard, composed
of gentlemen who boasted that among them they
could dispose of a rental of 100,000*l*. Annoyed at the epithet
of 'the show troop,' conferred upon them by their less fortunate comrades, they begged to be allowed to follow Rupert, and
in an evil hour for the cause which he served Sir John Byron,
their commander, granted their request.

The King's army was thus entirely deprived of the services
of its cavalry, a loss which was then of far greater importance
The King's
army left
without
cavalry. than it would be at the present day. The musketeers,
who supported their unwieldy weapons upon the
portable rests which formed part of their equipment,
were indeed habituated to take refuge, when attacked, among
the ranks of the pikemen; but it was hard even for the best
disciplined pikemen to resist on open ground a well-executed
charge of cavalry, and a regiment of infantry was therefore

---

[1] Wilmot's part in the battle is ignored by the Parliamentarians, but
his later absence from the field shows that there is truth in the Royalist
assertion that he was successful on the left. In Scotland it was reported
'that Prince Rupert and Ruthven routed both the wings of the Parliament.' *Baillie*, ii. 56. Compare *Spalding*, iii. 200. As Feilding's regiment is not mentioned by the Parliamentary authorities as taking any
further part in the battle, I have no doubt that his regiment was routed.
The fact that the reserve was routed, and not the two regiments in front
of it, makes it probable that Balfour and Stapleton must have slipped
aside, possibly to take advantage of some movement of the enemy, and
this view of the case is borne out by the statement of the Royalist authorities, that these regiments had never been charged, and were hidden in a
corner of the field. The Parliamentary accounts conceal the whole affair
in silence.

always unwilling, when within striking distance of the enemy, to undertake a march over open country without the protection of cavalry. Through the folly of the King's commanders, the only horse left on the field—the two small regiments under Balfour and Stapleton—were on the Parliamentary side.

The Parliamentary reserve of horse.

At first it seemed to Essex that, in the crash and whirl of disaster, all hope of retrieving the day was gone. Snatching a pike from a soldier, he placed himself at the head of the ranks, to die, if need be, on the field rather than on the scaffold. The regiments which stood firm justified the anticipations which Cromwell had formed of a Puritan soldiery. Amongst these were the Lord General's own regiment, which had been raised in the Puritan county of Essex, and Holles's regiment, which had been recruited in London, and was as noted for its Puritanism as for its courage.[1] Cromwell too, himself the very incarnation of the Puritan spirit, was at the head of an unbroken troop of horse.[2] It must have seemed to him as if his ideal of a Puritan army was already to some extent realised. "These were the men," said Strode, some days afterwards, "that were ignominiously reproached by the name of Roundheads, and by these Roundheads did God show Himself a most glorious God."

Resistance of the Parliamentary foot.

A Puritan soldiery.

The attack of the King's foot was met with a stubborn resistance. Balfour's horse, after routing two Royalist infantry regiments, found itself in presence of the enemy's cannon. Balfour called for spikes, but no spikes were at hand,

---

[1] In a later pamphlet describing the fight at Brentford, Holles's men are spoken of as 'those honest, religious soldiers.'

[2] The charge of cowardice subsequently brought against Cromwell by Holles is easily refuted, as in the narrative of Fiennes, which received the approbation of Essex and the chief commanders (E. 126, 38), Cromwell is distinctly named as one of those 'who never stirred from their troops, but they and their troops fought to the last moment.' In the letter, however, which precedes the narrative, Captain Cromwell is represented as flying. Probably this is a mistake for Cromwell's eldest son Oliver, who was a cornet in Lord St. John's regiment, and, according to Clarendon, St. John was amongst the fugitives.

and, contenting himself with cutting the traces, he wheeled round to do further service.   From the mass of Charles's infantry no more was to be feared.   Its centre had been pierced through by Balfour's charge, and from that time its right, though it stood firm, took no further part in the combat.[1]   Two regiments, indeed, took up a position round the cannon which Balfour had captured and abandoned, but they showed no signs of any disposition to advance.

The struggle on the field.

Charles himself could do nothing to improve the position of his troops.   He could neither command an army nor suffer anyone else to supersede him.   Personal bravery of the passive kind, indeed, he invariably showed. When his men were preparing to descend the hill, he rode up and down encouraging them to fight.   "Go in the name of God," he said to Lindsey, "and I'll lay my bones by yours.' Before the battle began, at the earnest request of his officers, he retired to the top of the hill.   But he could not long bear to remain in a position of safety, and he was soon to be found amongst his troops, sharing in the common danger, and adjuring them to show mercy to such of their enemies as fell into their hands.   To guide the issues of battle was not in his power, and Forth, brave soldier as he was, seems to have galloped off with Wilmot.   Each regiment failed or prospered as it might.   There was no attempt to organise the combined action of an army.

Charles's behaviour.

It was this failure of organisation which was disastrous to Charles.   The Royal Foot Guards—the King's Red Regiment, as they were sometimes called—were left unaided to bear the brunt of the day.   Above that regiment waved the royal standard, borne aloft by Sir Edmund Verney, the stainless Knight whose sad face still appeals for sympathy from the canvas of Vandyke.[2]   At the

Fate of the Royal Foot Guards.

[1] The attention of the reporters was so fully taken up with the stubborn fight which followed, that they give no clear idea of the general tactics of the battle.   It may, however, be gathered from the King's official narrative (E. 126, 24) that the regiments which saved the guns and were never put into disorder were on the right, though the narrative is by no means clear.

[2] The portrait is at Claydon.

head of the regiment was its own colonel, the Earl of Lindsey, resolved to do a colonel's work if he was not permitted to do that of a general. Isolated on the field, these brave men beat back all attacks for a time ; but the odds were sorely against them. Their musketeers were driven in, and the pikemen, charged in flank and rear by Balfour's and Stapleton's horse, and pressed hard in front by two regiments of foot, broke their ranks at last. The combat became a butchery. Verney was struck down, and the standard was wrenched from his dying hand. Lindsey, mortally wounded, fell into the hands of the enemy, to die a prisoner on the following day. The ruin of the King's hopes appeared to be complete. Only two of his regiments maintained their position on the field. The Parliamentary forces, flushed with victory, were already advancing to the attack, when they were checked by the return of the hostile cavalry. The shades of night were gathering, and Essex felt disinclined to continue the struggle. On the other side there was an equal disinclination to begin a fresh battle at such an hour. The horsemen were weary after their long pursuit, and the regiments had lost all cohesion as they straggled back man by man. Falkland, indeed, thought it still possible to end the Civil War at a blow, and urged Wilmot to attempt a decisive charge. " My lord," was Wilmot's reply, "we have got the day, and let us live to enjoy the fruit thereof." Perhaps Falkland was right, but the fact that Rupert did not, on his side, order a renewal of the attack goes far to show that it had little chance of success. At all events, the growing darkness made one brave deed possible. Captain Smith, a Catholic [1] officer of the King's Life Guards, hearing of the loss of the standard, picked up an orange scarf from the field and threw it over his shoulders. Accompanied by one or two of his comrades similarly attired, he slipped in amongst the ranks of the enemy, and found the standard in the hands of Essex's secretary. Telling him that so great a prize was not fitly bestowed in the hands of a penman, he snatched from

Return of the Royalist horse.

Recovery of the standard

---

[1] Rossetti to Barberini, Nov. $\frac{20}{30}$. *Roman Transcripts, R.O.*

him the precious symbol. Protected by his scarf, Smith succeeded in escaping hostile notice, and triumphantly laid the
recovered standard at the feet of the King. Charles rewarded
him with hearty thanks, and knighted him on the spot.[1]

The two armies, separated by the darkness, watched through
the long hours of the night under the nipping air of an early

Oct. 24.
The fight
is not
renewed. frost, which staunched wounds which, but for this
healing pain, might easily have proved mortal. In
the morning there was but little inclination on either
side to renew the battle. Essex had been reinforced by about
4,000 fresh men, including Hampden's regiment, but his inferiority in cavalry precluded all thought of an assault upon the
hill. The Royalists, on the other hand, were conscious of
the inferiority of their foot. The men shrank from a fresh
experience of an encounter with Puritan valour. Charles, too,
lost time by sending a messenger to offer pardon to such of his
opponents as would lay down their arms—those only who had
been proclaimed traitors being excluded from mercy. Of
course no such proclamation was allowed to reach the ears of
the soldiers. On the night of the 24th the Parliamentary army

---

[1] The foregoing account of the battle cannot, of course, lay claim to
absolute correctness, which is unattainable in any case, even when the
witnesses are producible to be examined ; but it is founded on a careful
comparison of the existing evidence. On the Royalist side we have,
besides Clarendon's account, Warwick's and Bulstrode's memoirs, the
narrative published in Carte's *Original Letters* (i. 9), the official statement, *A Relation of the Battle* (E. 126, 24), a letter of C. H. to Sancroft,
printed in Ellis's *Original Letters*, Ser. II. iii 301, and another from a
Royalist in London (*Harl. MSS.* 3,783, fol. 61). On the other side are
Ludlow's *Memoirs*, the account given by Fiennes (E. 126, 38), that of
Holles and his brother officers (E. 124, 26), and that contained in the
speeches of Lord Wharton and others (E. 124, 32). The story of Smith's
exploit comes from Ludlow. In *Britannicæ Virtutis Imago* (E. 53, 10),
written in 1644, after Smith's death, is a different story, said to be derived
from Dugdale, in which the orange scarf disappears, and Smith is said to
have put to flight six cuirassiers who were guarding the secretary. Smith
is there said to have wounded the person carrying the standard, as well as
one of the soldiers. For a discussion on the military position, see Col.
Ross's note referred to at p. 42, note 2.

was quartered at Kineton, and on the following day it with-

Oct. 25.
Essex retires to Warwick. drew to Warwick. As Essex was moving off Rupert made a dashing onslaught upon his rearguard, but no serious attack upon his main force was attempted.[1]

The claim of victory advanced by either party is little to be

Result of the battle. heeded. The promise of future success was un-doubtedly on the side of Essex. Only amongst the Parliamentary troops had there been that co-operation between infantry and cavalry which distinguishes an army from a fighting crowd. The immediate fruits of victory were reaped by Charles. He appointed Forth permanently to that nominal command of his forces which had hitherto meant

Oct. 27.
Surrender of Banbury. so little, and he pushed on unmolested towards London. On the 27th Banbury surrendered to him,

Oct. 29.
Charles enters Oxford. though its defence was entrusted to a whole Parlia-mentary regiment. On the 29th he entered Oxford in triumph at the head of his army, amidst the plaudits of citizens and scholars.

[1] *Clarendon,* vi. 88.

CHAPTER III.

TURNHAM GREEN.

DURING the days which had followed Charles's march from Shrewsbury, London had been deeply agitated. As soon as it was known that the armies were engaged [1] orders were given

1642.
Precautions
taken in
London.

by the Houses to close the shops, and to convey into the City the King's youngest children, Henry and Elizabeth,[2] who had fallen into the power of Parliament when Charles left Whitehall. The pretext given out for the latter step was the necessity of providing for the safety of the children, though the Royalists shrewdly suspected that they were to be kept as hostages in the event of a successful attack upon Westminster. During the next few days rumours and counter-rumours filled the air. The first set of fugitives asserted that Essex had received a crushing defeat, and those who arrived later asserted that he had won a brilliant

Oct. 28.

victory. Before long it was ascertained that the King was marching on without resistance. The spirit of the population of London rose with the danger. Armed men flocked in from the neighbouring counties. In addition to the chains which were now stretched across the streets, earthworks were thrown up to defend all the approaches, at which women and children laboured as heartily as the men.[3]

The danger which had fired some with resolution awoke a longing for peace in the minds of others. It was now evident that unless Charles were to gain a decisive victory the war

---

[1] Whitacre's Diary. *Add. MSS.* 31, 116, fol. 3b.

[2] *L.J.* v. 419.

[3] Giustinian to the Doge, $\frac{\text{Oct. 28}}{\text{Nov. 7}}$. *Venetian Transcripts, R.O.*

would be prolonged for some time to come. Especially to the
wealthy merchant and the wealthy landowner the

The Peace-party in the Lords. prospect of a long interruption of commerce, of
plunderings in town and country, was appalling.
In the City and in Parliament, above all in the House of
Lords, a Peace-party was quickly formed. Amongst the Peers
its most respectable member was the kindly Earl of Northum-

Northumberland. berland, always anxious for a quiet life and always
distrustful of enthusiasts. The support of the dis-

Holland. appointed courtier Holland brought it little credit,

Pembroke. and still less could it gain by the accession of Pembroke, who, when the King's strength appeared to be growing
in the summer months, had carried on a clandestine correspondence with Hyde, in which he offered his services
unreservedly to Charles,[1] and who, when in the autumn the
Parliament seemed likely to gain the upper hand, threw all the
influence of his great wealth on the side of the Houses. Now
that it was not altogether improbable that the King might
enter London in triumph, Pembroke's voice was raised loudly
for an accommodation.[2]

On October 29 a proposal to reopen negotiations for peace
was made in the House of Lords.[3] Two days later Edmund

Oct. 29. The Lords propose to negotiate. Waller urged the Commons to concur with the
Peers. The Peace-party which now formed itself
in the House of Commons and in the City counted

Oct. 31. Waller asks the Commons to concur with them. amongst its numbers many men in every way his
superior. Some of these, like D'Ewes, were strongly
Puritan in the guidance of their own lives. Others,
like Maynard and Whitelocke, were lawyers, startled

The Peace-party in the Commons. by every illegality, and ill at ease in the midst of a
state of war. They all shared in the common weak-
ness of desiring compromise, without rising to the height from
which an honourable compromise alone was possible. They
longed for peace, but there was no intellectual basis of peace
in their minds.

[1] The letters signed P. Herbert in the *Clarendon State Papers* (ii.
144–149) were written by Pembroke's son.
[2] *Special Passages.* E. 127, 12. [3] *L.J.* v. 424.

For the moment, however, Waller's proposal met with wide support. When Essex, who, with the broken remains of his army, had returned to London, gave his approval, on the condition that no unreasonable terms should be accepted, all obstacles appeared to be removed. On November 2 the Commons consented to the opening of a negotiation, on the understanding that there was to be no slackening in the preparations for defence.[1] Amongst those preparations they included a direct invitation to the Scots to enter England in order to suppress Newcastle's army. The admission of Catholics to its ranks, and the expected arrival of Danish troops in answer to the King's application made through Henderson and Cochrane, were held to constitute a danger sufficient to warrant an appeal to Scotland.[2]

Approval of Essex.

Nov. 2. A negotiation voted.

The demand that the King should lower his standard before he was admitted to negotiation was thus tacitly abandoned. On the 3rd Sir Peter Killigrew was despatched to request Charles to grant a safe-conduct to Commissioners empowered to negotiate. Killigrew found the King already on the march for London. Charles received the request of the Houses at Reading, but he was evidently in no hurry to comply with their wishes. After two days he declared that one of the Commissioners, Sir John Evelyn, being a proclaimed traitor, could not be admitted to his presence. As the fact was previously unknown, it was believed at Westminster that the proclamation of Evelyn's treason had been antedated, so as to serve as a pretext for postponing the opening of the negotiation till an attack had been made on the City. Even the Lords took fire at Charles's answer, and, declaring that the King had virtually refused to negotiate, gave the assent which they had hitherto refused to the invitation to the Scots.[3]

Nov. 3. A safe-conduct for negotiation demanded.

Nov. 4. The King at Reading.

Nov. 6. Is suspected of causing delay.

Nov. 7. The Scots invited to intervene.

On the 8th a deputation from the two Houses harangued

[1] *L.J.* v. 430. Yonge's Diary. *Add. MSS.* 18,777, fol. 47. Whitacre's Diary. *Add. MSS.* 31,116, fol. 5.

[2] Declaration of Parliament. *Rushw.* v. 393. See p. 39.

L.J. v. 437.

the citizens at Guildhall.   The citizens energetically responded
to the appeal.   By this time the new levies had reached the
number of 6,000 men.[1]   Essex had outstripped the

Nov. 8.
The Houses
appeal to
the City. King, and had brought up to London the relics of
his army.   From Parliament he received a vote of

Nov. 11. thanks.   The Commons had already offered him

Nov. 3. a gift of 5,000l.[2]

The terror of Rupert's name did far more to
quicken the ardour of the City than the eloquence of the
Rupert's
plunderings. members of Parliament.   It is true that he had been
recently repulsed in an attempt to storm Windsor
Castle, but it was not in his character of a soldier that he was
most dreaded.   It was his task to levy contributions and to seize
forage and provisions.   In the King's army such operations
were not branded with the name of pillage ; but whatever may
be the befitting language with which to characterise the proceedings of Rupert's troopers, there can be little doubt that
their work was done with no gentle hand.[3]   They had lately

---

[1] King to Calthorpe, Nov. 12.   *Tanner MSS.* lxiv. fol. 87.

[2] *Three Speeches.* E. 126, 44.   *L.J.* v. 441. *C.J.* ii. 833.

[3] The inhabitants of the country (Giustinian to the Doge, Nov. $\frac{11}{21}$,
Venetian MSS.) were compelled by the King to contribute ' a sosteni-
mento delle militie sue, le quali, la cavalleria in particolare, si nutriscono
per la maggior parte sopra il paese.'   Whitelocke's account of the proceedings of the soldiers at his own house may probably be taken as a fair
sample of the behaviour of the Royal troops : "Sir John Byron and his
brothers commanded those horse, and gave orders that they should commit
no insolence at my house, nor plunder my goods ; but soldiers are not
easily governed against their plunder.   They spent and consumed 100 load
of corn and hay, littered their horses with sheaves of good wheat.   Divers
writings of consequence and books that were left in my study, some of
them they tore in pieces, others they burnt to light their tobacco, and
some they carried away with them.   They broke down my park pales,
killed most of my deer, though rascal and carrion, and let out all the rest,
only a tame young stag they carried away and presented to Prince Rupert,
and my hounds, which were extraordinary good.   They broke up all
trunks, chests, and places, and where they found linen or any household
stuff they took it away with them, and cutting the beds, let out the
feathers, and took away the ticks.   They likewise carried away my coach
and four good horses, and all my saddle horses, and did all the mischief
and spoil that malice and enmity could provoke barbarous mercenaries to
commit."   *Whitelocke.* 65.

seized several waggon loads of cloth, coming from Gloucester
shire for sale in the London market. Lord Say's house,
Broughton Castle, and Whitelocke's house, Fawley Court, had
been plundered. In London few doubted that if Charles
entered the City he would abandon it to be sacked by his
soldiers.

On the 9th the excess of danger produced a revival of the
desire for peace. Sir John Evelyn begged that the King's
Nov. 9.
A petition to
be sent to
the King. treatment of himself might not stand in the way of
a negotiation. On this, permission was given to the
other Commissioners to wait on the King without
him. As but little confidence was felt in the result of diplomacy, Essex was ordered to take the field. That a better
discipline might be observed under his command than the
Royalist officers appeared to be able to enforce, he was
directed to exercise martial law. The stringent requirements of
the Petition of Right were thus set aside under the stress of
war.[1]

On the 10th Pym appeared at Guildhall to explain the
spirit in which overtures had been made to the King. He·said
Nov. 10.
Pym at
Guildhall. that the Houses hoped that, now that Charles had
had experience of the courage of his subjects he
would be more reasonable than he had been, and
that Parliament would be well pleased to establish any peace
which would secure their religion and liberty. Mere words,
however, would not suffice. " To have printed liberties," said
Pym, " and not to have liberties in truth and realities, is but to
mock the kingdom." [2]

When Charles replied to the petition of the Houses he
had already arrived at Colnbrook. He attempted
Nov. 11.
Charles's
reply. to gain an immediate advantage, by proposing that
Windsor should be surrendered to him as a place in
Nov. 12.
It contains
no proposal
for a cess-
ation. which the negotiations might be carried on, though
he expressed his willingness to treat elsewhere. The
Houses felt some surprise that the King had said
nothing about a cessation of arms, and after ordering Essex to

---

[1] *L.J.* v. 439. *Special Passages.* E. **127, 12.**
[2] *Two Speeches.* E. **126, 48.**

abstain from all acts of hostility, they sent again to call Charles's attention to his omission.[1]

There can be little doubt that the omission was intentional, and that Charles had no wish to be checked in his triumphant career. On the night of the 11th, before his message had been delivered at Westminster, he gave orders to Rupert to clear the way by an attack on Brentford, and on the following morning he wrote once more to the Houses, informing them that he would be in that town in the evening to hear what they had to say.[2]

Nov. 11.
Charles orders an attack on Brentford.

Rupert lost no time in obeying the instructions which he had probably dictated. On the morning of the 12th he burst out of the mist which lay heavily on the low ground by the river and fell upon Holles's regiment, which had taken up a position in advance of Brentford. The men fought worthily of the reputation which they had acquired at Edgehill; but the odds against them were too great, and they were compelled to fall back on the town, where Brooke's regiment was quartered. Here the two regiments long maintained an unequal fight. Many were slain or captured, many were driven into the river and drowned. At last Hampden arrived with fresh troops, but he could do no more than cover the retreat of the survivors. Rupert was left in possession of Brentford. Though the sentiments of many of the inhabitants were notoriously Royalist, Charles's soldiers made no distinction between friend and foe, and before nightfall they had thoroughly sacked the town.[3]

Nov. 12.
Rupert's attack on Brentford.

If Charles expected to deal as easily with London as he had dealt with the isolated regiments at Brentford, he must have been grievously disappointed with the result. All through

---

[1] *L.J.* v. 442.

[2] Clarendon (vi. 134) says that Rupert attacked without any direction from the King. Charles himself, however, in his letter of the 12th (*L.J.* v. 443), says that he had resolved to march on Brentford in consequence of information received on the night of the 11th.

[3] *England's Memorable Accidents.* E. 249, 19. Giustinian to the Doge, Nov. $\frac{18}{28}$. *Venetian MSS* D'Ewes's Diary. *Harl. MSS.* 164, fol. 245.

the evening of the 12th the City trained bands were streaming forth along the Western road. On the morning of the 13th

Succour sent from London.

Charles's way was barred by an army of some 24,000 men, drawn up on the common at Turnham Green. The Parliamentary force was probably about

Nov. 13. The Parliamentary army at Turnham Green.

twice as numerous as his own. Its composition was, no doubt, heterogeneous. Soldiers who had borne the brunt of war at Edgehill stood shoulder to shoulder with new levies which had never seen an enemy. Such an army might easily be defeated if it attempted complicated manœuvres, especially against an enemy strong in

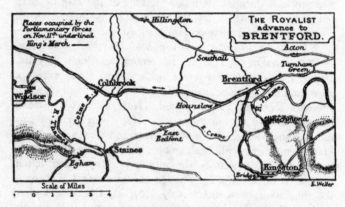

cavalry, but as long as it stood on the defensive it was irresistible. Its spirit was undoubted. Even those whose voices had been raised for peace had no wish to see London given over to pillage. The fear which inspired the half-jesting sonnet in which Milton implored the Royalist captain or colonel who might find his way to Aldersgate Street to spare the poet's home, as Alexander had spared the house once inhabited by Pindar, nerved the arms of hundred of men who were perfectly incapable of writing sonnets. Even Holland and Northumberland appeared in arms in defence of the City.[1]

The King's army would thus have been in a position of

---

[1] *Special Passages.* E. 127, 12.

extreme peril, if he had been in the presence of an enemy capable of profiting by his too rash advance. On the rear of his right flank, Kingston Bridge was guarded by a force of 3,000 Parliamentary troops, under Sir James Ramsay, and Essex was strongly urged to order Ramsay to fall on the King's rear. To this scheme the professional officers who had served in the Netherlands or in Germany were strongly opposed, and Ramsay was finally directed to fall back on the south side of the Thames to London Bridge, in order to aid in the defence of the City. Later in the day Essex was prevailed on to despatch Hampden to Acton, with orders to sweep round Charles's army and to place it between two fires. The professional soldiers again interposed, and Hampden was recalled There was much complaint in the army at its enforced inaction, but grounds are not wanting which warrant the belief that the General's final conclusion was probably the right one. A number of spectators had ridden out from London to enjoy the unwonted spectacle. Whenever their inexperience perceived signs of a forward movement in Charles's army, these holiday visitors galloped off to a safe distance, and it was observed that each successive flight was followed by disorder in the ranks. Was it likely that a force as yet so undisciplined would have retained its cohesion under the fierce charges of Rupert's horse, if he had caught it scattered and divided? [1]

However this may have been, the King was far too weak to take the offensive with any prospect of success. In the afternoon, after a few cannon shots had been exchanged, he drew off his men, and Brentford was reoccupied by Essex. The Parliamentary troops were at once surrounded by a hungry crowd, complaining that the Royalists had stripped them of everything. Fortunately the wives and sisters of the citizens who had stood to their arms on Turnham Green had not

It maintains a defensive position.

The King draws off.

Brentford reoccupied by Essex.

---

[1] *Whitelocke,* 65. Compare the pamphlets of the day, though these are not always to be relied on. Ludlow says that Holland dissuaded Essex from attacking. It is likely that the first-named Earl joined the professional soldiers on this point.

been unmindful of their needs, and hundreds of waggons were already on the way laden with the dinners which, but for Charles's sudden irruption, would have been quietly consumed at home.[1]

Charles, on his part, was able to claim some advantage. The Royalists of Kingston welcomed him, and gave him the com-

Charles gains Kingston.

Nov. 14. Essex throws a bridge of boats across the Thames.

Charles at Oatlands.

mand of the first bridge above the City. At Westminster it was believed that he intended to make his way into Kent, where he had many partisans among the gentry. Essex accordingly threw a bridge of boats across the Thames from Fulham to Putney, so as to be able to transfer his army to the southern bank. Charles made no attempt to force his way eastwards, but took up his quarters at Oatlands, where he remained for a few days.

Turnham Green was the Valmy of the English Civil War. That which seemed to Charles's admirers to be his triumphant

Nov. 13. Importance of the check inflicted on the King.

march from Shrewsbury had been stopped in the very outskirts of London. The Parliamentary army had not, it is true, achieved a victory, but it had gained time for reorganisation, so as to find some counterpoise for that invincible cavalry to which Essex had never yet been able to oppose a successful resistance. The check which Charles had suffered was the more important because it was no mere strategical defeat which had been inflicted on him. His conduct in ordering the attack upon Brentford whilst negotia-

Was his conduct in attacking Brentford blameworthy?

tions were pending was no doubt defensible on military grounds. A victorious general is not usually expected to throw away the advantages of his position because proposals have been made to treat, unless he has reason to believe that the terms offered to him will be such as he will be inclined to accept. Charles's error lay in forgetting that he was more than a victorious general. His only chance of permanent success lay in his being able to reconcile where Pym hitherto had been but able to divide. It is unnecessary to discuss whether Charles wished to make peace or not. The mere wish

---

[1] *A true and perfect relation.* E. 128, 17. *The humble petition of all the inhabitants of Brentford.* E. 128, 21.

to make peace with an unbeaten foe will always be followed by disappointment, unless it is accompanied by a clear perception of the strength of the cause for which he is contending.

The King's advance to Brentford after his acceptance of the offer of Parliament to negotiate was strongly resented at Westminster as an act of duplicity. "If your Majesty," said the Houses on the 16th, "had prevailed, it is easy to imagine what a miserable peace we should have had." [1]   Charles's reply, that he had only attacked Brentford because he was afraid of being surrounded by the enemy, [2] was so gross a perversion of geographical fact, that it is difficult to understand how he expected to gain for it even momentary credence.   He now, however, offered to renew the dropped negotiations, and, to give assurance of his peaceable intentions, he withdrew his army to Reading.

Nov. 16. Charles charged with duplicity.

Nov. 18. His reply.

Nov. 19. Charles at Reading.

It speaks much for the unpopularity of the war that such an answer was even taken into consideration.   For two days it was fully debated in the Commons.   That debate disclosed the fact that there were once more two parties in the House.   The Peace-party could now count on the support of one of the five members.   Holles had been disgusted with war since he had looked upon its calamities at Edgehill, and had survived the destruction of his regiment at Brentford.   Yet between Holles and Pym the difference was rather one of clearness of perception than of principle.   Both parties preferred peace to war, but neither party was ready to make those concessions which alone could make peace possible.   In fact, the division between the two was perfectly different from that which had divided parties in the

Nov. 21. Debate on the King's proposal.

The Peace-party and the War-party.

[1] The Parliament to the King, Nov. 16. *L.J.* v. 449. In *Special Passages* (E. 127, 12) we have a direct attack on the King, in which the usual theory that his advisers alone are at fault is abandoned. "This unkinglike accommodation," says the writer, "so to destroy his subjects when an accommodation was agreed unto, hath lost his Majesty the hearts of many of the blinded malignants that stood for him before, both in the City and parts adjacent."

[2] The King to the Parliament, Nov. 18. *L.J.* v. 451. *A continuation of Certain Passages.* E. 242, 31.

summer of 1641. Then members agreeing politically had been
found opposing one another on ecclesiastical subjects. Now
members who were agreed on ecclesiastical subjects differed
politically. Pym would have no peace which did not bring with it
Charles's complete submission to the directing power of Parliament and to a Puritan church. Holles and his friends would
have made concessions to Charles's claims to rule the State, but
they expected him to abandon his own ideal of church government. As there was not the slightest chance that he would ever
do anything of the kind, they did but beat the air.

Behind the controversy on the question of principle arose a
controversy on the question of confidence. The Peace-party,
like the Cavalier-party in the autumn of 1641, was inclined
to trust the King to do what they thought he ought to do.
Opinion of Pym. Pym had a deep distrust of the military element
around the King. He proposed that both armies
should be disbanded. King and Parliament would thus be left
face to face with one another, to come to terms as best they
might. Which of the two he expected to gain the upper hand
is evident from his asking that the Parliamentary proceedings
against delinquents should take their course, and that both
armies, before they broke up, should be bound by an oath to
accept the terms upon which King and Parliament should agree.
Stapleton followed with an attack upon the King's present advisers. "The principal men about him," he said, "are Digby,
Percy, and men of fortune,[1] which how desirous they are of
peace all men know." When the turn of Holles came to speak,
Opinion of Holles. it was found that he was ready to ask the King to
accept, in church matters, the conclusions to which
Parliament should come, upon the advice of the assembly of
divines, and to allow the punishment of such persons as had
been impeached before the outbreak of the troubles.[2]

---

[1] That is to say, 'adventurers.' We still say 'soldiers of fortune' in
this sense.

[2] Yonge's Diary. *Add. MSS.* 18,777, fol. 64–66. D'Ewes talks
about the proposal to disband the army being attacked by 'Strode,
Marten, and other violent spirits,' but gives no hint that it was supported
by Pym. D'Ewes is now too much of a party man to be trusted.

If these were the demands of the Peace-party, they afforded no more reasonable hope of winning Charles's assent than the proposals of their opponents. In the end it was voted

Nov. 22.
Demands of
the Houses.

that the King should be asked to return to his Parliament to settle liberty and religion, and to abandon delinquents to justice. The Lords demurred to the last demand, but the Commons were firm, and the Lords gave way.

The answer thus prepared was despatched to Reading. As might have been expected, it was contemptuously rejected

Nov. 24

Nov. 27.
End of the
negotiation.

by Charles. He had no longer any reason for remaining near London. Leaving a garrison behind him at Reading, he established himself at Oxford on the 29th.[1] From that time Oxford became the headquarters of Royalism in England.

It is unlikely that Pym expected any other result from his proposals. He knew now that he had Parliament at his back, and behind Parliament were all the forces, financial

Nov. 13.
The City
protests
against an
accommo-
dation

and military, of the City. On the very day on which the armies were facing one another on Turnham Green a deputation from the City, headed by a merchant named Shute, appeared at the bar of the Commons to protest against an accommodation. Two days later the City offered to maintain an additional force of 4,000 horse and dragoons. That there might be no dan-

Nov. 15.
Additional
City force.

Nov. 22.
Resignation
of Warwick.

ger of a divided command Warwick resigned the generalship of the London forces, to which he had been appointed whilst Essex was still far away. Essex was now at Windsor, and it was understood that as soon as the negotiations were broken off he would march against the King.[2]

The difficulties in the way of such a march were considerable. The country in front had suffered from the ravages of

Difficulty of
advancing.

the Royal army, and even if this had not been the case, it would have been by no means easy to undertake offensive military operations in the depth of winter. The

---

[1] *C.J.* ii. 858. *L.J.* v. 455, 456, 463. D'Ewes's Diary, *Harl. MSS.* 164, fol. 99.

[2] *L.J.* v. 454. *A continuation of Special Passages.* E 242 30.

main obstacle in Essex's way, however, was that he was unable
to pay his soldiers.   Unless the Commons could provide a
continuous supply of money, nothing vigorous could be done.

The Commons knew that voluntary loans would suffice no
longer.   Even the farce of appealing to the good-will of citi-

Nov. 25.
The Houses
resolve to
levy a tax. zens, who knew that they would be thrown into
prison if they failed to respond to the pressure, must
at last be abandoned.   Whatever constitutionalists
might say about the powers of the Houses to levy taxes without an Act of Parliament to which the Royal assent had been
given, it was plain that without taxation the war could not be
carried on.   Nor must this taxation be allowed to fall on
London alone.   On the 25th Pym, together with Lord
Mandeville, who had just become Earl of Manchester by his
father's death, was despatched by Parliament to the city to
announce the resolution which had been taken.   As the
burden is universal, said Pym, the aid must be universal too.[1]

The moment for the appeal was well chosen.   Not many
days before a Danish ambassador had arrived at Newcastle,

A Danish
ambassador
at New-
castle. bringing money and arms for the King.   He had
had an interview with Charles at Reading, and it
was understood that he had offered further aid in
his master's name.[2]   On the 26th came other disclosures.   An
intercepted letter from someone about the Queen revealed

Nov. 26.
The Queen's
plans re-
vealed. the hopes of her court.   The Prince of Orange had
advanced money to her.   No less than 1,200,000*l.*
had already been sent over to England, or was ready
to be sent.   The Queen was to land in person, perhaps in
Norfolk or Essex.   Charles—the letter was written before the
retreat from Turnham Green was known in Holland—could
surely spare men enough to invade Kent.   London would thus
be blocked up and isolated.   If it did not at once surrender,
it would be easy to induce the King of France to lend three
regiments of his Majesty's subjects which were in his service.[3]

---

[1] *Two Speeches.*   E. 128, 18.

[2] Fridericia, *Danmarks Ydre Pol. Hist.*, 1635–45, **314.**   Salvetti's
Newsletter, Dec. $\frac{2}{12}$.   *Add. MSS.* 27, 962, fol. 31.

[3] ——— to Nicholas, Nov. 22.   *Rushw.* v. 69.

This letter was enough to carry all opposition before it. The Lord Mayor called on the citizens for a fresh loan of 30,000*l.* to meet the immediate necessities of the State, and the citizens loyally responded to the appeal. On the 28th—a Sunday—the letter was read in the City churches. On the 29th Parliament agreed upon an ordinance directing the assessment of all persons in London and Westminster who had hitherto refused to contribute of their own will, in order that they might be taxed at a rate not exceeding five per cent. of their estates. The Houses had at last grasped the power of taxation.[1]

The City loan.

Nov. 29. Ordinance of assessment.

As might have been expected, this proceeding was denounced by the King in the bitterest terms.[2] His own conduct, however, was no less technically illegal than that of his opponents. If they had ordered the raising of money without the Royal assent, he had ordered the collection of a contribution from the country around Oxford without a Parliamentary grant. He expected to receive about 3,000*l.* a week from each county.[3]

Charles levies contributions.

Not long after the King's arrival in Oxford an explanation of the part taken by him in the recent negotiations was published in his name. The Houses were called on to part from their sins and schisms, by which God's judgments had been called down upon the land. It was true that Parliament was 'the representative body of the whole kingdom,' but the King was 'the soul of the whole commonwealth, elected and authorised by the power of God himself.' His government was established by lineal succession, and confirmed by the laws of the land.[4] The manifesto breathed the old spirit of Strafford.

His declaration.

---

[1] *Rushw.* v. 71.   [2] *Ibid.* 73.

[3] The contribution of Oxfordshire is mentioned in a *Paper of Advice,* Nov. 27. *Warburton,* ii. 69. Those of Berkshire and Buckinghamshire are mentioned under the date of Nov. 22 in *England's Memorable Accidents.* E. 242, 27.

[4] *His Majesty's propositions for peace.* E. 129, 4. The pamphlet speaks of the King in the third person, but it was printed by the University printer, and the author would have got into trouble if he had usurped the King's name without authority.

To defend such sentiments Charles would have to trust to the sword alone. He was, at least, in no danger of a sudden His military position. disaster. He had garrisons at Reading, Wallingford, and Abingdon, to check any forward movement which Essex might be inclined to undertake. His rear was guarded by one garrison at Banbury, whilst another garrison at Brill protected him from the Parliamentary forces in Dec. 5. Marlborough stormed. Buckinghamshire. The line of defence was completed on December 5, when Marlborough was stormed, and, after being ruthlessly plundered, was put into a defensible condition and entrusted to a Royalist garrison. It would thus be easy for Hertford to open com- Nov. 5? Evacuation of Worcester. munications with Oxford from the side of Wales, especially as Worcester had recently [1] been abandoned by the Parliamentary regiment which had been left behind by Essex when he marched to Edgehill. When the Royalists regained possession of the city, their disgust was aroused by the foul defilement of the Defilement of the Cathedral. Cathedral by the Parliamentary soldiers,[2] a defilement which offended every sense of decency far more than the violent destruction of the windows and the carvings at Winchester or Canterbury. In this case Puritan zeal had doubtless been strongly reinforced by the coarse disrespect for the decencies of civilised existence natural to men of the class from which many of the soldiers were drawn, especially as they belonged to a generation which, as the treatment to which the nave of St. Paul's had long been subjected bore sufficient witness, had outlived the tradition which enjoined special reverence towards a sacred edifice.

[1] About Nov. 5. *Special Passages.* E. 130, 10.
[2] Trevor to Ormond, Dec. 31. Carte's *Orig. Letters,* i. 14.

CHAPTER IV.

THE CRY FOR PEACE.

In strengthening his position at Oxford Charles was not merely aiming at security from attack. Having had the advantage of taking the initiative in the campaign which ended at Turnham Green, he had now the advantage of a complete strategical plan of operations for the campaign which he was now about to open. The attempt to penetrate to the heart of the enemy's position having failed, he resolved to substitute for it a scheme by which the enemy was to be surrounded and overwhelmed. He was himself to hold Essex in check from Oxford, whilst Newcastle pushed on at the head of the Northern army through the Midlands into Essex, and Hopton advanced from Cornwall to make his way through the southern counties into Kent. When these two armies had seized upon the banks of the Thames below London, they would find no difficulty in stopping the passage of shipping on the river, and, by the annihilation of its commerce, the great city, and with it the Parliamentary army, would be starved into submission.[1]

1642.
The King's strategical plan.

Though no evidence exists on the point, it is not altogether unlikely that the scheme originated with the Prince of Orange, as the first indication of it is to be found in a letter from some-one in the confidence of the Queen during her residence in Holland. If so it is not unlikely that it secured the approbation of Rupert, as he was always sensitive to the importance

[1] This, which is substantially the plan revealed in the letter referred to at p. 64, was communicated by Charles's agent Herne to the Venetian ambassador. Agostini to the Doge, Jan. $\frac{13}{23}$, 1643. *Venetian Transcripts,* *R. O*

of gaining London.   It is hardly probable that it was suggested by the Lord General of the King's army, the Earl of Forth.

The Earl of Forth.
Though it is true that he had been trained to war on a great scale, it is difficult to believe that if his brain had been the source of the King's plan of campaign, he would not have made a greater impression on his contemporaries than he did.   The plan, wherever it originated, had indeed the inherent weakness of directing a convergent attack upon a central position, from which the enemy, if he took the offensive vigorously, might crush the Royal armies in detail.   No strategy, however, could alter the fact that the position of London was a central one, and at all events those who now held that city had as yet shown no indication of the power of taking the initiative.

It was not, however, merely on its strategical weakness that the Royalist plan might possibly be wrecked.   For any opportunity of bringing together fresh armies both sides would have to depend upon the local organisation of the counties, and upon an appeal to the spirit of the local populations.   Even in the East and South of the country, where Parliament was supreme, the local feeling in the counties was far stronger than it is at present.   In the North and West, where Charles found his most devoted adherents, it was in almost exclusive possession.   Geographical considerations, too, were likely to tell against the King.   The deep indentations of the western coast especially hindered the growth of common patriotism, and the men of Cornwall, of Wales, and of Lancashire were therefore not united in feeling as were the inhabitants of Kent and Sussex with those of Suffolk or Northamptonshire.

Strength of local feeling.

The dangers likely to arise from the strength of local feeling were as yet unsuspected on either side.   In Cornwall, Hopton had for some time gained the upper hand.   Before he was ready to assume the aggressive the initiative had been taken by the few gentlemen in the county who had joined the Parliamentary side, and who formed the Parliamentary committee at Launceston.   Fancying themselves powerful because they were unmolested, they prepared to indict

Oct 13.
Hopton in Cornwall.

Hopton and his supporters at the quarter sessions at Lostwithiel as disturbers of the peace. Much to their surprise, upon their arrival in that town Hopton confronted them, bearing in his hand the commission which he had received from Hertford as Lieutenant-General of the Horse in the West, and calling upon all men to submit to the authority which, in virtue of that commission, he derived from the King. Puritanism had but little hold upon Cornishmen, and the majority of the population were as opposed as were the gentry to any innovations in the services of the Church. There was, no doubt, too, something of local patriotism in the prevailing dislike of religious changes to which Devonshire had submitted. Hopton accordingly now turned the tables on his adversaries. Not only was he acquitted of wrong-doing, but he persuaded the grand jury to declare the gentlemen at Launceston guilty of promoting a riotous assembly, upon which the sheriff was authorised to call out the forces of the county against them.[1]

Of all Hopton's supporters none threw himself more energetically into the cause than Sir Bevil Grenvile, the friend of Sir Bevil Grenvile. Eliot, the descendant, as family tradition boasted, of Rolf, the sea-king who conquered Normandy, and the grandson of that Sir Richard Grenvile who had perished in the *Revenge*. Grenvile was a type of all that was noblest in the resistance to a Puritan domination. "I cannot contain myself within doors," wrote this brave and tender-hearted gentleman to a friend, who begged him not to endanger his family by the course which he was taking, "when the King of England's standard waves in the field upon so just an occasion ; the cause being such as must make all those that die in it little inferior to martyrs. I am not without consideration, as you lovingly advise, of my wife and family ; and, as for her, must acknowledge she hath ever drawn so evenly in the yoke with me, as she hath never pressed before or hung behind me, nor ever opposed or resisted my will ; and yet, truly, I have not in this or anything else endeavoured to walk in any way of power with her but of reason; and though her love will submit to either, yet, truly, my respect

---

[1] *Clarendon,* vi. 239. Hopton's Narrative *Clarendon MSS* 1,738

(1)

will not suffer me to urge her by power, unless I can convince by reason." [1]

With support from such men as these Hopton was invincible in Cornwall.   At the head of his little army he drove
The Corn-
ishmen will
not leave
the county. the Parliamentarians before him, occupied Launceston and Saltash, and called upon his troops to
cross the Tamar.   The men utterly refused to follow
him.   Cornishmen summoned by the sheriff were bound to

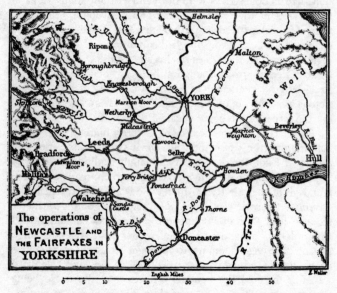

The operations of NEWCASTLE AND THE FAIRFAXES IN YORKSHIRE

keep the peace in Cornwall ; they were not bound to leave
the county to interfere in what was in that secluded district
considered to be almost a foreign country.   Hopton did not
attempt to thwart their inclinations.   Dismissing them with a
Nov.
Hopton's
new army. good grace, he called upon Grenvile and others to
raise a small force for permanent service by voluntary
enlistment.   In a short time he found himself at the
head of a body of 1,500 men ready to follow him where he

---

[1] Grenvile to Trelawny. *Parochial Hist. of Cornwall,* ii. 375.

would. Before the end of November he carried them into Devonshire,[1] occupied Tavistock and threatened Plymouth.[2]

As a commander Newcastle was not to be compared with Hopton, but he had a force of 8,000 men at his disposal. On

Dec. 1.
Newcastle
relieves
York.

December 1 he crossed the Tees, defeated the younger Hotham at Pierce Bridge, disarmed the Parliamentary levies in the North Riding, and relieved York. Cumberland, who had hitherto been the King's general in Yorkshire, retired from the command, and Newcastle had all the Royalist forces of the North under his orders. On the 6th Lord Fairfax, outnumbered and weakened by the desertion of

Dec. 6.
Tadcaster
fight.

some of his subordinates, turned upon the foe at Tadcaster. For a whole day he resisted all attempts to dislodge him, but powder and shot ran short, and on the following morning he fell back on Selby, where he

Dec. 7.
Fairfax re-
treats to
Selby.

would be in communication with the stores at Hull. Newcastle established himself at Pontefract, and by so doing cut the Parliamentary defence of Yorkshire in two. The clothing towns of the West Riding, with their strongly Puritan population, appeared to be beyond reach of help. Charles was overjoyed with the news. "The service I have received from you," he wrote to the splendid earl, "hath been so eminent, and is likely to have so great an influence

Dec. 15.
Charles
thanks
Newcastle.

upon all my affairs, that I need not tell you that I shall never forget it, but always look upon you as a principal instrument in keeping the crown upon my head. The business of Yorkshire I account almost done." Charles was but a bad judge of character, and he had little idea how small was likely to be Newcastle's success in face of real difficulty.[3]

Nor was it only in England itself that Charles's prospects appeared at Oxford to be hopeful. The Danish ambassador had continued to encourage him to expect succour from his

[1] Hopton's Narrative. *Clarendon MSS.* 1738 (1).

[2] *A perfect Diurnal.* E. 242, 35.

[3] Fairfax to the Committee of Safety, Dec. 10. *Bell's Memorials of the Civil War,* i. 25. D'Ewes's Diary. *Harl. MSS.* 164, fol. 226. The King to Newcastle, Dec. 15. *Ellis's Orig. Letters,* Ser. I. iii. 293.

master.[1] Unexpected news from France, too, flattered him with

His expec-
tation of
help from
abroad.

vain hopes. The great figure of Richelieu had disappeared from Continental politics. His death removed what had always been regarded at the English Court as the main obstacle to a kindly intercourse between Henrietta Maria and her brother, and it was hoped that his successor,

Nov. 24.
Dec. 4.
Death of
Richelieu.

Mazarin, would throw the influence of France into the right scale. The Queen herself was ready to recommend to her husband a course which would have

The Queen
recommends
the employment of Irish
soldiers.

alienated his subjects from him even more than an appeal to the swords of Danes or Frenchmen. Both she and Charles had been deeply irritated by the overtures made by Parliament to the Scots. If there were any danger of a Scottish invasion, wrote Henrietta Maria to her husband, let him win over the Irish Catholics to his side. Let him offer them the enjoyment of their estates and their religion, and they would furnish him with a plentiful supply of soldiers.[2]

No wonder that even before the whole extent of the disasters in the West and in the North was known at Westminster

Alarm at
Westminster.

Dec. 5.

the Houses took alarm. Their first impulse was to throw the blame on the dilatoriness of Essex. " It is summer," said Marten, " in Devonshire, summer in Yorkshire, and cold winter at Windsor." More practical men were aware that, before the army could stir, it was absolutely necessary to provide financial resources which would enable the commander to pay his soldiers regularly. On December 8, in spite of the opposition of constitutional purists,

Dec. 8.
Ordinance
for a general
taxation.

an ordinance extending to the whole of England the taxation which had recently been imposed on the City had passed through both Houses.[3] The measure was absolutely necessary, if a great catastrophe was to be averted. The estimated annual cost of the army exceeded 1,000,000*l.*, whilst that of the navy was more than 300,000*l.*[4]

---

[1] Agostini to the Doge, Dec. $\frac{9}{19}$. *Venetian Transcripts, R.O.*

[2] The Queen to the King, Dec. (?) *Letters of Henrietta Maria,* 148.

[3] D'Ewes's Diary. *Harl. MSS.* 164, fol. 243. *L.J.* v. 482.

[4] Yonge's Diary. *Add. MSS.* 18, 777, fol. 82.

In every direction the bounds of legality were being over-stepped, and each party had a sharp eye for the transgressions of the other.[1]   On the side of the King there was always the charge of rebellion to fall back on.   Amongst the prisoners taken at Brentford was John Lilburne.   On Decem-ber 6 he was indicted for treason before Heath, who had recently been made Chief Justice of the King's Bench.   Lilburne, who was never at a loss for an argument, boldly denied that he had waged war against the King.   He had taken arms to save his Majesty from evil coun-sellors.   The jury refused to take this view of his case, and brought in a verdict of guilty.   The judge sentenced him to death, and he would inevitably have been hanged if the Houses had not intervened with an energetic declaration that, if any of their soldiers were put to death, they would inflict the same punishment on all prisoners who might fall into their hands.[2]

Dec. 6.
Lilburne found guilty of high treason.

A similar collision arose on the King's appointment to of-fices which had hitherto been regarded as undeniably within his gift.   Parliament cancelled his nomination of sheriffs, which had been made in order to give heads to the Royalist gentry.   A less politically important office gave rise to a long contention.   On the 7th it was known in the House of Commons that Sir Charles Cæsar, the Master of the Rolls, was dead.   A resolution was come to that the House should name someone to fill the vacant post.   "I would," said the Speaker audibly, "you would name me."   The House took the hint, and named Lenthall.   The King, as might have been expected, refused to accept the nomination, and appointed Cul-pepper.   Culpepper could not fulfil the duties of the office in London, and as the Lords refused for the present to agree to

The Com-mons ques-tion the King's right to appoint sheriffs.

Dec. 7.
Double ap-pointment to the Mastership of the Rolls.

---

[1] Clarendon is never weary of attacking the Houses for their illegality. When his own party is concerned he takes a different view of the situation. In speaking of the refusal of the Cornish trained bands to enter Devon-shire on the score of illegality, he says that, ' however grievous and incon-venient soever this doctrine was discerned to be, yet no man durst presume so far upon the temper of that people as to object policy or necessity to their notions of law.'   *Clarendon*, vi. 243.

[2] *Rushw.* v. 83, 93.   *The examination of Capt. Lilburn.*   **E.** 130, 33.

take part in the appointment of anyone else, it was some little time before Lenthall gained possession of the post which he coveted.[1]

Not a few of the members took umbrage at these breaches of constitutional propriety ; but common sense was on the side of Pym when he refused to admit that the assessors of the new tax ought to be deprived of the power of administering an oath. "The law is clear," he said bluntly. "No man may take or give an oath in settled times ; but now we may give power to take an oath." [2]

Dec. 13. Pym's answer to the charge of illegality.

The question of immediate importance was not whether the taxes were legal, but whether they would be paid. If the burden imposed by them created a determined resistance, the King would have gained more than if he had won a victory in the field.

In the City of London the opposition to the new Parliamentary taxation assumed alarming proportions. Many of the wealthy merchants were Royalists at heart, and threw upon Parliament the blame of a war which was disturbing trade. Some of them vowed that, sooner than pay the tax, they would abandon business.[3] The hard times, bringing with them a loss of employment, made the war unpalatable to the lower classes. A petition was numerously signed calling on Parliament to make fresh overtures for accommodation on terms satisfactory to the King. On the 8th the Committee of both Houses for advance of money, which sat at Haberdashers' Hall, was besieged by a mob calling out for peace. Men known to be favourable to the Parliament were hustled and insulted. One gentleman who refused to sign the petition was told that, when the Cavaliers came, his house should be the first to be plundered. They were unarmed now, said some of them, but they would provide themselves with arms before long.

Dec. 8. The Royalist party in the City.

A petition for peace.

A mob at Haberdashers' Hall.

On the 12th there was a meeting of the Common Council

---

[1] D'Ewes's Diary. *Harl. MSS.* 164, fol. 243b. *C.J.* ii. 880. *L.J.* v. 481.

[2] Yonge's Diary, *Add. MSS.* 18, 777, fol. 92.

[3] Agostini to the Doge, Dec. $\frac{9}{15}$. *Venetian Transcripts, R.O.*

in the court adjoining Guildhall.   It had not been sitting long when the hall itself, as well as the yard outside, was filled with

Dec. 12.
Tumult at
Guildhall. an angry crowd clamouring for peace, and pressing to obtain the signatures of the Lord Mayor and Aldermen to their petition.   Cries of "Peace! peace!" were heard in every direction.   " Peace and truth ! " called out someone who took the unpopular side.   " Hang truth ! let us have peace at any price ! " was the prompt reply.   Some even threatened to break into the council chamber to drag out the Lord Mayor and the unpopular Aldermen, and to cut their throats. Others fell upon a few soldiers who were in the hall, wounded some of them, and snatched away their swords, bidding them go to the tavern.   " Spend your money you received from the State " they told the soldiers jeeringly, " for you shall have no more ! " At last a body of the City trained bands arrived, and order was restored.   The Common Council resumed its deliberations.

The resolu-
tion of the
Common
Council. The petition advocated by the mob was rejected, but the Council itself resolved to draw up two petitions asking for peace on reasonable conditions, the one to be directed to the King and the other to the Parliament.[1]

The hint thus given by the Common Council was taken by the House of Lords.   The Peers appointed a Committee to

Dec. 13.
The Lords
prepare
propositions
for peace. draw up propositions for peace, though they refused to receive the petition of the Royalist citizens on the ground that those who wished to present it were too numerous to be admitted to their bar.[2]   By the

Dec. 14.

Dec. 12.

Bears not to
be baited. Commons the keeper of the bear-garden had been committed to Newgate on the charge of obtaining signatures by means of threats, and an order was drawn up directing that no more bears should be baited during such distracted times,[3] an order which appears to have been very imperfectly obeyed.[4]

[1] Common Council Journal, Dec. 12. *Corporation Records*, xi. fol. 45.   Yonge's Diary. *Add. MSS.* 18, 777, fol. 91. *A continuation of certain Special Passages.* E. 244, 11. *The Image of the Malignants' Peace.* E. 244, 12. *An exact relation.* E. 130, 15.

[2] *L.J.* v. 488, 490.

[3] *C.J.* ii. 885.

[4] *The Actors' Remonstrance* (E. 86, 8) complains that whilst theatres

On the 14th the news of the retreat of Fairfax from Tadcaster reached Westminster, and it was accompanied by fresh

Dec. 14.
Bad news
from York-
shire.

information from Rotterdam of the activity of the
Queen in forwarding supplies to the Northern army.
Both Houses took alarm. There were twenty con-
victed recusants, it was said, amongst Newcastle's officers.

Dec. 16.
Alarm of the
Commons.

Measures
against the
Catholics.

Orders were at once given that all wealthy or
dangerous Catholics should be arrested, and their
estates sequestered. Nor was it only from the North
that danger was feared. Lord Herbert, the son of
the Marquis of Worcester, was raising a fresh army of
Welshmen, in addition to that serving under Hertford, and as
he was a Catholic, and had many Catholics in the army, his
movements were regarded with special alarm at Westminster.
About the middle of the month the Earl of Stamford, who had
maintained himself in Hereford as long as possible by plunder-

Dec. 14.
Stamford
leaves
Hereford.

ing the strongly Royalist population of the county,
evacuated his isolated position and fell back upon
Gloucester.[1] At the same time it was known in
London that Hopton, though some of the leading Devonshire

Hopton in
Devonshire.

Royalists had been surprised and sent up as prisoners
to London, was nevertheless able to hold the open
country up to the very walls of Exeter. So great was the
alarm that voices were heard in the Commons calling upon the
House to summon the Scots to bring immediate aid to their
English brethren. Such a confession of weakness, however,
did not as yet commend itself to the majority, and in the end
the Houses contented themselves with a declaration of their

Scottish
volunteers to
be enter-
tained.

readiness to entertain any Scottish volunteers who
might offer their services against an enemy whose
whole purpose was the suppression of the Protestant
religion.[2]

---

are closed the bear-garden is frequented. The date of this pamphlet is
Jan. 24, 164¾.

[1] Yonge's Diary. *Add. MSS.* 18, 777, fol. 96. Webb's *Civil War
in Herefordshire,* ii. 346.

[2] *L.J.* v. 495. *C.J.* ii. 891. D'Ewes's Diary. *Harl. MSS.* 164,
fol. 264b.

Something more than the addition of a few Scottish recruits to the army of Essex was needed if Charles's growing strength

Local orga-
nisation
needed. was to be kept at bay. Hitherto, outside those districts in which the King was present in person, the Houses had relied on something like the old county organisation, by placing authority in the hands of committees of the leading Puritan gentry in each shire. The arrangement had not worked well. The counties were too small to form the unit of the military system, and the plans of the committees were often liable to be thrown out of gear by the royalism of large numbers of the resident gentry. Hence a scheme had for some time been under discussion for the formation of associations comprising several neighbouring counties, so as to combine into active resistance the scattered elements of the Parliamentary party over a considerable extent of country. On December 15 an ordinance was passed for an

Dec. 15.
The Mid-
land Asso-
ciation. association of the midland counties, and this was followed on the 20th by another ordinance for an association of the eastern counties. The first com-

Dec. 20.
The Eastern
Association. prised the counties of Leicester, Derby, Nottingham, Rutland, Northampton, Buckingham, Bedford, and Huntingdon ; the second those of Essex, Suffolk, Norfolk, Cambridge, and Hertford. Stamford's son, Lord Grey of Groby, was appointed commander of the Midland Association, whilst the command of the Eastern Association, as yet removed from the perils of war, was left undetermined. On the 31st

Dec. 31.
Association
of Warwick-
shire and
Stafford-
shire. Warwickshire and Staffordshire were associated under the command of Lord Brooke.[1] The project was a hopeful one, at least for purposes of defence, but success was not to be assured merely by an improvement in administrative machinery. Each association would stand or fall in proportion to its ability to find a capable man to place at its head.

The necessity for increased organisation was brought home to the Houses by the progress of the war in the South and West. It is true that on December 13th Waller recovered

---

[1] *L.J.* v. 493, 505, 520.

Winchester, which had opened its gates to a small party of the
King's troops, and that on the 27th he recovered Chichester ;
Progress of   but, whilst Parliament was gaining ground in Sussex
the war in
the South   and Hampshire, it was in danger of losing London.
and West.   In the City the new taxation had stirred up the
bitterest feeling.   Though on one pretext or another the
chief promoters of the Royalist petition had been thrown into
prison, their followers had not been cowed.   On the 19th their
            petition was presented to the Lords by a chosen
Dec. 19.
The City   deputation, the numbers of which were not suf-
petitions. ficiently great to inspire alarm.   It was followed by
another petition which was presented in the name of the Lord
Mayor and the Common Council, and which was accompanied
by a copy of the petition which the Corporation of the City
proposed to send to the King, inviting him to return, and
assuring him that strict precautions should be taken against a
repetition of the tumults of the preceding winter.[1]

The next day the Lords sent down the propositions which
they had drawn up to be submitted to the King.   Charles was
            to be asked to bind himself to pass all such Bills as
Dec. 20.
The Lords' should be approved of by Parliament after consulta-
propositions. tion with the future assembly of divines ; to allow
Lord Digby and all persons impeached before January 1, 1642,
to stand their trials in Parliament, and to exclude Bristol,
Hertford, Herbert, Percy, Jermyn, and Wilmot from office and
from the Court ; to secure and vindicate the privileges of Parliament ; to give the Royal assent to Bills for securing the payment of the Parliamentary debt ; and to agree that all acts of
the Privy Council should be signed by those who had advised
them.[2]   There was also to be a new Militia Bill, and Charles
was to be asked to reinstate Northumberland as Lord High
Admiral.

Such were the propositions suggested by that House in
which the Peace-party was predominant.   They asked for
ministerial responsibility and for a Puritan settlement of the
Church—for all those concessions, in short, to which both

Charles and his partisans were most bitterly hostile. No wonder that those who kept their heads clear in the Commons thought it useless to engage in a negotiation on such terms. Vane led the way by asking the House to refuse even to take them into consideration. If Parliament began to treat with the King, it would grow careless of its own defence ; but the arguments of reason were borne down by the strength of the feelings enlisted in the cause of peace. To these feelings D'Ewes, with his imperturbable reliance upon phrases, gave expression. After repeating Pym's suggestion [1] that Charles's experience of the evils of war might make him more ready to treat than he had formerly been, D'Ewes asked his brother members how they expected to make head against the overwhelming forces in the field against them. The whole land was in confusion. No man would pay his rent. As the House had passed an ordinance to tax the subjects, it would be well to pass another to compel tenants to pay their rents. Poverty and famine were hastening upon them with winged feet. They were in danger lest the two armies might combine to make peace impossible. It would soon be a crime to be rich. D'Ewes sat down amidst loud applause, and the House voted that negotiations should be opened with the King. [2]

Dec. 22. They are considered by the Commons.

All the world, wrote one of Charles's partisans, was in favour of peace. [3] Those Lords who were understood to

---

[1] See p. 56.

[2] D'Ewes's Diary. *Harl. MSS.* 164, fol. 270b.

[3] The Verney correspondence presents the most touching evidence of the entire absence of anything like bitterness of feeling in a large group of men and women, amongst whom were warm partisans. The Royalist Edmund Verney, complaining to his brother that he had not received an answer to the letter of which an extract has been given at p. 5, writes as follows : "Although I would willingly lose my right hand that you had gone the other way, yet I will never consent that this dispute shall make a quarrel between us. There be too many to fight with besides ourselves. I pray God grant a sudden and firm peace, that we may safely meet in person as well as affection. Though I am tooth and nail for the King's cause, and shall endure so to the death, whatever his fortune be ; yet, sweet brother, let not this my opinion—for it is guided by my conscience

be the main supporters of the negotiation were greeted with shouts of "Peace! peace!" as they came out into Palace

Strong
desire for
peace. Yard. Pembroke and Northumberland, hat in hand, took up the cry, and called out "Peace! peace!" as loudly as anyone in the crowd.[1] In the Commons the Peace-party numbered Holles and Whitelocke, Selden and Maynard, amongst its members. It had the good

Weakness of
the Peace-
party. wishes of the vast majority of the nation, yet, for all that, it was from the first predestined to failure. There was not the smallest reason to suppose either that the terms which the Houses now offered would ever be accepted by the King, or that they would themselves be ready to accept any terms which the King was likely to propose.

It was this very impossibility of discovering terms of agreement which constituted Pym's strength. From the point of

The War-
party. view at which the man of the nineteenth century stands, it is easy to criticise his conduct severely. He and his followers, it may be thought, should have had more liberal views of ecclesiastical toleration, and should have been more ready to acknowledge that their adversaries who surrounded Charles at Oxford were fighting, as well as themselves, for conscience' sake. But it was not in the men of the first half of the seventeenth century to think anything of the kind. It was the tradition handed down from former generations, and held as firmly by those who were crying for peace as by those who were opposed to all negotiation, that there could be but one religion openly professed in the land. That which distinguished the War-party was its clear perception of the fact that, if the religion of England was to be Puritan, that object could only be attained by the sword. It was worse than waste of time, it was a slackening of the energies of the supporters of the Parliament, to attempt to establish Puritanism in England by negotiation with the King. Behind the question of what the

—nor any other report which you can hear of me cause a diffidence of my true love to you." E. Verney to Sir R. Verney, Feb. 24, 1643. *Verney MSS.*

[1] Forster to Chavigny, $\frac{\text{Dec. 29}}{\text{Jan. 8}}$, Jan. $\frac{5}{15}$. *Arch. des. Aff. Étrangères,* xlix. fol. 205, 212.

King might be persuaded to grant lay the question of personal confidence in his word. "The distrust of the few at the helm," shrewdly remarked the agent of a foreign court, "is not to be smoothed away. No one has so much eloquence as to persuade them to show confidence."[1]

Yet in spite of every objection the cry for peace was too strong to be resisted. On December 26, the Commons resolved to agree with the Lords' proposal that the negotiations should be opened. An attempt was to be made to come to terms with the King.

Dec. 26.
The Commons accept the proposal to negotiate.

No time was lost by the friends of peace. On January 2, before a formal treaty could be opened, the agents of the City arrived at Oxford with the petition of the Common Council, in which Charles was assured of protection if he chose to return to Westminster. At Oxford they found themselves in the midst of a population which might have been friendly a few months before,[2] but which was now dominated by the influx of Cavaliers. They were hooted as they passed through the streets, and it was with difficulty that they were preserved from actual violence. When at last they were admitted to the royal presence, Charles told them that he was glad of their coming, as he wished them to distribute amongst their fellow-citizens his declarations, which had hitherto been kept from their knowledge. On the 4th the agents were dismissed with the information that Charles would send an answer by Mr. Heron, one of his own servants, who was to accompany them on their journey. He asked which was the more numerous assembly in London, a Common Council or a Common Hall. On being told that the latter was the more numerous, he requested that his reply might be read there, as he wished as many as possible to be disabused and to know the truth.[3]

1643.
Jan. 2.
The agents of the City at Oxford.

Jan. 4.
The King's answer.

At least Charles could not justly complain that the citizens were not in a mood to listen even to reasonable terms. On January 3rd no less than 3,000 apprentices, many of them

---

[1] Salvetti's Newsletter, $\frac{Dec. 27}{Jan. 6}$. *Add. MSS.* 27, 962 K. fol. 40b.

[2] See p. 28.   [3] *L.J.* v. 458.

probably the very lads who had shouted lustily against the bishops a year before, came to Westminster with a petition for peace.[1]

Jan. 3.
The apprentices'
petition.

Petitions
for peace.

About the same time Bedfordshire, Essex, and Hertfordshire, the very counties in which the war spirit had risen the highest, agreed to petitions for peace.[2] The London press, usually so prolific of false accounts of victories, now began to cater for the popular taste by printing false accounts of pacific speeches, said to have been delivered by the King himself.[3] In the Commons, when Pym once more proposed to enter into a

Proposal
of Pym
negatived.

national association with Scotland to oppose that Catholic league which he believed to have been formed in support of the King, he met with no support. The Commons preferred to legislate directly for the extinction of Catholicism in England by the education of the children of Catholics in the Protestant religion, hoping that such a law would obtain the Royal assent when the King, at no distant date, was once more amongst them at Westminster.[4]

At last, on January 13, the Common Hall was gathered to hear Charles's answer to the City. It was a long diatribe against

Jan. 13.
Charles's
answer to
the City.

the arbitrary power illegally assumed by the men who had usurped his place. He called on all good subjects to throw off their yoke, and to begin by arresting the Lord Mayor and four of the leading citizens who had been guilty of treason. When this had been done, he would gladly return to London without the protection of his army.[5]

---

[1] *C.J.* ii. 917.

[2] *A petition of the County of Hertford; also the petition of the County of Bedford.* E. 84, 39. *The petition of the County of Essex.* E. 84, 40.

[3] *His Majesty's declaration.* E. 84, 38. *His Majesty's gracious answer.* E. 84, 41.

[4] Yonge's Diary. *Add. MSS.* 18, 777, fol. 112.

[5] *The humble petition of the City of London, with His Majesty's answer.* E. 84, 14. *The Kingdom's Weekly Intelligencer.* E. 85, 15. Agostini in his letter of Jan. $\frac{20}{30}$, says that armed men were at the door, but he does not say that anyone who had a right to enter was kept out by them. In explanation of his statement that two men who called out for peace were arrested, see the Lord Mayor's statement (*C.J.* ii. 927) that one man was arrested for being illegally armed.

After this Pym, who, together with other members of both Houses, was present in Guildhall, had no difficulty in con-

His terms rejected by the City.

vincing his audience that Charles had no thought of peace. The municipal spirit of the Londoners was roused, and of those who were present only two

Jan. 18.
Further attempt to circulate the answer.

raised their voices for the acceptance of such degrading terms.[1] A subsequent order from the King to the sheriffs to have his answer read in the halls of all the City Companies was frustrated by the interposition of the House of Commons.[2]

Pym was undoubtedly right in supposing that Charles had no serious thoughts of accepting a compromise. Herne, who

The King's intentions.

brought the royal answer from Oxford, assured the Venetian agent that Charles did not intend to give up a single point of his authority. In March he would have 40,000 men in the field. With these he would block the traffic of the Thames and force the citizens to throw off the existing government.[3]

If the war was to be carried on, the old difficulty of obtaining money must be resolutely faced. The taxation which had

Jan. 9.
The farmers of the customs refuse to lend.

been ordered produced little. The farmers of the customs had positively refused to lend. They alleged that trade was so ruined that the customs produced no more than 2,000*l.* a month. The Commons thought that this enormous falling off was due rather

Jan. 18.
And are dismissed.

to the disinclination of the farmers to levy money to be used against the King than to the decay of trade, and they dismissed them from their office. The new ones appointed in their place were ready to lend 20,000*l.*

---

[1] *Two Speeches.* E. 85, 7. In a speech purporting to have been delivered on the 17th Sir H. Garway says that the friends of peace were terrorised, and durst not appear. (*A speech made by Alderman Garway.* E. 245, 29.) On the other hand, in this account, printed at Oxford, it is stated that there was an overwhelming cry for peace on the 17th. This speech, however, as Mr. Firth has pointed out to me, is evidently one of the many forgeries which it was at this time thought expedient to issue from the Oxford press.

[2] *Rushw.* v. 120. *C.J.* ii. 941.

[3] Agostini to the Doge, Jan. $\frac{13}{24}$. *Venetian Transcripts, R.O.*

Such a sum would avail little unless the new Parliamentary
taxes could be raised, and as yet nothing had been obtained
Refusal to from this source. On the 20th Sir George Whitmore
pay taxes. and other wealthy citizens were imprisoned on their
refusal to pay. Sir Nicholas Crisp, one of the late farmers,
who was detected in carrying on a clandestine correspondence
with the King, succeeded in escaping to Oxford, but his plate
and money, to the value of 5,300*l.*, were seized by Parliament.[1]

In the midst of their financial difficulties the Commons
had been busily elaborating the propositions which had come
The peace down to them from the Lords. Impeachments, the
propositions date of which was earlier than January 1642, were to
in the
Commons. be proceeded with, and all subsequent to that date
were to be dropped. In spite of this decision, the name of
Newcastle was now placed alongside of that of Digby in the
worse category, although no charge had been brought against
him before the fatal date. Charles was to be asked to agree to
the disbandment of both armies before negotiations could be
opened, and Bills were rapidly hurried on for the regulation of
the Church in a Puritan sense. Amongst these was a Bill for
Bill for the the abolition of Episcopacy. Although it ought to
abolition of have been evident that to insist on such a Bill was
Episcopacy.
to place an insuperable obstacle in the way of peace,
the opposition to it, even of members of the Peace-party,
was extremely faint. One or two lawyers suggested that it
might be well to allow Episcopacy to stand, at least till the
House was prepared to substitute some other government for
Jan. 30. it. Even this gentle opposition found but little support, and before the end of January the Bill was
accepted by the Lords as well as by the Commons.[2]

If there had been anything to hope from the propositions
Progress of now ready to be presented, the balanced fortunes
the war. of the two parties might have reconciled both
Royalists and Parliamentarians to the idea of peace. If, during

[1] Whitacre's Diary. *Add. MSS.* 31, 116, fol. 16b, 19, 21, 21b. *C.J.*
ii. 935. D'Ewes's Diary. *Harl. MSS.* 164, fol. 277b.
[2] D'Ewes's Diary. *Harl. MSS.* 164, fol. 279. *C.J.* ii. 947.

the month of January, Charles's cause was prospering in the West, it was declining in the North.

After some hesitation, the Houses had nominated the wealthy but incapable Stamford to command the Western army.

Jan.
Stamford
sent to
command in
the West.

Early in January he arrived in Devonshire, bringing with him the troops with which he had failed to maintain himself in Hereford,[1] together with others which he had collected on the way. Hopton, who

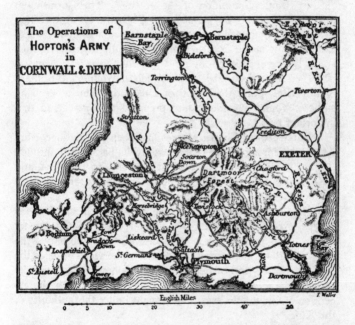

the month of January, Charles's cause was prospering in the West, it was declining in the North.

Hopton
retreats.

Rally of the
Cornishmen.

had found himself in want of supplies of every kind, had already retreated across the Tamar, where Stamford prepared to followed him. It was ill fighting Cornishmen in their own country. The trained bands which had refused to march into Devonshire now rallied round Hopton as soon as he touched Cornish soil. There was no such subordination on the other side as to render

[1] See p. 76.

Stamford's army really formidable. Ruthven, a Scottish officer

Ruthven disobeys orders. who commanded the garrison at Plymouth, with something perhaps of the contempt of the professional soldier for the titled commander to whom his obedience was due, pushed on hurriedly without waiting for Stamford.

Jan. 19. Royalist victory at Bradock Down. On January 19 Hopton and Grenvile fell upon him at Bradock Down, not far from Liskeard, and routed him utterly, taking 1,250 prisoners besides the guns and ammunition of the enemy.[1] The Cornishmen resumed the offensive. Saltash and Okehampton were carried by assault. Stamford retreated as hastily as he had advanced, and one wing of the Cornish army pursued the fugitives till they

Skirmish at Chagford. were checked by Sir John Northcote at Chagford, after a skirmish in which fell the young and brilliant Sidney Godolphin, the friend of Falkland. The other wing gathered round Plymouth, and prepared to lay siege to that important port.[2]

Nearer Oxford Charles's forces had been equally successful. At the beginning of the year Hertford had advanced through

Hertford reaches Oxford. the gap left by Stamford's march into the West, and with his Welsh regiments had joined the King at Oxford. To support these fresh troops it was neces-

Jan. 7. An attempt on Cirencester. sary to enlarge the circle within which contributions could be levied. An attempt made on Cirencester

Feb. 2. Cirencester taken. on January 7 was unsuccessful. On February 2 the town was carried by assault. The victors sacked the place, and carried off 1,100 prisoners to tramp wearily through the mire to Oxford. All Gloucestershire, with the exception of Gloucester, was thus brought under the authority of the King.[3]

In Yorkshire Newcastle had been less successful than his comrades in Gloucestershire and Cornwall. In December, when

---

[1] Hopton's Narrative, *Clarendon MSS.* 1738 (1).

[2] *Clarendon*, vi. 247. Grenvile to Lady Grenvile, Jan. 19. *Forster MSS.* D'Ewes's Diary. *Harl. MSS.* 164, fol. 289. *Special Passages.* E. 84, 17.

[3] *Rushw.* v. 130. *Warburton*, ii. 107. Massey to Fiennes, Feb. 11 *Add. MSS.* 18, 479, fol. 133.

he knew that Charles was anxiously expecting him to cleave his way to the Thames, the defeat of the Fairfaxes at Tad-

1642.
Dec.
Newcastle in
Yorkshire.

caster [1] seemed to have opened a path before him. His horse swept through Nottinghamshire, where the important town and castle of Newark were held by

Newark
he d for
the King.

Sir John Digby for the King ; and though an attempt to seize Nottingham failed, the possession of Newark made it easy to send supplies to Oxford. Yet before Newcastle could advance in person he was anxious

Sir W.
Savile in the
West Riding

to make himself completely master of the West Riding. The clothing towns of that district, cut off from succour by the retreat of the Fairfaxes behind the Ouse, were hard pressed. Strafford's nephew, Sir William Savile, dowered with something of his uncle's haughty and uncompromising temper, was sent to reduce them to submission. He entered Leeds and Wakefield without opposition, but at

Dec. 18.
He is re-
pulsed at
Bradford.

Bradford the stern Puritan spirit beat high, and, summoning their neighbours of Halifax to their aid, the townsmen prepared for resistance. On December 18, they foiled Savile's attempt to storm the town, and drove him to a hasty retreat.

Whilst Bradford was in expectation of a renewal of Savile's attack, succour arrived from an unexpected quarter. Sir

Sir Thomas
Fairfax.

Thomas Fairfax, the eldest son of the old lord, could not endure that the townsmen should be left to bear the brunt of war unaided. No more gallant spirit bore arms in the Parliamentary ranks. His frank nature and his sympathetic heart drew close the bonds which attach a soldiery to their leader. With a good eye for country, derived from his

Dec.
Fairfax at
Bradford.

experience in the hunting field, he was, like Rupert, ever foremost in the strife. If he was sometimes wanting in prudence, he was never deficient in dash,

1643.
Jan. 23.
Drives
Savile out
of Leeds

and for the present at least it was precisely this quality of dash of which his party stood most in need. Gathering a small force, the rider on the white horse, as he was fondly called, was despatched across

[1] See p. 71.

the enemy's country by his father, and before the end of December entered Bradford. Before long he was able to take the offensive, and on January 23 he drove Savile out of Leeds. Wakefield fell into his hands without further fighting.[1] Newcastle, baffled and disconcerted, fell back upon York.

In Cheshire Sir William Brereton, hardly less successful than Fairfax had been in the West Riding, had, on January 28th, succeeded in defeating the Royalists of the county at Nantwich. Thus, when negotiations were opened at Oxford neither side would be able to look upon an unbroken current of success. Charles's gain in the West was counterbalanced by his discomfiture in the North. To men less resolved to gain or lose all than were both Charles and his antagonists the path of compromise lay invitingly open.

Jan. 28.
Brereton's
success at
Nantwich.

[1] Lord Fairfax to a member of the House of Commons, Dec. 29, *Old Parl. Hist.* xii. 110. *The Rider of the White Horse.* E. 88, 23. See also for an account of these transactions in Markham's *The Great Lord Fairfax,* ch. iv.

CHAPTER V.

THE TREATY OF OXFORD.

ON February 1 the peace propositions, so carefully elaborated at Westminster, were laid before the King by the Commis-

1643.
Feb. 1.
The pro-
positions
presented
to the King.

Waller's
welcome.

Charles's
reception of
the Com-
missioners.

sioners appointed by the Houses. Amongst them was Waller, who had long been secretly working for him. "Though you are the last," cried Charles as he caught sight of the poet, "yet you are not the worst, nor the least in my favour." When, after this indiscreet speech, Northumberland began to read the propositions, he was continually interrupted by the King.[1] As far as words went Charles did not cast off all hope of an accommodation, if reasonable concessions were made to him. "They that principally contrived and penned them," he said of the proposals which had been brought before him, "had no thoughts of peace in their hearts, but to make things worse and worse. Yet I shall do my part, and take as much honey out of the gall as I can."[2]

Feb. 2.
His real
opinion.

In a letter to Ormond he expressed his real mind. "Certainly," he wrote, "no less power than His who made the world of nothing can draw peace out of these articles."[3]

Charles was a good critic but a bad statesman. The counter-proposals which he offered showed that he had made

Feb. 3.
His counter-
proposals.

no effort to look for honey to be taken out of the gall. He began by calling on his opponents to restore to him his revenue, his forts, and his ships, to recall all the declarations which they had issued in contravention

---

[1] *Whitelocke*, 67.　　　　　[2] *L.J.* v. 590.
[3] The King to Ormond, **Feb. 2.** *Clar. MSS.* 1654.

of the known laws of the land and of his own legal power, and to disclaim all right to imprison or to tax his subjects. Parliament was also to prepare a Bill which would preserve the Book of Common Prayer from the scorn and violence of the Brownists, Anabaptists, and other sectaries, in which he would be glad to see inserted a clause for the ease of tender consciences in accordance with his former declarations. All persons excepted from the general pardon were to be tried by their peers. Instead of the disbandment of both armies proposed by the Houses there was to be a cessation of hostilities during the negotiations, and there was to be freedom of trade between those who lived in the respective quarters of the Royal and the Parliamentary armies.[1]

After this reply no wise man could entertain any hopes of peace. Even the hint thrown out about tender consciences was too vaguely worded,[2] and was too unappropriate to a condition of things in which two religious parties were struggling on equal terms for the mastery, to produce the slightest effect. Anxious as the Lords were to proceed with the negotiation,

Feb. 7.
The Lords vote a cessation.

they felt that they could only do so by dropping out of sight for a time the question of principle which really divided them from the King, and they contented themselves with adopting Charles's proposal that a cessation of arms should come first, and that this should be

[1] *Rushw.* v. 165-169.

[2] In his declaration published after his reception of the Grand Remonstrance, Charles expressed himself in the following way : "For differences amongst ourselves, for matters indifferent in their own nature concerning religion, we shall, in tenderness to any number of our loving subjects, very willingly comply with the advice of our Parliament that some law may be made for the exemption of tender consciences from punishment or prosecution for such ceremonies, and in such cases which, by the judgment of most men, are held to be matters indifferent, and of some to be absolutely unlawful ; provided this can be attempted and pursued with that modesty, temper, and submission that, in the meantime, the peace and quiet of the kingdom be not disturbed, the decency and comeliness of God's service discountenanced, nor the pious, sober, and devout actions of those reverend persons, who were the first labourers in the blessed Reformation, or at that time, be scandalled and defamed." Husbands' *Collections*, 21.

followed by a diplomatic struggle which might lead to a general disbandment of the armies.

To the men who had hitherto disposed of the majority of the Commons this resolution of the Lords appeared to be a ruinous concession. A cessation of arms, they believed, would be altogether in the King's favour. The King was levying monthly contributions wherever his armies had the upper hand, and, whether from loyalty or fear, those contributions were duly paid. On the other hand Sir Gilbert Gerard, the Parliamentary Treasurer of the Army, had lately announced that he had not a penny left with which to pay the troops, and that it was absolutely necessary to establish that regular taxation about which so much had been said and so little done. Since this revelation, a committee had been sitting to devise an expedient;[1] but it needed but little sagacity to perceive that, if hostilities were suspended it would be more than ever difficult to induce even the warmest supporters of the Parliament to submit to taxation. Besides this, there was a strong conviction that delay would enable the King to gather from abroad those reinforcements which he was believed to be awaiting.

Feb. 8. Feeling in the Commons.

Feb. 1. Financial difficulties.

On both sides every effort had been made to secure a full attendance in the Commons. The Peers had induced a considerable number of members, who had long been absent from Westminster, to come up to vote for peace. On the other hand, members, who were also officers, forsook for a time their military charges to raise their voices against the dangerous pursuit of a phantom.[2] The highest vote recorded during the month of January was 102. In the division taken on February 8 the numbers reached 194.

Feb. 8. Full attendance in the Commons.

Yet, after all, the parties thus marshalled against one another were divided by no broad ground of principle. On both sides there was an agreement that the King's answer was no answer at all. Pym, who warmly supported an immediate disbandment, declared that the difference between the King and his people was not one to

Debate in the Commons.

Feb. 9.

---

[1] D'Ewes's Diary. *Harl. MSS.* 164, fol. 287.

[2] Agostini to the Doge, Feb. $\frac{10}{20}$. *Venetian Transcripts, R.O.*

be settled by the sword. He had too much confidence in his own cause not to believe that, if the arguments on which he relied were fairly heard, without the distraction caused by the presence of armed forces, they would bear down all opposition. He therefore asked that as soon as the armies had disappeared the propositions of the Houses should again be laid before the King, with such explanations as might seem necessary. When, after two days' debate, the vote was taken, it was found that, though there was a considerable minority which believed all diplomacy useless, the majority was for opening a negotiation on the subject of disbandment. On the 10th and 11th there

Feb. 11.
Disband-
ment to
precede the
negotiation
for peace.
was a discussion whether the Houses should offer to negotiate on the propositions themselves before the disbandment had taken place. Pym distinctly replied in the negative. "If they yield not to a disbanding," he said, "we shall have no hope of peace." Holles and Maynard must have known in their hearts that it was most unlikely that the King would yield at all, but they continued to hope against all probability. On a division, however, they were beaten, and the House resolved that the armies must be disbanded before another step was taken. In all probability Pym and Hampden had voted with Holles on the 9th, and now voted against him.[1]

There can be little doubt that the House had decided as rightly as it was possible for it to decide, unless it could rise

Feb. 16.
into a higher atmosphere of thought. To conduct a negotiation when the views entertained even by those who were most in favour of peace were diametrically opposed to those entertained by the King was plainly useless, and might be ruinous. The majority of the little group of Peers which now constituted the House of Lords thought otherwise. They

Compromise
proposed by
the Lords.
proposed a compromise. Let there be, at first, a mere cessation of hostilities. Let that be followed by a negotiation limited to twenty days, in which the demand of the Houses for a disbandment and the King's demand

[1] *C.J.* ii. 960. D'Ewes's Diary. *Harl. MSS.* 164, fol. 291b. Yonge's Diary. *Add. MSS.* 18, 777, fol. 145, 148. D'Ewes's prejudiced statements should be corrected by the last-named authority.

for a surrender of the forts and ships might be discussed. To this proposal the Commons gave way, though only by a majo-

Feb. 17.
And as-
sented to
by the
Commons.

rity of three. It was, perhaps, necessary in the face of the widespread agitation for peace to prolong the negotiation, futile as it was ; but so dissatisfied were some of those who had voted for breaking it off, that there was some talk amongst them of impeaching five of the Peace-party in the Upper House. Nothing, however, was done in the matter, and many days were spent in settling the

Feb. 28.
The new
proposals
ready.

details of the new proposals. It was only on February 28 that they were ready to be forwarded to Oxford.[1]

Whilst time was thus consumed at Westminster, Charles was looking anxiously but hopefully to the North for aid which

Jan.
Newcastle's
army in the
North.

would free him from the necessity of negotiating at all. Newcastle, it is true, had been compelled to fall back upon York by the successes of the younger Fairfax in the West Riding, but there was reason to believe that he would soon be in a position to take the field with advantage. From time to time he had been joined by officers of reputation who had been sent to him from Holland by the Queen, amongst

General
King
created
Lord
Eythin.

whom the most noted was General King, who, having known long service in the German wars, was at once accepted by the Earl as his military adviser, and was shortly afterwards created Lord Eythin in the Scot-

Feb. 2.
The Queen
sets sail.

tish peerage. On February 2 Henrietta Maria set sail in person for the Yorkshire coast. Arms, as occasion served, she had despatched to the army of Newcastle from time to time, and she was now bringing with her a fresh supply, together with a large sum of money, obtained by selling or pawning jewels, a sum which contemporary rumour, with probable exaggeration, reckoned at 2,000,000*l.* This time, however, a fierce storm swept over the North Sea, and for nine days the Queen, with her precious cargo, lay tossing on the waves. She never lost the high spirits which accompanied her

---

[1] Agostini to the Doge, $\frac{\text{Feb. 24}}{\text{March 6}}$. *Venetian Transcripts, R.O. L.J.* v. 608. *C.J.* ii. 969. *Rushw.* v. 170.

in every position in which she was placed, and she laughed
heartily as her attendant ladies were driven by the howling of
the wind and the creaking of the timbers to shout out, in confession to her chaplain, a catalogue of sins which was never
meant to reach the ear of their mistress. "Comfort yourselves,
my dears," she said, in unconscious imitation of the Red King;
" Queens of England are never drowned." [1]

At Oxford Charles was anxiously watching for news of the
safe arrival of his wife, whose energy had served him so well.

Feb. 12.
Charles's
anxiety.

The Queen
driven back,
and sails
again.
"Never woman with child," he wrote to Newcastle,
"more longed for anything than we for news from
you." [2]   Charles's longings were not immediately
satisfied.   Henrietta Maria at last regained a Dutch
port, and some days passed before she was again able
to put to sea, under Tromp's escort.

On the 22nd the Queen landed at Bridlington Quay.   On
the morning after she was awakened by the roar of guns.

Feb. 22.
Four Parliamentary ships, under Captain Batten,
were firing at the vessels which she had brought over,
and which were still laden with warlike stores.   The shot came

Feb. 23.
Is in danger
at Bridling-
ton Quay.
crashing through the houses of the little port.   The
one in which the Queen had passed the night was
specially exposed to danger, in all probability not
because Batten deliberately intended to injure her,[3] but
because it happened to be in the line of fire.   Springing from
bed, and hastily wrapping whatever first came to hand around
her, she hurried out in search of a place of greater safety.   On
her way through the street she remembered that her lap-dog
had been left behind, and in spite of the entreaties of her
attendants she riskéd her life by returning to seek for it.
Snatching up the little animal, she returned unhurt, and finally
took refuge in a ditch outside the town, where she was under
cover, though the bullets flew over her head or sprinkled
her with dust as they struck the ground.   At last a threat
from Tromp and the fall of the tide compelled Batten to

---

[1] *Mémoires de Madame de Motteville*, i. 209.

[2] The King to Newcastle, Feb. 13.   *Harl. MSS.* 6988, fol. 132.

[3] It is not very likely that he knew in what house she was.

desist.[1]   After a few days' rest she was conducted by Newcastle
March 5.
She goes to
York. to York, where she was to await an opportunity
of rejoining her husband with safety.

Charles was the more overjoyed at the last news
from his wife as he had been warned that a conspiracy had been
Alleged plot
against her. formed to seize her on her way from the coast, in
order to deliver her to the Parliament to be held as
a hostage.   Newcastle arrested Lord Savile and Sir Thomas
Gower on suspicion of complicity in the plot, whilst Lord Newport, who was charged with participation in it, sought safety in
flight.   As, however, Savile had no accusation made against him
after he was brought to Oxford, and as Newport was attempting
to make his way to the King when he was captured on the road
by the Parliamentary troops, and was ultimately thrown into
the Tower, there seems to be good reason to believe that both
Savile and Newport were, at least on this occasion, guiltless.[2]

On the day on which the tidings of the Queen's entry into
York reached Charles he received the articles of the proposed
March 1.
Articles of
cessation
presented to
the King. cessation at the hands of the Parliamentary Commissioners.   "Yesterday," he wrote to his wife on
the following morning, "there were articles of a
cessation brought me from London, but so unreason-
March.
Charles
comments
on them. able that I cannot grant them.   Yet, to undeceive
the people, by showing it is not I, but those who
have caused and fostered this rebellion, that desire
the continuance of this war and universal distraction, I am
framing articles fit for that purpose—only this, I assure thee
that the distractions of the rebels are such that so many fine
designs are laid open to us we know not which first to undertake ; but, certainly, my first and chiefest care is and shall be
to secure thee, and hasten our meeting." [3]

[1] *Mémoires de Madame de Motteville*, i. 210.   The Queen to the King,
Feb. 25.   *Letters of Henrietta Maria*, 166.   *Rushw.* v. 156.

[2] Savile's vindication has been published by Mr. Cartwright.   *Camden
Misc.* viii.

[3] The King to the Queen, March 2.   *Letters of Henrietta Maria*, 174.
Berwick Castle in this letter should, I have no doubt, be Belvoir Castle,
and Chester is evidently a misprint for Chichester.

In pursuance of the design which he announced to his wife Charles drew up the reply, which on March 6 he despatched to Westminster. He complained that the Houses had not granted freedom of trade during the cessation, and he asked that the ships which had been sent out to defend the realm might be placed under officers named by himself. Finally, he required that, during the cessation, no one should be imprisoned except in accordance with the known laws of the land.[1]

March 6.
The King's
reply to the
Houses.

These last words indicated something more than a benevolent desire to maintain the law. The City had lately responded to a fresh request for a Parliamentary loan by an offer of 60,000*l.* ; but its offer was accompanied by a request that the much-talked-of general taxation —the order of December 8 having been too vaguely worded to take effect[2]—might be actually put in force. The wish thus expressed had already been met. On February 24 an ordinance was voted imposing a weekly payment upon every county in England, and naming Commissioners who were to assess the owners of property at their discretion ; a scheme which seemed to be likely to be more productive than the levy of five per cent., which might easily lead to disputes between the owners of property and the assessors. If every county had been amenable to the orders of Parliament, the sum obtained would have exceeded 1,600,000*l.*[3] Even half of this sum would have been no inconsiderable revenue.

Feb. 26.
A fresh
City loan.

Feb. 24.
A general
tax imposed.

Charles was perfectly right in seeing that the difficulty of enforcing payment of taxation would be a weak point in his opponents' line of defence, and it was only natural that he should attempt to improve it to his own advantage, by suggesting that to imprison those who refused to pay the tax was as illegal as the tax itself. There were many who believed a demand for money made by anything short of an Act of Parliament to be unjustifiable, and many more who

Resistance
to taxation.

---

[1] *L.J.* v. 640.   [2] See p. 72.
[3] *L.J.* v. 619.   *Two Ordinances.*   E. 91, 36.

found it convenient to treat it as unjustifiable. The payment of the original five per cent. assessed upon London and Westminster [1] had been widely refused. So dull was trade, and so exhausted were the citizens by the continual calls upon their purses, that it was difficult to find buyers for goods seized in default of payment, and at last the Jews of Amsterdam were invited to send agents to England to purchase what few Englishmen would buy.[2] A beginning was thus made, and after a while money began to come in, though by no means in amounts equal to the expectations which had been formed by the promoters of the scheme.[3]

The situation was felt to be a serious one, all the more as the Parliamentary party had just suffered a considerable personal loss. In the Midland counties the King's cause had been steadily gaining ground, and before the end of February—in addition to Newark—Ashby-de-la-Zouch, Tamworth, Lichfield, Stafford, and Stratford-on-Avon were occupied by his forces.[4] The loss was the more severely felt at Westminster, as it opened the way for the southern march of Newcastle and the Queen.

Feb. The King gains ground in the Midlands.

In looking for a man who might stem the tide of disaster the Houses lighted upon Lord Brooke. His position as owner of Warwick Castle and his known staunchness to the Parliamentary cause had led to his appointment as commander of the recently associated counties of Warwick and Stafford, and he was now directed to take charge of the forces of those counties. After driving the Royalists out of Stratford he advanced to Lichfield, where the Cathedral and the close had been converted into a fortress, and were now garrisoned by the Royalists. Stepping into the street to watch the effect of a cannon shot aimed across the pool, the calm surface of which reflects the three graceful spires of the Cathedral, his appearance attracted the

Lord Brooke sent into Staffordshire.

March 2. He is killed at Lichfield.

---

[1] See p. 65.

[2] Agostini to the Doge, March $\frac{3}{13}$. *Venetian Transcripts, R.O.*

[3] There are books of payment in the Record Office. *Com. for advance of money*, A. 37–39; 46–52.

[4] The details may be gathered from the pamphlets of the month.

attention of the garrison. A shot from the central tower
pierced his brain and stretched him lifeless on the spot. The
Royalists triumphantly recorded the fact that the assailant of
the sacred precincts was slain on the festival of St. Chad, the
patron saint of the Cathedral, and that the fatal shot was fired
by 'dumb Dyott,' who, having been deaf and dumb from his
birth, might be regarded as a special instrument of Providence.
To his own party the loss was considerable. Those who were
beginning to censure Essex as a dilatory commander were
already casting their eyes on Brooke as a more energetic
successor. In modern times he will be chiefly remembered
as the author of that *Discourse on Episcopacy* which marks a
step in the progress of the doctrine of toleration.[1] Two days

March 4.
The Cathe-
dral sur-
renders.

after his death the garrison of the Cathedral surrendered to Sir John Gell, who had brought up reinforcements from Derbyshire. Yet, in spite of the
check thus inflicted on the Royalists, they continued to steal
gradually southward, and houses were from time to time
seized and garrisoned in unexpected quarters by the Cavalier
gentry.[2]

Every day brought news which convinced all but the most
stubborn that it would be unwise to weaken the defences of

March 7.
Orders for
fortifying
London.

March 9.
News that
Rupert has
marched
against
Bristol.

Parliament by listening to overtures from Oxford.
On March 7 Parliament, upon the proposal of the
Court of Common Council, ordered that London
should be fortified.[3] On the 9th a startling message
arrived from Essex, telling how Rupert, with 6,000
horse, had marched against Bristol, so that 'there
was likely to be little fruit of' the treaty. With the
full approbation of the Houses Essex now proposed to open
the campaign as soon as possible.[4]

---

[1] *Hist. of Engl.* (1603–1642), x. 35.

[2] *Special Passages.* E. 89, 17. *The last week's proceedings of Lord
Brooke.* E. 59, 19. Account of the Siege of Lichfield. *Harl. MSS.*
2,043, fol. 25. Agostini to the Doge, Feb. $\frac{10}{20}$. *Venetian Transcripts,*
R.O.

[3] Maitland's *Hist. of London,* i. 369.

[4] D'Ewes's Diary. *Harl. MSS.* 164, fol. 318.

Rupert's bold dash had already failed. Some of the leading merchants of Bristol had undertaken to open a gate to him
March 7.
Rupert's
failure. in the night, but the plot was discovered, and the
leaders captured, two of whom, named Yeomans and
Bourchier, were ultimately executed. Rupert returned hastily to Oxford, and in face of his numerous cavalry
Essex did not yet venture to stir.[1]

Just at the time when Rupert's attempt and failure were
known in London, the letter in which Charles assured the
March 10.
An inter-
cepted
letter. Queen that his only object in continuing the negotiations was to undeceive the people was intercepted
and published.[2] The phrase in which he expressed
satisfaction at the many 'fine designs' offered to him caught
the public ear, and for many a month, as one Royalist intrigue
after another came to light, the newspapers took good care to
remind their readers that it was one more of his Majesty's 'fine
designs.'

It was not by the Commons alone that Charles's answer of
the 6th was regarded as unsatisfactory. To abandon
The Lords
alienated by
Charles. the navy to him and to renounce the power of imprisonment was to surrender at discretion, and the
Peers, long urgent for peace, now felt it to be hopeless, and
threw in their lot with the party of resistance.[3]

Yet, even so, those who in their hearts knew that the prolongation of the war was inevitable were loth to pronounce the
fatal word which would put an end to this futile negotiation.
March 11.
The City
demands an
association. The Common Council, on the other hand, angry
with such trifling, called for the formation of that
association for which Pym had asked on the eve of
the King's march to Edgehill.[4] Disastrous as was a policy
which would divide more sharply than before the already divided
nation, the only alternative to it was a policy of reconciliation
based on religious toleration, and, unhappily, neither Charles
nor his adversaries had conceived the idea of any such solution.

[1] *A brief relation of a plot against Bristol.* E. 93, 3.

[2] See p. 95.

[3] Agostini to the Doge, March $\frac{10}{20}$. *Venetian Transcripts, R.O.*

[4] See p. 39.

Conciliation in respect to the material objects in dispute was alone possible as yet, and what little of this there was came from the side of the Parliament.

March 18.
Fresh over-
tures made
by Parlia-
ment.

On the 18th fresh instructions were forwarded to Oxford by the Houses, empowering their Commissioners to offer a reasonable compromise on the question of the custody of the forts and ships. "The passages of this day," wrote D'Ewes, "gave me the first hopes I had received for divers months last past that God of His infinite mercy would be pleased to vouchsafe a speedy peace to this almost half-ruined kingdom, for the articles propounded were so full of equilibrancy as that there was no probability to the contrary but that his Majesty would readily accept them." [1]

D'Ewes
hopes for
peace.

The very equilibrancy, as D'Ewes termed it, of the new proposals was sufficient to set Charles against them. He was asked to entrust the forts and ships to persons nominated by himself on condition that they should possess the confidence of Parliament. [2] He first objected to the proposed articles of cessation, and then, rejecting the compromise of the Houses, asked that the forts and ships should be entrusted to those in whose hands he had himself placed them before the outbreak of the troubles, at the same time professing himself to be ready to remove his nominees if just cause should be shown for his so doing. [3] As this arrangement would place the Tower in the hands of Byron, Portsmouth in the hands of Goring, and Hull in the hands of Newcastle, even the warmest supporters of an understanding with the King must have felt that their hopes were at an end.

March 23.
Charles
criticises
the cessa-
tion, and,
March 28,
asks for
the forts
and ships.

Indeed, even before Charles's claim to the ships and forts was known at Westminster, it was generally recognised that the treaty would come to nothing. Lords and Commons agreed in taking measures for carrying on the war in earnest. On March 27 they passed an ordinance sequestrating the estates of all who gave assistance to the King. The

March 27.
Ordinance
of seques-
tration.

---

[1] D'Ewes's Diary. *Harl. MSS.* 164, fol. 334.
[3] *Rushw.* v. 175.   [2] *Ibid.* 177, 200.

policy of confiscation, announced on September 6, and partially
enforced on October 15,[1] was thus made generally applicable.
D'Ewes, it is true, mourned over the fact that the 'fiery spirits'
were now as supreme over the Peers as they were over the
Commons, and consoled himself with the remembrance that
superiority of character was on the side of peace. In the
Commons at least most of the men of great estates were on
the side of an accommodation, whilst the supporters of Pym
were 'mean or beggarly fellows,' who, having been mechanics,
and being men of mean fortune, were therefore 'not so sen-
sible of the destruction of the kingdom as those who had estates
to lose.' It did not occur to D'Ewes to ask whether Charles's
exorbitant demands had anything to do with the ascendency
which Pym had now regained.[2]

Pym was bent on placing the Parliamentary finances on a
sound basis. The tax of five per cent., the monthly contributions, and the rents of sequestrated estates might perhaps be sufficient if all England could be compelled
to pay. As this was impossible, Pym proposed an excise upon all commodities bought and sold. Such a proposal
was certain to rouse the warmest opposition. If the incidence
of an excise is not more oppressive than that of other taxes, it
is at least more widely felt. A member rose to express his
astonishment that a motion should be made in that House to
revive a tax which, when the King had attempted to impose it
in 1628, had been declared by the Commons to be destructive
to trade. Pym then proposed to restrict the new tax to super-
fluous commodities. One member after another refused to
accept it even on these terms, one speaker expressing his astonishment 'that he who pretended to
stand so much for the liberty of the subject should propose

March 28.
*Pym pro-
poses an
excise.*

*His motion
rejected.*

---

[1] See pp. 17, 37.
[2] *C.J.* iii. 21. D'Ewes's Diary. *Harl. MSS.* 164, fol. 344b, 346.
There is an odd entry on fol. 338b to the effect that the Lords on March
22 acquainted the Commons that they had sent to Oxford to ask the King
for payment of the expenses of firing for the use of the King and Parliament. If this means, as I suppose it does, the warming of the Houses at
Westminster, it is not strange that the King would not pay.

such an unjust, scandalous, and destructive project.' Pym's motion was lost, but the time would come before long when it would be found necessary to adopt it.[1]

In spite of the rejection of Pym's project, the evident hopelessness of an accommodation had given the War-party the ascendency in the Commons. On March 30 the Commons, in the teeth of the opposition of the Lords, offered a deadly insult to the Queen. They sent a committee, of which Marten was a member, to arrest the Capuchins at Somerset House, and to tear down the images—the idols, as they scornfully named them—in the chapel.[2] A picture by Rubens, valued at 500*l.*, which stood over the high altar, was cast into the Thames.[3] The feeling against the Queen was growing daily amongst Pym's adherents in the Commons.

March 30.
Expulsion of the Capuchins.

Destruction of images in the Queen's Chapel.

By none was Charles's obstinacy felt, as its consequences developed themselves, more than by those who, on either side, were sincerely desirous of peace. On March 19 Roe had poured his troubles into the sympathising ear of Falkland. "If," he wrote, " you can agree the cessation, which is the popular part, the articles will follow almost by necessity, and this rule only I will lay, that if you must or shall make war successfully, you must set peace in the first rank, you must show that she is ravished from you, and your arms are only employed to rescue the beloved of all men."

March 19.
Despondency of Sir T. Roe.

Roe's subsequent letter of April 6 shows the effect produced on him by the news of the King's demand for the ships and forts. "It may appear great presumption in me," he wrote, "to give any opinion either of the state of your treaty in hand or of your proceedings therein ; but if indignation could make a poet against nature, the passions of a troubled spirit may excuse any errors of a well-affected zeal. I cannot bear to inform you that the last message of his Majesty hath utterly discomposed even all those who seriously pursued and grasped after the hopes of accommodation. They

April 6.

---

[1] D'Ewes's Diary. *Harl. MSS.* 164, fol. 346b.
[2] *Ibid. Harl. MSS.* 164, fol. 348b. *L.J.* v. 687.
[3] Salvetti's Newsletter, April $\frac{7}{17}$. *Add. MSS.* 27, 962 K. fol. 83b.

pretend to have no ground nor subject left them to continue their endeavours. There is another party who triumph and proclaim that it is you that decline the peace by refusing the cessation which, though I know it be in some points disad vantageous to his Majesty, yet, considering the popularity of such an expectation, I cannot conceive the inconveniences of equal weight to the general opinion which would have been gained to your part by yielding, which is often the true way to perfect victory." [1]

At Westminster Holland spoke almost in the same language. He assured D'Ewes that both he and others had urged their friends at Oxford to implore the King rather to yield to some present inconvenience than to let slip this opportunity of making peace. If only, he added, 'the two Houses' could 'return into their old way of advising and debating, the King would find so many sure friends in either House, as those violent spirits who had raised this un-natural and bloody war would be brought low in the esteem of all men, and' his Majesty would then be restored 'to all his ancient and undoubted power and rights.' Holland sadly ac-knowledged that his counsel 'had been nothing at all regarded.' [2] Charles, in fact, if he desired peace, desired it only on his own terms, and was entirely unconscious of the importance of win-ning the sympathy of his more moderate opponents. His eye was fixed on the progress of the military operations.

*April 8.
And of
Holland.*

Charles's position at Oxford was an isolated one, and be-tween him and each of the supports on which he counted there was some Parliamentary force which must be over-powered before the Royalist plan for the summer's campaign could be carried out As long as Stam-ford held Devonshire Hopton's advance was impossible, and Rupert's failure to capture Bristol, together with the devotion of Gloucester to the Parliamentary cause, interposed a bar against the progress of the Welsh levies of Lord Herbert.[3] Further north, Brereton, in Cheshire and Lancashire, main-

*March.
The military
position.*

[1] Roe to Falkland, March 19, April 6. *Harl. MSS.* 1,901, fol. 62b, 64.

[2] D'Ewes's Diary. *Harl. MSS.* 164, fol. 367b. [3] See p. 76.

tained a superiority over Lord Derby, whilst the Hothams in Hull and the Fairfaxes in the West Riding continued to hold their own against Newcastle. If the Parliamentarians held the broken circumference of a circle round the King, the Royalists held a still more broken circumference of an outer circle beyond. The efforts of the Royalists of this outer circle to overpower the resistance of the intermediate zone with a view to an ultimate advance on London, gave a kind of unity to those local and desultory combats which bewilder the historian.

During the first fortnight of March Sir William Waller, who had been down to Gloucestershire to strengthen the position

Sir W. Waller in Gloucester-shire.

which had been weakened by Stamford's march into Devonshire, had been engaged in making good his footing. On the 15th he secured Bristol. Having reduced Malmesbury on the 21st, he threw himself on the 24th on Lord Herbert's Welshmen at Highnam, and dispersed or captured all who escaped the sword.[1]

Bristol and Gloucester having been thus secured, Waller assumed the offensive. Ross and Newnham, Monmouth and

April 5. He occupies Monmouth and Chep-stow.

Chepstow fell into his hands ; but he did not venture to advance further westward. Not only was the Welsh population hostile, but he learnt that Rupert's younger brother, Prince Maurice, had been sent from Oxford with Lord Grandison to fall upon his rear. Sending his foot and artillery across the estuary of the Severn, he passed through the enemy's lines, and slipped into Gloucester

April 11. Returns to Gloucester.

at the head of his cavalry. The places which he had occupied in Monmouthshire fell back into the hands of the Royalists. If Waller had not accomplished all that he had hoped to do, he had at least secured the important district of which he was in charge. He had also shown that Parliament possessed a general whose wariness was united with that agility in which Essex, with all his sterling qualities, was terribly deficient. The name of ' William the

---

[1] Mr. W. P. Price, in a letter addressed to the *Gloucester Journal,* July 4, 1868, and which has since been reprinted, shows that there was considerable slaughter, from the evidence of local tradition and the dis-covery of skeletons.

Conqueror,' which was now applied to him, marked the estimation in which he was held.[1]

In the North, Newcastle and the Queen were more successful than Herbert had been in the West. Money was sadly wanting to the Parliamentary army in Yorkshire, and there was none to spare in London to send to its support. Amongst its commanders, too, there were some who had taken arms from political rather than from religious motives, and who therefore felt themselves ill at ease as the cause for which they fought showed itself as more distinctly Puritan. Amongst these were Sir Hugh Cholmley, the governor of Scarborough, and the two Hothams. Of the three, Cholmley appears to have had the nobler nature, and to have been actuated by the purer motives. In the years of passive resistance he had refused to pay ship-money, and had been disgraced by Strafford. Like most of the Yorkshire country gentlemen he had nothing of the Puritan in him, and having taken service under Parliament in the belief that the war would soon lead to a constitutional compromise, he was bitterly disappointed at the failure of the Oxford negotiators to reach any basis of agreement.

March.
State of
Yorkshire.

March 25.
Sir Hugh
Cholmley.

Whilst Cholmley's mind was in this state, the Queen invited him to a conference at York. He accepted the invitation, and returned to Scarborough resolved to embark in a treason which might easily assume in his eyes the character of loyalty to the sovereign whose castle he had been guarding against its true owner. On March 25 he informed the garrison that from that time they were to hold the fortress for the King. Their apparent acquiescence lulled him into security. On March 31, during his absence on a second visit to the Queen, Bushel, one of his officers, persuaded the soldiers to return to their allegiance to Parliament. On the following day, however, Cholmley reappeared before the walls

March 25.
Deserts
the Parliamentary
cause.

Scarborough
Castle
gained for
the King.

[1] Nicholas to Rupert, April 6. *Warburton*, ii. 159. Waller's operations in the West are given in detail in Webb's *Civil War in Herefordshire*, i. 235, 249.

with 1,500 men, and Bushel was compelled to surrender the fortress which he had won.[1]

The Hothams did not as yet follow Cholmley's example ; but they showed little interest in the Parliamentary cause, and

April 2.
The Fair-
faxes in
Leeds.

did all that lay in their power to thwart the operations of Lord Fairfax and his son.   The Fairfaxes, thus deserted, abandoned the country about Selby, and threw themselves—not without loss—into Leeds, where they were soon besieged.[2]

In proportion as Newcastle gained ground in Yorkshire it became necessary to hold out a hand to him from Oxford, to enable him, when his immediate task was accomplished, to make his way southwards.   The loss of Lichfield had been felt by the Royalists as weakening the King's hold upon the Midlands, where it most concerned him to be strong.   On

March.
Northamp-
ton sent to
recover
Lichfield.

the receipt of the news, therefore, Northampton had been despatched from his station at Banbury to retake it.   From a life of ease and luxury this wealthy nobleman had been roused by the outbreak of the war to throw himself heart and soul into the royal cause. In Warwickshire his name had been from the first a tower of

March 19.
Battle of
Hopton
Heath.

strength to the King.   On March 19 he met Gell's forces on Hopton Heath, about two miles from Stafford.   After a sharp conflict he drove the enemy before him ; but in the moment of victory, as he was charging too far in advance, his horse was killed under him, and his helmet struck from his head.   The Parliamentary soldiers who surrounded him offered him quarter.   " I scorn," was the disdainful reply, " to take quarter from such base rogues as you are." Irritated by this contemptuous rejoinder, a soldier dashed at him with a halbert and silenced him for ever.

Death of
Northamp-
ton.

Whilst the King's horse were pursuing the fugitives in a course as headlong as that which had cost them so dear at Edgehill, Brereton arrived on the field with fresh

---

[1] *Rushw.* v. 264.   *Memoirs of Sir H. Cholmley*, 36.   Memorials touching Scarborough.   *Clar. MSS.* 1669.   *Certain letters sent from Sir John Hotham*, 100, d, 47.   *Certain informations.*   E. 97, 3.

[2] Letter of Fairfax in Whitacre's Diary.   *Add. MSS.* 31, 116, fol. 126.

Parliamentary troops, and enabled some at least of his beaten

A doubtful
victory. comrades to hold their ground.   Both sides claimed the victory.   The Earl's body remained in the hands of the enemy, and, unless the constant asseveration of the Royalists is to be mistrusted, Gell and Brereton were so dead to all honourable feeling as to refuse to deliver it up to the slain nobleman's son, except in exchange for the guns and prisoners which had been captured by the Royalists.[1]

Charles resolved to send Rupert to complete the work which had been interrupted by Northampton's death.   On

April 3.
Rupert at
Birming-
ham. April 3 the Prince reached Birmingham, then a small town noted for its Puritanism and its iron-work.   When the Civil War broke out it threw itself with more than ordinary ardour into the Parliamentary cause.   It furnished Essex with 15,000 sword-blades, and cast into prison two messengers who brought an order to forge weapons for the King.   When Charles was on the march to Edgehill the men of Birmingham intercepted and carried off the plate which followed him.   Though their town was an

April 3. open one, they now refused to allow Rupert a passage through it, and fired on the approaching troopers.   After a brave resistance they were driven back, and the Royalists gained possession of the town.   In spite of Rupert's order to spare the beaten foe, the place was sacked and many of the houses were set on fire.   Twenty thousand pounds, it was said, would be insufficient to repair the damages.   The Earl of Denbigh, the honest squire who had risen to fame as Buckingham's brother-in-law, and was now fighting in the Royalist ranks, was slain in the attack.[2]

As Rupert marched on loud cries reached him from distressed Royalists.   Lady Derby implored him to hasten to the

Rupert
summoned
to the
North. assistance of her husband, who was fighting an unequal battle in Lancashire.   Capel, who was maintaining the King's cause in Shropshire, urged him to advance against Brereton, who held almost all Cheshire for the Parliament.   If Nantwich, he said, were taken,

[1] *Rushw.* v. 152.   *Clarendon*, vi. 280.
[2] The evidence on both sides is collected by *Warburton*, ii. 151.

Manchester would soon fall, 'and after that, between Oxford and Scotland, the King's affairs would have little impediment.'[1]

Rupert struck for the nearest object. On April 10 he laid siege to Lichfield Close and Cathedral.[2] When that had fallen,

Siege of
Lichfield
Close. and its resistance could hardly be prolonged, he would be able to hold out a hand to Derby and Newcastle, and to conduct to Charles the Queen and the military stores in her keeping. The resistance was, however, prolonged till the 21st, and when the Cathedral was at last surrendered Rupert's services were needed in the South. His scheme of a northern march had to be abandoned for the present.

On April 8 the Houses refused to agree to a cessation on the King's terms, and required a positive answer to their original

April 8.
Will the
King agree
to a dis-
bandment? demand for a disbandment.[3] On the 12th Charles replied by asking, as he had asked before, that his revenue, magazines, ships, and forts should be re-

April 12.
His final
terms. stored to him, and placed under the charge of the persons trusted by him, unless just and legal exceptions could be taken against them ; that all members of either House expelled since January 1642 should be restored ; and, finally, that, in order that Parliament might be secured against tumultuous assemblies, it should be adjourned to some place not less than twenty miles from London. From the Parliament thus reconstructed he expected Bills for punishing those who, in the press or in the pulpit, had used seditious language against himself or against the laws, and especially those who had justified the taking of arms against the King. To make these terms more acceptable he offered to throw over the Catholics, and to consent to a Bill for the better discovery and speedier conviction of recusants, as well as for the compulsory education of their children in the Protestant faith.[4]

As a matter of course these proposals were rejected. On April 14 the Houses refused to accept them as a basis of

---

[1] Capel to Rupert, April 6.   *Add. MSS.* 18, 480, fol. 37.
[2] *Rushw.* v. 148.   [3] *Ibid.* v. 191.   [4] *Ibid.* v. 259.

negotiation. "Let us not trouble ourselves," said Marten
bluntly, of this and of another message which had recently
April 14.
The mes-
sage re-
jected. been delivered, "to send away an answer; but
rather answer them with scorn, as being unworthy
of our further regard." [1] The Commissioners were
recalled from Oxford, and the long and fruitless negotiation
was brought to an end.

[1] D'Ewes's Diary. *Harl. MSS.* 164, fol. 363. *C.J.* iii. 45.

CHAPTER VI.

IRISH AND SCOTCH MOVEMENTS.

THE paragraph relating to the Catholics in Charles's final reply was peculiarly disgraceful. In the hour of trouble he had joyfully accepted their services, yet he was now ready to abandon them to their enemies at a moment when he was stickling for every jot of his own prerogative.

1643.
April.
Charles's
treatment
of the
Catholics.

The fact was that Charles, as was so often the case with him, was floating between two irreconcilable policies. The first, which was embodied in his message, was the policy of Hyde, who had just been advanced to a seat in the Privy Council, and had been named Chancellor of the Exchequer in succession to Culpepper. The strict execution of the law of the land, in reliance on the support of a complete Parliament, which was to be freed by its removal to a distance from Westminster from the dictation of a London mob, was the groundwork of Hyde's system. If that system was very far from being all that the circumstances of the time demanded, it was at least straightforward and complete in itself, whilst it appealed to the reverence for law and the reverence for Parliaments which are the most abiding characteristics of political Englishmen.

His two
policies.

Hyde as a
counsellor.

With such principles Hyde had no objection to dabble in what ordinary men would speak of as plots and conspiracies. He could not understand that a trust imposed by the Houses at Westminster was binding upon the conscience at all. Those who, like Cholmley, surrendered to the King fortified places which they had engaged to guard for Parliament were simply restoring to its legitimate owner property, of which, in a moment of weakness, they had accepted the charge at the hands of a gang of robbers. Whilst the negotiations were still in progress preparations had been made at Oxford to secure a prize in comparison with which Scarborough Castle was as nothing. Charles knew that a large number of the inhabitants of London were anxious for peace, and he was ready to offer any assistance in his power to enable them to shake off the yoke of the usurpers.

Accordingly, on March 16, Charles addressed to Sir Nicholas Crisp and other citizens a commission of array, by which

March 16. A commission of array for London. they were authorised to appoint officers and to select from amongst their loyal fellow-citizens such as were fit to be brought under military discipline. The commission, however, was retained at Oxford till an opportunity should occur of conveying it safely to London. In the meanwhile the poet Waller undertook the completion of the

Origin of Waller's plot. political arrangements, and offered to act as intermediary between the citizens and such members of either House as might be ready to declare for the King on a fitting occasion.[1] That the correspondence between Oxford and London was to pass through the hands of Falkland is a sure indication that the plan had the concurrence of Hyde.

In substance the policy of Hyde was the policy of Charles. The King was as indisposed as his adviser to make any real

Charles concurs with Hyde, concession to those whom he regarded as actuated by the basest motives. Of a broader, more genial statesmanship there was no thought with either. Where Charles stood apart from Hyde was in his willingness to accept aid from any quarter, and in his fond belief that men of every religious or political principle might be brought to sacrifice themselves for him without exacting corresponding advantages in return. He fancied especially that he could

but adopts a policy of his own. so use the Catholics as to avail himself of their services, though he never intended to bind himself to them further than he was conveniently able to do.

Hence arose a second policy, the details of which were

---

[1] *State Trials,* iv. 628.

never communicated to Hyde, a policy which was certain to clash with the one which Charles ostensibly adopted. In a later

Charles and the Catholics. generation it would be possible to be a convinced Protestant and to support the claims of Catholics to complete religious liberty, but such breadth of judgment was hardly possible as yet, and Charles at least laid no claim to it. As far as England was concerned, the weakness of the Catholics was such as to make them well pleased with anything short of the worst treatment, but it was otherwise in Ireland, and it was to the Irish Catholics that Charles was now looking. As yet, indeed, he did not ask them for direct aid, but he hoped so to conciliate them as to enable him to bring away from Ireland the English army which had been serving against them. On April 9, only three days before

His expectations from Ireland. Charles announced his readiness to abandon the Catholics of England to the cruelty of the law, Sir Nicholas Byron, writing by his direction, informed Capel 'that his Majesty did shortly expect succour from Ireland, which was for a time to be kept secret.'

No doubt Charles wished to keep his project secret. Unless he could veil his Irish plans in darkness, it would be hard for him to secure the sympathy of any considerable section of the London citizens. Unluckily for him, Byron's letter was intercepted, and its contents were before long known at Westminster.[1]

For more than a year the Irish insurgents had been doing their best to come to an understanding with Charles. In

1642.
March 22.
Overtures from Ireland. March 1642, just after they heard that he had given his assent to the Act of Confiscation,[2] the Catholic gentry of the Pale despatched Colonel Reade to England as the bearer of their assurances of loyalty.

Colonel Reade tortured. The unfortunate messenger fell into the hands of the Puritan government at Dublin, and was put to the torture in the vain hope that he might be brought to acknowledge Charles's participation in the rebellion.[3] The

[1] D'Ewes's Diary. *Harl. MSS.* 164, fol. 242b.

[2] *Hist. of Engl.* (1603-1642), x. 173.

[3] Reade's examinations in Gilbert's *Hist. of the Irish Confederation*

insurgents, however, knew that in the main they must depend on themselves and not on Charles. On the very day on which

The Synod of Kells.

Reade was stretched on the rack a synod of the clergy of the province of Armagh, meeting at Kells, called for an organisation which might give unity to the

May.

Assembly at Kilkenny.

The Supreme Council.

scattered forces of the insurrection.[1] In May an assembly in which the clergy took counsel with the principal Catholic laymen was held at Kilkenny. It was then resolved to choose a Supreme Council of nine members to act as a Provisional Government of revolutionary Ireland, on the understanding that a General Assembly, which would practically be an informal Parliament of the insurgent population, should meet as soon as possible.[2]

To the step thus taken the Lords Justices replied, on May 28, by prohibiting all intercourse with the Catholics. On June

June 21.

Catholics excluded from the Dublin Parliament.

21, the House of Commons at Dublin, now a purely sectional body, resolved that all persons refusing the oath of supremacy should in future be debarred from taking their seats, and expelled forty-one of its members as traitors.[3] The two religions were thus divided by a sharper line than ever, and in Ireland the division of religion was nearly, if not quite, coincident with the division of race.

Before the end of July the Catholics made another effort to lay their case before the King, requesting Ormond to

July 31.

Petition to the King.

forward their petition to him. Ormond, however, placed it in the hands of the Lords Justices, by whom it was carefully suppressed.[4]

Of the war, which formed a lurid background to these consultations and schemes, no detailed account is possible.

do not show this, but Castlehaven (*Memoirs*, ed. 1684, p. 39) says that his brother, ' who heard it from Reade himself as he was brought out of the room where he was racked,' told him that Reade ' was much pressed to tell how far the late King and Queen were privy or concerned in the Irish rebellion.' See Mr. Gilbert's Preface, p. xxxiv.

[1] Gilbert's *Hist. of the Irish Confed.* i. 790.

[2] *Ibid.* i. 86.   [3] *Ibid.* ii. 45.

[4] Petition of the Irish Catholics. Carte's *Ormond*, v. 352.

There was no strategy on either side. It was an affair of skirmishes and sieges, of raids over the wide expanse of pasture land for the purpose of sweeping off the herds of cattle which were the main wealth of the people. Wherever an English force could penetrate, its track was marked by fire and the gallows. Exasperated at the Ulster murders, and seeing in every Irishman a murderer or a supporter of murderers, the English soldiery rarely gave quarter, and, unless the accounts of their enemies are entirely devoid of truth, when they did give it it was often violated. The peasants retaliated by knocking stray soldiers on the head, and by slaughtering parties too weak to resist. Yet whenever in the summer of 1642 the Irish forces were commanded by officers of rank and authority, they were distinguished for humanity under circumstances of no slight provocation. The garrisons of fortified posts captured by the Irish were uniformly allowed to find their way in safety to a place of refuge.[1] On the whole the balance of advantage was on the Irish side. Seldom able to cope with the English in the field, and extremely deficient in artillery, they had been defeated in May by Ormond in a comparatively considerable engagement at Kilrush, and in several other encounters in different parts of the country. Numbers were, however, on their side, and the English troops, ill supplied with pay and depending on plunder for their support, dwindled away, till garrison after garrison was compelled to surrender. In the course of the summer two soldiers of note arrived from the Low Countries, where they had occupied distinguished posts in the service of the King of Spain. One of these, Colonel Thomas Preston, was appointed by the Supreme Council to command its army in Leinster ; and Owen Roe O'Neill, the heir of the ancient chieftains of his race, immediately upon his arrival in Lough Swilly, was accepted by the whole native population of Ulster as its natural leader.[2]

Marginal notes: Progress of the war. — Preston and Owen O'Neill.

[1] Though the *Carte MSS.* of this year are composed almost entirely of letters and documents on the English side, I cannot remember any instance in them to the contrary.

[2] This paragraph is based upon Bellings and the author of *The Aphor-*

In the course of September, therefore, the Lords Justices had but a dismal tale to recount. In the county of Limerick only one garrison held out. In the county of Cork only a few places, mainly on the coast, still made head against the enemy.

Sept. 1.
Account by the Lords Justices.
Further east, Waterford and Wexford were in the hands of the Irish, who hoped to make of the latter port another Dunkirk, a nest of privateers darting forth to prey on English commerce. In Ulster, Monro, the rude soldier who had harried Strathbogie in 1640, had taken up his quarters at Carrickfergus ; but neither he nor the Earl of Leven, who arrived subsequently to take the command, was inclined to engage in any difficult military undertaking. The English Parliament had promised to send money to support the Scottish army, but the outbreak of the war in England prevented it from fulfilling its obligations. After a short stay in Ireland Leven returned to his native country, leaving Monro behind him at the head of the troops as his major-general.

" Thus," wrote the Irish Council on September 1, " are the rebels plentifully supplied with arms and munition, while we

Sept. 1.
Despondency of the Irish Council.
want both, for our arms are much broken, decayed, and grown unserviceable, inasmuch as we have not sufficient now in any degree to arm our men fully, though grown so defective in our numbers. And now the only advantage we hitherto had of our enemies, being arms and munition, they are now like to have of us, which, added to their other advantage of numbers of men, renders our condition very lamentable. Neither is it to be marvelled that their provisions should increase, and ours not so, in respect they have the wealth and natural commodities of the whole kingdom in their hands. They have the merchants and traders of the principal ports travailing for them and their supply of arms, munition, and all other provisions, by sea and land, at home and abroad, and the very inhabitants of the few ports we have,

---

ismical Discovery, tested and completed by the mass of material in the *Carte MSS.* Mr. Gilbert's valuable selection of documents published in the appendix to his two books will not relieve even a writer who treats Irish history as briefly as I have done from the duty of working in that mine of information.

being Papists, do the like. We on the other side have not the quiet use of any land in the kingdom, nor anything but what we fight for, out of the few towns we have." [1]

By the end of September the Irish Council were in somewhat better spirits. Lord Lisle, the son of the Earl of Leicester, had been sent to Ireland at the head of 1,500 men. He had relieved Trim, and had marched by way of Kells to Virginia. "He still proceeds"—such is the account given by the Government—"in burning, wasting, spoiling, and destroying all the country about him, and all the rebels' corn, hay, and turf, and depriving the rebels of all the cattle he can, so as to take from them all means of lodging, food, and fire; which course, God willing, we to our power intend to hold in other parts, as knowing that nothing conduceth more certainly to the destruction of the rebels; yet we see we shall be wonderfully disabled therein by those extremities of want under which we now suffer, and whereof we are in danger to be swallowed up, if not speedily supplied from thence, our want of powder and match being such and so great as we much fear the Lord Lisle will hardly have sufficient to retreat hither." [2]

It is no wonder that a policy so desolating, and at the same time so ineffectual, found some opposition in the ranks of the Irish Government itself. Ormond had long known himself to be distrusted by the Lords Justices, or, to speak more plainly, by Sir William Parsons, who was the guiding spirit of the party of confiscation and destruction. He had many relatives engaged on the opposite side, and he knew Ireland too well not to wish to see all reasonable concessions made to the just complaints of the Catholic nobility and gentry. Even if he had not been bred up in the school of Strafford, he would have been drawn by his feelings as an Irish statesman to repose confidence in Charles, and to distrust the English Parliament, which treated Irish grievances with

Marginal notes:
Sept. 29. Lisle's expedition.

Sept. 29.

Conciliatory tendencies of Ormond.

---

[1] The Irish Council to the Commissioners for Irish affairs, Sept. 1. Gilbert's *Hist. of the Irish Confed.* ii. 55.

[2] The Irish Council to the Commissioners for Irish affairs, Sept. 29. *Carte MSS.* iii. fol. 532.

contempt. Yet he had never allowed his political views to affect his conduct as a soldier, and as commander of the army he had lost no opportunity of attacking the insurgents

Aug. 30.
Ormond
created a
marquis. though to some extent he sympathised with them in their misfortunes. Charles had been grateful to him, had supported him in the claim which he had put forward to the appointment of officers in opposition to the Lord Lieutenant, and on August 30, before leaving Nottingham, had raised him to the dignity of a marquis.[1]

The question of the attitude to be taken towards those whom the Dublin Government designated as rebels was grow-

Oct. 24.
Meeting of
the General
Assembly at
Kilkenny. ing more pressing every day. On October 24, the day after the battle of Edgehill, the General Assembly of the confederate Catholics met at Kilkenny. Every county and every borough, not actually in the power of the enemy, had chosen its representatives. To all intents and purposes the body thus produced was a Parliament of the Irish nation, though it met in a single House, and though, out of respect for the King, it disclaimed the title of Parliament for an Assembly which had not been summoned by his writs.

The Assembly thus constituted proceeded to remodel the Supreme Council, which was thenceforward to consist of

Nov.
The
Supreme
Council
remodelled. twenty-five members.[2] Under it there was to be a Provincial Council in each province, and a Council in each county. All these Councils were to exercise judicial as well as administrative functions. On the ecclesiastical question the Assembly pronounced a decided opinion. The Roman Catholic Church was to re-enter upon its rights, and the Roman Catholic bishops and clergy were to be held as the true possessors of all ecclesiastical property, though, much to the disappointment of the monks, abbey lands were not to be restored by the lay impropriators, many of whom were sitting in the Assembly itself. Whether the Protestants in Ireland were to be allowed liberty of religion was a point on

[1] *Carte MSS.* v. fol. 573.

[2] At first it was to have been twenty-four, but Castlehaven was added to it. *Castlehaven's Memoirs,* 59.

which the Assembly did not touch, and which it perhaps reserved for future negotiation. On the land question the Assembly was equally reserved. On the one hand, it refused to acknowledge the results of popular violence. Land was to be held to be the property of him who had possessed it on October 1, 1641. Where, however, the owner was an enemy or a neutral, his rents were to be sequestered for the promotion of the public cause.[1] It is, however, impossible to doubt that, if the efforts of the Assembly had been crowned with success, it would have found itself powerless to reinstate the English and Scottish colonists on the lands which they had recently lost, and it is not very probable that Catholic Ireland would have granted to Protestants a toleration which was denied to Episcopalians in Presbyterian Scotland, and had lately, when Charles's authority was supreme, been denied to Presbyterians in Episcopalian England.

"Irishmen, unanimous for God, the King, and the country," was the motto chosen for the seal of the confederate Catholics.[2]

The motto of the confederates.

Unless the unwonted unanimity of Irishmen could be preserved, the Assembly would hardly succeed in carrying out the work which it had undertaken, and there were already signs that the unanimity which it proclaimed was but skin-deep. The land policy proclaimed was a policy of landowners, and was unlikely to conciliate those who had formed the strength of that agrarian revolution which had well nigh swept the English out of Ulster. Owen O'Neill, the darling of the Ulster population, came indeed to Kilkenny, and accepted an appointment as general of the Ulster forces from the Supreme Council ; but there was little real amity between him and the leaders of the Government of the Confederacy, especially as Phelim O'Neill, who was his rival in the North, and who claimed as well as himself the chieftainship of the sept, had lately married a daughter of Preston, with whom Owen O'Neill was by no means on good terms.[3]

---

[1] Acts of the General Assembly. Gilbert's *Hist. of the Irish Confed.* ii. 73.

[2] *Pro Deo, rege et patria, Hiberni unanimes*, or, in some specimens, *Hibernia unanimis.*

[3] Gilbert's *Cont. Hist. of Affairs in Ireland*, i. 53.

For the present, however, no actual division showed itself. A fresh petition was forwarded to the King, and this one at least reached his hands.[1] By the time that he received it he had grave reason to be displeased with the Lords Justices.

Fresh petition to the King.

In the course of October [2] Reynolds and Goodwin, two members of the English House of Commons, had been despatched from Westminster, with 20,000*l.* in their hands, as a committee to examine into the state of affairs at Dublin. Not only had the Lords Justices permitted these rebels, as Charles styled them, to be present at the sittings of the Privy Council, but they had given their support to a preacher who had declaimed against the King's marriage with an idolatress.[3] It was only to be expected that Charles should do all that was in his power to secure his own authority in Dublin.

A deputation from England.

As yet, however, Charles did not venture directly to attack Parsons. All that he could do was to prevent him from becoming more powerful than he was. At the end of November Leicester was at Chester, hoping at last to cross the sea to take in hand the Lord Lieutenancy, to which he had been appointed so long before. It was absolutely certain that if he once reached Dublin he would take part with Parsons against Ormond, with whom he had a personal quarrel. On November 29, therefore, Charles, immediately after his arrival at Oxford, wrote to request his presence there, on the transparent pretext of wishing to take his advice. After a long delay Leicester most unwillingly set out for Oxford, understanding clearly that it was not intended that he should ever hold authority in Ireland.[4]

Nov. 29. Leicester forbidden to go to Ireland.

Shortly after Leicester's virtual recall the officers of the English army in Ireland, driven to despair by the impossibility

---

[1] Petition, Dec. *Bellings,* ii. 129.

[2] From D'Ewes's notes of a letter from Reynolds and Goodwin (Diary, *Harl. MSS.* 164, fol. 111), it appears that they arrived on Oct. 29.

[3] Carte's *Ormond,* ii. 325.

[4] Leicester to the Speaker of the House of Lords [?], Dec. 20. *Carte MSS.* iv. fol. 134.

of obtaining payment for their services, drew up a remonstrance calling attention to their hard condition.[1]   The news that the

army which had been sent out under the authority of the English Parliament was dissatisfied with its position appears to have roused Charles's interest in the events which were passing beyond the sea.   He had allowed the petition in which the Irish Catholics had asked that their grievances might be heard to remain unanswered for

1643.
Jan. 11.
Charles
orders the
opening of
negotiations.

many weeks.   On January 11 he issued a commission to Ormond, Clanricarde, and others to meet the Catholic leaders, in order to report to him on their complaints.[2]

If Charles had resolved to enter on this negotiation with an honest intention to face the enormous difficulties of the Irish problem, he might well have been appalled by the hopelessness of the task which he had undertaken.   Until religious differences ceased to exasperate nations to war, not only the prejudices but the legitimate apprehensions of Englishmen of every party would stand up like a wall against a policy which would have established so near the shores of England a Church and a Government unavoidably hostile to her own religion and institutions, and unavoidably allied with the Continental powers who were her bitterest rivals.   Even those who may be inclined to wish that the experiment had been tried must be well aware that it could not have been tried with the good-will of any Protestant Englishman of the seventeenth century.

Charles meddled with no such high matters.   What he wanted was so to pacify the Irish Catholics as to be able to uti-

lise the English regiments in Ireland for service against the English Parliament.   He informed Ormond that his affairs in England would be ruined if he agreed to the abrogation of the penal statutes in Ireland, but that there would be no difficulty in executing them with laxity. There must be no independence in the Irish Parliament.   He

[1] Remonstrance of the officers (undated).   Ormond to Nicholas, Dec. 19.   Carte's *Ormond*, v. 395, 399.

[2] Commission to Ormond and others, Jan.   The King to the Lords Justices, Jan. 11.   Gilbert's *Hist. of the Irish. Confed.* ii. 139.

could not agree to restore the Plantation lands occupied before
his own accession, but the whole subject might be referred to
Commissioners after the conclusion of the main treaty. He
would not promise that the Irish should be governed by their
own countrymen, but he would consent that Irishmen should
be qualified to hold office, 'because it will always be his
Majesty's choice whom he will entrust with those charges, and
if some of the more subordinate ministers be Irish, so long as
they shall be controllable by the major part of the English, the
danger will be less, and by degrees his Majesty may with more
safety reduce the frame of government to its former condition.' [1]

It is unnecessary to say that the commission to treat was
received with grave disapprobation by the Lords Justices and
the English Committee. What was of more importance, the officers of the army raised some objections,
though in the end they were persuaded by Ormond
to withdraw their opposition. Weary of expecting
those supplies which the English Parliament was unable to give,
the officers were easily induced by Ormond to turn to the King
for the redress of their grievances.[2]

*Jan. 30.
Reception
of the com-
mission at
Dublin.*

Charles's next step was likely to test the strength of his authority in Dublin. On February 3 he wrote to the Lords Justices, rating them soundly for their presumption in
allowing members of the English Parliament to be
present at the sittings of the Council, and ordering
the immediate exclusion of the intruders.[3] Finding
it impossible to win over the army, Reynolds and
Goodwin left Dublin shortly before an order for their arrest
arrived from Oxford.[4]

*Feb. 3.
The Par-
liamentary
Committee
excluded
from the
Council.*

[1] Memorial for the Irish treaty. The King to Ormond, Jan. 12.
Carte's *Ormond*, v. 1.

[2] Tucker's Journal. Gilbert's *Hist. of the Irish Confed.* ii. 155, 188.
Ormond to Clanricarde, Feb. 3. Ormond to the King, Jan. 31. Carte's
Ormond, v. 370, 432.

[3] The King to the Lords Justices and Council, Feb. 3. Carte's
Ormond, v. 393.

[4] *Ibid.* ii. 413.

In the meanwhile the risk of a military disaster was increasing daily. On January 20 Preston had taken Birr

Jan. 20.
Birr Castle
taken.

Castle, an important post in King's County.[1] The Lords Justices did what they could. The 20,000*l.*

brought by Reynolds and Goodwin were almost spent, but, having raised a small amount of money by a forced loan of plate, they resolved to send out Lord Lisle at the head of a force of 1,500 men. Rather than allow Lisle, who was

Feb. 18.
Ormond
takes the
command
of an ex-
peditionary
force.

closely allied with Parsons, to have such a force under his orders, Ormond declared his intention of taking the command himself.[2] Owing to his superiority in artillery, Ormond defeated Preston at Ross, on March 18, but his supply of provisions

March 18.
Battle of
Ross.

was too scanty to enable him long to keep the field. Before the end of the month he was back in Dublin,

followed by a half-starved army, clamorous for pay and food. The Lords Justices pleaded with the English Parliament for money, but in such a time of necessity they pleaded in vain. Ormond had learned by this time that the soldiers, disgusted with continual ill-treatment, were ready to throw themselves into the arms of the King.[3]

Some weeks passed after the receipt of the King's commission to negotiate before the negotiators were brought face to

March 17.
Opening of
a negotia-
tion at
Trim.

face. At last, on March 17, the day before the battle of Ross, Commissioners from both sides met at Trim. The Remonstrance of Grievances, presented by the Irish Catholics, is a document worthy of

The Remon-
strance of
Grievances
of the Irish
Catholics.

attention. Its author spoke of the incapacities under which they laboured ; of the exclusion of their sons from university education and from pub-

lic employment ; of the tricks and chicaneries of Protestant officials bent upon making their own fortunes, of whom Parsons was one of the worst ; of the boasts of Parsons and others that the Catholics should be forced to change their

---

[1] Articles of agreement, Jan. 20. Gilbert's *Hist. of the Irish Confed.* ii. 145.

[2] Tucker's Journal. *Ibid.* ii. 200.

[3] Ormond to the King, Feb. 8. Carte's *Ormond,* v. 393.

religion ; of wagers laid by persons in high position that within a year there should be no Catholic left in Ireland ; and of the intention of the English Parliament to introduce laws for the extirpation of the Catholic religion in the three kingdoms. Then came an attack upon the dependence of the Lords Justices upon the English House of Commons, and of their misconduct which had forced the lords of the Pale to take arms in self-defence. The remonstrance then proceeded to deal with the Confiscation Act of the English Parliament. The Irish Parliament, it declared, was entirely independent of the English, and the latter had no right to make laws for Ireland. As for the Irish Parliament as constituted under the Lords Justices, it was but a collection of their own partisans, in which the large majority of the members did not dare to appear. In conclusion, the Irish Commissioners asked for a free Parliament, in which all matters of interest might be discussed, unhindered by Poynings' Act.[1] A Parliament mainly composed of Catholics, in short, was to draw up Bills for the settlement of Ireland, to be presented to the King for his acceptance. In recognition of the favours shown to them, the Irish Catholics were ready to send an army of 10,000 men in defence of the King's prerogatives.

Whilst this remonstrance was speeding over the sea to Charles, a missive of a very different character was forwarded to him by the Lords Justices and that section of the Irish Council which adhered to them. The picture here drawn of past history was very different from that which had been drawn by the Irish Commissioners. The Irish were the rebels, and they were the Royalists. The Irish, they declared, did not really care for their religion, but were ungrateful for the care which the English had taken of them, and had repaid it by the massacre of no less than 154,000 men, women, and children. Astounding as this statement was, there was one point in the argument of the Lords Justices which had been passed over entirely by the Irish Commissioners. If the Irish, after all that had passed, were suffered

March 18.
Opinion of the Lords Justices.

---

[1] A remonstrance of grievances, March 17. Gilbert's *Hist. of the Irish Confed.* ii. 226.

to consolidate their power, would they allow the English to live on an equality with themselves? It was a mere question, therefore, which race was to reduce the other to slavery, and the Lords Justices were not alone in preferring to be masters rather than to be slaves. Cynicism, however, has seldom gone further than the cool anticipation of slaughter which followed. "They remember," say the writers, "that in the best of former times the Irish did so exceed in number, as that the governors never could or durst fully execute the laws for true reformation for fear of disturbance, having some hope always by civil and fair entreaty to win them into a civil and peaceable life; so as if peace should now be granted them before the sword or famine have so abated them in number as that in reasonable time English colonies might overtop them, and so perhaps frame the residue into English manners and civil course of life, by trades and other good industry, to take comfort in a quiet life, the English do plainly foresee it can never be safe to cohabit with them, secure for England to enjoy them, or likely that themselves—separate from the English— can ever digest into a people good to themselves or profitable to their King and country." No peace, the Lords Justices repeated, could be safe or lasting 'till the sword have abated these rebels in number and power.' [1]

Whether Charles took either of the two policies thus offered to him into serious consideration it is impossible to say. The memorial which he had sent to Ormond in January [2] shows that his wish was to come to terms with the Catholics without offering to them any real power. Though it could not be doubted that this policy would in the long run fail signally, it might offer some immediate advantage. If it was dangerous for Charles to accept the 10,000 men named by the Irish Commissioners, it might not be dangerous to gain time by discussing the Irish grievances, in order to enable him to bring over from Ireland that English army on which he now knew that he could depend to fight his battles

Charles and the two policies.

[1] The Lords Justices and part of the Council to the King, March 16. Cox, *Hib. Anglicana*, App. iv.

[2] See p. 120.

in England. On March 31, therefore, he dismissed Parsons
from the Lord Justiceship, and appointed in his room Sir
Henry Tichborne, the gallant defender of Drogheda.
Sir John Borlase, as too old and inefficient to be
dangerous, kept his place.[1]

March 31.
Tichborne
succeeds
Parsons
as Lord
Justice.

On April 23, Charles followed up this step by
formally authorising Ormond to treat for a cessation
of arms for one year. In a private letter accompanying the commission he bade the Marquis to
'bring over the Irish army to Chester,' as soon as
the cessation had been agreed upon.[2]

April 23.
Ormond to
treat for a
cessation
and to
bring over
the army.

If Charles's Irish negotiation was unlikely to facilitate
his objects in England, it was still less likely to facilitate
his objects in Scotland. For some time Scottish
Commissioners, among whom Loudoun and Henderson were conspicuous, had been urging him
to assent to their appearance as mediators in the
English civil war, on the basis of an assimilation of the government and discipline of the Church of England with those of
the Church of Scotland. Charles had naturally repelled these overtures,[3] and had rejected the request
of the Commissioners to be allowed to visit London
on their return to their own country. Their language
had, however, alarmed him as to the possibility of an
alliance between the Scots and his enemies in England, and he had been listening to advice of a very different
character given him by Hamilton through his brother Lanark.

Feb.
Scottish
Commis-
sioners offer
to mediate
in England.

March 22.
Their over-
tures re-
jected.

April.
Return of
the Com-
missioners.

As usual, Hamilton had the fullest confidence in his own
power of intrigue. There were noblemen enough in Scotland,
he urged, who were jealous of the predominance of
Argyle and the clergy. Let Charles, above all things,
avoid any attempt to coerce Scotland, and there would be no
difficulty in raising up a party strong enough to hinder her
from giving military aid to the English Parliament.

Hamilton's
advice.

[1] Lascelles, *Liber Munerum*, Part ii. 7.
[2] The King to Ormond, April 23. Commission to Ormond, April 23.
Gilbert's *Hist. of the Irish Confed.* ii. 266.
[3] *Clarendon*, vi. 337–366.

Such advice was too consonant with Charles's nature to be lightly rejected by him. He gave directions to six Scottish noblemen, who happened to be at Oxford, to return to their native country and to do everything in their power to stir up political opposition to Argyle.[1]

April.

Montrose, in the meanwhile, had come easily to the conclusion that Hamilton was no match for Argyle in the field of Parliamentary statesmanship. He was already with the Queen at York, asserting vehemently that there was a good understanding between the leaders of the two Parliaments, and arguing that, unless he were allowed to anticipate the blow, a Scottish army would, before long, cross the border in support of the enemies of the King. Argyle being at present unprepared for war, a sudden attack made by himself at the head of the forces which the Royalist nobility would be able to muster would change the state of affairs.[2] Aboyne would be able to dispose of the whole strength of the Gordons, and, with the warm approval of Nithsdale, Antrim might be despatched to Ireland to bring over a force of Macdonells, the deadly enemies of the Campbells.[3]

Montrose proposes to begin a war in Scotland.

To counteract Montrose, Hamilton, taking with him Traquair, with whom he was now cordially acting, hastened to York to urge upon the Queen the superiority of his own plan. Henrietta Maria, it may be supposed, sympathised with the brilliant Montrose rather than with his saturnine rival, the more especially as Montrose proposed to act in combination with the Catholics and semi-Catholics of Scotland and Ireland ; but she was bound by her husband's orders, and the Scots who were present in her court were, for the most part, naturally averse to a scheme which would expose their country to the hazards of civil war. "Montrose," they said, "is a generous spirit, but hath not so good a head-piece as Hamilton." Montrose was therefore

May.
Hamilton's plan finally adopted.

---

[1] *Certain informations.* E. 101, 2.

[2] *Wishart,* cap. ii.

[3] This seems to be the explantion of the letters seized with Antrim and printed in *A declaration concerning the rise and progress of the grand rebellion in Ireland.* E. 61, 23.

dismissed with fair words, but with the understanding that Hamilton's advice was to be followed.[1]

It was part of the plan of Hamilton and Traquair that the Scots were to be assured that in no case would their Presby-

Comparison between the two policies. terian Church be endangered. Such a proposal was, as far as Scotland itself was concerned, wise and conciliatory. Where Charles was at fault was in failing to see that this policy would break down unless he acted in its spirit in England and in Ireland as well as in Scotland. To give it success in Edinburgh, it was necessary that he should be ready to make concessions to Puritanism in London. A policy which attempted to overbear the religion of half England by means of armies reinforced by troops set free in consequence of an understanding with Irish Catholics, would be fatal to a policy of conciliation in Scotland. Montrose's advice was, as matters stood, the best, not because it was in itself admirable, but because it was in accordance with the system created by the Irish cessation and the breach of the negotiations at Oxford. Charles would almost certainly have prospered if he had set himself earnestly to conciliate those of his enemies whom it was possible to conciliate ; and he might possibly have prospered if he had carried on war unsparingly with all the forces at his command. The mixture of weak military operations with weak diplomacy was fatal to his hopes.

[1] Poyntz to Ormond, June 1. Carte, *Orig. Letters,* i. 19.

CHAPTER VII.

READING AND STRATTON.

It would be some time before regiments from Ireland could be made available by Charles. In the meanwhile he had to bear the brunt of an assault upon his central position at

1643.
April 13.
Essex leaves
Windsor.

Oxford. On April 13, the day after that on which the King issued the message which had brought the ne-gotiations to a close, Essex advanced from Windsor to lay siege to Reading, a siege which, in the common belief of his army, was but the preliminary to that of Oxford itself.

On the 15th the Parliamentary army swept round the southern outskirts of Reading, and seized on Caversham

April 15.
And lays
siege to
Re ding.

Bridge, in order to bar the way against a relieving force from Oxford. A Royalist post on Caversham Hill was easily stormed, and the preparations for an attack on the town itself were carried briskly on. Sir Arthur Aston, the governor of Reading, was a Catholic, and as such failed to command the entire confidence of his soldiers, of whose want of all military qualities he bitterly complained. The place was, however, strongly fortified, and Essex proceeded with his usual deliberation, risking the lives of his men as little as possible. The arrival of Lord Grey of Wark from Hertford-shire, with a reinforcement 5,000 strong, enabled him to complete the investment. London kept him well supplied with provisions, and the country around was favourable to his cause.

Charles
summons
Rupert.

Eagerly did Charles call on Rupert, who was still engaged at Lichfield,[1] to hasten back to the succour of the beleaguered garrison. Powder was running short within

---

[1] See p. 108.

the walls, and Aston had been disabled by a blow on the head from a falling tile.

Lichfield surrendered on the 21st, and Rupert at once turned his horses' heads southwards. On the 24th he over-

April 24. Charles leaves Oxford. took his uncle. Charles was already on his way to Reading, and though he no longer hoped to raise the siege, he expected to be able to open a way for the escape of the garrison. When he approached Caversham he learned that Colonel Feilding, on whom, when Aston was laid aside, the command of the garrison had devolved, had already hung out a flag of truce, and had offered to surrender

April 25. But fails to relieve Reading. the town. An attempt made by the King to seize Caversham bridge was defeated by a Parliamentary force so inferior in numbers to his own, that the Puritan soldiers were able to boast, with even more than their usual assurance, that this success was a clear evidence of Divine intervention in their favour. It is possible, however, that the attack, made after negotiations had been opened, was not pushed home.

As soon as the musquetry fire was heard in Reading some of the officers of the garrison urged Feilding to sally out to Charles's assistance. Feilding replied that his honour was engaged to keep the truce, and that if the King himself were to knock at the gate and command him to break his word he would disobey him.[1]

On the 26th, by the permission of Essex, the request of the garrison for leave to capitulate was laid before the King. As

April 26. Capitulation of Reading. the defenders of Reading were to be allowed to march out with the honours of war, Charles, who had hoped for nothing better even in the event of a successful attack, willingly gave his approbation, and on the 27th the Royalist troops left the town. On the pretext that some of the soldiers carried out arms contrary to the capitulation, some of them were attacked and robbed as they passed

[1] The pamphlets in the volume of the Thomason Tracts, E. 99, should be compared with Rupert's correspondence in *Add. MSS.* 18, 980, fol. 38–52, the greater part of which has been printed by War burton.

the gates, though the Parliamentary officers did their best to stop these outrages.

Feilding met with a bad reception at Oxford. His kins-man, Basil Feilding, who had recently succeeded to the earldom of Denbigh, was fighting on the side of the Houses, and a suspicion easily grew up that the governor of Reading had been bribed or influenced by family ties to surrender the place. He was brought before a court-martial and sentenced to death. The King, who is said to have been irritated by one of the articles of the capitulation, according to which deserters from the Parlia-mentary ranks found in Reading were to be handed over to Essex, wished to carry out the sentence. At once there arose a violent contest amongst his followers. On one side it was maintained that Feilding was a low-minded traitor, whilst the other side was equally confident that he was innocent of the crime laid to his charge. Between the two parties Charles vacillated. Twice Feilding mounted the scaffold, and twice he was withdrawn ; the second time at the pleading of the young Prince of Wales, who had been urged to this work of mercy by Rupert himself. Feilding was ultimately deprived of his regiment ; and though he fought bravely as a volunteer, and was afterwards appointed to a con-siderable command, he bore the stigma of treachery to the end of his life.[1]

Feilding condemned to death.

May 13. Feilding is spared.

Whilst Essex was occupied with the siege of Reading the course of military operations had been on the whole favourable to Parliament. On April 25 Waller surprised Hereford,[2] whilst farther west Chud-leigh, after failing on the 23rd to overpower Hopton at

April 25. Hereford taken by Waller

---

[1] *Rushw.* v. 266. *Clarendon*, vii. 39. News from London, June $\frac{8}{18}$. *Archives des Aff. Étr.* xlix. fol. 264. The suspicions which attached to Feilding on account of his relationship with Denbigh are alluded to by the Venetian agent, who says that he and other officers were 'ben affetti per le corrispondenze di parentella nel Parlamento.' Agostini to the Doge, May $\frac{5}{15}$. *Venetian Transcripts, R.O.* See also *A continuation of certain Special Passages* (E. 101, 17) where it is stated that Feilding was bribed with 16,000*l.*   [2] *Rushw.* v. 263.

Launceston, succeeded on the 25th in driving him back from
the bleak heights of Sourton Down.

Repulse of Hopton by Chudleigh.

    The news of Chudleigh's success reached the
House of Commons on the 29th. It was accompanied by some letters written by the King which had
been taken in Hopton's baggage, in which Charles
urged that commander to hasten to his succour with
all possible speed. The King's failure to relieve Reading, the
intercepted letters, and every indication which spies could
bring, led to the conclusion that Charles could not hold out at
Oxford before a resolute attack. Yet on the very day that the
captured letters reached Westminster a jarring note
in the song of triumph was struck. Stapleton and
Goodwin had come up from Reading to warn the
Houses that without pay for his army Essex could not
move.

April 29. The King's weak position at Oxford.

Essex cannot move without money.

    Honest and devoted as he was, Essex was not the man to
conduct to a successful end the enterprise which he had undertaken. Methodical by nature and by his training in the Dutch
service, he had none of the inspiration of genius or of the
daring energy which goes far to supply its place. He could
lead his troops to victory if the conditions were favourable ; if
they were unfavourable he could not grapple with the obstacles
in his path, and snatch the prize from the grasp of obdurate
nature.

    As yet there was no disposition in the Houses to throw
blame on their commander. The great majority of the
members only thought of providing for him the money which
he needed. Yet the spirit which eventually brought about the
discharge of Essex from his functions was already making
itself felt, the spirit which regarded hesitancy as treason and
lukewarmness as a crime. The Lord General's
bitterest critic was Henry Marten. Hating all
shams and unrealities, and ever ready to speak out
the thought which lay unformed in the minds of others, he
had nothing but scorn for those who thought it possible to
proceed in the ways of peace. A letter which Northumberland
had written to his wife whilst he was still negotiating at Oxford

Henry Marten and Northumberland.

had fallen into the hands of Marten, who tore it open to see
whether it contained indications of treachery.   On April 18

April 18
Northum-
berland
cudgels
Marten.

the wrathful Earl, meeting Marten at a conference,
taxed him with his ungentlemanly conduct, and on
receiving the reply that he was 'no whit sorry,'
struck him on the head with a cane.   Each House
took up the cause of its own member, but it was impossible
either for the Lords to defend the blow given by Northumberland or for the Commons to defend Marten's conduct ; and,
after some altercation, the subject was allowed to drop.[1]

Marten and those who agreed with him soon found a safer
mode of displaying their zeal.   The irritation caused by the
King's defiant attitude first expended itself on inanimate

April 24.
The de-
struction of
monuments
ordered.

April 25.
Iconoclasm
at West-
minster.

objects.   On April 24 the Commons appointed a
committee, at the head of which was Sir Robert
Harley, with instructions to destroy superstitious or
idolatrous monuments, and on the following day
painted windows, the glory of medieval art, were
crashing, and the heads of images, the monuments
of medieval devotion, were flying off in Westminster
Abbey and St. Margaret's.[2]   Not to be behindhand, the
Common Council ordered the destruction of Cheapside Cross,

May 2.
Cheapside
Cross de-
stroyed.

and on May 2 that monument of the affection of a
great king, who could have taught Charles to yield
to his people without losing their respect and obedience, was levelled to the ground amidst signs of public rejoicing.[3]

Something more was needed to defeat Charles than these
acts of barbarous iconoclasm.   On May 1 Pym moved that a

May 1.
Pym moves
to send
committees
to Scotland
and Hol-
land.

committee of members of both Houses might be
sent to Holland to acquaint the States with the true
position of affairs in England, and that another committee similarly composed might be sent to Scotland
'to acquaint that State how affairs stood here, and to
demand their aid.'   It was Pym's reply to the King's employ-

[1] D'Ewes's Diary. *Harl. MSS.* 164, fol. 372b.

[2] *C.J.* iii. 357. *Certain informations.* E. 100, 10.

[3] *The Downfall of Dagon.* E. 100, 21. Agostini to the Doge,
May $\frac{5}{15}$. *Venetian Transcripts, R.O.*

ment of a bevy of Scottish noblemen to raise a Royalist party in their own country.[1] Marten cried out that Parliament should assume sovereign authority before sending ambassadors to contract an alliance.[2] Pym had too much worldly wisdom to allow so unnecessary and so dividing a question to be raised. He and his followers protested loudly against a course which would lead 'to the utter subversion of this monarchy and the dethroning of the King.' The proposal to open communications with Scotland was adopted, though, apparently in consequence of the lukewarmness of the Peers, nothing was done for some time to carry out the resolution of the Commons. It may be that Pym was the more earnest in rejecting Marten's proposal as, in conjunction with Say, Manchester, Salisbury, and Hampden, he had recently opened a secret negotiation with the Queen, urging her to procure her husband's assent to the propositions which had been rejected at Oxford, and had assured her that till they had her answer Essex should not advance. If Pym expected either to obtain Henrietta Maria's consent to a treaty on his own terms, or to delude her into the belief that Essex could march against Oxford if he wished, he little knew the woman with whom he undertook to deal. She replied in a way which was calculated to keep her correspondents in hope, while she strained every nerve to forward to her husband the supplies of which he was sorely in need.[3]

A secret negotiation.

It was high time for help to come if Oxford was to be retained. Charles had no want of men to serve him, but he found it hard to provide them with ammunition. In the beginning of May his correspondence with his wife exhibits him as chiefly anxious to secure a

Charles needs ammunition.

---

[1] See p. 125.

[2] D'Ewes's (*Harl MSS.* c. 164, fol. 381b) reports that Marten asked that no message should be sent 'in the condition we were now in, but that we should give ourselves power to send as from ourselves, and to declare publicly that we will take the people into our protection.' The language is obscure, but taken with the context it can only bear the meaning which I have assigned to it.

[3] The Queen to the King, May 5. *Letters of Henrietta Maria*, 193, 197.

safe line of retreat.   Henrietta Maria hastened off the convoy
of arms and munitions which she had been preparing.   On

May 13 it arrived safely at Woodstock.[1]   Essex had
missed his opportunity, and Charles was now in a
position to defy any force which could be brought
against him.   On the 17th the Commons despatched
to Reading 15,000*l.*, which they had borrowed from
the City, and applied themselves seriously to the

*May 13.
Arrival of
the Queen's
convoy.*

*May 17.
Money sent
to Essex.*

preparation of an ordinance for levying and excise.   Even if
Charles's army had been in a far worse condition than it was,
the money would have reached Essex too late.   Disease had
broken out amongst his troops, and was rapidly thinning his
ranks.[2]

The Parliamentary leaders seem to have been hardly aware
of their danger.   Now and then some of Charles's schemes
came to light, and attempts were, in consequence, made at
Westminster to meet them by an appeal to those
foreign States whose favour the King was endeavouring to win.   More, however, was needed than an effort to
countermine Charles's unskilful diplomacy.   The main weakness of the Parliamentary armies was very similar to the main
weakness of the Royalist army at Edgehill.   Essex, whatever
his defects may have been, was at least a general
over his own army ; but it was only in name that he
was a general over the other armies of the Parliament.   Each separate force, supported from local resources,
and controlled by local commanders, set his authority at
nought on the rare occasions when he attempted to exercise
it.   Nor is there reason to suppose that he had the intellectual
capacity for exercising it effectively.   During the whole of his
career he never showed any sign of ability to regard a campaign as a whole, in which the activity of each separate force
is to be combined for the achievement of a common end.
"We," said Marten, when in the midst of the perils preceding
the execution of Strafford he called for union amongst the

*A message
to Scotland.*

*Essex with-
out general
authority.*

---

[1] *Mercurius Aulicus.*   E. 103, 10.

[2] *L.J.* vi. 43, 49.   *Merc. Aulicus.*   E. 102, 8.   *Joyful news from
Plymouth.*   E. 102, 9.   D'Ewes's Diary.   *Harl. MSS.* 164, fol. 389b.

members of Parliament, "are honest, disjointed fellows." In the campaign of 1643 the Parliamentary troops might well have been described as honest, disjointed armies.

The Parliamentary military organisation was still to be created. The traditions of organisation served the Royalists well. What-

Royalist organisa-tion. ever might be wanting amongst them, there was at least the combination of distant forces on a precon-certed plan. Therefore the balance of the war, which in the last week in April appeared to be inclining in favour of Parliament, began in the third week in May to incline in favour of the King. Preparations were vigorously made for taking up Charles's original scheme of moving forward his two wings from Yorkshire and Cornwall. The arrival of the Queen's convoy at Oxford was but the fruit-fruits of the offering which she had brought to her husband. On May 18 she wrote that she would

May 18. The Queen hopes to advance. soon be on the march. It was necessary, however, that she should remain in the North till Leeds had been taken, so that Newcastle might be set free to relieve the Earl of Derby, who was hard pressed in Lancashire. When that had been successfully effected, and she was herself enabled to move, she would clear Lincolnshire, and that task once accomplished would appear at Oxford at the head of 1,000 foot and 1,500 horse.[1]

After Lancashire had been succoured the southward march of Newcastle might be expected to begin. Tidings were already on their way from the West which showed that Hopton had already overcome the initial difficulties of an eastward march from Cornwall. Encouraged by Chudleigh's success on Sour-

Stamford takes the command in Devonshire. ton Down,[2] Stamford placed himself at the head of the army under his command, and resolved on carry-ing the war into Cornwall. As he could dispose of 6,800 men, whilst Hopton and the Cornish leaders at Launce-ston had with them less than half the number, he determined to despatch the greater part of his horse to Bodmin in order to suppress any attempt to muster the trained bands there. With

---

[1] The Queen to the King, May 18. *Letters of Henrietta Maria,* 203.

[2] See p. 131.

his infantry and a few remaining horse he established himself
May 15.
Stamford at
Stratton. near Stratton, in the extreme north-west of the county,
in a position apparently strong enough to secure
him from attack, at least till his cavalry returned.

The ground occupied by Stamford was well chosen. A
ridge of high ground running from north to south parallel with
the coast dips sharply down, and rises as sharply again to a
grassy hill, from the southern end of which there is a still deeper
cleft through which the road descends steeply to the left into
the valley in which lies the little town of Stratton. On the top
of this hill, the sides of which slope in all directions from the
highest point to the edge of the plateau, the Parliamentary army
lay. Beyond this plateau the ground falls away in all directions,
more especially on the eastern side, where the position was
almost impregnable if seriously defended. The ascent from the
west was decidedly the easiest, but an earthwork had been
thrown up on this side, the guns from which commanded the
whole of the approach from this quarter.[1]

Undismayed by the odds against them, Hopton and his
comrades resolved to break up from Launceston in order to
May 16.
The Battle
of Stratton. seek out the enemy. As they approached Stratton
on the morning of the 16th they had the advantage
of having amongst them one to whom every inch of
ground must have been perfectly familiar. But a few miles to
the north, on the bleak hillside above the waves of the Atlantic,
lay that house of Stow from which Sir Richard Grenvile had
gone forth to die in the ' Revenge,' and where doubtless the Lady
Grenvile of a younger generation was watching anxiously for
the return of him who had ventured his life in the King's quarrel.
It would have been strange if on this day of peril the ordering
of the fight had not fallen into Sir Bevil Grenvile's hands.[2]

---

[1] The earthwork, of which a great part is still in existence, does not
command the steep part of the slope on the other three sides, though the
guns would be available against an enemy after he had once established
himself on the plateau. I do not know whether the work was thrown up on
this occasion, or was of far earlier origin, and though I have made inquiry
in various quarters, I have failed to obtain any information on the subject.

[2] A tablet removed from the battle-field to the wall of the Tree Inn,
at Stratton, states that ' in this place the army of the rebels, under the

The little army of Royalists consisted of but 2,400, whilst their adversaries could number 5,400, well provided with cannon and ammunition.   The attacking force was divided into four

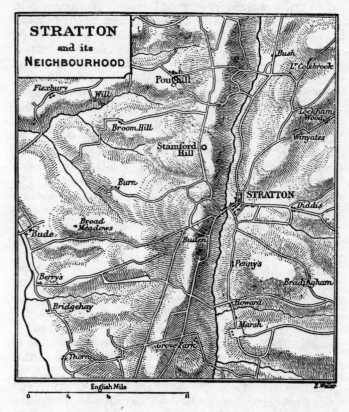

bands, prepared to storm, or at least to threaten, the hill from every side.   For some hours every effort was in vain against superiority of numbers and superiority of position.   At three in

command of the Earl of Stamford, received a signal overthrow by the valour of Sir Bevil Grenvile and the Cornish army on May 16, 1643.' The prominence given to Sir Bevil is, it may be presumed, not entirely due to local or family feeling.

the afternoon word was brought to the commanders that their scanty stock of powder was almost exhausted. A retreat under such circumstances would have been fatal, and the word was given that a supreme effort must be made. Trusting to pike and sword alone, the lithe Cornishmen pressed onwards and upwards. Their silent march seems to have struck their opponents with a sense of power. The defence grew feeble, and on the easier western slope, where Grenvile fought, and on the northern, on which Sir John Berkeley led the attack, the outer edge of the plateau was first gained. Immediately the handful of horse which had remained with Stamford turned and fled, the commander-in-chief, it is said, setting the example. In vain Chudleigh, now second in command, rallied the foot for a desperate charge. For a moment he seemed to make an impression on the approaching foe, but he incautiously pressed too far in advance, and was surrounded and captured. His men, left without a commander, at once gave way and retreated to the farther part of the plateau. By this time the other two Royalist detachments, finding resistance slackening, had made their way up, and the victorious commanders embraced one another on the hard-won hill-top, thanking God for a success for which at one time they had hardly ventured to hope. It was no time to prolong their rejoicings, as the enemy, demoralised as he was, still clung to the heights. Seizing the cannon which had been abandoned in the earthwork, the Royalist commanders turned them upon Stamford's cowed followers. The frightened men had no one to encourage them to deeds of hardihood, and, following the example of the cavalry, they too dashed down the slope in headlong flight. Of the Parliamentary soldiers, 300 had been killed, and 1,700 were taken prisoners, besides Chudleigh and thirty of his officers. All the cannon with a large store of ammunition and provisions fell into the hands of the victors. From that day the spot on which the wealthy Earl demonstrated his signal incompetence as a leader of men has been known as Stamford Hill.[1]

---

[1] My account is founded on Hopton's Narrative, *Clarendon MSS.* 1738 (1), and its reproduction in *Clarendon*, vii. 87, but it is modified by personal observation of the locality. The Ordnance map is inaccurate.

The entire collapse of the Parliamentary army had an unexpected effect upon Chudleigh. As a soldier he must have
despised the poltroons who had deserted him, and
have felt a corresponding admiration for the prowess
of his antagonists. His own proclivities were Royalist.
At the beginning of the war he had made his way to Oxford to
offer his services to the King, but it was not forgotten there
that, at the time of Strafford's trial, he had been the bearer of
messages between the army and the Court, and that his evidence on the army plot given before a Parliamentary committee
had told heavily against the King.[1] Taking umbrage at the
cold looks and bitter words with which he was received, he
had transferred his services to the Parliament, and returning now
to his natural allegiance, he deserted a cause which he had
only adopted through pique. He attempted to persuade his
father, Sir George Chudleigh, who was in command of the
cavalry which had been despatched to Bodmin, to follow his
example ; but the old man contented himself with resigning
his commission, lest even a suspicion of his son's treachery
should attach itself to his person.[2]

*Chudleigh
joins the
Royalists.*

It was easy, at Westminster, to lay the whole blame of the
disaster upon Chudleigh's treason. It was none the less necessary to oppose a barrier to the advance of Hopton.
Before many days were over all Devonshire, with
the exception of Bideford and Barnstaple in the north, and of
Plymouth, Dartmouth, and Exeter in the south, fell easily into
his hands. All eyes were turned on Waller, whose tried
generalship was at that time supposed to be capable of meeting
any difficulty, and by the orders of Essex he prepared
to march towards Devonshire. Yet signs were not
wanting that even Waller's generalship might prove insufficient.
The growing strength of Charles at Oxford was making itself
felt on the Severn and the Wye. On May 20 Waller was compelled to abandon Hereford after a brief occupation,[3] and on the
29th he failed in an attack upon Worcester, which he probably
wished to secure as an outlying post to defend the Severn valley

*Hopton's
advance.*

*Waller sent
against him.*

---

[1] *Hist of Eng.* 1603-1642, ix. 314 ; x. 2.
[2] *Clarendon.* vii. 91.   [3] See p. 130.

after he had marched westwards. Fresh enemies, too, threatened him in another direction. A force under the command
of the Marquis of Hertford, in which Rupert's bro-

Hertford's army at Salisbury.

ther, Prince Maurice, occupied a prominent position, left Oxford on the 19th and occupied Salisbury, with the evident intention of holding out a hand to Hopton as he advanced.

Together with the tale of disaster from the West more cheerful tidings reached Westminster from the North. By a
dashing night attack the younger Fairfax had sur-

May 21. Wakefield surprised.

prised Wakefield, though it was held by a force far superior in numbers to his own. The blow was well aimed, but it could not affect Newcastle's preponderance in Yorkshire. Fairfax had 1,400 prisoners to exchange—among them the double-traitor Goring—and that was all. He was compelled to abandon Wakefield almost as soon as it was taken, whilst Newcastle firmly established himself at Pontefract, and occupied Rotherham and Sheffield.[1]

If Charles was superior to Essex in strategy, he was far inferior to Pym in diplomacy. Whilst Pym sought as ever to combine homogeneous elements of resistance, Charles pursued his usual course of attempting to combine in his favour elements of attack which were mutually repugnant. Just as he had failed to see that an understanding with the Irish Catholics would make it difficult for him to secure the neutrality of the Scottish Presbyterians, he now failed to perceive that the negotiation which he was still carrying on with the King of Denmark for aid, on the basis of the cession of Orkney

The proposed cession of Orkney and Shetland.

and Shetland to that King whose ancestor had once pledged the islands to the Scottish Crown, would rouse the national feeling of the Scots against himself. Henrietta Maria, however, through whose hands the negotiation passed, was shrewd enough to doubt whether the abandonment of Shetland and the Orkneys was likely to be helpful to Hamilton in his attempt to form a Royalist party in Edinburgh.[2]

---

[1] *Dugdale's Diary. Special Passages.* E. 103, 7. *Merc. Aul.* E. 104, 21.

[2] See p. 125.

"Please," she wrote to her husband in announcing the contents of the despatches from Denmark, "to resolve something

May 27.
Henrietta
Maria's re-
marks. thereupon. There is no time to be lost ; and send back someone to conclude what you will do, whether you are satisfied to give the islands, about which I should make no difficulty, it only being a thing which concerns Scotland. Care must be taken that the Scots do not avail themselves of this opportunity to take offence. Therefore, if you are willing to give them, I would make a secret contract with the King of Denmark to deliver them to him when your business is settled, and tell him the reason why you do not do it at this instant, and that if the King of Denmark agrees to that, he that shall go shall treat with him about the place where he shall land his forces and where his ships shall come, and do this quickly and without delay." [1] Charles followed his wife's counsel, and worded his promise to cede the islands in terms so cautious that Christian shrank from risking a fleet and army on so uncertain a security.[2]

In the field of domestic intrigue the Queen seemed likely to be more successful. Amongst those who were now attracted to Royalism by their natural affinities were the two Hothams, both of whom were also influenced by jealousy of the Fairfaxes.

April 15.
Treachery
of the
Hothams. On April 15 Captain Hotham—as the son of the Governor of Hull was styled—wrote to Newcastle, telling him that he had 'found out a way to do his Majesty real service,' and holding out hopes that 'such a considerable party' would be brought to the King 'as hath not been yet.' [3] In a subsequent letter he asked that Sir Marmaduke Langdale might be sent to confer with him. "I have no doubt," he added, "he is instructed to treat as with gentlemen who value their honour above anything." In the end Hotham gave Newcastle to understand that he and his father were ready to carry out the design agreed on—a design which appears to have embraced the betrayal of Hull and Lincoln—though it

---

[1] The Queen to the King, May 27. *Letters of Henrietta Maria,* 208.

[2] Fridericia, *Danmarks ydre politiske historie,* 316.

[3] Hotham to Newcastle, April 15. *A new discovery of hidden secrets.* E. 267, 11.

would take some time to carry it into practice. Above all, it would be necessary 'to hinder Colonel Cromwell's marching hither.'[1]

Colonel Cromwell's name was already a terror to those who were inclined to play fast and loose with the Parliamentary cause.

Cromwell in the eastern counties.

Whilst Essex contented himself with indicating the causes of his own failure, Cromwell, in his lower sphere, set himself to make failure impossible. He had early recognised that the weakness of the Parliamentary army was above all a weakness in cavalry, and he determined that the troop which he commanded as a captain, and the regiment which he subsequently commanded as a colonel, should fear no comparison with Rupert's high-spirited cavaliers. The men whom he selected from the Puritan freeholders and farmers of the eastern counties were such as had thrown their whole hearts into the religious strife, and were also ready, for the sake of victory, to submit to the iron discipline which he imposed on them. To trust in God and to keep their powder dry—the popular summary of his requirements—in other words, to combine practical efficiency with enthusiasm, was the secret of the marvellous success of Cromwell's soldiers. As for himself, he was an ideal cavalry officer on the field of battle, as fiery as Rupert in the charge, as cautious as Essex in preparation, with a never-failing presence of mind, which was all his own, and which never allowed him to be carried away by the excitement of victory or to be depressed by the weight of adversity.

By the end of April, Cromwell had stamped out whatever sparks of Royalism were to be found within the bounds of the Eastern Association, and, as Hotham feared, was soon fighting his way through Lincolnshire, where the Royalists from Newark dominated the county. Delivering Crowland from attack, he

May. Proposed attack on Newark.

pressed for a combined attempt upon Newark, and an arrangement was made early in May for the co-operation of Stamford's son, Lord Grey of Groby, the commander-in-chief of the forces of the Association, with the Lincolnshire gentry and with Sir John Gell, who was at

[1] Hotham to Newcastle, April 26, 31. *Tanner MSS.* lxii. fol. 83, 90. Compare *Letters of Henrietta Maria,* 221

that time posted at Nottingham. The plan came to nothing.
Local jealousies were too strong to admit of common action.
It needs no explanation to account for the reluctance of the
force at Lincoln to move as long as the younger Hotham was
in the place, and Grey, whose father's house was not far from
Leicester, refused to stir for fear of exposing that town to
danger. "Believe me," wrote Cromwell to the Committee of
Lincoln, "it were better, in my poor opinion, Leicester were
not, than that there should not be found an immediate taking
of the field by our forces to accomplish the common ends."

The entire subordination of private and local aims to the
common ends was one of the secrets of Cromwell's success. If
others failed him, he would not make that an excuse for remiss-
ness. On the evening of May 13 he found himself with twelve
troops of horse, 'whereof some so poor and broken that you

May 13.
Skirmish
near
Grantham.

shall seldom see worse,' opposed to double their
number, two miles from Grantham on the Newark
road. Without counting heads, he gave the word to
charge. The spirit of their commander gave force to the followers, and the larger host broke and fled before the smaller.
"With this handful," wrote Cromwell, in recounting the event,
"it pleased God to cast the scale."[1] The whole fortune of the
Civil War was in that nameless skirmish. A body of Puritan
horsemen had driven twice their number before them as chaff
before the wind, and as armies were then constituted superiority
in cavalry was superiority in war.

Whatever the future might have in store, Cromwell knew
well that the Eastern Association could not be saved by twelve
troops of horse. Not without reason had he striven to rouse the
neighbouring commanders to combine for an attack upon Newark,
the connecting link between the Royalism of Yorkshire and the
Royalism of Oxford. The brilliant surprise of Wakefield by the
younger Fairfax did not blind Cromwell to the inherent weakness of the Parliamentary cause in Yorkshire, and he knew that,
if once the defenders of the West Riding were overpowered,
Newcastle would soon be at Newark, and that it would need all
the resolution of the inhabitants of the Association, and far

---

[1] Cromwell to the Lincolnshire Committee, May 13. *Carlyle*, Letter X.

more harmony between its commanders than had been hitherto displayed, to bar his road to London. Like Essex, Cromwell

May 28.
Cromwell in straits for money.

was in desperate straits for money. It profited him little that on May 26 his native county of Huntingdon was added to the Eastern Association.[1] "Lay not," he wrote to the men of Colchester, "too much on the back of a poor gentleman who desires, without much noise, to lay down his life and bleed the last drop to serve the cause and you. I ask not your money for myself. I desire to deny myself, but others will not be satisfied."[2] Voluntary contributions are but a slender staff on which to lean. In two months the whole of the payments from the five counties which composed the Association reached no more than 3,372*l.*, of which the share borne by the single county of Cambridgeshire, in which Cromwell's influence was the highest, was little less than 2,000*l.*[3]

At the close of May the outlook of the Parliamentary party was depressing. Devonshire had been overrun in the West, and

The military situation.

in the North the Royalists were growing in strength. In the valley of the Thames Essex continued inactive, his army wasting away with sickness and desertion. The military situation reacted on the political, and in May the time appeared to Charles to have arrived when the Commission

May.
Waller's plot.

of Array, which he had issued in March to the leading Royalists in London,[4] might be put in execution. That Charles had a considerable party in the City is beyond doubt, and it is equally beyond doubt that large numbers there, without being distinctly Royalists, would welcome any change which would bring the blessings of peace within their reach.

Accordingly on May 2 Charles authorised one Chaloner, a linendraper of some repute in the City, to collect money for

Employment of Chaloner

objects of which we have no detailed account, but which were evidently connected with the great design of throwing off the Parliamentary yoke. Waller, vain and incapable, but flattering himself that he was fitted to play

[1] *L.J.* vi. 63.
[2] Cromwell to the Mayor of Colchester, May 28. *Carlyle*, Letter XI.
[3] *Tanner MSS.* lxii. fol. 70.   [4] See p. 111.

a conspicuous part on the political stage, busied himself in winning over personages of high social position, whilst his brother-
in-law, Tompkins, undertook to keep up communications between the Parliamentary group of Royalists
at Westminster and the more active spirits in the City.

*and of
Tompkins.*

On May 19 Alexander Hampden, a cousin of the member
for Buckinghamshire, was despatched from Oxford, ostensibly
to call upon the Houses to return an answer to the
message of April 12,[1] in which Charles had demanded the immediate surrender of the ships and
forts. In the communication brought by Hampden, the King
threw the blame for all misfortunes which might befall the
country upon those by whom his reasonable offers were refused.
Such, he added, was 'his strength of horse, foot, and artillery,
his plenty of ammunition, which some men lately might conceive he wanted, that it must be confessed that nothing but
the tenderness and love to his people, and those Christian im-
pressions' with which his heart was touched, 'could move him
once more to hazard a refusal.'[2]

*May 19.
Mission of
Alexander
Hampden.*

In the Upper House there was a majority in favour of the
acceptance of any possible compromise. Conway and Portland, like Waller in the House of Commons, had
only remained at Westminster to further Charles's
objects, whilst Northumberland and Holland, Bedford and Clare, were only too anxious for an opportunity of
bringing the war to a close on any terms short of a complete
surrender. Yet even these peers refused to accept
Charles's proposal as a basis of negotiation, though
they imagined that advantage might be taken of his
message to make fresh overtures of their own. The
House of Commons not only turned a deaf ear to this unpractical suggestion, but took a step which, if it were persisted in,
would make peace impossible. A member having asked that
all Papists in arms should be declared traitors, Henry Darley
rose to make a far more startling proposition. "For
my part," he said, "I desire to speak plain English. I
think that the principal Papist now in arms against us is the

*Peace-party
in the
Lords.*

*May 23.
Their re-
ception of
the King's
message.*

*The Queen
impeached.*

---

[1] See p. 108.   [2] *L.J.* vi. 57.

Queen." He then moved that she should be impeached, and, after a feeble opposition, his motion was carried without a division. Pym was sent to lay the impeachment before the peers.[1]

Evidently the House was influenced by the King's boastful reference to the store of ammunition with which the Queen's energy had provided him. Its leaders acted under a sense of impending danger, the depth of which they were as yet unable to fathom. Either Alexander Hampden or some

The Earl of Dover's letter. one who accompanied him had brought from Oxford a letter written by the Earl of Dover to his wife in London, entreating her to come away with her children as soon as it was possible to do so. There was something in the tone of the letter which excited suspicion, and on May 22, the day before the Queen's impeachment was voted, the Commons ordered that Hampden should be detained in custody.[2]

Slight as the indication was, it had served to awaken the suspicions of the Committee of Safety. Shortly after Hampden's arrest a certain Hassell arrived in London as the bearer

Hassell's rash language.

May 28. A spy set.

May 31. Arrest of Waller and Tompkins. of a fresh message from the King. He was foolish enough to boast that within ten days London would be set on fire, and his rash speech was carried to the Committee. It was known that Hassell was intimate with Waller and Tompkins, and a clerk in the service of Tompkins was induced to act as a spy upon his master. On the 30th he brought sufficient information to justify further action, and on the early morning of the 31st both Waller and Tompkins were arrested.

The 31st was one of those days set apart for the monthly fast which had been observed ever since the outbreak of the war. At the time of the morning service the congregation at

---

[1] *C.J.* iii. 98. D'Ewes's Diary. *Harl. MSS.* 164, fol. 390b.

[2] On June 6 D'Ewes states that the seizure of Dover's letter gave the first hint of Waller's plot, and that it took place about a fortnight before. An exact fortnight would be May 23, but we may safely assume that the discovery happened on the 22nd, and the arrest of Hampden would be thus accounted for.

St. Margaret's was disturbed by messengers from the Speaker, calling on the members of the Commons who were present
A sermon interrupted.
to attend him immediately in the House. D'Ewes, who refused to obey the summons till the sermon was at an end, found, when he left the church, that the streets were guarded by soldiers. The Westminster trained bands were not all devoted to the Parliamentary cause, and he overheard some of them muttering that the plot had been invented in order to give an excuse for fresh taxation. D'Ewes himself was at first inclined to share this opinion, but, welcome as a belief in Pym's trickery would have been to his mind, he soon came round to the opinion that Parliament and the City had escaped a great danger.

Conway, in fact, with his military instincts, had put the vague design originally entertained into a practical shape. A
Conway organises the plot.
secret association was formed in the City, no member of which was to be acquainted with the names of more than three others amongst the associates. It was calculated that in London itself about one-third of the population was Royalist, whilst in the suburbs the proportion rose to four-fifths. Royalists as well as Parliamentarians were to be found in the trained bands, detachments of which guarded in turn the new fortifications. A night was to be selected on which the Royalists on guard were in a majority. They would then seize upon the magazines of arms and powder, and upon the principal military positions. Lord Mayor Pennington and his chief supporters in the City would be seized in their beds, and at Westminster Say and Wharton, Pym, Hampden, Stapleton, and Strode were to share their fate. The King was to send a force of 3,000 men to the neighbourhood of London. To this force the gates were to be thrown open, and with its help rebellion would be crushed and the civil war at an end.

To give an aspect of legality to the design Charles had forwarded to London the Commission of Array which had been issued in March.[1] It had been entrusted to the beautiful and

[1] See p. 111.

high-spirited Lady Daubigny, whose husband had been slain at Edgehill, and who was visiting Oxford with a pass from
the Houses on business connected with her husband's estate. Concealing the important document in her bosom, in the well-founded assurance that no rude Parliamentary soldier would search for it beneath her dress, on her return to London in the company of Alexander Hampden, she had handed it over to Chaloner. Chaloner in turn had surrendered it to Tompkins, in whose cellar it was ultimately found by the Parliamentary searchers.[1]

The King's commission brought by Lady Daubigny.

In the eyes of Charles and Falkland, through whose hands the correspondence with the conspirators passed, these proceedings were no more than legitimate acts of defence against successful treason. It was because this view of the case was very far from being complete that Waller's plot, as it came to be called, was fatal to the Royal cause. "You must show," Roe had written a few weeks before, "that peace is ravished from you, and your arms are only employed to rescue the beloved of all men."[2] By entering on this plot at a time when he was offering to negotiate, Charles showed that he considered his opponents as rebels to be crushed, not as adversaries to be conciliated. The result was a deepening of the gulf, already far too deep, by which the parties were divided. Charles was coming to be regarded at Westminster, no longer as a sovereign led astray by evil counsellors, but as a conspirator against the peace and safety of the nation. This feeling was a few days later rendered even more bitter by news from Ireland. On June 5 a letter from Parsons was read in the House of Commons, in which the late Lord Justice detailed the circumstances of his supersession, and on the same day it was known that Charles had despatched Lord Taaffe to Kilkenny, and had

Effect of the discovery of the plot.

May 31.

June 5. News from Ireland.

[1] According to the statement in the *State Trials* (iv. 628), it was found in Tompkins's cellar. For its having been in Chaloner's hands, and for the date of Lady Daubigny's journey, see D'Ewes's Diary. *Harl. MSS.* 460, fol. 11; 164, fol. 49; 165, fol. 101b.

[2] See p. 102.

thereby placed himself in direct communication with the Irish rebels.[1]

After this revelation everything was possible for Pym.   On the 6th he made his report on Waller's plot.   Lords and

June 6.
Pym's
report on
the plot.

Parliamentary covenant voted by the Commons.

Commons alike were carried away by their indignation.   The imposition of a vow or covenant, which a few days before had little chance of acceptance, was now voted by the Commons with scarcely a dissentient voice.   Those who took it engaged themselves to support the forces raised in defence of Parliament against those raised by the King, 'so long as the Papists now in open war against the Parliament shall by the force of arms be protected from the justice thereof.'[2]

The assembly of divines authorised by the Lords,

June 9.
who also accept the Parliamentary covenant.

On the same day the Lords accepted an ordinance, authorising the meeting of the proposed assembly of divines, to which they had long opposed a steadfast resistance ; and on the 9th the new covenant was taken by every one of the sixteen peers then present in the House, after which it was sent forth with the authority of both Houses to be signed as a test of loyalty to the cause which the Houses were defending.   For the time, at least, the Peace-party was annihilated.   Charles's intrigue had made it possible for Pym to impose a test which gave coherence to his followers, though it separated

June 15.
A day of thanksgiving.

them fatally from their fellow-countrymen in the opposite ranks.   June 15 was observed as a day of public thanksgiving for the recent deliverance, and on that day the covenant was freely taken in the City.   Yet those who rejoiced knew that the time of anxiety was not at an

June 14.
The licensing of the press.

end.   An ordinance passed the day before for the more stringent enforcement of the censorship of the press was a sure token that the Houses did not consider that they had yet reached a port of safety.[3]

[1] D'Ewes's Diary. *Harl. MSS.* 164, fol. 395.   [2] *Rushw.* v. 325.
[3] *L.J.* vi. 96.

CHAPTER VIII.

THE ROYALIST VICTORIES.

WOULD the sword be able to make good the defiance which the Houses had flung in the face of the King? Essex had at last been reinforced, and had broken up from his quarters at Reading. On June 10 he occupied Thame. Three days later his army was still further increased, and he was able to send his advanced guard to Wheatley, in the immediate neighbourhood of a Royalist post on Shotover Hill.[1] It is hardly likely that so cautious a strategist as Essex contemplated an attack on Oxford as long as it was held by forces not inferior to his own, and he probably intended no more than to protect Buckinghamshire from plunder, and to interpose an obstacle in the way of the Queen's march from Yorkshire. In the meanwhile he allowed his own troops to scatter themselves over a wide extent of country, so as to invite attack by an enemy whose cavalry was far superior to his own.

Hampden, it is said, warned Essex of the risk to which he was exposed. For purposes of attack the Parliamentary army was insufficient, and on the 17th a force of 2,500 sent by Essex to capture Islip, retreated without striking a blow. Such vacillating tactics were dangerous when Rupert was within striking distance. On the same afternoon he rode out of Oxford at the head of a select body of some 1,700 men, of which the greater part was cavalry. He had learned from Colonel Hurry, a Scottish deserter, that a sum of 21,000*l.* was on its way to

Marginal notes:

1643. June 10. Essex at Thame.

June 13. He occupies Wheatley.

June 17. Essex fails to take Islip.

Rupert's foray.

[1] *Merc. Civicus.* E. 106, 13. *A continuation of certain passages.* E. 106, 6.

Thame from London, and he resolved to strike for the prize. An hour after midnight the tramp of his band was heard by the sentinels at Tetsworth ; shots were fired and an alarm given. Two hours later, as the sky was whitening before the dawn, he surprised a few of Essex's soldiers at Postcombe. In the early morning light he surrounded Chinnor, and fell suddenly upon a party of new-levied men who were soundly sleeping in the hamlet. Some fifty poor wretches were shot down or knocked on the head as they attempted to escape, and 120 surrendered themselves as prisoners.

June 18.

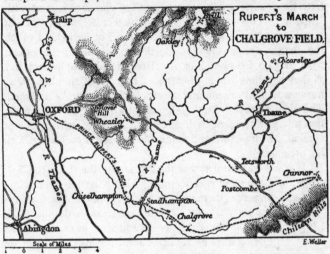

It was now time to look out for the expected convoy. Rupert's proceedings, however, had been too noisy for secrecy. The drivers were warned by a countryman, and they turned the heads of their team into the woods which clothed the sides of the Chiltern Hills, where, now that the enemy had been fully roused, Rupert could not venture to follow.

Through his own want of judgment Rupert had missed his prey. Sweeping round as he returned under the hills to the left, as if loth to hurry back, he at last, skirmishing as he went with the gathering foe, directed his march upon Oxford. Sending forward his foot to Chiselhampton

Chalgrove Field.

Bridge to guard the line of retreat, he faced with his horse on Chalgrove Field the now increasing numbers of the enemy, roused by the tidings of his presence from the villages round. Amongst them, though as yet he knew it not, was Hampden, who slept that night at Watlington, and who, roused from his sleep by the cry of alarm, had thrown himself as a volunteer amongst the ranks of the first comrades with whom he met. The Parliamentary troops were indeed insufficient to combat Rupert with any prospect of success, but they hoped that by threatening him they might hold him back till succours could arrive from headquarters. It was dangerous to play such a game with Rupert. "This insolency," he said to his comrades, "is not to be borne." He was the first to leap the hedge behind which the enemy was drawn up. By the confession of the gallant troopers who followed him, the Roundheads fought that day as they had never fought before. The odds of numbers were, however, against them, and after a while they broke and fled. This time Rupert did not gallop off in wild pursuit. Knowing that a large force sent by Essex would soon be on the place of combat, he drew rein and made his way safely to Oxford with his prisoners.[1]

It is not with Rupert that the thoughts of the visitor to Chalgrove Field are mainly concerned. Hampden's is the abiding presence there. With his head bowed low over his horse's neck the warrior-statesman had ridden off, early in the fight, sorely wounded in the shoulder.[2] For six days he lay at Thame in agony from which on June 24 he was only released by death.[3]

Hampden wounded.

June 24. Hampden's death.

---

[1] *His Highness Prince Rupert's late beating up of the Rebels' quarters* is the best authority. There is no copy in the British Museum library, but there is one in the Bodleian, and one in the possession of Mr. Madan, who kindly lent it to me. Compare D'Ewes's Diary, *Harl. MSS.* 164, fol. 233 ; *A true relation*, E. 55, 11 ; and the letter of Essex, E. 55, 19.

[2] For the discussion whether the wound was inflicted by the enemy or by the bursting of a pistol see *Notes and Queries*, 3rd. Ser. iii. 11, 71. That this utterly unimportant point should have been made the subject of partisan contention is one of the marvels which are only to be met with in writings relating to the Civil War.

[3] Mr. Firth, in *The Academy* of Nov. 29, 1889, has conclusively shown

So little was it Hampden's habit to put himself forward in
political life, that the historian is apt to ask himself whether,
after all, he deserved the fame which has crowned him. Other
men outstripped him in the senate and in the field. He seldom
spoke in the House of Commons, and never at any length. As
a soldier he won no battles and reduced no fortresses.[1] Yet
the impression which he made upon his contemporaries cannot
be lightly set aside. Friend and foe are of one mind in recog-
nising his power. A thoroughly loyal man, without even the
infirmity of ambition, his first and last thought was his duty to
his country. Inspired with the loftiest and most enduring courage, ready to throw himself into the breach in peace or war
whenever occasion demanded the sacrifice, he had too high a
reverence for the virtue of subordination to resist the authority
which he regarded as lawful. He was never heard to murmur.
The belief that he regarded the generalship of Essex as too cautious and hesitating was so widely spread that it cannot be altogether false, but he never attempted, even indirectly, to weaken
his authority. He doubtless felt—for such men feel rather
than reason—that insubordination was worse than bad generalship, and he made no exception when his own person was
concerned.[2]

that Clough's narrative of Hampden's last days found in the *Gentleman's
Magazine* for May 1815, is a nineteenth-century forgery. The belief that
we possess the words of Hampden's last prayer must therefore be abandoned.

[1] Lord Nugent indeed has a long account of an early siege of Reading,
in which Hampden plays a conspicuous part, but that siege has no foundation in fact, the authority for it being one of the many lying pamphlets of
the time.

[2] The following letter, the last written by Hampden, as far as we
know, before he died, is very characteristic of the quiet self-possession of
one who, placing duty above everything else, expected others to do the
same. His cousin Cromwell would have penned a far more fiery appeal,
but hardly one more effectual : "Sir, my Lord General hath written to
the county of Essex to call in the well-affected people to his assistance,
and hath entreated the help of the Deputy Lieutenants in it. The work
is so necessary and so hopeful that I cannot but improve the interest I
have in yourself for the promoting of it. The power of Essex is great, a
place of most life of religion in the land, and your power in the county is

That Hampden, if he had lived, would have brought about
a peace on terms satisfactory to both parties is an idea which
could only arise amongst those who misunderstand alike his
character and the political situation. His ideas on Church and
State were such as ought to have made it easy for him to come
to an understanding with Falkland, but he never could have
come to an understanding with Charles. The constant intrigues, the reliance on foreign aid, the plots and conspiracies
which occupied so large a space in Charles's statesmanship,
built up a wall of separation between him and Hampden which
could never be passed over. If there was still a lurking hope
in Hampden's mind that Charles might be won over from his
evil counsellors, it was never likely to be more. For the present open war was the path of duty. To tear asunder the web
of mingled violence and deceit which was ennobled by the name
of constitutional right was the work to which Hampden had
devoted himself, in all modesty, but with all the vigour of a
well-balanced nature, and there is no reason to suppose that if

great too. The difficulties of this war needs the utmost of both. Our
army wants both men and money, and therefore their help in this way
proposed would be very seasonable. I know you need not be moved to a
thing that you apprehend for the good of the cause. Such I conceive this
business for the good of the kingdom in general, and so of Essex in particular. Consider of it, and you will find it deserves your serious and
hearty endeavours. It will be a service acceptable to my Lord General,
and you shall further engage your affectionate cousin and servant, Jo·
Hampden." Hampden to Sir T. Barrington, June 9. *Barrington MSS.*
The letter from Essex himself in the same collection is also noteworthy.
"I desire," he writes, "such may appear in this cause as have most
interest in it, such of whose constancy and courage we may be assured,
men of religious lives and affections, fittest to bear arms for truth of
religion, men of estates to defend those estates that the enemy seeks to
devour. The employment is not too mean for the best men ; and then we
shall hope for success when such put their hands to the work ; for assure
yourselves the looseness and inconstancy of the soldiers amongst others is
one cause of the continuance of the war." It is evidently wrong to attri-
bute to Cromwell the sole credit of an attempt to fill the regiments with
pious men. What distinguished him was that he succeeded in doing what
others only attempted. I have, however, seen a statement in a contemporary pamphlet to the effect that none of Hampden's officers had ever
sworn excepting in a court of justice.

he had lived longer he would ever have learned to place confidence in Charles.

Two days after the skirmish at Chalgrove Field Charles replied to the Parliamentary covenant in a strain of fierce defiance.

June 20. Charles declares the Parliament no longer free. In a proclamation issued on June 20, in order to lead up to the conclusion that the Houses were in durance to arbitrary power, he recited a whole catalogue of the illegalities of which Parliament had been guilty, though they were in truth no more than the necessary consequences of its virtual assumption of sovereign authority. Parliament being no longer free, all who abetted it in its usurpation were liable to the penalties of high treason, though with the exception of five lords and thirteen commoners any one of these persons presenting themselves at Oxford would be welcome, 'until by the adjournment of the Houses to some fit and free place, or otherwise, due course be taken for the full and free convention in Parliament of us and all the members of both Houses.' [1]

Such a proclamation was one of those half-measures which combine the maximum of irritation with the minimum of advantage. From this day the Houses at Westminster were regarded at Oxford merely as a pretended Parliament, consisting, as the wits never ceased to assert with wearisome iteration, of three Houses—the Common Council, the House of Commons, and the House of three Lords. Officially they were treated by the King as non-existent, and as being therefore incapable of addressing to him a petition or of sending to him a Bill. At the same time Charles did not as yet propose, as with a slight stretch of authority he might well have done, to gather round him at Oxford a Parliament of his own, from which he might have derived constitutional support.

For the moment Charles was content to rely on his military preponderance. It seemed as if the unwieldy host of Essex might be subjected to any indignities. On the 25th a body of cavalry under Hurry, who had been knighted for his services at Chalgrove Field, swept round the rear of the Parliamentary army as Rupert had swept round it a

June 25. Wycombe plundered.

[1] *L.J.* vi. 108.

week before, defeated Stapleton's horse, and plundered Wy-
Panic in London. combe. So great was the alarm, that in London itself a rumour spread that the City was in danger. From all parts men ran hastily to their posts on the line of defence. When the Commons met on the morning of the 26th
June 26 The Commons remonstrate with Essex. there was a general disposition to throw the blame on Essex. A sharp letter was written to him by Pym, telling him that men were safer under the King's protection than under his, and bidding him tender the
June 28. Essex tenders his resignation. new covenant to his troops.[1] To this letter Essex replied by offering a resignation which it was naturally impossible to accept at such a time.[2] Whatever doubts might be entertained of Essex's ability, there could be no question of his fidelity, and fidelity was, at the moment, too
Causes of his failure. rare a virtue to be despised. His extreme weakness in cavalry, combined with the effect of the sickness which had broken out on the low ground round Thame, in consequence of the persistent bad weather, was the real cause of the ruin of a force of which high hopes had been entertained.[3] A Cromwell might have provided a remedy ; Essex was capable of using the means which were in his hands, not of creating new forces when the old ones failed.

During the weeks which witnessed for a second time the decay of Essex's army the attention of the Houses had been
June 12. Waller denounces Conway and Portland, directed to a prolonged inquiry into the ramifications of the late plot. On June 12 Conway and Portland were denounced by Waller as having taken part in the conspiracy. There is strong reason for believing that the charge was true,[4] but Waller was so abject

---

[1] *C.J.* iii. 144. D'Ewes's Diary. *Harl. MSS,* 164, fol. 233.

[2] D'Ewes's Diary. *Ibid.* 165, fol. 100b.

[3] *A remonstrance to vindicate Robert Earl of Essex.* E. 71, 7.

[4] Conway's complicity may be assumed as proved by Clarendon's admission. As to Portland, his denial appears in his examination of July 1 (*Hist. MSS. Com. Rep.* v. 94). There is, however, in existence a letter of Waller's written to Portland, which leaves in my mind very little doubt that Portland was the liar. " My Lord," he writes, after justifying his own conduct, " I beseech you this business was never meant for your knowledge either by the Lord Conway or Sir Hugh Pollard. The only

in his terror that when Conway and Portland bluntly denied the truth of the accusation public feeling was strongly in their favour. It seemed more probable that Waller should have lied than they. Waller even lost ground by including *and North-* Northumberland in his charges, as having indeed *umberland.* refused to take part in the plot, but as having done so, not because the plot was wicked, but because it was likely to fail. Waller, however, acquitted himself so badly when confronted with Northumberland, that the tide of opinion *June 30.* ran still more strongly against him than before.

Trial of
Tompkins
and other
conspirators.
On June 30 Tompkins, Chaloner, Alexander Hampden, and three others were tried by a court-martial sitting at Guildhall under the presidency of *July 5.* the Earl of Manchester. On July 3 Tompkins and *Tompkins* *and Chal-* Chaloner were sentenced to death, and in their case *oner exe-* *cuted.* the judgment of the court was carried into execution two days later.[1] Hampden fell ill, and ultimately

reason I imparted it to your Lordship was that by you I might be instructed how far that Lord Conway might be trusted, with whom Sir Hugh so often urged me to speak ; this you might perceive by some strangeness towards you when first we met at Pollard's chambers and often after, when that lord whispered to me apart, which for the most part he did when he mentioned the Earl of Northumberland, so that but for me, I think—nay, I am confident—you had never known anything of this business, which was by them prepared for another ; and therefore I cannot imagine why you should wed it so fast as to contract your own ruin by concealing it, and persisting unreasonably to hide that truth which without you already is and will every day be made more manifest. Can you imagine yourself obliged in honour to keep that secret which is already revealed by another, or possible it should still be a secret which is known to one of the other sex, though for a time denied ? No, my Lord, be most assured that if you still persist to be cruel to yourself for others' sakes that deserve it not, it will nevertheless be made appear ere long, I fear, to your ruin." Waller to Portland. June ? Sanford's *Studies of the Rebellion*, 563. This letter appears to me to be inconsistent with Portland's statement that Waller wanted him to join in making a false accusation. In that case Waller might have painted in high colours the advantages of the immunity which he would gain by so doing, but he would not have entered into details which the recipient of his letter must have known to be entirely false.

[1] *Rushw.* v. 325.

died in confinement. The lives of the other three were
spared.

As a member of the House of Commons, Waller could
not appear before a court-martial without leave given by

July 4.
Waller at
the bar of
the House.

the House. On July 4 he was brought to the bar
to show cause why that leave should be refused.
No more effective speech was ever delivered by a
prisoner. Dressed in deep mourning, 'as if he had been going
to execution itself,' he made no attempt to excuse his fault,
disclaiming, probably with entire disregard of truth, all knowledge of the military arrangements made by the other conspirators, and dwelling solely on two points on which he knew
his fellow-members to be most sensitive, their dislike of creating
a precedent for handing themselves over to the judgment of
soldiers. This pleading was not entirely in vain. Waller was
expelled the House, but he remained in prison for many months,
untried and unsentenced, till the throng of events had almost
blotted out the memory of his crime.[1]

Like Conway and Portland, Lady Daubigny persisted in
denying all knowledge of the plot. Lady Sophia Murray,

Lady Dau-
bigny and
Lady
Sophia
Murray.

charged with carrying on a correspondence with
Falkland, refused to be examined at all. "I do not
mean," she said boldly to the Committee of Safety,
"to give an account to such fellows as you are." A

June 29.

few voices were raised in the House for sending the
two ladies before a court-martial, but in the end
respect for their sex prevailed, and no further attempt was made
to inflict any penalty upon them.[2]

Conway and Portland were equally fortunate. The feeling
of the Lords was strongly against allowing members of their

July 31.
Liberation
of Conway
and Port-
land.

House to be convicted on the testimony of a single
witness, and on July 31, after a detention of seven
weeks, they were liberated on bail.[3] Their enforced
absence from their places had weakened the Peace-
party amongst the peers at a critical moment.

[1] D'Ewes's Diary. *Harl. MSS.* 164, fol. 144. *C.J.* ii. 166. *Rushw.*
v. 328. Waller's final liberation will be spoken of in the proper place.
[2] D'Ewes's Diary. *Harl. MSS.* 165, fol. 100–102.   [3] *L.J.* vi. 161.

During those weeks the wave of calamity which had been gradually rising burst upon the Houses like a flood.   Early in

June, indeed, it seemed for a time as if Cromwell's hope of gathering the forces of the Northern Midlands for the rescue of the Fairfaxes from Newcastle's overwhelming power was at last to be realised.   Some 6,000 men under Lords Grey of Groby and Willoughby of Parham, Cromwell, Gell, the younger Hotham, and others were gathered at Nottingham,[1] with the view of a march into Yorkshire. Local feeling was once more too strong for Cromwell's ardour on behalf of the common cause.   The appearance of a strong body of Royalists in the neighbourhood served as an excuse for remaining at home, and a letter bearing the signatures of five commanders, amongst which that of Cromwell, though doubtless not with his own goodwill, is to be found, announced to Fairfax that Newcastle's army in Yorkshire had been so weakened that their own presence in Yorkshire was quite unnecessary.   Fairfax in reply told them that they were entirely misinformed, and that the ' Popish army ' was strong enough to ruin him, whatever report might say.[2]

The letter of the commanders was in the handwriting of Captain Hotham, and doubtless it conveyed his sentiments. He was longing to carry out the treacherous compact which he had made with Newcastle.[3]   He was, however, anything but a good conspirator.   His soldiers were as turbulent and unprincipled as himself.   The warmest supporters of the Parliamentary cause complained bitterly that their homes were marked out for plunder by these marauders. To the remonstrances of Hutchinson, the leader of the Puritans of Nottingham, Hotham replied with scorn.   " I fight for liberty," he said, " and I expect it in all things."   Gell's men were scarcely better disciplined, and Lord Grey was weakly compliant.   Hutchinson found in Cromwell a man to whom disorder was as detestable as to himself.   The two watched

June 2.
A gathering at Nottingham.

June 2.

Hotham's conduct at Nottingham

---

[1] *Mercurius Aulicus.* E. 55, 14. *Certain informations.* E. 55, 4.
[2] Gell and others to Lord Fairfax, June 2. Bell's *Mem. of the Civil War,* i. 46.
[3] See p. 141.

Hotham's proceedings closely, and soon discovered that he
was in constant communication with the garrison at Newark.
His conduct grew more insufferable than ever. Quarrelling
with Lord Grey's men about the possession of some oats, he
offered to fight them to settle the dispute, and he turned his
cannon upon Cromwell himself. Cromwell and Hutchinson
laid their narrative of his proceedings before the Committee of
Safety, and the Committee passed the intelligence on to Essex.
Essex ordered the arrest of Hotham, and sent Sir John
Meldrum, a Scottish officer of tried ability and character, to
take the command of all the forces then at Nottingham. On June 18, the day of the fight at Chalgrove
Field, Hotham was seized and lodged as a prisoner
in Nottingham Castle.[1]

June 18.
*Hotham's
arrest and
escape.*

    The captive was carelessly guarded, and escaped to Lincoln,
where he had the audacity to justify his conduct in a letter to
the Speaker. He explained that he was still faithful
to the House, but complained 'Colonel Cromwell
had employed an anabaptist against him, and that
one Captain White had been employed against him, who was
lately but a yeoman. The valour of these men had only yet
appeared in their defacing of churches.'[2] The genuine Cavalier
spirit was plainly to be detected here.

June 24.
*Justifies
himself.*

    To the Queen, Hotham showed himself in his true colours.
Since the 16th she had been at Newark, at the head of the
small army which she was at last conducting to
Oxford. "You will pardon two days' stop," she
wrote on the 27th to her husband. "It is to have
Hull and Lincoln. Young Hotham . . . is escaped,
and hath sent to me that he would cast himself into my arms,
and that Hull and Lincoln shall be rendered."[3] The Queen's
hopes, however, were not realised. On the day when her letter
was written, orders were despatched by the House of Commons

June 27.
*The Queen
hopes to
have Hull
and Lincoln.*

    [1] *C.J.* iii. 138. *Memoirs of Col. Hutchinson* (ed. Firth), i. 220. The
Parl. Scout. E. 56, J.
    [2] D'Ewes's Diary. *Harl. MSS.* 164, fol. 234.
    [3] The Queen to the King, June 27. *Letters of Henrietta Maria.*

commanding the traitor's appearance at Westminster.[1]   When
they arrived at Lincoln he was no longer there.   Going to Hull
to confer with his father, his movements excited suspicion.
On the 28th the Mayor of Hull received information of the

June 29.
Arrest of
the two
Hothams.

plot, and captured him in his bed.   The fortifications were at once placed in the safe hands of the
citizens themselves.   Sir John learning what had
taken place, flung himself on horseback and succeeded in
effecting his escape, but he was knocked off his horse at
Beverley and brought back as a prisoner to Hull.   Father and
son were carried on board a ship and sent off by sea to London.[2]

If the Hothams had succeeded they would probably have
been welcomed at Oxford as effusively as Hurry had been.

July 4.
Royalist
opinion
of the
Hothams.

As it was, the imprisonment of the man who had
first bid defiance to the King was almost a matter of
rejoicing.   "The rebels," wrote Nicholas, "have
seized him, his son, their wives and children, and
sent them all prisoners to the rebellious city, London, where
the justice of God will, I believe, bring him to be punished by
the same usurped power that at first did encourage him in his
first act of rebellion ; for falser men than he and his son live
not upon earth."[3]

The arrest of the Hothams was carried out just in time to
save the Parliamentary cause in the North from ruin.   Whilst
Hotham was embarrassing his colleagues by his turbulence at
Nottingham, Newcastle, after parting with the Queen, gathered
his forces for a final blow at the thinned and hard-pressed

June 22.
Howley
House
stormed.

ranks of the Fairfaxes in the West Riding.   On
June 22 he stormed Howley House, the residence
of Lord Savile.   A week later he led his troops to
Bradford.   The Fairfaxes knew that their scanty stock of provisions would avail them for no more than a twelve days' siege.
On the morning of the 30th they marched out to oppose the
10,000 men of Newcastle's array with a force of which only 4,000
were armed soldiers, though it included an indefinite number

[1] D'Ewes's Diary. *Harl. MSS.* 164. fol. 234b.
[2] *Rushw.* v. 275.
[3] Nicholas to Ormond, July 4. *Carte MSS.* vi. fol. 11.

of countrymen armed with scythes and pitchforks, and who were at that time known as clubmen.[1] Advancing along the

June 30.
Battle of
Adwalton
Moor.

ridge of Adwalton Moor, they soon found themselves opposed by the enemy coming in the opposite direction. Although for a time it seemed as if the high spirit of the younger Fairfax would keep the foe at bay, superiority of numbers told at last against him. His left wing was broken, and his whole force was then driven off the hill. The old Lord Fairfax reached Bradford in safety ; his son retreated to Halifax. With the chivalrous devotion which endeared him to all that knew him, Sir Thomas threw himself before nightfall into Bradford to share his father's fate. The

Despair of
the Fair-
faxes.

prospect was indeed gloomy. Not one of the towns in the neighbourhood was capable of standing a siege. As far as was then known in Bradford, Sir John Hotham was still master of Hull, and Sir John had declared openly that if the Fairfaxes retreated thither he would shut the gates against them.

Suddenly a ray of light beamed upon the overborne warriors out of the deepest gloom. A messenger found his way into Bradford, and told how the citizens had risen against the

June 30.
Lord Fair-
fax invited
to Hull.

Hothams, and how anxiously they longed for Lord Fairfax to come amongst them to assume the vacant command. The old man rode off at once to Leeds, to secure it, if possible, on his way to Hull. Sir Thomas remained at Bradford in the post of danger and of honour ; but after a short resistance he cut his way out, leaving behind him most of his followers, and even his wife, as prisoners in Newcastle's hands. When Bradford was lost, all other towns in the West Riding, Leeds, Halifax, and Wakefield, were of necessity abandoned. After many a hard bout, weary and

July 4.
The Fair-
faxes in
Hull.

wounded, Sir Thomas reached Hull on July 4, finding that his father, who had ridden in advance, was already safe within the walls, and was installed as governor of the town. His own little daughter, who in after years was to be joined in an ill-assorted union with the profligate Duke of Buckingham of the Court of Charles II., was

---

[1] D'Ewes's Diary. *Harl. MSS.* 164, fol. 118.

amongst the missing. The fatigues of that long ride had been too severe for her childish frame, and she had been left dying, as her father verily believed, in a wayside house.

Sir Thomas's domestic anxieties were soon relieved. On the day after his arrival he recovered his child, restored to health by a night's sleep, and before long his wife rejoined him, sent to him with all courtesy by the stately Newcastle, who was too gallant a cavalier to make war on ladies.[1]

To have saved Hull was much, far more than in all probability the Fairfaxes could have imagined at the time. Yet, at least they knew that, with the level expanse before them offering no vantage ground to the enemy, and with the broad Humber behind them opening out into that sea which was dominated by the Parliamentary navy, it would go hard with them if they failed in maintaining the post which had been confided to them by its own citizens.

For the present Newcastle could boast that, with the exception of Hull, all Yorkshire was in his hands. It seemed that his part at least of Charles's strategical plan was now easy of fulfilment, and that the victorious army of the North would soon press heavily upon the Eastern Association, if not on London itself. Whatever use Newcastle might make of his victory, the Queen could hardly be now prevented from making her way to Oxford. 'Her she-majesty, generalissima, and extremely diligent with 150 waggons to govern in case of battle,' as she jestingly described herself, was full of spirit and vigour. With no slight contempt for the bitter tongues of her adversaries, she placed her little army under the command of Jermyn. Everything had not, however, fallen out precisely as she wished and expected. The failure of the Hothams to secure Hull had been a grievous disappointment, and it was followed by another disappointment at Lincoln. Two brothers named Purefoy, who held commands in the city, introduced within its walls some sixty Royalist soldiers in disguise. A timely letter

[1] *Rushw.* v. 279. Fairfax's *Short Memorial* in the *Somers Tracts*, v. 382. Rushworth puts the arrival of the messenger from Hull at Leeds, but Sir Thomas is hardly likely to have been mistaken in placing it at Bradford.

from the Mayor of Hull, however, had warned the garrison of its danger ; the Purefoys were arrested and the intruders captured or slain.[1]

On July 3 the Queen set out for Oxford. By this time Essex had abandoned Thame and had established himself at

July 3.
The Queen
sets out for
Oxford.

Aylesbury. If he had any thought of intercepting the Queen's march, it was frustrated by Rupert, who was already to the north of him at Buckingham. So wide

Essex at
Aylesbury.

was the sweep of Rupert's horse that some members of Parliament, summoned by Essex to consult with him at this critical moment, were unable to reach his camp.

July.
He removes
to Brickhill.

After attempting in vain to bring Rupert to an engagement near Buckingham, the Parliamentary commander drew off to Brickhill, on the borders of Bedfordshire, in order at least to keep open his communications with London. His second attempt to take the aggressive was irretrievably shattered. In a letter written on the 9th he complained

July 9.
His in-
feriority
in cavalry,

that the infantry of the Royalists always retreated before him, but that their cavalry was ubiquitous. Rumour spoke of want of discipline as being equally in fault with the defective character of the Parliamentary cavalry, and complained that Essex was far too indulgent

and indul-
gence to
his officers.

to inefficient officers. He was wanting, in short, in that ferocity of discipline which in a great commander cuts sharply asunder the ties of personal attachment.[2] His letter closed with a proposal that terms of peace, upon the lines which had been rejected at Oxford when Charles was comparatively weak, should be offered again now that he was comparatively strong, and that, if these were refused, his Majesty should be asked to withdraw himself from the field, in order that the

A chivalrous
proposal.

two armies might settle the quarrel in a pitched battle.[3] His chivalrous unpractical proposal met with no response in any quarter. The wits in the City asked whether

---

[1] *Rushw.* v. 277. D'Ewes's Diary. *Harl. MSS.* 165, fol. 107.

[2] For instance, the *Parliament Scout* (E. 60, 8) says that 'some captains of horse . . . had suffered their horse and men to be taken prisoners thirty and forty at a time, themselves being in bed.'

[3] Essex to the Speaker of the House of Lords, July 9. *L.J.* vi. 127.

Essex, who appeared to be afraid of fighting the King, was also afraid of fighting the Queen. It is to the credit of Essex's thorough loyalty of purpose that no taunts drove him to falter in his allegiance to the cause which he had conscientiously espoused.

In the Commons Pym pointed out temperately, but decisively, the radical weakness of Essex's suggestion, by reminding his hearers that every overture hitherto made to Charles had invariably been rejected; and the House of Lords, in which, since the arrest of Conway and Portland, the Peace-party had been considerably weakened, agreed with the Commons in refusing to reopen a useless negotiation, as being, in the words of Pym, 'full of hazard and full of danger.' On the other hand, a reinforcement of 500 horse for the Lord General was voted without opposition.[1]

July 11. *Parliament refuses to negotiate.*

However quickly this new cavalry force might be brought together, it would be too late to hinder the junction of the forces with those of her husband. On the 11th, Rupert welcomed Henrietta Maria at Stratford-on-Avon. That night—so at least it was believed after a lapse of a quarter of a century—the wandering Queen was the guest of Shakspere's granddaughter.[2] Like the last Frenchwoman before herself who had wedded an English king, she was bringing succour to her husband, sore bestead amidst his foes. It is hardly likely that the figure of that predecessor arose before her mind that night as the great poet had graven it for ever, soured and embittered by the strokes of fate, angry with all except herself, and stranded, bereft of all she loved and honoured, on the sands of a generation which knew her not. Such sorrow, such loneliness, such bitterness of spirit was one day to be her lot, as it had once been the lot of Margaret. For the present there was no boding fear with Henrietta Maria. Was she not about to see once more the husband whom she loved, even though he was less resolute and altogether weaker

The Queen met by Prince Rupert.

[1] D'Ewes's Diary. *Harl. MSS.* 164, fol. 123. Lenthall to Essex, July 13. *Tanner MSS.* lxxi. fol. 168. News from London, July $\frac{13}{23}$. *Arch. des Aff. Etr.* xlix. fol. 276.

[2] *Warburton*, ii. 227.

than herself? On the 13th the royal pair, parted for fifteen anxious months, met on the historic ground of Edgehill. Her

July 13.
The meeting
of Charles
and Henri-
etta Maria.

first request of Charles was that he would raise Jermyn to the peerage. Till she had his promise for that, she told him, no doubt with an arch smile on her merry lips, she would not speak to him alone. Jermyn had served her well. During the hazards of her enterprise he had acted as her man of business, seeing to the purchase of arms and conducting negotiations for advances of money. For the world and its calumnies the sprightly Queen cared nothing at all.[1]

Of course Henrietta Maria had her way, and Jermyn became a peer. On July 14 she rode into Oxford [2] by her husband's

July 14.
They enter
Oxford.

Good news
from the
West.

side, amidst the ringing of bells and the shouts of men, raised all the more lustily because there were tidings from the West of a victory as complete as that which, little more than a fortnight before, had been gained by Newcastle on Adwalton Moor.

The consequences of Stamford's defeat at Stratton had evolved themselves rapidly. In Devonshire, Plymouth, Dartmouth, and Exeter, on the south, Bideford and Barnstaple on the north, were constant in their allegiance to Parliament ; but

June.
Hopton in
Devonshire.

the gentry, as everywhere else, were for the most part Royalist, and the whole of the remainder of the county submitted to Hopton as he advanced east-

He joins
Hertford
and Prince
Maurice.

Skirmish at
Glaston-
bury.

wards. Early in June he effected a junction at Chard with Hertford and Prince Maurice. At the approach of the combined force, numbering rather more than 6,000 men, Taunton surrendered, and the garrison of Bridgwater fled without striking a blow. The garrison of Dunster Castle sent in its submission about the same time. At Glastonbury there was a skirmish with a small body of horse, the relics of the cavalry

---

[1] Warburton (ii. 229), who gives the anecdote on the authority of the scattered notices which he calls Rupert's Diary. He takes the half-jesting words of the Queen much too seriously. Jermyn's services are set forth in his patent in Dugdale's *Baronage.*

[2] Dugdale's *Diary.*

which had served Stamford so ill at Stratton. Such men were easily defeated and driven through Wells and over the Mendips.

So far everything had gone well with Hopton. If his mind was weighed down with anxiety, it was not from fear of the enemy. The horsemen who followed Hertford and Maurice were full of energy and courage, but they were desperate plunderers. As a commander of those Cornish soldiers who were as stainless in this matter as even Cromwell's troopers, Hopton was gravely dissatisfied with the evil which he was powerless to stay, and he was all the more vexed because he was himself a native of Somerset, and they were his own friends and neighbours who complained in vain of the ravages to which they were subjected.[1]

Prince Maurice's robber horsemen at least knew how to fight. At Chewton, to the north of the Mendips, they found themselves in presence of Waller's army, which had for some little time been established at Bath. The advantage remained with the Royalists, but neither army was as yet prepared to engage in serious hostilities. Waller especially was unwilling to abandon the defensive. His army was weak and ill-provided, and he feared to leave Bristol unprotected. West Somerset was, in the main, hostile to him, whilst East Somerset, a land of small freeholders and thriving industries, was favourable to the Parliamentary cause.

It was after the fight at Chewton that Waller received from Hopton a proposal for a private interview. "Certainly," replied Waller, "my affections to you are so unchangeable, that hostility itself cannot violate my friendship to your person. But I must be true to the cause wherein I serve. The old limitation, *usque ad aras*, holds still, and where my conscience is interested all other obligations are swallowed up. I should most gladly wait upon you, according to your desire, but that I look upon you as engaged in that party beyond the possibility of a retreat, and consequently uncapable of being wrought upon by any persuasions. And I know the conference could never be so

Marginal notes:

Royalist plunderers.

June 12. Fight at Chewton Mendip.

Waller at Bath.

June 16. Correspondence between Hopton and Waller.

---

[1] Hopton's narrative. *Clarendon MSS.* 1,738 (4).

close between us but that it would take wind, and receive a
construction to my dishonour. That great God who is the
searcher of my heart knows with what a sad sense I go on upon
this service, and with what a perfect hatred I detest this war
without an enemy; but I look upon it as sent from God, and
that is enough to silence all passion in me. The God of
Heaven in His good time send us the blessing of peace, and
in the meantime assist us to receive it! We are both upon
the stage, and must act such parts as are assigned us in this
tragedy. Let us do it in a way of honour and without personal
animosities." [1]

Such was the temper in which the nobler spirits on either
side had entered on the war. The quarrel had its roots too

---

[1] *Clarendon St. P.* ii. 155. This letter is rightly ascribed by the
editor to Waller. He says that it 'is the last of six polite letters, all rough
drafts written in the same hand and on the same paper. They appear,
most of them, to have been sent from the chief commander of the
Parliament forces in the West to Sir Ralph Hopton, whose name is
written on the back of the paper in the same hand.' He is wrong here,
as a careful examination shows that the name on the back can only
mean that the person who copied them got them from Hopton, or from
a collection which had been in Hopton's possession. No. 1 is written to
Lord Arundell of Wardour about the custody of his children taken at
Wardour Castle, probably by Waller, who, as Mr. Firth reminds me, had
the custody of Arundell's children. Nos. 2, 3, and 4 speak for themselves. The first begins: 'My Lord, upon the assurance of your Excellency's parole;' the second, 'Noble Sir;' the third, 'Sir, I have had
the honour to receive a letter from your Highness.' Undoubtedly 'Your
Excellency' was Hertford, 'Noble Sir' Hopton, and 'Your Highness'
Prince Maurice. The first two are on the subject of the exchange of
Colonel Lunsford—i.e. Colonel Herbert Lunsford, who had been taken
prisoner by Waller when he captured Malmesbury. The third letter, to
Prince Maurice, is on a general exchange of prisoners. These letters
must have been written by Waller after the junction of the three commanders, and hardly earlier than the skirmish at Chewton Mendip. No.
5, to the same person as No. 2, is to Hertford. Hopton, probably in
answering No. 3, expressed a wish to see Waller, and it is to this
request that Waller's letter from which an extract is printed above is an
answer. Waller's last letter is printed in Polwhele's *History of Cornwall*,
i. 98, and evidently taken from a different copy from that in the *Clarendon
MSS.* It is there signed by Waller and addressed to Sir Ralph Hopton
at Wales, i.e. Wells. It is also dated "Bath, June 16, 1643."

deep to be settled otherwise than by the sword. The Royalist
commanders were now the first to move. Sweeping round by
way of Frome to Bradford-on-Avon, they threw themselves

March of
Hertford
and Hopton

between Waller and London, and at the same time
threatened Bath by way of the valley of the Avon,

Waller's
defence.

by which the approach is easiest. In Waller, however, they had to deal with an able tactician, by the

July 3.
Skirmish at
Monkton
Farleigh.

confession of his opponents 'the best shifter and
chooser of ground when he was not master of the
field.' On July 3 they succeeded in drawing a small
body of the enemy out of Monkton Farleigh on the high
ground to the north of the river, but Waller's main army
was on the other side of the valley under Claverton Down,
and they neither dared to cross the river in the face of the
enemy nor to pursue their way to Bath leaving him in the rear.

The whole of July 4, the day on which the war-worn
Fairfaxes were riding into Hull, was spent in manœuvring.

July 4.
The armies
manœuvre.

At last the Royalists abandoned the line of the
river and betook themselves to Marshfield, apparently
hoping to reach Bath more easily from its northern
side along the ridge of Lansdown.

When the morning of the 5th dawned the Royalists perceived that Waller still blocked the way. The road by which

July 5.
Battle of
Lansdown.

Hopton hoped to pass was for some three miles the
main road from Chippenham to Bristol. At Tog
Hill another road branches off to the left, dips
steeply down into a valley, and then ascends with a winding
course on the opposite side till it reaches the north-western
end of Lansdown. The height once gained, a level road runs
along the ridge till the ground falls sharply down to Bath. If
the Royalist army could gain possession of this ridge all else
would be comparatively easy. Essex was lying in hopeless
inactivity at Aylesbury, and from him Waller had no aid to
expect.

As the Royalists pushed on through Cold Ashton to Tog
Hill they could see that Waller intended to contest any attempt
to scale the heights of Lansdown. His cannon were planted
behind a breastwork, and horse and foot were ranged so as

to command every available approach. As he remained immovable when Hertford and Hopton drew up their forces at Tog Hill, the order to retreat was given. The sight of the retiring enemy was too much for Waller to endure. Keeping his infantry at their posts, he sent his horse and dragoons in pursuit. Amongst them was a newly formed regiment of London cavalry, under Sir Arthur Hazlerigg, known popularly as the Lobsters, from the complete armour in which they were encased on back and breast. At Cold Ashton they found the

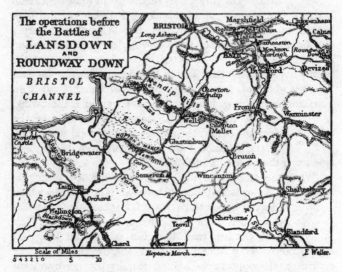

enemy halted. The charge of the Lobsters was successful for a time, but in the end superior numbers told, and the Parliamentary horse was driven back to its old position on the edge of Lansdown. The victors followed as far as Tog Hill, and drew up to examine the position once more.

To descend into the valley and to climb the guarded heights was a formidable task, but the sight of the enemy posted in apparent security only exasperated the Cornishmen. "Let us fetch off those cannon," they cried to their officers. The officers assented, and the nimble feet which had stormed

the heights of Stratton were once more in motion, working
their way upwards through the woods on either side, in
which the enemy had placed musketeers to hold the ground.
The horse, advancing along the road, was less fortunate.
It was charged and driven back. Then Sir Bevil Grenvile,
who was stationed with his regiment at Tog Hill, gave
the word to advance, and descended into the valley.
Placing his pikemen in the centre, his horse on the open
ground to the right, and his musketeers on the left, he steadily
pushed on. It is possible that Grenvile was protected by the
very steepness of the ascent, and that Waller's cannon could
not be sufficiently depressed to strike the ascending force.
The bend of the road to the right was undoubtedly in his
favour, as it gave him the shelter of a stone wall running
almost at right angles to the enemy's fire.[1] It was only on
approaching the top that the road, sweeping round once more,
made straight for Waller's position. Then came the real
struggle of the day. Five times did the Parliamentary cavalry
charge with all the advantage of the slope, and five times it
charged in vain. At last the whole Royalist force surged over
Waller's breastworks. The moment of victory was also the
moment of sorrow. Of the 2,000 horsemen which had
marched out of their quarters in the morning, 600 only were
still in the saddle when the day was gained. The Cornishmen
were saddened by the fall of their beloved leader, Sir Bevil
Grenvile, struck down in the thick of the fight. Waller too,
if beaten, was still formidable. He had withdrawn his cannon
in time, and had placed them behind a stone wall a little in
the rear of his old position, breaking it into gaps to serve as
embrasures. For the rest of the day shots were occasionally
fired from either side, but neither army ventured to charge the
other. As night fell the Royalists, 'seated,' as one of those

---

[1] The shelter of the stone wall is mentioned in a contemporary narrative,
but it was only after a visit to the spot that I understood the importance
of the bend in the road, which is not noticed by any of the authorities.
The space to the left is now filled with trees. Only a few are represented
in *Thorpe's map of the environs of Bath*, issued in 1771, and I suspect that
in 1643 the woods were at some little distance from the road.

present expressed it, 'like a heavy stone upon the very brow of the hill, which with one hasty charge might well have been rolled to the bottom,' watched for every sign of an attack under the cover of night. About eleven, a volley of musketry was poured into their ranks, and then all was still. A soldier creeping forwards found that the enemy's line was deserted. Waller had retired to Bath. "We were glad they were gone," wrote a Royalist officer, "for if they had not, I know who had within an hour."

The victorious army was too shattered to press on in pursuit, and the powder remaining to it was too scanty to make a siege of Bath possible. Disputes in their own ranks arose to diminish the efficiency of the force. The Cornishmen had had the honour of the day, and they were inclined to depreciate the services of the cavalry, which had been called on to fight on unfavourable ground. Hazlerigg's Lobsters, too, had shown themselves to be possessed of better military qualities than were to be found in the cavalry of Essex's army. "Indeed," wrote a Royalist who took part in the battle, "had our horse been as good as the enemy's, the rebels had never gone off the field unharmed." [1]

The retreat of the Royalists in the morning was saddened by an unexpected misfortune. Hopton, who had been slightly wounded on the day of the fight, was struck down and seriously injured by the explosion of a waggon which contained almost the whole of the remaining stock of ammunition. If the Cornishmen loved Grenvile as the most genial of their countrymen, they revered Hopton as a capable commander and as a man of unstained probity. "Our horse," was the mournful comment, "was bad before, but now worse; our foot drooped for their lord whom they loved, and that they had not powder enough to defend him." That night they spent at Marshfield, and the two following at Chippenham, that their wounded general might have the needful rest. Then, on an alarm that the

July 6.
Hopton wounded by an explosion.

---

[1] Narratives by Hopton and Slingsby. *Clarendon MSS.* 1,738 (2), (4). Waller and Hazlerigg to Lenthall, July 12. *Tanner MSS.* lxii. fol. 164. *The Parliament Scout.* E. 60, 8.

enemy was approaching, they hurried on to Devizes, suffering heavily from Waller's attacks upon their rear. On the 10th

July 9.
Hopton at Devizes.

Waller took up a position on Roundway Down, a chalk height about a mile to the north of Devizes

July 10.
Waller on Roundway Down.

commanding the road to Oxford. A convoy of ammunition coming from Oxford under the charge of the Earl of Crawford fell easily into his hands, but he was unable to hinder the escape of the whole of the Royalist cavalry, which rode off with Hertford and Prince Maurice in the direction of Salisbury.

Waller might well think that Hopton's Cornishmen were delivered into his hands. On the morning of the 11th he laid

July 11.
Siege of Devizes.

siege to Devizes. What Hopton could do he did bravely, giving his orders from his sick-bed. His foot were still more numerous than those of the enemy, and by his direction barricades had been thrown up at the entrances of the streets. The town was, however, unfortified ; of powder there was but little remaining, and the stock of match was entirely exhausted. Fertile in expedients, Hopton ordered the ropes which supported the sacking of the beds of the townsmen to be collected and boiled in resin. Yet, if Hopton could provide match he could not provide powder, and unless succour should arrive the resistance of Devizes could not be long pro-

July 12.

tracted. "The Cornish," wrote Waller and Hazlerigg, "defend it bravely. We hope that God will scatter, if not destroy, this mighty army of the West. He hath wrought wonders for us, and we hope the Lord will keep us from that great strength they expect from Oxford." The evening of the

July 13.
Battle of Roundway Down.

13th was fixed for the general assault. In the afternoon the heights of Roundway Down were crowned by a large body of horse. Prince Maurice had returned from Oxford, bringing with him a considerable reinforcement commanded by Wilmot. Waller at once drew off his men from before the town to meet the new enemy. Hazlerigg impetuously charged up the hill, but on the steep slippery down the courage of the Lobsters was exerted in vain. Their repulse struck terror into the western horsemen, the relics of Stamford's force, who formed the weakest part of Waller's army. The whole of the Parliamentary cavalry rushed madly down the hill side, 'where never horse went down or up before.' Waller joined in the flight, and his infantry, abandoned by their comrades and their geneıal, knew their case to be hopeless when they saw Hopton's Cornishmen sallying out to take them in the rear. Of 1,800 footmen 600 were slain and the remainder led off as prisoners. For all practical purposes Waller's army was annihilated.[1]

[1] Slingsby's Narrative. *Clarendon MSS.* 1,738, (2). Waller and Hazlerigg to Lenthall, July 12. *Tanner MSS.* lxii. fol. 164. A few details may be gathered from the contemporary newspapers.

CHAPTER IX.

BRISTOL AND GAINSBOROUGH.

ALTHOUGH the news from Roundway Down, following close upon the news from Adwalton Moor, was a terrible blow to the Parliamentary leaders, it brought with it no thought of surrender. It rather gave life to that scheme for calling in the Scots which they had long entertained, but which even the House of Commons had hitherto shrunk from putting into execution.

1643.
July.
The effect of the news at Westminster.

There can be little doubt that between Pym and Argyle a good understanding had for some time existed. It was under Argyle's influence that the various bodies which together acted as the government of Scotland resolved on May 10 to summon a Convention of Estates— a kind of informal Parliament—to meet on June 22 without the royal consent.[1]

May 10.
A Convention of Estates summoned.

Against this resolution Hamilton had pleaded in vain. When it was taken he characteristically dissuaded Charles from standing upon his dignity and prohibiting the meeting. It was possible, he thought, that the Convention might, after all, decline to interfere in England, and it was certainly not likely that it would pay any attention to orders from the King commanding it to abstain from sitting.[2]

Hamilton's opposition.

June 5.
He dissuades the King from prohibiting the Convention.

Straightforwardness, unhappily, was never to be counted on in Charles, and some time before the Convention met a fresh discovery filled with alarm the minds of even the most trustful. Although the counsel given by Montrose at York had been rejected by the King, it had

May.
Montrose's plans.

[1] *Baillie*, ii. 68. [2] Information to the King, June 5. *Burnet*, 226.

probably not been so decisively rejected as to lead its author to
suppose that his plan might not be taken up again if Hamilton's
mission failed.   However this may have been, there can be no
doubt that Montrose's plan of action contemplated, not merely
a rising in Scotland against the Presbyterian Government, but
the bringing over of Irish Catholic troops as well. Of the Scottish Royalists, Nithsdale and Aboyne had been prominent at the
conference at York, whilst Antrim, whose vanity and incapacity
had once drawn down upon him the weight of Strafford's sarcasm, was also present to expound the chances of obtaining aid
from Ireland.   Towards the end of May, Antrim, as he was
landing in his native country, was captured and carried before
Monro.

In Antrim's pocket were found compromising letters from
Nithsdale and Aboyne, and subsequent examinations elicited

Discovery
of Antrim's
correspon-
dence.

an acknowledgment that plans existed for a rising in
Scotland, to be backed by the Irish Catholics. There
was indeed no evidence that the plans had been actually adopted by Charles, but the undoubted fact that he was at
the time engaged in negotiations with the confederates at Kilkenny would be accepted as a confirmation of the worst sus-

Rumours in
Scotland.

picions.   It was freely stated in Scotland that Antrim
had offered to bribe Monro with 5,000*l.* to join that
English army in Ireland which Charles intended to employ
against the Parliamentary forces in England, and that if this
offer were refused the English and Irish were to be incited to
join together in order to fall upon the Scottish troops in Ulster.[1]
It was also believed that, when Monro's army had been got rid
of, the combined forces were to cross over to Cumberland, where
they would receive support from Nithsdale, whose family was
powerful on the Western Borders, whilst Hamilton would strike
a blow for the King in the centre of Scotland, and Montrose
would rouse the North.[2]   Baillie, in reporting what he heard,

---

[1] If this appears too visionary, it must be remembered that there is
undoubted evidence that a similar proposal was made some months later.

[2] Antrim's correspondence was published by the English Parliament
on July 15 in *A declaration of the Commons.* E. 61, 23. Compare
Baillie, ii. 74.

did not give full credence to every part of the story, and it is evident from the place assigned in it to Hamilton that it represents rather the intentions of the schemers than a definite plan accepted by the King. Opinion in Scotland was, however, certain to outrun the actual facts on which it was based, and it was

June.
Meeting between Montrose and Huntly.

still more inflamed when it was known that in the early days of June Montrose was at Aberdeen, holding close conference with Huntly, whose son, Aboyne, had been an active participator in the consultations at York.[1]

After this there was no hesitation in Scotland. On June 9, the detection of the plot was announced by the Council. The

June.
Effect in Scotland.

thought of the necessity of an alliance with the English Parliament gained ground at once. Even if Antrim's correspondence could have been explained away, Charles's understanding with the Kilkenny Catholics was incompatible with an understanding with the Edinburgh Presbyterians. Under the influence of the recent

The elections in Scotland.

disclosures the elections to the Convention were held. The gentry of the counties and the townsmen of the boroughs sent up representatives all but unanimously in favour of a military alliance with the Parliament at Westminster. When on June 22 the Estates met, it was to

June 22.
Meeting of the Estates.

no purpose that Hamilton offered in the King's name to allow them to proceed to domestic legislation if they would consent to abstain from military

June 26.
They declare themselves a free Convention.

preparations. On the 26th they declared themselves a free Convention, and two days afterwards they ordered that copies of the documents seized from Antrim should be forwarded to Westminster.[2]

The news of the discovery outran the official information. On June 27 it was known in the English House of Commons.

June 27.
Excitement at Westminster.

Coming, as it did, so shortly after the detection of Waller's plot, it raised a feeling of intense horror. "The discovery of this plot," wrote D'Ewes, than whom no man had been more forward as an advocate of

---

[1] Spalding. *Hist. of the Troubles*, ii. 252.
[2] *Acts of the Parliament of Scotland*, vi. 6.

peace, "did more work upon most men than anything that had happened during these miserable calamities and civil wars of England, because it seemed now that there was a fixed resolution in the Popish party utterly to extirpate the true Protestant religion in England, Scotland, and Ireland." [1]

On the day on which these words were written Lords and Commons agreed that a deputation of members of both Houses should be sent to Scotland. As yet, however, no proposal to ask for military assistance was made. There was a natural disinclination to see a Scottish army once more on English soil, and the Scots were but asked to contribute counsel and advice, and to send a select number of ministers to take part in the Assembly of Divines which on July 1 was at last to meet at Westminster. [2]

Members of the Houses to be sent to Scotland.

Whatever hesitation remained was swept away by the news of disaster from Adwalton Moor and Roundway Down. Waller's defeat had taken place on July 13. On the 19th orders were given to the Earl of Rutland—Lord Grey of Wark had pleaded illness as incapacitating him from the mission—to proceed to Edinburgh together with the younger Vane and three other members of the House of Commons, and to make a demand for an army of 11,000 men. If the request were granted—and there was but little expectation of a denial—Pym's policy of rallying all Puritan men to the defence of the Puritan cause would receive a fresh development.

July 19.
Instructions to the Commissioners.

Extension of Pym's policy.

Much as might be expected from the aid of a Scottish army, some time must elapse before it could actually cross the border. Pym was well aware that unless the English Parliament could do something for its own preservation there would be nothing left for the Scots to succour.

On the one hand, in spite of the growing belief in the inefficiency of Essex, he persuaded the Commons to order the levy of 6,500 horse to be added to the Lord General's army, whilst at the same time the City, where the feeling against Essex was especially strong, was

Fresh cavalry to be raised for Essex.

[1] D'Ewes's Diary. *Harl. MSS.* 164, fol. 400.
[2] *C.J.* iii. 146.

authorised to place all troops which it might hereafter raise
for its defence under the command of its own militia committee.[1]   On July 22 the excise ordinance, which
had long been under discussion, and which was in
reality an ordinance for increased customs as well,
was issued by the authority of both Houses.[2]

The City to
command its
own forces.

July 22.
The excise
ordinance.

These measures could not affect the immediate
military situation.   Waller had already found it impossible to
maintain himself at Bath, and, abandoning the place which had
hitherto served him as headquarters, was making his
way to London by devious ways.   On July 18 Rupert,
at the head of a strong force, marched out of Oxford, and, joining
the victors of Roundway Down, sat down before Bristol on
the 23rd.   The great commercial city, second to
London alone amongst English ports, was coveted
by the Royalists as giving them near access to the
wealth-bearing sea.   They knew too that the richest of its
merchants were on the side of the Crown, and it was a point
of honour at Oxford to avenge the deaths of Yeomans and
Bourchier, the two citizens who had been executed by the
order of Essex and of the Houses, as the prime-movers of the
plot to admit Rupert in the preceding spring.

Bath
abandoned.

July 23.
The siege
of Bristol.

On the morning of the 26th a general assault was made.
On the Somerset side, where the Cornish troops were posted,
the ground was unfavourable, and the attack was
repulsed with heavy loss.   On the Gloucestershire
side, where Rupert commanded in person, a body of
his troops slipped over the outer defences at a spot which was
weakly guarded.   Much, however, still remained to be done,
when the governor, Nathaniel Fiennes, offered to surrender,
and Rupert thus found himself in possession of the prize at
which he aimed.[3]

July 26.
Assault and
surrender.

Whether Fiennes was in reality able to offer further resistance is a question difficult, if not impossible, to answer satis-

---

[1] *C.J.* iii. 171.   [2] *L.J.* vi. 145; *Ordinance*, E. 61, 28.
[3] *Rushw.* v. 285.   *Clarendon*, vii. 110.   A true relation of the late
fight.   E. 61, 6.   *Wednesday's Mercury.*   E. 61, 9.   Journal of the siege
in *Warburton*, ii. 236.   Slingsby's Narrative.   *Clarendon MSS.* 1,738 (3).

factorily at the present day. He was not a soldier by profession, and was therefore devoid of that special sense of

*Alleged
cowardice
of Fiennes.*

military honour which sometimes prompts a soldier
to prolong a defence long after ultimate success has
ceased to be within his reach. He knew that
there was a strong party in Bristol hostile to himself and to
the cause for which he fought, and he can hardly be blamed
if he treated as non-existent the chance that succours might
reach him from the army of Essex.[1] Upon his return to

*Court-
martial on
Fiennes.*

London he was violently attacked by Prynne, and by
Prynne's friend, Clement Walker, as a coward and a
traitor ; and a court-martial, before which he was
ultimately brought, sentenced him to death, though only on
the ground of improper surrender, thus tacitly exonerating him
from the charges of cowardice and treason. The penalty was
remitted by Essex, and Fiennes was merely excluded from
military service, for which he was obviously unfit.

For the present the question which agitated London was
rather that of the capacity of Essex himself for command.

*July 22.
Essex un-
popular in
London.*

Rude caricatures, in which the Lord General was
represented in an easy-chair holding a glass of wine
in one hand and a pipe in the other, were scrawled
on the street walls.[2] The great city was, however, far from

*July 23.
Suppression
of a rising
in Kent.*

being despondent. On July 23 its troops suppressed
a rising in Kent, which had been fostered by the
opponents of Parliamentary taxation and of the
religious changes introduced into the churches by the order of

*July 27.
Waller's
reception in
the City.*

the Parliament. On the 27th the City received
Waller enthusiastically at Merchant Taylors' Hall,
forgetting his defeat in his staunchness to the cause,
and petitioned Parliament to place him in command of a new
army, to be raised in the City itself. On the 29th the Houses
accepted the proposal, and on the same day they assented
to another scheme of no less importance. Sir John Conyers,
the lieutenant of the Tower, had asked for leave of absence to
transfer his family to Holland, or, in other words, for leave to

---

[1] A relation by Col. Fiennes. E. 64, 12. *State Trials,* iv. 185.

[2] News from London, $\frac{\text{July 27}}{\text{Aug. 6}}$. *Arch. des Aff. Étr.* xlix. fol. 289.

withdraw himself from the side of the Parliament in the civil
war. Permission was granted, and the custody of the Tower

The Tower
entrusted to
the City. was given to the Lord Mayor and the two sheriffs.
For all purposes of defence the City was thus placed
in the hands of its own authorities.[1]

The independent military position now assumed by the
City was but commensurate with the great sacrifices which it

Strong anti-
royalist
feeling in
the City. had made, and was still making. Many motives, no
doubt, combined at this moment to make the
citizens impervious to the discouraging influence of
the recent defeats. Charles had just prohibited his loyal
subjects from carrying on any trade whatever with rebellious
London,[2] and the tidings from Scotland of the discovery of
Antrim's correspondence,[3] together with the knowledge that
Charles's Irish negotiations were steadily progressing, served to
fan the flame of religious enthusiasm. Charles, it was true, as
he was about to receive the Communion at Oxford, had recently

Charles's
declaration. interrupted the service to make a solemn declaration
of his resolution to maintain the Protestant religion
'without any connivance of Popery,' but when the news was
told in London it was received by the citizens with derisive
incredulity.[4]

Inspiriting as the zeal manifested in the City was to Pym,
a grave danger lay in the general distrust of Essex with which
it was accompanied. The choice of Waller as the City
commander threatened to embitter the antagonism which

Ill-feeling
between
Essex and
Waller. existed between the two generals. Essex was convinced that Waller had drawn his disaster upon
himself by disobedience to orders, whilst Waller was
equally convinced that Essex had been remiss in suffering the
Royalists to march unchecked to Roundway Down.

Of this ill-feeling the leaders of the Peace-party were not
slow to make use. They thought it possible that Essex might

---

[1] *A declaration of the proceedings at Merchant Taylors' Hall.* E. 63,
10. *C.J.* iii. 169, 177, 181, 187. *L.J.* vi. 154.

[2] *Three speeches.* E. 63, 8.

[3] It was published in London on July 15. See p. 176, note 2.

[4] *The Kingdom's Weekly Intelligencer.* E. 63, 1.

be brought to declare against the continuation of the war, and they knew that if he declared for peace at the head of his army, resistance to his commands would be impossible. Essex, however, was of too loyal a nature to take part in a mere intrigue. On the 28th he addressed to the Houses an unexcited statement of the position in which he was. He explained that he had but 3,000 foot and 2,500 horse fit for service. If he was expected to do anything he must have reinforcements, and money must be punctually provided. He then touched upon the sore point. Men must not be attracted by promises of higher pay to a new army as long as the old one was in its present condition. Nor should any commander in England receive a commission except from the Lord General himself. The causes of the disaster in the West should be fully investigated.[1] Every word in this paper was thoroughly reasonable. Unity of command and unity of plan were the indispensable conditions of success. If the mutual distrust which had kept back the commanders in the Northern Midlands from hurrying to the succour of the Fairfaxes in Yorkshire was to be repeated in the South, a more crushing blow than that of Adwalton Moor would not be long postponed.

Hopes of the Peace-party.

July 28. Demands of Essex.

Though Pym was already suffering from the disease which was before long to put an end to his labours, he roused himself to profit alike by the zeal of the City and by the devotion of Essex. It might have been well if Essex could be superseded by a more spirited commander, but if that could not be, the powers for which he asked must be willingly accorded to him. By August 2 all his demands, save one, had been granted. The inquiry into the cause of the failure in the West, which would only have given rise to dangerous recriminations, was refused, but Waller, who was to be placed at the head of an army raised in defence of the home counties, was to receive his commission from the Lord General, who would thus be set free to operate in the West. To forget the past and to join in united action was the charge which the Commons, under the sway of Pym, gave to the rival com-

August 2. Pym's intervention.

[1] Statement by Essex, July 28. *L.J.* vi. 160.

manders, a charge all the more imperative now that the loss of Bristol had come to emphasise its necessity.[1]

Whilst the Commons were bending their energies to the prosecution of the war, the Lords, amongst whom the Peace-

The Lords prepare propositions for peace.

party had now recovered its preponderance, seized the opportunity of the General's discontent once more to draw up propositions for peace. To gain the support of Essex was the one thing necessary, and, instead

August 3. Holland and Pym apply to Essex.

of acquainting the Commons with the propositions, the Peers hurried Holland off to the Lord General's quarters to urge him to stand firm on the side of peace. The Commons, on the other hand, as soon as they understood the state of the case, added Pym's name to a committee which had already been appointed to carry to Essex the resolutions of the preceding day, no doubt intending that Pym should use his tact and authority in opposition to Holland.[2]

What passed between Pym and Essex we have no means of knowing; but if Holland, as he can hardly fail to have done,

The Lords' propositions.

exhibited a copy of the propositions which commended themselves to the majority of the Lords, Pym's task would be considerably lightened. The position

---

[1] *C.J.* iii. 188–193.

[2] "I was at Westminster, intending to have gone into the House, till I understood, first from the Earl of Holland and afterwards from the Earl of Bedford, that the propositions which the Lords' House was in preparing to be sent to his Majesty for adding (*sic*) of peace to his kingdom . . . should not be communicated to the House of Commons till to-morrow. . . . After some debate the House appointed Mr. St. John and some others to go speedily to the Lord General to desire him to grant the commission to Mr. Waller. . . . This was the public pretence for which these men were sent to the Lord General; but the secret end, they being most of them very violent spirits, was to draw off my Lord General, if they could, from his good inclinations to peace; but the Earl of Holland went before them to settle and confirm the said Lord General in that good resolution." D'Ewes's Diary. *Harl. MSS.* 165, fol. 134b. There is no direct evidence that Pym's name was added to the committee in consequence of Holland's mission, but as the motion was made after the committee had received its instructions, and was resisted in a division in which 21 voted against it and 27 for it, it seems reasonable to conclude that this was the case. *C.J* iii. 193. See also *Clarendon*, vii. 172.

assumed by both Houses at the time of the negotiations at Oxford was to be entirely abandoned. Charles was again to be placed in possession of his revenues, of his navy, of his forts and magazines. Hull and Plymouth, Portsmouth, and the Tower of London itself would be his without striking a blow, in mere confidence that he would entrust them to such persons as would be faithful both to himself and to the Parliament. Parliament was to be reconstituted by the readmission of all expelled members, so as to place the Royalists in a majority in the House of Lords, and to secure the triumph in the House of Commons for a majority which would be composed of the pure Royalists and of some at least of the members of the party of peace. The Assembly of Divines, which had been in session ever since the beginning of July, was to be treated as non-existent, and a new Assembly, which would be summoned with the King's approbation, was to take in hand the settlement of the Church. There were to be provisos for the maintenance of the privileges of Parliament, and for the disbandment of the armies, as well as for the trial of delinquents accused before January 1, 1642.[1] Such propositions as these were not a com-

Essex refuses to adopt them.

promise but a capitulation, and Essex, dissatisfied though he was, was in no mood to capitulate. When Pym returned to London he brought with him the assurance that he had no military interference to dread.

Abandoned as they were by Essex, the majority of the Lords resolved to persevere. On the 4th they obtained the assent of their own House to their propositions, and at once

August 4. The Lords accept the propositions.

August 5. The Commons resolve to consider them.

demanded a conference in order to lay them before the Commons.[2] On the following morning the benches of the Lower House were unusually crowded. Members who usually abstained from attendance on the debates flocked to Westminster on hearing that negotiations for peace were to be discussed. At a division taken two days before only 52 members had been present. No less than 163 took part in the first division on the 6th. By a majority of 29 it was resolved to take the Lords' proposition into consideration.[3]

[1] *Hist. MSS. Com. Rep.* v. 98.   [2] *L.J.* vi. 171.   [3] *C.J.* iii 196.

In the City the news of this vote created the greatest con-
sternation. The quarrel had long ceased to be one which a
Parliamentary majority could decide. Even if the
propositions had been far more equitable than they
were, to treat at that moment would, by discouraging
all military effort, make further resistance impossible. Unless
D'Ewes was misinformed, it was resolved at a meeting, in which
Lord Mayor Pennington took a prominent part, to make use of
force, in case of necessity, against a party which was itself looking to the Lord General and his army for aid. Northumberland and Holland in the Lords, Holles, Pierrepont, Lewis,
Evelyn, Grimston, and Maynard in the Commons,
were to be summarily arrested. It was, however, resolved, before proceeding to such extremities, to try the effect
of mob intimidation.[1]

The day after this resolution was taken happened to be a
Sunday. The pulpits rang with invectives against the advocates
of peace. Placards were set up calling on all well-
disposed persons to go to Westminster on Monday
morning, assuring them at the same time that 20,000
Irish Papists were about to land in England. Baseless as the
assertion was, but for the King's negotiations at Kilkenny it
could hardly have obtained credence so readily.[2]

Before the propositions were again taken into consideration
on Monday morning, a petition urging their rejection[3] was presented in the name of the Common Council. At the
same time Palace Yard was filled with a mob of some
5,000 men shouting angrily against the proposed
treason to the commonwealth. The Lords threatened to ad-
journ till order was restored, and called upon the other House
to join them in suppressing the tumults. The Commons, however, contented themselves with relying on the promise of the
Lord Mayor to keep order for the future, and the lords of the
Peace-party, knowing that the sword of Essex was no longer
available, gave up all hope of further resistance. As Holland,

Marginal notes:
Consterna-
tion in the
City.

Violent
resolutions.

August 6.
The City.
roused.

August 7.
A mob in
Palace
Yard.

---

[1] D'Ewes's Diary. *Harl. MSS.* 165, fol. 145.
[2] Yonge's Diary. *Add. MSS.* 18,778, fol. 11.
[3] *Rushw.* v. 356.

Bedford, and Clare passed out of the House they were assailed with angry cries and scornful gestures, but no bodily injury was inflicted on them. In the Commons the propositions were definitely rejected by a majority of seven in a House larger by ten than that which had taken part in Saturday's division. Some timid members of the previous majority had absented themselves, and every effort had been made to secure additional votes on the other side. A few who had voted for peace on the 5th voted against it on the 7th.[1]

The peace propositions rejected.

On the following morning the approaches of the House were beset by a crowd of women, with white ribbons in their hats, shouting for peace and crying out against Pym and Say. The next day they came back in greater numbers and with more determined purpose, having, according to one account, a number of men disguised amongst them. After presenting a petition for peace they pressed on to the door of the House, battering it for an hour, and vociferously demanding that Pym, Strode, and the other Roundheads should be delivered to them in order that they might throw them into the Thames. At last the guards attempted to clear the passages by firing powder. The women, seeing no one hurt, imagined that they had no bullets to fear, and, filling their aprons with stones and brickbats, began to pelt the soldiers. The endurance of the soldiers was at an end, and they fired—this time with loaded arms—killing two men, one of whom was encouraging the crowd. The women were not to be frightened by the killing of men, and continued shouting, "Give us those traitors that were against peace, that we may tear them to pieces! Give us that dog Pym!" At last a small body of Waller's horse came to the rescue from the City. The women at once rushed at the new-comers, calling them Waller's dogs, and attempted to tear the ribbons from their hats. In self-defence the men laid about them, at first with the flat of their swords, and then, when this did not clear the way, with the edge. Some of the women were trampled down, and a few were wounded. When the rest saw blood flow they shrank back. A troop of horse coming up finally drove them away with as little violence as possible, though

August 8. The women in Palace Yard.

August 9. A violent mob of women.

[1] D'Ewes's Diary. *Harl. MSS.* 169, fol. 145.

unfortunately a young woman passing from one side of Palace Yard to the other was accidentally shot by a trooper. One at least of those who were wounded subsequently died.[1]

D'Ewes, who witnessed the scene, contrasted bitterly the harsh treatment of the women with the leniency shown to the men two days before. He took no notice of the fact that the women threw stones and brickbats, and that the men contented themselves with ugly looks.

As soon as these tumults were quieted the Commons adopted a statement of the reasons which had led them to reject the propositions. Their special arguments were of little value. The assertion with which they concluded was incontrovertible. " We could not," argued the Commons, " in this time of imminent and pressing danger, divert our thoughts or our time from those necessary provisions as are to be made for the safety of the kingdoms to the framing of new propositions, we having so lately presented propositions to his Majesty, and by his answer received no satisfaction, that we cannot, at least with any

August 10. Reasons given by the Commons for rejecting the propositions.

---

[1] D'Ewes's Diary. *Harl. MSS.* 165, 146b. Yonge's Diary. *Add. MSS.* 18,778, fol. 13. *Certain Informations.* E. 65, 8. *Rushw.* v. 357. *Lightfoot's Works,* xiii. 9. D'Ewes's remarks are characteristic of the temper in which he wrote : " No man can excuse the indiscreet violence of these women, but the remedy used against them by the procurement of John Pym and some others, who were enemies to all kind of peace, was most cruel and barbarous ; for, not content to have them suppressed by the ordinary foot guard, which had been sufficient, there were divers horsemen called down, who hunted the said women up and down the back Palace Yard, and wounded them with their swords and pistols with no less inhumanity than if they had been brute beasts, of which wounds some of the poor women afterwards died ; and one of those horsemen, being a profane fellow, and bearing an old grudge to a religious honest man, named John Norman, who sold spectacles without Westminster Hall gate on the east side thereof, did shoot his daughter to death as she was peaceably going upon an errand, for which wilful murder the said father could never to this day procure justice to be done upon the malefactor." The account given in *Rushworth* says : " Unhappily a maidservant, that had nothing to do in the tumult, was shot as she passed over the churchyard. The trooper that did it was sent to the Gate House in order to his trial for her death, but he alleged that his pistol went off by mischance."

hope, present others at this time, when we have cause to doubt his late success will make his royal assent more difficult." [1]

This was, after all, the true reason why there could be no negotiation. Those who believed that even the continuance of civil war with all its miseries was better than the abandonment of the cause for which they were contending must fight on to the end. "In all the propositions tendered to us by the Lords," said Glyn in the critical debate, "there is no care for religion;" [2] and Glyn's words only gave utterance to the general opinion of those by whose votes the propositions had been rejected.

The necessity of strengthening the defence to the uttermost was becoming more visible every day. Whilst the Houses were debating, the King had been making rapid strides both in the North and in the West. On July 22 Parliament had confirmed Lord Fairfax in the government of Hull,[3] but it was hardly thought likely at Westminster that Hull could stand in the way of Newcastle's southern march. On the 25th the Commons gave assurance to the Committee which managed the affairs of the Eastern Association that they should not be left without support,[4] and directions were also given to Meldrum and Cromwell to hasten to the assistance of Lord Willoughby of Parham, who had surprised Gainsborough on the 20th, and who was threatened by a strong force of cavalry under Charles Cavendish, Newcastle's young and gallant kinsman.[5]

Progress of the Royalists.

July 22. Fairfax at Hull.

July 25. Meldrum and Cromwell to support Willoughby at Gainsborough.

Strategically, the position of Gainsborough was of no slight importance. Standing as it did in the way of Newcastle's advance, whether he wished to support his friends at Newark or to assail his enemies at Lincoln, its seizure by the Parliamentary commander was not likely long to pass unchallenged. When

---

[1] *Hist. MSS. Com. Rep.* v. 98.

[2] Yonge's Diary. *Add. MSS.* 18,778, fol. 10.

[3] Husband's *Collection*, 242.

[4] Lenthall to the Committee of the Eastern Association, July 25. *Tanner MSS.* 62, fol. 188.

[5] *Special Passages.* E. **62, 8.**

Cromwell received orders to advance to Willoughby's assistance he had just stormed Burghley House, and cleared Stam-

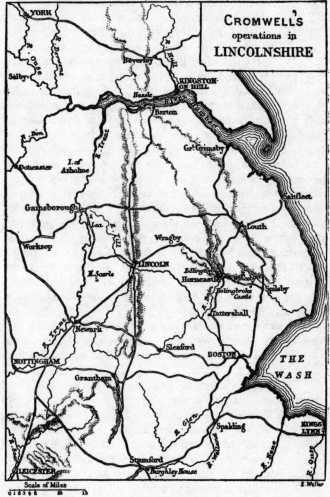

ford and its neighbourhood of the Royalists. On July 26, leaving his infantry behind him, he hurried northwards with

600 horse and dragoons.   At Grantham he was joined by
Meldrum from Nottingham, and a body of troops from Lincoln

July 14.
Cromwell
takes
Burghley
House.
July 28.
Gains-
borough
fight.

met him at North Scarle.   The combined forces now
under Meldrum's command were strong enough to
be safe from a flank attack from Newark, and on the
morning of the 28th they came up with Cavendish's
horse, posted on the edge of a sandy plateau, where
the ground slopes steeply down, a little to the north
of Lea on the road to Gainsborough.   Picking their way with
difficulty amongst the rabbit holes, they gained the upper level,
and, charging the main body of the Royalists, drove them in
headlong rout.   For six miles the horsemen from Lincoln and
Nottingham chased the flying enemy as Rupert had swept the
rout before him at Edgehill.   Cromwell was not among the
pursuers.   Looking round as soon as the enemy began to fly,
he perceived that Cavendish had kept one regiment in reserve,
and was preparing to fall upon the rear of the unthinking
victors.   Rallying his own troops, he allowed Cavendish to
pass him, and then galloping after him charged the Royalist
commander from behind.   In an instant Cavendish's regiment
was driven headlong down the hill, and he himself, the young
and gallant flower of a noble family, was knocked off his horse
in a bog at the foot of the slope, where he was killed by one of
Cromwell's officers.

  The day's work was not yet at an end.   Powder and provisions were being thrown into Gainsborough, when news was

Gains-
borough
relieved.

brought that a small Royalist force was approaching
from the north.   Taking with them 400 of Willoughby's foot, the Parliamentary commanders sallied
out to meet it.   In an instant they found themselves face to
face with Newcastle in person, at the head of a complete army.

Appearance
of New-
castle's
army.
Cromwell's
retreat.

Willoughby's men fled at once.   Meldrum's cavalry
remained to bear the brunt.   Cromwell, who was in
command of the main body, threw out two parties
under Captain Ayscough and Major Whalley, with
orders to retire alternately.   "To the exceeding glory
of God be it spoken," say the official recorders, "and the great
honour of these two gentlemen, they with this handful faced

the enemy so, and dared them to their teeth, in the least, eight or nine several removes, the enemy following at their heels, and they, though their horses were exceedingly tired, retreated in this order near carbine shot of the enemy." The whole force reached Gainsborough with the loss of only two men.[1]

Unimportant as it was in its immediate results, this skirmish of Gainsborough, as an indication of the future course of events,

Indications of future victory. was second to none of the more hard-fought battles of this eventful year. Here at least was that which Essex had failed to create or to discover, a cavalry as highly disciplined as it was enterprising. Here, too, was a commander capable of making the utmost use of his materials, prompt in action, sober in judgment, undaunted in the hour of adversity. Potentially, the combat at Gainsborough was the turning point of the war. For the moment it led· to nothing. The best of cavalry under the ablest of commanders was useless behind stone walls, and Cromwell rode off, leaving

July 30. Gainsborough capitulates. Gainsborough to its fate. On the 30th it capitulated to Newcastle.[2] Willoughby's force melted away, and he was forced to abandon Lincoln and to retire discomfited to Boston.

Cromwell realised the danger to the full. "It's no longer disputing," he wrote to the Committee at Cambridge, "but out

August 6. Cromwell calls for help. instantly all you can. Almost all our foot have quitted Stamford ; there is nothing to interrupt an enemy but our horse, that is considerable. You must act lively ; do it without distraction. Neglect no means." Stamford he was soon driven to abandon as untenable. Sending his foot to Spalding in order to hold out a hand to Willoughby, as well as to guard the fen country round Boston, he took up his own quarters at Peterborough, that he might check Newcastle's advance into the associated counties.[3] It was not

---

[1] Ayscough, Cromwell, &c. to Lenthall, July 29. *Tanner MSS.* lxii. fol. 194. Cromwell to Bacon, &c. July 31. *Carlyle*, Letter XII.

[2] Dugdale's *Diary.*

[3] Cromwell to the Committee at Cambridge, August 6, 8. *Carlyle,* Letters XIV. XV. There is a letter of the same date to the Deputy Lieutenants of Essex amongst the *Barrington MSS.* now in the British Museum.

merely the fortune of the associated counties that was at stake. If Newcastle could break through Cromwell's scanty band of troopers, London, and with it the whole Parliamentary cause, would be gravely imperilled.

The Houses had not been unmindful of Cromwell in his danger. On August 9, three days after his almost despairing

August 9.
Measures
taken by the
Houses.

letter was written, and two days after the rejection of the peace propositions, the Commons resolved that the infantry of the associated counties should be raised to 10,000, and that such of the divines of the Assembly as had their homes in those counties should go down to rouse the people to be stirring in their own defence. Scarcely less important was the resolution to appoint Manchester as the commander over the army of the Eastern Association. Something had been done by the appointment of Meldrum, and the failure in July had at least not been disgraced by those intestine discords which had produced the failure in June. Meldrum, however, good soldier as he was, could not speak with the authority of an English earl, even though that earl had as little knowledge as Manchester had of the ordering of armies in the field. On the 10th the Lords concurred, and a request was sent to Essex

August 10.
Manchester
to command
the army of
the Eastern
Association.

to give a commision to Manchester as Major-General of the army of the associated counties,[1] a request with which Essex at once complied. On the same day, to mark the sense entertained by the Houses of the growing dangers of the situation, an ordinance appeared authorising the pressing of men to serve as soldiers.[2]

It was not merely from the north that London was threatened. Scarcely had Bristol fallen, when a force under

August 4.
Dorchester
taken by
Carnarvon.

Prince Maurice was despatched by the conquerors to push on that advance along the line of the southern counties which had always formed part of Charles's strategy. On August 4, Carnarvon, riding in advance of the main body, summoned Dorchester to surrender. The place was well fortified, and Puritanism was strong amongst its townsmen, but the terror of Bristol was upon them. The King's soldiers, they had been told, were no ordinary warriors.

[1] *C.J.* iii. 199 ; *L.J.* vi. 174.   [2] *L.J.* vi. 175.

They 'made nothing of running up walls twenty feet high.'
Under the influence of unreasoning panic Dorchester sur-
Dorsetshire
overrun
by the ·
Royalists. rendered without firing a gun. Weymouth and
Portland Island followed its example. Sir Walter
Erle, who was besieging Corfe Castle, abandoned
the enterprise and shut himself up in Poole. In a few days, with
the exception of Poole and Lyme, the whole of Dorsetshire
was in the hands of the Royalists.[1]

As the Houses opposed Manchester to Newcastle, they
now opposed Waller to Maurice and Carnarvon. On August 7
August 7.
Waller
receives a
commission
from Essex.

A new army
to be raised. a commission from Essex arrived appointing Waller
to command the forces to be raised in the City.[2]
On the following day the Commons sent a request
to Essex to place Waller as Major-General in command of a new army of 11,000 men.

The King's strategy was thus to be met by counter-strategy.
Essex, with the main army of the Parliament, was to be opposed
Defensive
strategy. to the main army of the King. Waller on the left
was to meet the army of Maurice, whilst Manchester
was employed to ward off the forward march of Newcastle.
The plan had against it the inherent weakness which attaches
to all purely defensive measures, and the still more serious
weakness arising from the fact that the greater part of the three
armies as yet existed only upon paper.

---

[1] *Clarendon*, vii. 163. Erle to Lenthall, August 6. *Tanner MSS.*
62, fol. 218.

[2] *L.J.* vi. 172.

CHAPTER X.

GLOUCESTER AND NEWBURY.

So little were the Parliamentary armies prepared to offer adequate resistance to the forces now arrayed against them, that posterity has pointed with singular unanimity to the first week in August as marking the instant when a virile resolution on the King's part would probably have changed the fortunes of the war. To understand why that resolution was not taken by Charles is to understand why his adversaries, rather than himself, became masters of the field.

1643.
A critical moment.

Both sides had known how to avail themselves of the local feeling which was still strong in England. It was a feeling which had proved of excellent service as long as the struggle remained local. Fairfax's Yorkshiremen had fought hard against Yorkshiremen under Newcastle, and Hopton's Cornishmen, when the fate of their own county was at stake, had overpowered Stamford's mixed multitude at Braddock Down and Stratton. The startling victories of the Royalists in June and July had made it incumbent on Charles to play a bolder game, and to combine his scattered forces for an attack on the central position of the enemy. Was it to be expected that the men who had hitherto served him well would march at his bidding far from their own homes, and would remember that they were Englishmen first, and Yorkshiremen or Cornishmen only in a secondary sense?

Local feeling on both sides.

Before the end of August it was evident that the men of the North were not to be relied on for general service. Newcastle found that his Yorkshire levies refused to leave the county as long as their own fields and houses were en-

dangered by forays from Hull. Whether he wished it or not,
Newcastle was forced to lay siege to Hull as a preliminary to
further operations,[1] and Hull, open as it was to the
sea, where the Parliamentary fleet was supreme,
would hardly be overpowered as easily as Bristol,
to which access by sea could readily be prevented.
Manchester, it seemed, would have leisure to recruit his army.

*August.
Newcastle
draws back,
and lays
siege to
Hull.*

To the men of the West, Plymouth was all that Hull was
to the men of the North. The Cornishmen who had followed
Hopton to victory would follow him no longer.
They made up their minds to return home, that
they might protect their county from the hostile garrison of Plymouth.[2]

*Return of
the Cor-
nishmen.*

Hull and Plymouth saved the Parliamentary cause.
Charles's original design of advancing on three lines was
necessarily postponed till it was too late to make
the attempt with effect. Even his own army was
confronted with a difficulty similar to that which checked
Newcastle and Hopton. There was some hope that powerful
assistance might be obtained from Wales, but the
Welsh refused to cross the Severn as long as
Gloucester remained untaken.[3] The attack upon the fortresses
in the rear of the Royalist advance was imposed upon Charles
by necessity.

*Hull and
Plymouth.*

*Conduct of
the Welsh.*

Scarcely less fatal than the predominance of local over
national patriotism was the ever-increasing discord between
the Royalist commanders. Alike in the cabinet and in the
field, those who wished to carry on the war with a view to
eventual peace, and who wished to preserve intact the constitutional gains of the early months of the Long Parliament, found themselves opposed by men who cared
nothing for the constitution, who as counsellors
dragged the King into foreign alliances and Irish negotiations,

*Divisions
amongst the
Royalist
leaders.*

---

[1] *Lives of the Duke and Duchess of Newcastle, by the Duchess*, ed.
Firth, 56. Compare *Clarendon*, vii. 176, note 1. Sir Philip Warwick
thought that Newcastle did not wish to go where he would no longer be
the first personage ; but this may be scandal.

[2] *Clarendon*, vii. 152.   [3] *Ibid*. vii. 157, and vii. 176, note 1.

and who in carrying on the war were soldiers first and citizens afterwards, if indeed they were citizens at all. At Oxford, Digby and Jermyn were the main props of a disastrous policy which found its chief advocate in the Queen, so ardent in her husband's cause, yet so ignorant of all that it befitted her to know. In the camp the two foreign princes, Rupert and Maurice, were the hope of those who believed war to be the affair of soldiers only, and who derided the claim of civilians to be treated with even common consideration.

Scarcely had Bristol surrendered, when the controversy, long smouldering, burst out into a flame. Rupert was in

Dispute between Rupert and Hertford. command of the troops which had been brought from Oxford. Hertford, on the other hand, had, early in the war, been appointed Lord-Lieutenant of the counties in which Bristol was situated, and he therefore regarded Rupert as a mere auxiliary in the army of which he was, in virtue of his office, nominally in command, though Hopton was its real leader. In the face of these claims, Rupert had signed the articles of capitulation without consulting Hertford, and Hertford, to vindicate his authority, had named Hopton as governor of the city without consulting Rupert. Rupert immediately wrote to the King, without mentioning Hertford's action, to ask for the governorship for himself, and Charles, ignorant of the facts, at once complied

August 1. Charles at Bristol. with his nephew's wishes. So bitter was the feeling aroused, that Charles visited Bristol to allay the storm. Hopton, as ever, anxious to remove the causes of strife, offered to accept the post to which Hertford had named him, as Lieutenant-Governor under the Prince; and Charles, on the transparent pretext of needing Hertford's counsels, carried him to Oxford and not long afterwards raised Hopton to the peerage.

The conduct of Maurice was even worse than that of his

Dispute between Prince Maurice and Carnarvon. brother Rupert. Carnarvon, after subjugating Dorsetshire, was doing his best to win over the population by equitable treatment and the good discipline which he maintained. His promises of protection were freely given to all who desired them. No sooner did

Maurice appear upon the scene as Carnarvon's superior officer, than fields and homesteads were recklessly abandoned to the plunderings of the Prince's followers. Indignant at the wrong done to those to whom he had plighted his word, Carnarvon hurried to Charles to complain of his nephew's misconduct. Charles may have sympathised with Carnarvon, but he had no remedy to offer. Maurice was the King's nephew and Rupert's brother, and he must not be called to account. He was to continue in command of the force which, now that Dorsetshire had submitted, was to be employed to reduce the ports of Devonshire.[1]

Whilst Charles was still at Bristol it was resolved, after mature deliberation, that the main army, instead of advanc-
Gloucester to be besieged. ing upon London should undertake the siege of Gloucester. Again and again it has been repeated that this resolution was the ruin of Charles's cause. No doubt, if he had had his whole army well in hand—if his main body, pushing steadily along the valley of the Thames,
Was this resolution ruinous to Charles? could have been supported by a forward movement of Newcastle against the Eastern Association on his left, and if Hopton or Maurice could have swept across Hampshire and Sussex on his right, it would have been desperate folly to linger round an isolated fortress like that of Gloucester. If, however, this could not be done—if Charles had neither the authority nor the firmness of purpose requisite—if the cries of the populations of Yorkshire on the one side, and of Devon and Cornwall on the other, were not to be disregarded—if Newcastle must needs tarry round the walls of Hull, and Maurice round the walls of Exeter and Plymouth, it was only in consistency with the general operations of the army that Charles should clear away the enemy's force behind him, to prepare for a united advance on some future day. No doubt, when that day came, it would probably be found that the time for successful action had passed away, but it was also true that when Charles resolved to besiege Gloucester it had already passed away. For him to advance to London unsupported was plainly useless.[2]

[1] *Clarendon*, vii. 192.   [2] *Ibid*. vii. 176, note 1.

Nor were there wanting reasons for the belief that the siege of Gloucester was a less formidable task than it ulti-
Condition of Gloucester. mately proved to be. A letter from Massey, the governor of the town, had on August 1 been read in the House of Commons. "Our wants," he wrote, "are so great, and this city so averse to us, that our power cannot
Massey's complaints. enforce men beyond their wills, which I had done, and would do, if our regiment might have equalled the city in strength ; but now, what with the general discontent of both, of the city soldiers and our own, we stand at present as betrayed unless speedily your care prevent it. Alderman Pury and some few of the citizens, I dare say, are still cordial to us, but I fear ten for one to incline the other way. If your supply come speedily you may have hopes to call Gloucester still yours ; if not, I have lost mine, for above ourselves we cannot act."[1]

It is difficult to avoid the conclusion that Massey's despairing appeal was intended to cover a contemplated act of treachery.
Probable treachery of Massey. There is strong reason to believe that he was already in communication with the Royalists, and that he had indicated his intention to surrender Gloucester to Charles if only he would appear in person before it.[2]

Before Charles arrived Massey had changed his mind. The Puritan minority had gained the mastery over the city.
August 5. Massey resolves to resist. Preparations for defence were earnestly made, and on August 5 a messenger was despatched to entreat the Houses for speedy aid.[3]

On August 10 Charles summoned Gloucester. A soldier

---

[1] Massey to Lenthall, July. *Tanner MSS.* 62, fol. 197.

[2] "Governor Massey wrote to Major Legge that if the King came before the town he would bring him in with a thousand men." Journal of the siege, *Warburton*, ii. 280. Compare Nicholas to the King, August 8. *Ibid.* 278, and *Clarendon*, vii. 158.

[3] Corbet's *Hist. Relation*, 41, in Washbourn's *Bibl. Gloucestrensis*, vol. i. D'Ewes's Diary. *Harl. MSS.* 165, fol. 149b. *Clarendon*, vii. 176, note 1, where it is suggested that Massey wanted to lure the King on to besiege Gloucester. In the face of his letter to Lenthall this seems improbable.

and a citizen, 'with lean, pale, sharp, and bald visages,' delivered the reply. The city, they said, was at his Majesty's orders as soon as they were signified by both Houses of Parliament. With scant knowledge of etiquette, the messengers wheeled round as soon as the words were spoken, turned their backs on the King, and, clapping on their heads hats in which the offensive orange ribbons were conspicuous, stepped briskly away. There was loud laughter amongst the giddy crowd of courtiers. The wiser few knew that this strange scene had its serious side. Gloucester must be won by force if it was to be won at all.[1] To Charles, even if he had hesitated before, it was now a point of honour to push on the siege, especially as a messenger from Newcastle had recently arrived to assure him more strongly than before that it was impossible for the Northern army to march southwards till Hull was taken.[2]

August 10. Gloucester summoned.

The siege to be pushed on.

Before the siege had lasted a week Charles was called away to Oxford. Of the few peers remaining at Westminster, seven abandoned their seats soon after the disappearance of all chance of peace. Three of them, Portland, Conway, and Lovelace, had remained to act in the King's interest, and were sure of a welcome at Oxford. Clare had never taken an active part in the struggle, and he ought to have no reason to complain of his reception. The other three, Northumberland, Bedford, and Holland, had opposed the Court at the opening of the civil war, but had latterly appeared as advocates of peace, and had taken an active part in the Parliamentary resistance.

August 16. Charles visits Oxford.

Seven peers leave Westminster.

With characteristic caution Northumberland betook himself to his country seat at Petworth, to learn how it fared with others. Bedford and Holland made straight for Oxford. Much to their surprise, they were stopped at Wallingford by the governor, who informed them that they could go no farther till the King's pleasure was known.

Northumberland at Petworth.

Bedford and Holland stopped at Wallingford.

All considerations of prudence were in favour of giving a

[1] *Clarendon*, vii. 161. Journal of the siege in *Warburton*, ii. 281.
[2] *Clarendon*, vii. 176, note 1.

warm welcome to the deserters; but the Queen was furious, and the jealousy always felt of new converts was strong amongst the old supporters of the Crown.   Never was the belief in the hopelessness of the Parliamentary cause stronger at Oxford than at the opening of the siege of Gloucester.   "I cannot

A lady's
letter. choose," wrote a lady, not long before the flight of the peers, to her cousin, who, being a member of the House of Commons, had remained constant to his duties at Westminster, "but let you know my opinion of your condition, which I think is so ill that it were want of friendship in me to conceal it.   You have been all this year thought a violent man against the King, and the taking of the oath [1] has confirmed it.   He says himself that all that took it would be glad of his ruin, and it is the opinion of most that are about him. God hath blessed him above all your expectations, and he is now in so good a condition that he need not fear the Parliament, though they have gone all the ways in the world to destroy him.   They have neither wanted men, money, nor towns till now, but you see how they have prospered.   I believe the main party of them have well provided for themselves and will leave you in the lurch.   Whatever your conscience has been heretofore, I now believe you see your error ; for it is impossible that you can still continue in so much blindness. God hath given you too large a proportion of sense.   Look upon the King from the beginning, and think with yourself, if God's blessing had not gone with him, whether it had been possible he could have been in such a condition as he is now in.   I know many that would be glad to make their peace and give good sums for it, and such persons as you would not believe would leave you, and will not be accepted of." [2]

State of
opinion at
Oxford. The letter of a clever woman is more likely to reflect the sentiments of the world in which she moves than are the stately periods of official document.   Opinion at Oxford was convinced that complete

---

[1] I.e. the Parliamentary covenant.

[2] Dorothy Leeke to Sir R. Verney, July. *Verney MSS.* Compare the letters of Lady Denbigh to her son in the *Hist. MSS. Com. Rep.* iv 260.

success was now easy, and regretted the delay at Gloucester as unnecessarily postponing the day of triumph. This latter sentiment reached its height in the mind of the Queen, who had thrown all her weight into the scale for an immediate advance upon London, and was mortified to find that her husband, as she believed, had followed Rupert's advice in preference to hers. In the mood in which she was she had nothing but contempt for the renegade peers, who had fled to Oxford for safety after demonstrating their incapacity to forward the royal cause at Westminster.

Charles, therefore, resolved to visit Oxford to pacify his wife, and to take a resolution upon the conduct to be observed towards the fugitives. He found the Queen's views everywhere in the ascendant. The whole Council, with the exception of Hyde and Savile, urged that Bedford and Holland should be treated with scorn. Hyde strongly argued on the other side, on the obvious ground that to receive the fugitives well would be to encourage others to follow their example. Charles took a middle course, which combined every possible disadvantage. The Earls were to be allowed to come to Oxford, but every one was to be left to treat them as he thought best. As might have been expected, they met with nothing but cold looks, and, finding that the King had already returned to Gloucester, they, together with Clare—who had now joined them—followed him there to offer their services in the field. Rupert, who had more sense than the Queen, brought the three to kiss the King's hands. Charles received them without friendliness, but without discourtesy. Clare and Bedford accepted their position for the present ; but the foolish Holland, to whom Jermyn had given hopes of restoration to the post of Groom of the Stole which he had formerly held in the royal household, writhed under the treatment to which he was subjected. Refusing to acknowledge that he had committed an offence by siding with rebels, and imagining that Charles would, without any request of his or any form of apology for the past, replace him in an office which had once been his, and which was still vacant, he

August 16. The King visits Oxford.

The Earls at Oxford.

August 18.

Their reception at Gloucester.

became a laughing-stock to the whole Court.   Northumberland, who had been watching affairs from a distance, was not
encouraged to follow Holland's example by the tidings which
reached him in his stately seclusion at Petworth, and ultimately
found his way back to his place in the Parliament at Westminster.   No one else amongst the friends of peace attempted
the thankless journey to Oxford.[1]

Whilst Charles's Court was thus distracted by petty jealousies,
in London all thoughts were set upon the momentous task of
the relief of Gloucester.   Now that Pym was sure of
Essex, nothing was to be left untried to provide him
with the money and the clothing which his soldiers
sorely needed.   Two thousand recruits were, if necessary, to
be pressed to fill his ranks, and six regiments of London
trained bands to be sent forth under his standard.   The formation of Waller's new army could wait till Gloucester was
safe.   To supply pay for the special service an ordinance was
issued on the 18th commanding every inhabitant of
London rated on the subsidy books, to advance as
a compulsory loan a sum equivalent to no less than
fifty times the amount of his subsidy.[2]

Essex to relieve Gloucester.

*August 18.
A forced loan of fifty subsidies.*

At the moment when the Houses were entering on this
vital struggle, the Commons took care to put in evidence that
loyalty to the royal person which was every day
becoming more shadowy.   A clergyman, named
Saltmarsh, having printed words to the effect that
' it were better that one family were destroyed than the whole
kingdom should perish,' his language was called in question in
the House.   Marten, to whom conventionalities were ever
hateful, justified the expression.   It would be well, he said
plainly, to extirpate the royal family and utterly to subvert
monarchical government.   Prudence demanded that plain
speaking of this kind should be silenced, and
Marten was expelled the House and committed to
the Tower.   He did not, it is true, remain in confinement more than a fortnight, but he would no longer have the

*August 16.
The royal family assailed.*

Marten expelled the House.

[1] *Clarendon,* vii. 182, 241.   *Warburton,* ii. 272.   [2] *L.J.* vi. 190.

opportunity of uttering inconvenient truths in his place in Parliament.[1]

Marten's imprisonment would not alter the fact that the

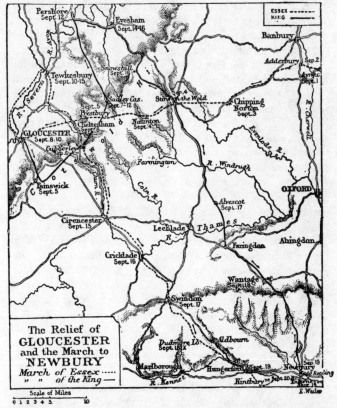

The Relief of
GLOUCESTER
and the March to
NEWBURY
March of Essex ......
" " *of the King* ——

Scale of Miles
0 1 2 3 4 5   10

Houses were engaged in a life-and-death struggle with the King. London was now about to throw its sword into the scale. Wherever Londoners had fought they had quitted themselves like men. At Edgehill, at Brentford, and at Lansdown they had borne the brunt of the enemy's

Preparations in London.

[1] D'Ewes's Diary. *Harl. MSS.* 165, fol. 180b. Yonge's Diary. *Add. MSS.* 18,778, fol. 15.

attack, and their defeat at Roundway Down was probably due to a defect of leadership rather than to a failure in their own courage. London now made itself ready for a supreme effort. Every shop was closed, that no man might plead the calls of business as a bar to the fulfilment of duty. The pulpits rang with exhortations to go forth to the help of the Lord against the mighty. Patriotic and religious emotions beat in unison.

On August 22 Essex reviewed 8,000 men on Hounslow Heath, ready to start on the perilous enterprise. On the 26th he set out from his last station at Colnbrook. As he marched on fresh reinforcements joined him, and after a few days he was at the head of about 15,000 soldiers, well clothed and well provided. No longer condemned to aimless manœuvres, their hearts beat high in the prospect of definite work. Essex pressed steadily on by way of Aylesbury, sweeping round Oxford to the north. Soon he found himself in an enemy's country, in which Wilmot's cavalry hung about his left flank. Wilmot's attacks were repelled without difficulty, and on September 4, as the Parliamentary army entered Gloucestershire at Stow-on-the-Wold, it had to bear a fiercer and more sustained attack from Rupert. Rupert's cavalry, however, with all its vigour, was no match for a complete army, and it was compelled to retire baffled from its gallant attempt. An effort made to induce Essex to negotiate was as unsuccessful as the effort to defeat him. He had no commission, he said, to treat, but to relieve Gloucester. "No propositions!" was the cry caught up by rank after rank at the appearance of the messenger.[1]

August 26.
March of Essex.

Sept. 4.
Failure of Rupert's attack.

Rupert had calculated that Essex would hardly advance so far. On the open uplands of the Cotswolds his superiority in cavalry could make itself felt, and the flocks, which formed the wealth of the district, had been already swept off by the King's foragers. The march of the Parliamentary army was a rough one for soldiers unused to war. Food and water were alike scarce. "Such straits and

Essex on the Cotswolds.

---

[1] This is from the *Perfect Diurnal,* and must therefore be received with more caution than statements by eye-witnesses.

hardships," wrote a sergeant in one of the London regiments, "our citizens formerly knew not ; yet the Lord that called us to do the work enabled us to undergo such hardships as He

The Royalists before Gloucester.

brought us to." There was no such spirit as this in Charles's camp before Gloucester. The nobler hearts were weary of the conditions under which they were fighting. Carnarvon had turned back from Dorsetshire, sickened with the cruelty and perfidy of his comrades. Chillingworth, after attempting by day to turn his knowledge to account by suggesting a mode of directing the siege works after the fashion of the ancient Romans, found relief by night in disputing with Falkland on religious subjects in a smoky hut.[1] Falkland, who, when 'sitting amongst his friends often, after a deep silence and frequent sighs, would with a shrill and sad accent ingeminate the word "Peace ! peace !" and would passionately profess that the very agony of the war, and the view of the calamities and desolation which the kingdom did and must endure, took his sleep from him and would shortly break his heart,' was exposing himself recklessly to danger, partly, perhaps, as he said, 'that all might see that his impatiency for peace proceeded not from pusillanimity ;'[2] partly, too, because he had lost all sympathy with the world in which he lived.

The citizens of Gloucester were holding out bravely. Vague rumours reached them on August 29 that Essex was

Rumours in Gloucester.

coming to their relief. On September 3 an arrow shot over the wall by one of the besiegers bore a paper which told them that Waller, their god, had forsaken them, and that Essex had been beaten. On the morning of

Sept. 5.
The siege raised.

the 5th, when their scanty supply of powder had dwindled to three barrels, the besieged descried a commotion in the Royalist army. A blaze amongst the huts of the besiegers soon told them that their danger was

[1] Sunderland to Lady Sunderland, August 25. *Sydney Letters,* ii. 669. Sunderland's assertion that Chillingworth advocated Socinianism merely means that he wished to apply the test of reason to revealed religion, not that he favoured the Socinian doctrine on the Trinity.

[2] *Clarendon,* vii. 233.

at an end, and before long Charles's army was in full retreat in the direction of Painswick.

The night before had been rough and stormy, and the sound of the cannon fired by Essex from Prestbury Hill to give the joyful intelligence of his approach had not been heard by the beleaguered citizens. With the light of the morning Essex learned that he had not come in vain, as he looked over the green valley of the Severn, and descried the grey tower of the cathedral standing out amidst the drifting smoke from the burning camp, and the dark masses of the Royalist army in full retreat. There was no need for him to hasten now. Driving a small force of the enemy out of Cheltenham, at that time a petty market town, he gave his troops the rest which they sorely needed. On the 8th he marched into Glou-

Sept. 8. Essex enters Gloucester.

cester amidst the ringing cheers of the citizens, who but for him would have been at the mercy of their enemies. The spirit in which the defence of the city and the operations of the relieving army had been conducted was summed up in words soon to be inscribed on one of the renovated gates which had been injured by the Royalists' shot : ' A city assailed by man but saved by God.' [1]

Baffled just as he fancied himself certain of success, Charles had been driven from Gloucester. Local tradition tells how,

Sept. 6. Charles at Painswick.

seated on a stone by the wayside at Painswick, he was asked by one of his sons when they were to go home. "I have no home to go to," is said to have been the desponding reply.[2] If the words were truly reported they can hardly have been more than the expression of a passing feeling. Disappointing as his failure to take Gloucester

The military position.

had been, Charles had now the hope of securing a prize far more valuable than Gloucester. His intention in breaking up from before the city had been to fight Essex, not to avoid him.[3] If he had offered battle

---

[1] The pamphlets which give a contemporary account of the march of Essex and the siege of Gloucester are collected in Washbourn's *Bibliotheca Gloucestrensis.*

[2] Rudder's *Hist. of Gloucestershire,* 592.

[3] The King to Rupert, September 5. *Warburton,* ii. 286.

in front of Gloucester he would have had every disadvantage
to contend with. His superiority of cavalry would have availed
him little amongst the hedgerows of the valley, whereas everything would be in his favour on the wide expanse of the
Cotswolds. He was even in a better position now than he
would have been if he had left Gloucester some days earlier,
and had supported Rupert with his whole army at Stow on-the-
Wold. He was in easy communication with his base of operations at Oxford, whilst the enemy, short of supplies, was cut
off from London. Whoever may have been the adviser on
whom the direction of Charles's movements depended, he had
shown himself to be a strategist of no ordinary skill. If the
soldierlike qualities of the royal troops could make good the
expectations of the King, Essex could hardly escape a great
disaster, far more decisive than Waller's disaster at Roundway
Down.

During the few days which followed the raising of the siege
the Royalist army was encouraged by favourable news from the
West. Before the end of August the townsmen of Barnstaple

August
28–31.
Surrender
of Barn-
staple and
Bideford.

Sept. 4.
Surrender
of Exeter.

and Bideford were disgracefully beaten by Sir John
Digby at Torrington, and surrendered the two
towns without further resistance. An attempt made
by Warwick to relieve Exeter from the sea failed,
and on September 4 the chief city of the West gave
itself up to Prince Maurice. To the westward of
Poole, the only places still holding out against the
King [1] were Lyme, Dartmouth, and Plymouth, with the isolated
post of Wardour Castle, which, earlier in the year, had been
wrested by Ludlow from the brave and beautiful Lady Blanche
Arundell.

That Plymouth was not already in his hands was a source
of great disappointment to Charles. The governor, Sir Alex-

Sir A.
Carew
attempts
to betray
Plymouth.

ander Carew, was one of those who, like Cholmley
and the Hothams, had taken up arms for the Parliament on political grounds. As the conflict assumed a more distinctly religious shape he grew
discontented with his employers, and attempted to signalise

------

[1] *Clarendon,* vii. 194.

his desertion of their cause by betraying to the Royalists
the fortifications on the mainland and on Drake's Island.
Unluckily for the success of the plan, his own garrison turned
upon him and sent him as a prisoner to London.[1] Plymouth,
like Hull, was thus secured against treason. As seaport towns
their capture by an enemy who had not the command of the
sea was a matter of no slight difficulty. Exeter and Bristol
had fallen because they were placed upon rivers and could be
beleaguered on every side. Hull and Plymouth could not be
so treated. Charles's northern wing, under Newcastle, and his
southern wing, under Prince Maurice, would be detained
around them as Wallenstein had been detained by the siege of
Stralsund.

Whatever might be the ultimate importance of the resistance
of these towns, the attention of men was for the present fixed

Sept. 7.
Charles
at Sudeley
Castle. on the valley of the Severn. On September 7, the
day before Essex entered Gloucester, Charles took
up his quarters at Sudeley Castle, to block the way
by which Essex had arrived from London, and by which he

Sept. 11.
Manœuvres
of the two
armies. might be expected to return. On the 11th he learned
that Essex had quitted Gloucester and had occupied
Tewkesbury. For a few days the armies did their
best to outmanœuvre one another. Essex appeared to be
aiming northwards, either with the purpose of attacking
Worcester, or of reaching friendly Warwickshire by a march
along the valley of the Avon. Charles, who had nothing to
gain by assuming the offensive, attempted to block his way up
that valley by posting himself first at Pershore and afterwards
at Evesham. By so doing he left the road to London open

Sept. 15.
The sur-
prise of
Cirencester. to his adversary. On the 15th Essex turned sharply
southwards to Cirencester, and surprised two newly
levied regiments which were intended to raise the
Royalist standard in Kent, together with a large quantity of

Retreat of
Essex. provisions, of which his men were sadly in need.
He then hastened on in a south-westerly direction
to gain the road running through Hungerford and Newbury to

---

[1] *Certain Informations.* E. 67, 3. Letter from Plymouth, August
29. D'Ewes's Diary. *Harl. MSS.* 165, fol. 165.

London, which lies out of striking distance from Oxford on the south, as the road by Warwick lies out of striking distance on the north.

Either through Rupert's error or his own, Charles had allowed the enemy to slip away, and there was nothing for him to do but to follow, bending his course to the left of the line taken by Essex in order to cut him off on the road to London.[1]

Charles therefore marched steadily on for Newbury, Rupert with his cavalry hurrying in front and heading back Essex to Hungerford on the morning of the 18th, after a sharp skirmish on Aldbourn Chase. On the 19th Charles slept at Newbury, the bulk of his army lying in the open fields on the south of the Kennet, and thus occupying the road from Hungerford by Kintbury, by which Essex would most probably have marched if Newbury had been undefended. Essex, however, on arriving in the evening of the 19th, though he established his artillery and baggage under a strong guard near Hamstead, not far from the Kintbury road, took up his own head-quarters at a cottage near Enborne Street,[2] from which began an ascent to a long ridge,

The race for Newbury.

*Sept. 18.
Skirmish on Aldbourn Chase.*

[1] Byron distinctly asserts that the mischief would have been averted 'had Prince Rupert been pleased to credit his intelligence.' *Clarendon MSS.* 1,738, 5. According to Warburton's account (ii. 288), founded on what he speaks of as a note to Rupert's Diary, the fault lay with the King I have not been able to discover where this diary at present is, but Warburton's view that Rupert did not follow Essex, after he heard of the enemy's movement, because he was without orders to do so, is difficult to accept. Could Charles really have expected his cavalry to remain fixed in a certain position, though its commander knew that the enemy was on the march?

[2] In all that I have to say about this battle I have had the advantage, not merely of studying Mr. Money's *Two Battles of Newbury*, a work written with great local knowledge, but also of a visit to the site of the battle in 1883, undertaken under Mr. Money's guidance, and of a very lengthy correspondence on controverted points subsequently. The battle presents difficulties which, even after the most complete study, both of the locality and the authorities, are incapable of a positive solution. More than is usually the case, the authorities are disconnected with one another, and the modern writer has to put together, as best he may, narratives which are absolutely isolated, usually without any clear reference to the

lying on the whole parallel with the Kennet, and throwing out
a succession of rounded spurs towards the Kennet on the
The field of battle. north, and towards the En Brook on the south. On
the southern slope the ground was mainly open, En
borne Heath on the western end being succeeded farther to the
east by Newbury Wash, as that part of the common was styled.
The western end of the central height was cut up by copses and
deep lanes intersecting one another, whilst the greater part of the
northern slope was covered by inclosures. In the evening of
the 19th some of Essex's troops made their way up to the point
where one of the lanes, leading from Skinner's Green, opens out
upon Newbury Wash, but they found that the Royalists had
already planted their ordnance at this important point, and had
sent up a small force of horse and dragoons sufficient to guard
the post at that late hour. They consequently drew back,
leaving the work of breaking through till the next day.[1]

Essex knew that the morning light would bring with it no
easy task. His main plan of action was plainly dic-
Sept. 20.
Essex's plan. tated to him by the lie of the ground. As he could
not pass through Newbury, he must make his way
amongst the hedges and lanes, avoiding the open ground of

locality or time. It will be seen that on some points, especially in rejecting the victorious charge which he supposes to have been delivered by
Essex at the end of the day, I differ from Mr. Money. On the other
hand, the points on which I have given way before his local knowledge
are very many.

[1] The Royalists declared that they did not occupy the ground till the
next day, but the simple narrative preserved in Yonge's Diary (*Add. MSS.*
18,778, fol. 54) leaves no doubt of the fact. Compare *A letter from our
quarters at Reading*, September 23. E. 69, 2. The main authorities for
the battle, besides two narratives preserved by Yonge, and afterwards
embodied to some extent in the newspapers, are, on the Parliamentary
side, *A true relation of the late expedition* (E. 70, 10), which is the official
account, and Sergeant Foster's *A true relation of the marchings of the two
regiments of the trained bands*. E. 69, 15. From the Royalists we have
A true and impartial relation (E. 69), which, as Mr. Money pointed out
to me, is shown by an edition, of which there is a copy in the Bodleian, to
have been written by Lord Digby, and the account of Lord Byron in the
Clarendon MSS. (1,738, 5), which was, however, only written in 1647.
There is also an anonymous narrative in *Add. MSS.* 18,980, fol. 120

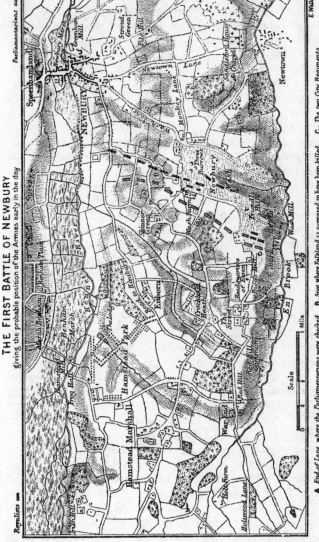

THE FIRST BATTLE OF NEWBURY

giving the probable position of the Armies early in the day

E. Waller

A. *End of Lane, where the Parliamentarians were checked.*   B. *Spot where Falkland is supposed to have been killed.*   C. *The two City Regiments*

Enborne Heath to his right, till he reached the point at the entrance to Newbury Wash where his reconnoitring party had recoiled before the King's guns on the preceding evening. To do this, strong as he was in infantry, was comparatively easy, and it was also comparatively easy to push on from hedge to hedge on the slope of the hill to his left. Success here, however, would not open the road to London. The road lay over the open ground of Newbury Wash, and of Greenham Heath beyond. Even if the King's guns could be taken or silenced, how was the Parliamentary army to make its way onward in face of the rush of Rupert's horse, both in numbers and in quality so superior to their own? This was the real problem to be faced, and faced at once. No delay, no skilful manœuvres to gain more favourable ground, were any longer possible. Food was running short with Essex, and unless he could defeat Charles famine would drive him to surrender.

As plainly as the offensive was dictated to Essex, the defensive was dictated to Charles. To bar the way was the one thing needful, and anything which might weaken his force for that object would expose him to unnecessary risk. In this spirit were his orders given. On the morning of the 20th part of his army occupied the road from Kintbury along the Kennet valley, whilst the other part, with Rupert and the larger part of the cavalry, established itself across the road over Newbury Wash. To seek out Essex as he struggled through the lanes would be in the highest degree dangerous.

It was not by the Kintbury road that Charles's right was exposed to danger. Its commanders had forgotten that to keep on the defensive requires skill and forethought, and they had neglected to secure those slopes cut up by hedges, which if once in the possession of the Parliamentary foot would command their own position in the valley. Early in the morning, Essex, whilst his main body was still struggling amongst the lanes, had despatched a party to seize the hedges on his left. The surprised Royalists saw the hill above them crowned with the advancing enemy. Sir Nicholas Byron, at the head of a brigade of infantry, to which a body of horse, under the command of his nephew, Sir John Byron, was attached, hurried up the hillside to retrieve the ground. For long the combat raged from bank to bank, from hedge to hedge. Amongst the hundreds who fell, unwept and unlamented save by those of whose tears History in her haste takes no account, perished one whose memory is still green in England. That morning had found Falkland rejoicing greatly. At Gloucester he had courted death in vain. The longed-for hour had struck at last. Dressing himself in clean linen, as one who had leisure to think of the seemliness of his own attire, because he alone of all in those hosts had set his mind on something else than the winning of victory, he bemoaned the misery of his country. He was weary of the times, he said, but he would ' be out of it ere night.' [1] Placing himself as a volunteer under Sir John Byron, he noticed that his commander drew rein before a gap in the hedge, through which the bullets were flying thick and fast. Byron, whose object was to beat the enemy, waited till the gap had been widened. Falkland, whose object was to die, spurred his horse at the opening. Horse and man rolled lifeless on the ground before the other side was reached. The battle raged on, the Royalists, for a time at least, steadily gaining ground. [2]

The fight amongst the hedges.

Death of Falkland.

On the Royalist left, where Rupert and his cavalry were stationed, impatience had almost proved as ruinous as neglect. Whilst Essex himself, with the main part of his army, was pushing up the lanes leading to the entrance to the Wash, Rupert was unable to endure the mere patient waiting which would have enabled him, when the right moment came, to throw himself on the enemy's columns at their exit from the lanes before they had time to deploy on the open ground. The uninclosed land to his left, leading to the wider expanse of Enborne Heath, tempted him on.

The Parliamentary centre ascends the hill.

[1] *Whitelocke*, 73.

[2] " The enemy had beat our foot out of the close, and was drawn up near the hedge. I went to view ; and as I was giving order for making the gap wider my horse was shot in the throat, so that I was forced to call for another horse. In the meantime my Lord of Falkland, more gallantly than advisedly, spurred his horse through the gap, where both he and his horse were immediately killed." *Byron's narrative.*

Bidding a force of infantry to follow, he galloped off at the head of a numerous and imposing body of horse. When Enborne Heath was gained he could descry Essex's reserves strongly posted amidst inclosures, and beyond them, on the north of the position, the baggage waggons and artillery near Hamstead. It was indeed hopeless to attack a force so strongly guarded. On Enborne Heath itself, however, were two regiments of the London trained bands with horse on either flank.[1]

To charge the Parliamentary horse and to drive them off the field was the work of a few minutes. Cut off from support,

The fight on Enborne Heath.

with neither horse nor cannon to rely on, the two trained-band regiments, composed of men whose only knowledge of the operations of war was derived from the bloodless contests of the Artillery Garden, found themselves exposed on open ground to the discharges of the enemy's cannon and to the rush of Rupert's horse. They bore the trial nobly. Closing up their ranks as the ripping cannon-

[1] After a long discussion, Mr. Money has convinced me that the 'little heath' mentioned in Digby's narrative was Enborne Heath. Crockham Heath is too low and too easily commanded to have been the scene of this part of the fight. Digby's statement that the Parliamentary horse was routed on this 'little heath' is confirmed by a Parliamentary newspaper. "Our regiment," it is there said, "made the right wing of the army, and we were flanked with horse, who, being charged by the enemy, wheeled off and left us." *Certain Informations* (E. 69, 17). This combat early in the day is evidently the same as that described by Sergeant Foster of the London trained bands (E. 69, 15). He says that his regiment ran up after Lord Robartes' soldiers had begun to skirmish, that is to say, quite at the beginning of the fighting. "Our two regiments of the trained bands," he adds, "were placed in open campania," i.e. on open ground, "upon the right wing of the whole army." The incident about a Royalist regiment calling out 'Friends! friends!' is mentioned by Sergeant Foster and the *Cert. Inf.*, thus showing that they are speaking of the same combat, so that the absence of any allusion to the defeat of the horse by Foster cannot be regarded as fatal to the identification between the fight described by him and that described by Digby. Later details, it is true, do not entirely agree, as the fight seems to have gone on longer than Digby admits, and the Royalist foot, according to Foster, did take part in the fight, which Digby denies. Perhaps Digby was not himself present in this part of the battle, which would account for considerable discrepancy.

shot tore them asunder, the London apprentices and tradesmen stood like a wall whilst the fierce horsemen dashed up against their pikes in vain. Many a saddle was emptied by the musketeers within the square. At last an attempt was made to gain by fraud what force could not accomplish. Each regiment in both armies was clad in the colour which the fancy of its colonel dictated. There were men in blue, in green, in red on either side. To distinguish those who fought under Essex, each soldier in his ranks had placed in his hat a green spray plucked from the hedges. A regiment of Royalist cavalry now rode up, with similar sprays in their hats, crying out 'Friends! friends!' as they approached. The Londoners were too shrewd to be beguiled by the counterfeit, and a sharp fire of musketry drove off the tricksters. For some time the fight went on, the Royalist infantry, which at first had cowered for shelter under cover of a hill, being brought up to the charge, and ultimately the Londoners retreated in good order off the heath, and took up a position on the cultivated ground, from which no serious attempt was made to dislodge them.[1]

Already, whilst Essex's right was thus engaged, his centre had pushed up the hill. For hours there was a deadly struggle amongst the lanes and hedges. Each field was a fortress, to be captured or defended. At last two regiments of Parliamentary horse—perhaps because the enemy's cavalry was weakened by the absence of so many regiments on Enborne Heath—pushed out, under Stapleton, from the end of a lane upon the open ground of the Wash, and drove back a Royalist regiment by which they were assailed. They were too few in number to hold the ground, and they drew back waiting for reinforcements. As other regiments came up there were fresh charges, and a determined resistance. At last Stapleton's regiment was broken and driven back into the lane. Already the Royalist horse was following up its victory and

Fight in the centre.

---

[1] Here again both Digby and Foster substantially agree. "We were glad," says the latter, "to retreat a little way into the field." Digby speaks of the result as 'the forcing the foot to retreat into their strength, though unbroken.' The field, however, is, as distinguished from 'closes,' open ground.

pouring after the fugitives, regardless of the Parliamentary musketeers who lined the hedges on either side. Caught in a trap like the French chivalry at Poitiers, the dashing Cavaliers perished almost to a man, shot down without hope of defence in the deep trench between the banks. The battle was restored, and the approaches to the Wash were once more the scene of embittered strife.

The Royalist commanders had failed to do more than keep Essex's centre in check. Their attack on his right on Enborne

Royalist attack on the Parliamentary left. Heath had profited them little. In the afternoon, massing large forces on their own right, they directed a fresh attack on his left in the valley of the Kennet. The eye of the veteran Skippon, who acted that day as second in command of the Parliamentary army, caught sight of them as he was encouraging his men upon the hill. Hurrying down, he drove back the enemy, and returned with the assurance that the army would not now be assailed in the rear nor its baggage pillaged. Again the battle raged along the whole line from the Kennet to the En Brook. An attempt by

Essex gains ground. the troops left behind by Skippon in the valley to seize a ford over the Kennet failed ; but, on the whole, the Parliamentary army gained ground. When night fell it had not only occupied a great part of the inclosures which had been hotly disputed earlier in the day, but had even established itself on the edge of Newbury Wash.

For all that, nothing decisive had been achieved. The King's troops still stretched across hill and valley, barring the

No decisive victory. way to London. As each soldier in Essex's army laid himself wearily down on the bloodstained ground, it was in full conviction that if surrender or starvation was to be averted another battle, as vigorously contested as that which had just died away, must be fought on the morrow. The sentinels heard, or thought they heard, the rolling sound of

Sept. 21. The King retreats. fresh guns brought up to be placed in position. When morning dawned all uncertainty was at end. The Royalist positions were empty ; Charles had withdrawn his troops into Newbury under cover of the night. The way to London was open at last.

The King's ammunition had failed him,[1] and it seemed to him that he had no choice but to retreat. It may be that, weak as was the fire of the cannons and muskets of those days, a resolute body of horse, with pikemen in support, might have kept back Essex's hungry soldiers till food absolutely failed ; but neither Charles nor his followers were in any mood for such an adventure. The unlooked-for prowess of the Londoners and the terrible slaughter of their own leaders had been so discouraging that there was little thought of renewing the conflict on unequal terms.

Each side claimed the victory, but if up to the moment of Charles's retreat the Parliamentarians had failed to gain their object, at least they had shown themselves the better soldiers. To the great Royalist historian of the war there seemed to be something contrary to the order of nature in their achievement. On the King's side unequal fate cut down 'persons of honour and public name,' whilst amongst his adversaries it was only known that 'some obscure, unheard-of colonel or officer was missing,' or that 'some citizen's wife bewailed the loss of her husband.' It is indeed unnecessary for those who respect humanity above any single class to hold that the lives of all men are of equal value to their fellows. The loss of the leader is greater than that of the led, and the fall of the worthy general or statesman is more deeply felt than that of hundreds of the toilers but for whose hearty co-operation neither general nor statesman would have saved himself from failure. The charge against the Royalist gentry is that they had ceased to lead. The contrast between the infantry which followed Essex and the infantry which followed Charles is their bitterest condemnation. They could fling themselves upon death with romantic heroism, but they had lost touch of the middle and lower classes. They could not inspire the common man with their own courage,

A disputed victory.

Clarendon's complaint.

---

[1] Byron was incredulous, but under the date of September 23 the *Perfect Diurnal*, a Parliamentary newspaper, says that some officers from the army told the Houses that ' before half the fight was over their '—i.e. the Royalists'—' powder and shot was so far spent that they were not able to answer us one shot for three.'

because they had no living faith in which he was able to share. They could point sarcasms at the narrowness and harshness of popular Puritanism, but a nation cannot live upon sarcasms, and the culture which raised the higher minds amongst them above any possibility of accepting Puritanism as a standard of life was entirely inaccessible to the rank and file of their followers.

On the battle-field of Newbury death had dealt hardly with the noblest of the King's supporters. A monument, which has recently been erected not far from the actual scene of the battle, gracefully couples with that of Falkland the names of Carnarvon and Sunderland, who fell in the struggle either on the Wash or on Enborne Heath. Unhappily, modern political partisanship, stretching across the ages, has attempted to awaken the now silent feuds of the past, and has refused to commemorate the deaths of any except those who fought on the royal side on that memorable day. Such an exclusion is especially unjust to Falkland. By assigning to him a memorial which would be suitable to a Rupert, it deprives him of his special claim to the loving memory of future generations. His glory was that when other eyes persisted in seeing nothing but party divisions, he had persisted in seeing England as a whole, and that he had thus ceased to be in accord either with the party which he had joined or with the party which he had deserted. It was because he could sympathise with neither that he flung away his life by an act which can hardly be distinguished from suicide. He could not, like Wolfe, die happily because the enemy had taken to flight. All that he asked of the enemy was to lodge a bullet in his body. He had ceased to hate, though he had not yet learnt to love. History, which takes note of the aspiration as well as of the accomplishment, cannot but think of Falkland as of one whose heart was large enough to embrace all that was noble on either side. It sees in him a prophet whose vision of peace was too pure and too harmonious to allay the discords of his own day, and whose longings could only be satisfied by the reconciliation which was to be accomplished long after he had ceased to breathe.

The Falkland monument.

Little recked Essex of dreams or visions. Finding the way open before him, he pushed on steadily. A sudden attack by

A skirmish near Aldermaston.

Rupert in a deep lane near Aldermaston threw his rearguard into a momentary panic, but Rupert was beaten off, and on the 22nd Essex, without further

Sept. 22. Essex reaches Reading.

difficulty, entered Reading. The King, after throwing a garrison into Donnington Castle, retired to Oxford. After the fight at Newbury it was at least plain that Charles needed more force than he had at his disposal to overpower the resistance of London, whilst it was equally plain that the Parliamentary armies were not as yet adequate to the task of crushing Charles. Much, therefore, depended on the result of the struggles round Hull and Plymouth ; much, too, depended on the result of the negotiations which, during these weeks of balanced warfare, Charles was carrying on in Ireland, and the Houses were carrying on in Scotland.

CHAPTER XI.

THE IRISH CESSATION AND THE SOLEMN LEAGUE AND COVENANT.

AID had not come to Charles from Ireland as speedily as he had once thought possible. Loyal as the confederate Catholics

1643.
May.
Progress
of the nego-
tiation in
Ireland.

professed themselves to be, they were not inclined to neglect the interests of their country and of their religion merely to give Charles the opportunity of entering Westminster in triumph. They asked that a free parliament might meet at Dublin—a parliament, that is to say, in which, as matters stood in Ireland, the vast majority

June 1.

of the members would be Catholics. On June 1, however, Ormond informed them that they must be content to rely 'on what they may gain from the King upon humble and reasonable propositions to be made by their agents, which may be fit for his Majesty to grant.' In the meanwhile, to afford an opportunity for a peaceful negotiation at Oxford, there must be a cessation of hostilities, and they must themselves contribute a sufficient sum to enable the King's army in Ireland to subsist without plundering. At the same time Ormond pointed to the rock on which the negotiation was likely to be wrecked. To allow a free parliament to meet would be, 'in the construction of some, in effect, to make them judges of their own actions, and to entrust them to make laws for them who have had little cause to trust to the provision they shall make for their future security, for few but themselves are like to be of that parliament, as the times are now composed, and how unequal that course would be they who are indifferent do foresee.' [1]

---

[1] Ormond to Barry, June 1. Gilbert's *Hist. of the Irish Confed.* ii. 284.

Time was fighting for the Irish confederates. Before the end of June the Castle of Galway capitulated to their army in Connaught, and Sir Charles Vavasour was defeated by Castlehaven in Munster. On June 21 Ormond, knowing how hopeless his military position was, and perhaps wishing to establish beyond dispute the necessity of coming to terms with the insurgents, told the Lords Justices that he was ready to break off the negotiations if they could find any possible way of maintaining the troops.[1] The Lords Justices were at their wits' end. An attempt to draw money or supplies from the impoverished citizens of Dublin ended in complete failure, and on the 24th Ormond set out, with at least the tacit consent of the Government in Dublin, to attempt to come to terms with the enemy. He found the Supreme Council less yielding than he had hoped, and after nearly three weeks spent in fruitless diplomacy, he resolved to try the fortune of arms once more. At the head of 5,000 men he threw himself on Preston, and captured a few strong places; but Preston wisely avoided a battle, and Ormond, unable to feed his soldiers, was compelled to retire to Dublin.[2]

Irish successes.

June 21. Ormond's offer to the Lords Justices.

June 22.

July. Warlike operations renewed.

The resumption of negotiations was now a matter of necessity. It was the less distasteful to Ormond as he now knew that the King was prepared to discuss the proposed free parliament with Irish agents, as soon as they had agreed to a cessation.[3] It was the least of the obstacles to this policy that a certain number of members of the Irish Privy Council were bitterly opposed to it. Before the end of July Sir William Parsons, Sir John Temple, and two other councillors were arrested by Charles's orders, on various charges, but practically for having sided with the English Parliament against the King.

July 2. The King consents to listen to the demand for a free parliament.

Imprisonment of four councillors.

It still remained to be seen whether the Irish would con-

[1] Ormond's motion, June 21. Order by the Lords Justices, June 22. *Ibid.* i. 156; ii. 290.

[2] Carte's *Ormond*, ii. 501.

[3] The King to Ormond, July 2. *Carte*, v. 453.

sent to any terms whatever. At Kilkenny the feeling of the
lords and gentlemen of Norman or English descent was favour-

Views of the
Supreme
Council.

able to an understanding with the King which
would restore to the clergy of their Church the
jurisdiction which they had formerly exercised, would
hand over to themselves under parliamentary forms the actual
government of Ireland, and would secure the co-operation of
the royal troops against the common enemy, the Puritan Scots
in Antrim.[1]

Such views, attractive as they were, suffered from one fatal
defect. They presupposed that Charles, if he gained the
victory over his enemies in England, would have either the
will or the power to support in Ireland the system which now
found favour at Kilkenny.

Very different opinions prevailed amongst a numerous
section of the Irish clergy, and amongst the northern popula-

Nationalist
opinions.

tions, whose military chief was the energetic and
experienced soldier, Owen O'Neill. These men
rallied round Scarampi, who had recently arrived as a Papal
delegate to give all possible encouragement to the insurgents,
and to provide for the full recognition of the claims of his
Church. In an argument drawn up by some persons who were
possessed of his confidence,[2] the notion of trusting to Charles
is denounced with plain-spoken severity. "We should undoubtedly," they urged, "carry on our work to establish the
Catholic faith, the authority of Parliament, and the security of
our country, by arms and intrepidity, not by cessations and
indolence. For this there are the following reasons : That
peace will ever be made between the King and the Parliament
is improbable, nor would it be to our advantage, for if they
combined we should be necessitated to surrender. It is likely,
however, that before long one side will become powerful
enough to dictate to the other. If the Parliament prevail,
which God forbid, all Ireland will fall under their arbitrary

[1] Bellings' reasons in favour of a cessation, July. Gilbert's *Hist. of the
Irish Confed.* ii. 319.

[2] Mr. Gilbert (*ibid.* ii. 321) prints it as proceeding from Scarampi
himself, who is, however, spoken of in it in the third person.

power ; the swords of the Puritans will be at our throats, and we shall lose everything except our faith. Should the King triumph, we may expect much from his goodness and kindness, and much from the Queen's intercession. It is uncertain, however, what laws or terms may be imposed on us under such circumstances. The King, should he succeed by the aid of the Protestants, would be, in a manner, engaged to them. They, as usual, would oppose freedom of religion in Ireland, and insist on the punishment of our ' rebellion,' as they style it, to enable them to seize our properties and occupy our estates. It would probably be thought a sufficient concession to the Queen to allow us to return to the miserable position in which we were before the war. On the other hand, if we now adopt proper measures, the party eventually triumphing in England will find us in arms, well provided, with increased territories, and stronger in foreign succours. Thus they would not so readily invade us or swallow us up, so as to leave us without the free exercise of our faith or some share in the administration of the kingdom. By God's assistance our arms may perhaps carry matters so far that we may obtain or insist on many other advantages."

It was the banner of Irish nationality which was here un-folded, and those who upheld it were at least not afraid to look Irish na-tionality. in the face the stern fact that no English party would willingly tolerate the organisation of the Roman Catholic Church in Ireland or the organisation of a purely Irish government. If the opportunity of England's divisions was to be seized to any profit, Ireland must become a nation strong enough to hold its own. To gain for itself the sentiment of patriotism, to cherish, in defiance of all assailants, its own tradi-tions and its own beliefs, would be worth many a struggle and many a defeat, if only through suffering it might be attained.

Such a prize is not easy of achievement, and it was not within reach of Irishmen in the seventeenth century. They Difficulties over-estimated the help which they were likely to in its way. receive from the Catholic world, torn asunder by a war in which the nations which were most strongly Catholic were being borne down by the nations which were less strongly

Catholic, or which were not Catholic at all. What was still more fatal, they over-estimated their own power of cohesion, and they failed to understand that England's resistance was, at least to some extent, based on a righteous foundation. No race, no nation, can live entirely for itself. The achievement of nationality is but the stepping-stone to a still wider development of the social feelings of humanity, and by throwing themselves athwart that stream of European progress, of which the impelling force was Protestantism, Irishmen had taken up a position of hostility to the development of other countries than their own. Above all, the independence of a Papal Ireland would have been a standing menace to Protestant England. Nothing like this had been the case when Scotland shook itself free in the fourteenth century. There was political and military danger to England, but there was no danger to its intellectual and spiritual life. Add to this that Englishmen, little mindful of their own cruelties exercised upon Irishmen, were filled with the bitterest indignation by the Ulster murders; and that, even if the Ulster murders had never taken place, they could hardly be expected to welcome a settlement which would have left their own kindred beyond the Irish Channel exposed to ruin. It is, therefore, no matter for surprise that all English parties combined to treat the Irish claims, even in their most moderate form, as absolutely inadmissible. "Out of Ireland," wrote a pamphleteer, when the news of Ormond's resolution to take the field arrived in London, "it is informed that, notwithstanding all the means which hath been practised either privately or publicly by the Papists there to make a pacification and cessation of arms between the Protestants and Irish rebels, yet the Protestants will not be brought to condescend thereunto, because they know it will tend, not only to the utter ruin of themselves, but of all the Protestants in England and Scotland also." [1]

Necessity, however, was for the time too strong even for such considerations. The negotiations were resumed after Ormond's military failure, and on September 15 articles of

---

[1] I omitted to take down the reference to this extract, and have been unable to verify it.

cessation for twelve months were at last signed. A limited
district on the East coast, and another limited district round

August.
Progress
of the
negotiation.

Cork, and such fortresses in the North and West as
were held by the King's garrisons were to remain
in the hands of the English commanders. All the

Sept. 15.
The cessa-
tion.

rest of Ireland was to be left to the Catholic Confederation. If the Scots under Monro chose to
conform to the cessation they were to participate in
its benefits ; if not, Ormond with his army was to stand aside
whilst the whole power of the Confederation was brought
against them, and Charles was even to be requested to allow
Ormond to assist the Irish in overpowering them.[1] Upon
these conditions the Supreme Council agreed to pay 800*l.* to
relieve the garrison of Naas, and 30,000*l.* in money or cattle to
be expended upon the regiments which were about to be
carried beyond sea to support Charles in England.[2] In due
course of time the Confederates were to send agents to Oxford
to discuss the political questions at issue with Charles in person,
and it was fondly hoped that this discussion would lay the
foundations of a permanent peace.

It was characteristic of Charles that he did not see that
these negotiations with the Irish Catholics put an end to

Montrose at
Gloucester.

all hope of winning a party at Edinburgh. Almost
at the time when the cessation was being signed
Montrose appeared in Charles's camp before Gloucester, and
pleaded with him to sanction that immediate appeal to arms in
Scotland which had now become his only feasible policy.
Montrose was now able to inform the King that he had received
from the Presbyterian leaders the offer of the command of the
army which was about to cross the Tweed, an offer which left
no shadow of doubt either as to their intention to invade
England, or to their conviction that Montrose himself was the
merest slave of ambition. With that strange reverence for
legality which never forsook him, Charles refused to strike the

---

[1] The rumours in Scotland three months before (see p. 176) were therefore only a little premature, if indeed they were that.

[2] The Articles of Cessation. Gilbert's *Hist. of the Irish Confed.* ii.
365.

first blow, and Montrose found himself once more discarded as a harebrained lad. Hamilton, with his soft diplomatic wiles, which never harmed anyone but him who practised them, was still in favour. "I will pro-test," he had recently said to Montrose's urgent entreaties to use force now that fair words had been shown to be useless, "but I will not fight." Whilst Charles dismissed Montrose, he created Hamilton a duke.[1]

Montrose and Hamilton.

Amongst the Presbyterian leaders Argyle at least was clear-sighted enough to perceive that Charles's triumph over Pym would inevitably be followed by a reaction in Scotland, supported by the bulk of the nobility through jealousy of the new organisation of the middle classes and of the power of the Presbyterian clergy.

Argyle favourable to an alliance with the English Parliament.

Indirectly the Scottish Presbyterian clergy were rendering to their country a political service of no common order. Every new social class as it rises into power needs, in proportion to its previous ignorance, a strictness of discipline which becomes unnecessary as soon as it has learned to bear lightly the responsibilities of its new position. That discipline in England was afforded to the middle classes by the rule, grasping, unscrupulous, and im-moral as it was, of Henry VIII. In Scotland it was by the Presbyterian clergy that the middle classes were organised, and the organisation thus given enabled them to throw off the yoke of the feudal nobles and ultimately to assert their own predominance.

Political services of the Pres-byterian clergy.

It was with little thought of the political result of their rule that the clergy strove to maintain themselves in the position to which they had been elevated. To them the support of religion was all in all, and, strict as they were in the matter of doctrinal orthodoxy, their strictness was still greater with respect to the observance of the Ten Commandments. They strove by means of church discipline, enforced in the most inquisitorial manner, to bring a whole population under the yoke of the moral law. To a later generation, which disbelieves in the existence of witches, and which has ceased, at least according

[1] *Wishart*, ch. ii. and iii. *Burnet*, 241.

to the Genevan interpretation of the command, to keep holy
the Sabbath-day, there is something very shocking in hearing
that severe penalties were inflicted upon those who infringed
in the slightest and most innocent manner the rule which
guarded the sanctity of the Lord's Day, and still more that in
the course of a few months no less than thirty unhappy women
were burnt alive as witches in Fife alone.[1]   These things have
passed away, as for a great part of European mankind the
monastic rule of the Middle Ages has passed away.   Discipline
for discipline, the Scottish system was the nobler of the two.
It was not a rule for those alone who sought counsels of perfection, whilst the mass of mankind was left to content themselves with a lower standard of morality.   In Scotland there
was to be a parity of moral law as there was to be a parity of
ministerial office.   The fierce ruffians who in the sixteenth
century had reddened the country with the feuds of noble
houses, the rude peasants who wallowed in impurity, were
made to feel the compulsion of a never-resting, ever-abiding
power, which pried into their lives and called them to account
for their deeds as no lay government, however arbitrary, could
venture to do.   Therefore the Scottish people has rightly
venerated as its saviours those to whom it is mainly owing that,
even in that race after material wealth which set in amongst a
people whose soil was poor and whose climate was ungenial, it
has ever kept in honour the laws of righteousness.

The Scottish clergy were likely to be the last to perceive
that what was possible in Scotland was impossible in England,
or that a nation whose middle classes had been disciplined under the Tudor monarchy, and had already
ceased to feel alarm at the pretensions of the nobility,
would never place itself under the Presbyterian
system.   Such considerations were entirely alien to
the thought of the seventeenth century.   It was,
therefore, with natural eagerness that the Northern
clergy urged the assimilation of the English to the Scottish
Church.   They had pressed it on Charles in their negotiation

The Scottish system impossible in England.

The Scottish clergy wish to impose it upon England.

---

[1] *Baillie*, ii. 88.   It should be remembered that the Royalist annalist
(*Spalding*, ii. 271) shows no sign of horror.

in the spring, and they were certain to press it on the Parliamentary diplomatists in the summer.

The error, fatal as it was, as long as it was persisted in, to a
permanent good understanding between the two nations, was

Nature
of their
mistake. hardly likely to appear in its true colours to a clerical
body.   It would never occur to them that the politi-
cal development of the English people would render
them hostile to a strict inquisition into the moralities of domestic life, and that their superior social organisation would make
them intolerant of a masterful ecclesiastical rule.   They were
the less likely to pay attention to the essential difference in the
character of the two peoples, because the Parliament at Westminster which now implored their aid was quite ready to accept
Presbyterianism in its more showy, but in reality less important,
aspect.   Little difficulty would be made about the abolition of
Episcopacy, or about the establishment of a Presbyterian ministry.   No one, however, who had studied the Root-and-branch
Bill, which was brought in and dropped in the summer of 1641,[1]
could doubt that the English Parliament would refuse to surrender that control over the clergy by the laity which had been
the most abiding result of the Tudor rule, or would resist to the
uttermost the ever-present despotism of the Presbyterian church
courts.   Yet, as every Scottish minister knew, it was in these
two points, and not in the mere absence of bishops, that the
essence of Scottish Presbyterianism was to be found.

On August 7 the English Commissioners arrived at Leith.
Of the two named by the House of Lords, Grey had refused to

August 7.
Arrival of
the English
Commis-
sioners. come, and Rutland had pleaded illness.   Of the four
commoners, the younger Vane was conspicuously the
first in ability and authority.   These four were as-
Marshall
and Nye. sisted by two ministers—Stephen Marshall, who was
the mouthpiece of the Presbyterian party, which was
predominant amongst the Parliamentary clergy, and his son-in-
law, Philip Nye, who had been the minister of a congregation
at Arnheim, where, in common with the leaders of some other
congregation- in the Netherlands, he had developed opinions

---

[1] See *Hist. of England*, 1603-1642, ix. 407.

on the subject of church government which, without being distinctly in accordance with those of the Separatists, accorded far greater liberty of action to individual congregations than the Presbyterians were willing to allow. The popular language, always disinclined to admit of fine distinctions, classed Nye and his friends with the Separatists under the common name of Independents, an appellation which had been for many years growing into use amongst the Separatists themselves.

The Scottish clergy, to whom Nye's presence was unwelcome, were well pleased to hear that the preparation of the State papers, which were to be presented in the name of the Commissioners, had been entrusted to Marshall in conjunction with Vane. Nevertheless, the negotiation at first took an unsatisfactory turn. The Scots soon pointed out that the English demand for aid was unaccompanied by any suggestion of uniformity in religion. For a moment it seemed as if the idea of sending military aid would be abandoned. At a meeting, at which the chief Scottish laity and clergy were present, there was for some time a general concurrence of opinion that the Scottish army should cross the Tweed to offer its mediation to both parties, and not to give direct assistance to the English Parliament. A few words from Johnston of Warriston, however, sufficed to convince the authors of this scheme of the futility of the course proposed. Yet, though the Scots were now inclined to give way, further discussion with the English Commissioners only served to bring into prominence the essential difference between the two nations. "The English," wrote Baillie, "were for a civil league, we for a religious covenant." The English, in short, did not seem to understand that they had come as suppliants. They fancied that, distracted as they were by civil war, they could take the destinies of their national Church into their own hands as firmly as their fathers had done when they were united under Henry or Elizabeth.

August 8. Opening of the negotiations

Such a claim to independence was more than Scotsmen would admit. Henderson, to cut the dispute short, drew up a covenant on the lines of the national covenant of 1638, in order that the two nations might bind themselves to join together for the pre-

Henderson's draft of the Solemn League and Covenant.

servation of themselves and their religion.[1]   A vow was to
be adopted in common by both 'that we shall all and each
one of us sincerely, really, and constantly, through the grace of
God, endeavour in our several callings and places the preservation of the true Protestant reformed religion in the
Church of Scotland, in doctrine, worship, discipline, and government, and the reformation of religion in the Church of
England, according to the example of the best reformed
Churches, and as may bring the Churches of God in both
nations to the nearest conjunction and uniformity in religion,
confession of faith, form of church government, directory for
worship and catechising, that we and our posterity after us
may, as brethren, live in faith and love.'[2]   To this draft the
English Commissioners took exception. "They," wrote Baillie,
"were, more than we could assent to, for keeping of a door open

Vane's amendments.

in England to Independency."[3] All that Vane could
hope for, unless his mission was to fail entirely, was
to keep a door open for the assumption by the English Parliament of a control over the national religion. His
subtle mind suggested a means by which this end might be
effected. He suggested two amendments, by which the contested
clause should pledge the nations to preserve 'the Church of
Scotland in doctrine, worship, discipline, and government *according to the Word of God*, and the reformation of religion in
the Church of England according to *the same Holy Word and*
the example of the best reformed Churches,' whilst the remaining words were left as Henderson had penned them.[4]   Hen-

---

[1] *Baillie*, ii. 88.

[2] Henderson's original draft has not been preserved. The form above
given is, with the omission of the two phrases subsequently referred to
about 'the Word of God,' that in the *Acts of the Parliament of Scotland*,
vi. 42, which was accepted at Edinburgh after the insertion of Vane's
amendments, but is earlier than the form finally agreed on in England,
which is the one usually printed.

[3] *Baillie*, ii. 90.

[4] The story of Vane's amendments is given by Burnet, and his
authority may not be considered in itself sufficient, especially as there is
no direct evidence of the actual amendments. We know, however, from
Baillie, as quoted above, that there was a struggle about keeping a door

derson could hardly object to the proposed change, and he may reasonably have argued that the general sense of the passage would stand in the way of any serious deflection from the Scottish model.

Other clauses provided for the abolition of Episcopacy in England, the maintenance of the rights of the two Parliaments and of the stipulations of the treaty of 1641, and the bringing to trial of incendiaries and malignants. The Solemn League and Covenant, as the amended document was styled, was at

August 17. The Solemn League and Covenant adopted by the Convention of Estates.

once adopted by the Assembly, and on August 17 it was ratified by the Convention of Estates.[1] The Convention at once proceeded to order the levy of a general taxation, and informed the Commissioners that they expected a monthly payment of 30,000*l.* from the English Parliament, 100,000*l.* to be paid in advance

---

open for Independency, and the first ' according to the Word of God ' has the aspect of a phrase fitted in on second thoughts. That phrase is one which would be familiar to Vane. It occurs in clause 185 of the Grand Remonstrance. " We hold it requisite," the House of Commons there declare, " that there should be throughout the whole realm a conformity to that order which the laws enjoin according to the Word of God." More recently, on June 12, 1643, the ordinance for calling the Assembly of Divines had declared the intention of the Houses to be ' that such a government shall be settled in the Church as may be most agreeable to God's Holy Word, and most apt to procure and preserve the peace of the Church at home, and nearer agreement with the Church of Scotland and other reformed Churches abroad.' Guthry, in his *Memoirs* (1702), 117, says that the Commissioners on their arrival ' presented to the Assembly a letter from the divines assembled at Westminster, together with a declaration from the Parliament of England, both to one sense, viz. that they purposed to extirpate Episcopacy root and branch, and to introduce that which they should find most agreeable to the Word of God.' Guthry alleges that he objected to this as insufficient. Guthry, however, is inaccurate here. The declaration of the Lords and Commons (*L.J.* vi. 140) has nothing in it about the Word of God. Neither has the supplication of the divines (*Spalding*, ii. 260). Guthry may, however, have confused language spoken by the Commissioners with that of the letters which they brought. On the whole, therefore, I think I am justified in conjecturing that Henderson's draft is represented by the form in the Acts of Parliament, with the omission of the two phrases.

[1] *Baillie*, ii. 95. *Acts of the Parliament of Scotland*, vi. 41.

before a Scottish army crossed the Tweed.   In reliance upon
the readiness of the English to consent to this demand, they
appointed the Earl of Leven, the Alexander Leslie
of earlier wars, as commander of the forces to be
raised.   On August 26 they adjourned themselves,
leaving a Committee to govern Scotland till they met
again.[1]

Financial demands.

Leven to command.

August 26. The Convention adjourned.

On the very day on which the Scottish Estates
were adjourned a copy of the Solemn League and
Covenant reached Westminster, and was at once forwarded by the House of Commons to the Assembly
of Divines.

The Solemn League and Covenant at Westminster.

That body, which, having met on July 1, had now been in
session in the Chapel of Henry VII. for nearly two months,
was a very different body from the General Assembly
which exercised supreme authority over the Scottish
Church.   Composed of 120 clerical and 30 lay
members,[2] the latter having been selected from the two Houses,
it was the creature of Parliament, and was only authorised to
give advice upon subjects on which Parliament desired its
opinion.   It comprised the flower of the Puritan clergy, whilst
the few Episcopalian members who had been originally nominated either refused to take part in its deliberations or were
expelled upon charges of royalism.   Of the lay members only
a few gave themselves the trouble to attend.   At first it had
been entrusted with the task of revising the Thirty-nine
Articles, but its attention was now to be directed to a subject
of far more pressing importance.

The Assembly of Divines.

Every clerical assembly has strong tendencies towards
Presbyterianism in its unwillingness to submit to the regula-
tive authority of bishops, especially when bishops are
appointed by the State without regard to the prevailing clerical opinion.   Yet, though the Assembly
was quite willing to assent to the abolition of Episcopacy, it showed its jealousy of a foreign Church by refusing
to ask any man to engage to maintain the Church of Scotland,

August 28. Amendments by the Assembly.

---

[1] *Acts of the Parliament of Scotland*, vi. 47.

[2] See the annotated list in Masson's *Life of Milton*, ii. 515.

except so far as in his conscience he should 'conceive it to be

August 29. according to the Word of God.' On the next day it defined the Prelacy which it would engage to exterminate as that which consisted in archbishops and bishops. The Assembly evidently intended to reserve to itself perfect freedom as to the form of church government which was to take the place of the old Episcopacy.[1]

In adopting the first amendment of the Assembly the Commons, perhaps to avoid giving offence to the Scots, transferred it from the text to the margin. One change of their own was carried without difficulty. Ireland was to be brought into covenant with England and Scotland, and, as far as words could effect anything, that land of Catholics was to be brought under the yoke of Puritanism.[2] On the amendment relating to the definition of Prelacy there was more hesitation. Glyn and Maynard, who as members of the Peace-party disliked the additional barrier which would be raised between the Houses and the King, did their best to induce the Commons to leave open a door for the settlement of the Church on the basis of modified Episcopacy. Pym, in reply, asked whether, admitting such a system to be useful as medicine for the disease of the Church, a sick man who saw a murderer approaching would 'cast away his medicine and betake himself to his sword, or take his medicine and suffer himself to be killed?' Surely he would rather 'prevent and remedy the present danger.'[3] To Pym the exact form of church government was a matter of indifference ; but at the time when he was speaking he knew that Gloucester was still unrelieved, and he thought that it was not worth while to throw away the hope of Scottish assistance for the sake of the most admirable of church governments. If the King was able to overcome the resistance of London, he would make short work of modified Episcopacy. The Commons rallied to Pym's view, and accepted the proposal of the Assembly.

Marginal notes:
Sept. 1. Discussions in the House of Commons.
Sept. 2.
Pym's argument.

---

[1] Journal of the Assembly, in *Lightfoot's Works*, xiii. 10.

[2] *C.J.* iii. 223.

[3] Yonge's Diary. *Add. MSS.* 18,778, fol. 29.

On another point the House was less complaisant. The Scots had proposed that the new Covenant should include an

The Commons refuse to confirm the treaty of 1641.

oath to observe the treaty of 1641. When this clause was reached Whitelocke asked that the articles of that treaty might be read. Lenthall objected that it would take four hours to read it. "What, Mr. Speaker," called out Sir Robert Pye, "do you mean that we shall swear to that which must cost us four hours to read?"[1] The objection proved insuperable, and the clause was omitted.

On September 7 the Covenant thus amended was sent to the Lords. Before it left their House Commissioners,

Sept. 7. The Covenant before the Lords.

amongst whom the most prominent were Henderson, Johnston of Warriston, and Lord Maitland, the future Earl of Lauderdale, arrived to forward the alliance

Arrival of the Scottish Commissioners.

between the two nations. By mutual arrangement the amendment which related to the Church of Scotland was got rid of, as offensive to the Scots.

The Covenant amended.

The words, 'according to the Word of God,' were omitted, so that Englishmen would merely bind themselves to aid in the defence of that Church without giving an opinion upon the alleged scriptural basis of every one of its institutions. On the other hand, the phrase, 'according to the Word of God,' was retained in relation to the coming reform of the English Church, and the Assembly's explanation of the Prelacy to be abolished was re-transferred from the margin to the text. Thus altered, the Covenant was accepted by the Lords, and it was arranged that on September 25 it should be sworn to at St. Margaret's by the House of Commons and the Assembly of Divines.

Of the two members of the Assembly who had taken part in the negotiations at Edinburgh, Marshall had for the present

Sept. 25. Nye's address.

remained in Scotland ; Nye was, therefore, pointed out as the proper person to open the proceedings at St. Margaret's. Nevertheless, it was significant of the temper which prevailed at Westminster, that one whose principles were so little in accordance with those which prevailed in Scotland should not have been passed over. It was

[1] D'Ewes's Diary. *Harl. MSS.* 165, fol. 165.

well known that the sermons which he had been called on to deliver at Edinburgh had given little satisfaction to a critical audience of convinced Presbyterians. He now seized the opportunity of reminding his English hearers that the Covenant did not bind them to a servile imitation of their Northern brethren. " If England," he said, " have attained to any greater perfection in so handling the Word of righteousness and truths that are according to godliness, so as to make men more godly, more righteous ; and if in the Churches of Scotland any more light and beauty in matters of order and discipline by which their assemblies are more orderly ; or if to any other Church or person it hath been given better to have learned Christ in any of His ways than any of us, we shall humbly bow and kiss their lips that can speak right words unto us in this matter, and help us unto the nearest uniformity with the Word and mind of Christ in this great work of Reformation." [1]

In this spirit the members of the Assembly swore to maintain the Covenant. In this spirit 112 [2] members of the House

The Covenant taken by the House of Commons and the Assembly.

of Commons, who were present on that day, gave in their adhesion. Henderson, who spoke later, took no exception to Nye's words. Substantially, he doubtless thought, agreement had been secured. Yet, whatever the future might have in store, it was something that the ideal of Nye, which was no other than the ideal of Robinson, should have been upheld in such a place and on such an occasion. At least between

Character of the Covenant.

Puritan men the Covenant, as finally accepted, was no narrowing formula tightening the bonds of orthodoxy. Unhappily it had another side. It emphasised the separation between those who were Puritans and those who were not. Pym, whether or not he had understood the full import of his words, had spoken truly. The Covenant was not medicine to heal the wounds of the Church, but a sword to divide. After all that had passed and was passing still, how

---

[1] *The Covenant, with a narrative of the proceedings.* E. 70, 22.

[2] Yonge's Diary. *Add. MSS.* 18,778, fol. 56. This disposes of the longer list given by Rushworth as evidence of the presence of members who figure in it on this particular occasion.

could it well be otherwise? Yet, divisive as the Covenant was, it merely emphasised the division which was harsh enough already. Especially had Charles's understanding with the Irish deepened the lines of controversy. "Most of all," wrote Baillie of his own countrymen, "the Irish cessation made the minds of our people embrace that means of safety."[1] What was true of Scotland was also true of England.

Effect of the Irish cessation.

[1] *Baillie*, ii. 103.

CHAPTER XII.

WINCEBY AND ARUNDEL.

ON September 25 Essex arrived in London. On the 26th he received the thanks of both Houses.[1] A review was held in

1643.
Sept. 25.
Return of
Essex.

Finsbury Fields of all the London trained bands which had remained at home at the time of the recent expedition. Essex received a warm welcome,

Sept. 26.
He is
thanked by
Parliament.

but there were no offers of permanent service.[2]

The 28th was appointed for the re-entry of the

Review
of the
London
trained
bands.

London troops which had fought at Newbury. Gladly would Essex have kept around him the army which had served him so well, but the citizen soldiers

Sept. 28.
Return of
the City
regiments.

had gone forth for the special object of relieving Gloucester, and now that their task was accomplished they were eager to be back to their shops.

Royalist critics, who had at first boldly claimed the result of the battle as a victory for the King, had recently contented themselves with suggesting that Essex ought to pass under a triumphal arch constructed of his favourite tobacco pipes, and with asserting that large bodies of citizens had been sent out by night in order to fill the gaps made in the regiments by the charges of the Royal cavalry.[3] Such figments made no impression on the dense crowd which shouted its heartfelt welcome as the long military array stepped proudly through the streets on its eastward march.[4] That night there was a proud

[1] *C. J.* iii. 255.
[2] *Merc. Civicus.* E. 69, 8. Agostini to the Doge, $\frac{\text{Sept. 29}}{\text{Oct. 9}}$. *Venetian Transcripts, R.O.*
[3] Newsletter, $\frac{\text{Sept. 27}}{\text{Oct. 7}}$. *Arch. des Aff. Étr.* xlix. fol. 306.
[4] *The True Informer.* E. 69, 14.

joy in every household from which a son or a brother had gone
forth, save where those mourners dwelt whose sorrow was
none the less real because those who had fallen bore no lordly
names.

If there was joy in homely dwellings, there was anxiety
with those who were entrusted with the conduct of affairs.
The army of Essex was again reduced to those scanty numbers
which had made it insufficient for all offensive operations. He
found it necessary to fall back upon Windsor.   On October 3

Oct. 3.
Reading
occupied
by the
Royalists.

the Royalists reoccupied Reading, where Sir Jacob
Astley was installed as governor.   Charles could
hardly have been in a better position if he had been
the undoubted victor at Newbury.   In the West his

Oct. 6.
Surrender of
Dartmouth.

arms were no less prosperous.   On October 6 Dartmouth surrendered to Prince Maurice, whilst the
far more important port of Plymouth was in grievous danger.[1]

It was not a time when the Parliamentary generals could
afford to remain at variance.   An understanding was, in ap-

Oct. 7.
Reconcilia-
tion of
Essex and
Waller.

pearance at least, patched up between Essex and
Waller, the latter agreeing to take his instructions
from the Lord General, and being empowered to
raise an army for service in the West.[2]   Essex, too,
was well aware of his need of a force upon which he could
permanently rely.   He told the citizens that they must choose

Demands
of Essex.

between three courses.   Unless they could either
discover a fountain of gold or find volunteers who
would be content to serve without pay, they must make
peace.[3]

The difficulty of finding money for Essex was the greater
because the citizens were at the same time called upon to find

Oct. 6.
Money for
the Scots.

money for the Scots.   On October 6 many thousand
pounds were subscribed to enable Parliament to
fulfil its obligations to its Northern allies.   Something more than money was, however, needed if the intervention of the Scots was to answer the expectations formed in
England.   Unless the power of the Royalists could be limited

[1] Dugdale's *Diary*.   [2] *L.J.* vi. 247.
[3] Agostini to the Doge, $\frac{Sept. 29}{Oct. 9}$.   *Venetian Transcripts, R.O.*

in Lincolnshire and the Midlands, a Scottish army in the North would be cut off from the co-operation of the English Parliamentary armies in the South, and might be overwhelmed before assistance could arrive.

It was with the object of putting an end to those local quarrels which had been so disastrous in the early part of the summer [1] that Manchester had been appointed in August to command the forces of the Eastern Association. For some

August.
Siege of Lynn.

weeks, however, he was detained in Norfolk by the siege of Lynn, which had declared for the King, and

Sept. 16.
Lynn surrenders.

it was only on September 16, when the town capitulated, that he was set free for service farther north. [2]

Sept. 20.
Lincolnshire in the Association.

On the 20th Lincolnshire was added by a Parliamentary ordinance to the Eastern Association. [3]

Sept. 5.
Cromwell sent into Lincolnshire.

For the conduct of siege operations a large body of cavalry was unnecessary. On September 5, therefore, Cromwell, who had for some little time been at Cambridge, was despatched [4] by Manchester to encourage Lord Willoughby of Parham to hold out in Boston and the Fens. Cromwell, however, had more arduous work in view. On September 2 Newcastle, who had

Sept. 2.
Newcastle besieges Hull.

been created a marquis in reward for his victory at Adwalton Moor, [5] had laid siege to Hull. The Fairfaxes were holding bravely out, but they found

Sept 18.
Escape of Fairfax's horse.

the horses of Sir Thomas's cavalry a sore burden to their straitened garrison. On the 18th some of Cromwell's troops appeared at Barton, on the Lincolnshire side of the Humber, and the horses from Hull were gradually passed over the river with their riders. On the

---

[1] See p. 192.

[2] *A relation of the siege of King's Lynn.* E. 67, 28.

[3] *L.J.* vi. 224.

[4] Harlakenden to Barrington, September 5. *Barrington MSS.* Cromwell was not at the siege of Lynn at all, which is a strong argument for the spuriousness of the *Squire Papers.* See Part 3 of the *English Historical Review.*

[5] The patent is dated October 27, but he is styled Marquis in a letter addressed to him by Lord Widdrington on October 12 (E. 71, 22), and the title was probably offered to him earlier.

22nd Cromwell was himself in Hull, bringing with him a store of muskets and powder.[1]   The day on which he arrived had been

Sept. 22.
Cromwell in
Hull.

appointed by the beleaguered garrison to be held as a day of fasting and humiliation, and it may well be imagined how devoutly Cromwell joined in the prayers for Divine assistance put up to Heaven amidst the booming of the cannon.   In those anxious moments began his tried brotherhood in arms with the younger Fairfax.

Cromwell did not remain long in Hull.   On the 23rd Lord Willoughby paid an equally brief visit to the besieged garrison ; and on the 26th Sir Thomas crossed over to the Lincolnshire side with the twenty troops of horse which were still left in the town.[2]   Shortly afterwards the three commanders met at Boston.

At Boston Cromwell had hoped to find money from the Association, but money there was none,[3] and in the beginning

Oct. 2.
Cromwell
at Lynn.

of October he arrived at Lynn to confer with Manchester.   However the financial difficulty was arranged, Cromwell was able to return to Lincolnshire with the knowledge that Manchester with the main body of infantry would soon follow.

On October 9 Manchester joined Cromwell and Fairfax,

Oct. 9.
Manchester
joins Cromwell and
Fairfax.

Oct. 11.
Winceby
fight.

finding them engaged in the siege of Bolingbroke Castle.   On the evening of the 10th a small body of Fairfax's horse was driven in by a force advancing upon Horncastle from the West, which proved to be commanded by Sir John Henderson, the governor of Newark.   On the following morning Henderson, at the head of a strong body of horse and dragoons,

[1] Letter of T. May, September 19.   *A true relation from Hull.*   E. 69, 13.   *Certain Informations.*   E. 70, 7.

[2] *Hull's managing of the kingdom's cause.*   E. 51, 11.

[3] "Colonel Cromwell tells me he wept when he came to Boston and found no monies for him from Essex and other counties.   He saith he regards monies as little as any man, but for his troops, if they have not monies speedily, they are in an undone condition.   He says he wonders how I will be able to see the troops of horse and dragoons, and have little or no money for them."   Harlakenden to Barrington, October 2.   *Barrington MSS.*

pushed on through Horncastle to the relief of the besieged garrison. Cromwell, if it had been possible, would have avoided a conflict, as his horses were worn out by a month of hard work ; but to retreat to Boston was to court disaster, and the Puritan troopers, pealing forth a battle-psalm as they rode, advanced towards the enemy. The two forces were about equal in numbers. They met near Winceby, a little hamlet on a ridge of ground which runs away past Horncastle to the northward. Cromwell, who led the van, dashed into a charge. At the first onset his horse was shot under him, and as he struggled to disengage himself he was thrown violently to the ground by the rush of a Royalist trooper. Recovering his footing, and flinging himself on the first horse which came to hand, he was soon in the thick of the fight. The enemy, checked in his career, fell back on his supports. Another charge from Fairfax turned the whole force to flight. Through Horncastle rushed pursuers and pursued, the Puritan sword rising and falling not in vain. After Horncastle was passed the fugitives scattered. Of those who were not slain or taken prisoners many were drowned in the waters of the Fens, and the scanty remnant at last found refuge behind the walls of Newark.[1]

The cavalry action at Winceby—Manchester's foot took no part in the combat—fulfilled the promise of the retreat at

Spirit of the two parties.

Gainsborough. The gallant gentlemen who followed Charles were not sufficiently numerous to constitute an army, and levies collected at random, and partly, at least, by compulsion, had no spirit in them which could match the disciplined enthusiasm of the soldiers of the Eastern Association. "The commission of array," one of the dying Royalists is reported to have said, "brought us hither full sore against our wills ; we were as true servants to the Parliament, to our religion and liberties, as any in England. . . . We die as true friends to the Parliament as any."[2]

---

[1] *A true relation of the late fight.* E. 71, 5. *The weekly account.* E 71, 18. Widdrington to Newcastle, October 12, in *A true and exact relation.* E. 71, 22. Manchester to the House of Lords, October 12. *L.J.* vi. 255.   [2] *The Parliament Scout.* E. 71.

At Hull the same causes were producing the same results. Newcastle was not without brave and devoted followers, but the greater part of his army had been swept up from town and village sorely against their wills.[1] Newcastle was a gallant gentleman, but he was no soldier, and his military adviser, Lord Eythin, was a Scot, and as such was not likely to inspire the Yorkshire villagers with warlike ardour. The besieging army melted away before the toils and hardships to which they were subjected. "You often hear us called the Popish army," jested Newcastle, when Fairfax let the water of the Humber into his trenches, "but you see we trust not in our good works."[2] Every day the besieged grew stronger in courage and resolution. The women of Hull volunteered to carry earth to strengthen the fortifications. On October 5 a reinforcement of 500 men, sent by Manchester, landed on the quay. On the 11th, the day of Winceby fight, a general sally of the garrison drove the besiegers out of several of their forts, and captured a huge cannon, one of the pair known familiarly either as Gog and Magog, or as the Queen's pocket pistols. On the morning of the 12th Newcastle raised the siege. Hunger and desertion together with the enemy's fire had cost him half his force. On the 20th Lincoln surrendered to Manchester, and it was hardly likely that the remaining Royalist garrisons in the county would hold out long.[3] The failure of Newcastle to take Hull had far greater influence upon the progress of the war than the failure of Charles to take Gloucester. Yet, important from a strategical point of view as these events were, they were still more important as revealing a soldier-like capacity in the Parliamentary ranks, and a heartiness of co-operation between the Parliamentary leaders.

Would Essex and Waller join hands in the South as Manchester and Fairfax had joined hands in the North? Yet more urgent was the question whether they could find an army which they could

Marginal notes:
Newcastle before Hull.

Oct. 12. The siege of Hull raised.

Oct. 20. Lincoln taken.

Difficulties of Essex and Waller.

---

[1] *Slingsby's Diary* (ed. 1836), 99.   [2] *Warwick's Memoirs*, 265.
[3] *The True Informer.* E. 74, 1. *Hull's managing of the kingdom's cause.* E. 51, 11.

oppose to Charles. If the spirit of the soldiers of the Eastern Association was to be found at all in the South it was to be found in London, and the Londoners were far from being eager to abandon their busy industry for the life of a professional soldier. "Can the plough go," wrote a contemporary pamphleteer, "when there are no men to hold? It's an ill trade that is driven when the master is in the country."[1]

The citizens unwilling to serve permanently.

For the time the reluctance of the citizens was overcome by the feeling aroused by the loss of Reading. Seven regiments of trained bands from London and the suburbs offered to join Essex and Waller in an attempt to retake so important a military position, which had been abandoned to the enemy by the defection of the Londoners, and which in hostile hands was a serious menace to the commerce of the great city. Orders were issued that if any member of the appointed regiments failed to appear at the rendezvous his shop should be closed, and himself expelled from the circuit of the fortifications.[2]

City regiments offer to retake Reading.

The march to Reading was to have begun on October 18. Before that day arrived it was known in London that on the 15th Rupert, accompanied by Hurry, had sallied out of Oxford, and, leaving Sir Lewis Dyves to throw up fortifications at Newport Pagnell, was plundering Northamptonshire and Bedfordshire.

Oct. 15. Rupert marches out of Oxford.

The occupation of Newport Pagnell was even more serious than the occupation of Reading. Not only did it cut the communication between London and the North, but it threatened the Eastern Association itself. The proposed march to Reading was promptly abandoned, and the seven London regiments followed Essex on the northern road as readily as they would have followed him on the western.[3]

Occupation of Newport Pagnell.

---

[1] *The Parliament Scout.* E. 71, 25.

[2] *Merc. Civicus.* E. 70, 19. *Certain Informations.* E. 70, 29., *Declaration of the Committee for the Militia.* E. 71, 17. *The True Informer.* E. 74, 1.

[3] The Committee at Cambridge to Barrington, October 17 ; Sanders to Barrington, October 18. *Barrington MSS. Merc. Civicus.* E. 72, 10.

Dyves gave way before the approaching storm. On the 28th

Oct. 28.
Newport
Pagnell
abandoned
by the
Royalists, he abandoned the rising fortifications of Newport Pagnell. On the 30th they were occupied by a detachment of the army of Essex, whilst another detachment busied itself with throwing up defences at St. Albans. Whatever might happen elsewhere

Oct. 30.
and occu-
pied by
Essex. the line of communication with the North must be firmly held if the Parliamentary cause was to be saved.[1]

It was the more important that a strong garrison should be posted at Newport Pagnell as the Royalists had fortified

Royalist
garrison at
Towcester. Towcester.[2] Waller, with about 5,000 men, was posted at Farnham, to guard against a possible attack from the West.

The difficulty of raising money was even greater than that of levying soldiers. Two of the judges, indeed, Berkeley and

Fines on
Berkeley
and Trevor. Trevor, were opportunely fined for their part in the ship-money judgment, and 16,000*l.* was thus obtained

Sept. 21.
Seizure of
the royal
revenue for the immediate necessities of the armies.[3] On September 21 the revenues of the King, the Queen, and the Prince were seized, so far as seizure was

Oct. 9.
Seques-
trating
ordinance. practicable, for the use of the Parliament ; and on October 9 an ordinance directed that the lands and houses of such members of either House as had absented themselves, or of other persons who neglected to pay the Parliamentary taxation, should be let, in order that the rent might serve as a security for the repayment of loans.[4]

It was not enough to satisfy the soldiers of Essex and

Oct. 15.
The Lords
take the
Covenant. Waller ; the Scots must be satisfied as well. On October 15 the little group of the peers who remained at Westminster took the Covenant, and on

Oct. 16.
Money re-
quired for
the Scots. the following day an ordinance was passed to authorise a loan of 200,000*l.* Of this a third part, or 66,666*l.* 6*s.* 8*d.*, was required at once, if the Scottish army of 21,000 men was to cross the Tweed. On the 27th the

---

[1] *Merc. Civicus.* E. 74, 14.   Dyves to Prince Rupert, October 28. *Add. MSS.* 18,980, fol. 133.

[2] *The True Informer.* E. 74, 21.

[3] *L.J.* vi. 264, 273.   [4] *Ibid.* vi. 227, 250.

Houses, finding that there was no chance of raising even this amount voluntarily, passed an ordinance for the levy of a

Oct. 27.
A forced
loan. forced loan, and sent Vane and Marshall to acquaint the City with their resolution.[1] On November 1 the

Nov. 1.
Instructions
for Commis-
sioners
with the
Scottish
army. Houses issued instructions to the Commissioners who were to accompany the Scottish army,[2] and, on November 4, 50,000*l.*, as a first instalment of the money due, was actually sent by sea to Leith.[3] Nor

Nov. 4.
Money sent. was it only for the army which was to enter Northumberland that the English Parliament engaged itself to provide. The maintenance of the Scottish army in Ireland was now of the gravest importance for the issue of the struggle in England, and it was therefore actually to receive those supplies from Westminster which had been promised long ago.[4] The Irish cessation, so bitterly denounced, had at last appeared as a grim reality. On

Oct. 23.
Landing of
regiments
from Ire-
land. October 23 an English regiment, set free by the cessation from service in Munster, had landed at Minehead, and before long another regiment from the same quarter appeared at Bristol.[5] At first it was firmly believed that the two regiments were composed of Irish rebels who had been brought over to massacre Protestants in England, as two years before they had massacred them in Ulster. Even when the truth was known the indignation excited was hardly lessened. If the first to arrive were Englishmen, it was said, Irish Papists would follow close upon their heels, or, at all events, would have free scope in Ireland to complete their bloody work upon the Protestants there. No single action of Charles's did so much to weaken his authority as the introduction of these troops from Ireland. In Lincolnshire it made the conciliatory action of Manchester far more easy than it otherwise would have been. A large number of gentlemen who had hitherto appeared as supporters of the

---

[1] *L.J.* vi. 257, 279.   [2] *Ibid.* vi. 288.
[3] *The Scottish Dove.* E. 75, 21.   *The Parliament Scout.* E. 75, 22.
[4] *L.J.* vi. 289.
[5] *Letter from Bridgwater,* October 27.   E. 74, 20.   *Merc. Civicus.* E. 74, 14.

royal cause now professed their readiness to take part against it.[1] At Oxford it gave an excuse to Holland to make his escape and to return to Westminster. The silent contempt of London was a welcome exchange for the scornful hostility of Oxford.

The ill-feeling in London was much increased by the knowledge that appointments recently made at Oxford portended a struggle in which all thought of concealment would be flung aside. Cottington, who was almost openly a Catholic, had recently become Lord Treasurer, and the energetic and unscrupulous Digby had succeeded Falkland as Secretary of State. In Digby Charles had a man to whom he could confide secrets of which it was well to keep the honourable Nicholas in profound ignorance.

Oct. Promotions at Oxford. Cottington and Digby.

Under these circumstances, the belief, which had always been strong, that Charles had made himself the instrument of a terrible Popish conspiracy was raised to absolute conviction. It is at least significant that the news of the Irish cessation was followed by a resolution to hurry on the proceedings against Laud, which had been allowed to sleep for nearly two years. To those who can look back calmly at the past it may appear inexplicable that the Houses thought it worth while to prosecute an old man who seems to us to have been absolutely harmless. He at least could never have stepped forth, as it was once feared that Strafford would step forth, to lead the King's armies to victory. The anger which was aroused against Laud was of a different kind from that which had been aroused against Strafford. In him was seen the embodiment of that spirit which was leading men who called themselves Protestants to seek the co-operation of Irishmen and Catholics. Few could divest themselves of the belief that Laud had been the centre of a dark and hideous conspiracy, which was now exploding around them at every point.[2]

Oct. 19. Laud's impeachment to be proceeded with.

---

[1] *The Scottish Dove.* E. 75, 21.

[2] A curious reason for proceeding against Laud is given in *The Complete Intelligencer* (E. 75, 32). "Certainly the sparing of him hath been a great provocation to Heaven, for it is a sign that we have not been so

Therefore it was that the rancorous hatred with which Prynne had ransacked the Archbishop's cell in May, and had carried off every scrap of paper from which he could hope to extract evidence against him, at last bore fruit in October. On the 19th the Commons voted to present to the Peers further articles against the Archbishop, and on the 23rd the Peers ordered him to send in his answer. The proceedings thus launched would take their course, and it was at least better for Laud that he should meet his enemies face to face, rather than that, as had been barbarously proposed earlier in the year, he should be sent to New England to be baited as a bear at the stake by the separatists who had once fled before him.[1]

The dread of a union between Cavalier and Papist which did so much to wreck Charles's cause, was baseless enough so

Expected union between Catholics and Cavaliers. far as the bulk of Charles's supporters were concerned ; but it was not baseless as regarded Charles himself. The regiment of English soldiers from Ireland, which had landed at Minehead, and had passed on to Bristol, was only the forerunner of the larger force, obtained by the connivance of Irish Catholics, which was to make it possible for the King to take up once more his original plan of operating against London with three armies. If the old western army, under Prince Maurice, was engaged at Plymouth, and the old northern army was kept at bay by Manchester and the Fair-

Armies to be formed un ler Hopton and Byron. faxes, two new armies might be created. Hopton, who had now recovered from his wounds, was available to lead a force, partly composed of 2,000 English soldiers from Munster, through the southern counties into Sussex and Kent ; whilst Sir John Byron, who had recently been created Lord Byron, was to take the command of a small army in Cheshire, which was to be reinforced by 4,000 English soldiers from Leinster. His first work would be to

careful to give the Church a sacrifice as the State. We could soon revenge our own injuries upon Strafford, but we have been slow and behind in revenging the cause of God upon Canterbury, he having corrupted our religion, banished the godly, introduced superstitions, and embrewed both kingdoms at first in a tincture of blood, and all this unnatural war of ours hath its rise and growth from this unhappy seedtime of his designs."

[1] History of the Troubles and Trial. *Laud's Works,* iv. 19, 24.

overpower Brereton, who had occupied Wem, and was pushing
Capel hard in Shropshire, and then to deliver Lancashire, which,
with the exception of Lord Derby's home at Lathom House,
was now entirely in the hands of the local Parliamentarians.
After that he might either lend help to Newcastle in Yorkshire,
or might fall upon the forces of the Eastern Association.

So much might be easily learned by any of the principal
military commanders at Oxford. What remained was communicated in confidence to Ormond, who was now named
Lord Lieutenant of Ireland. A better choice could
hardly have been made if Charles had sought with a
single eye to mediate between infuriated Catholics
and infuriated Protestants. A worse choice could hardly have
been made if he merely needed a man to play off one party
against the other, and to win by intrigue what it was hopeless to
obtain by force.

Oct. 19.
Ormond
to be Lord
Lieutenant
of Ireland.

Never did an unhappy official receive more intricate instructions than those which were now transmitted to Ormond. In
the first place he was to induce the Irish to lend ships
to transport the English soldiers to England. He
was then to turn his attention to the Commissioners
who were to be sent to Oxford by the Catholics to negotiate a
permanent treaty of peace. If possible, he was to delay their
coming, and if that could not be done he was to urge the
Supreme Council not to bind them to put forward extravagant
claims. It would be a still more important service if Ormond
could succeed in preventing Monro and his Scottish army in
Ulster from coming to England to fight for the Parliament as
Ormond's own army was coming to England to fight for the
King.

Oct. 19.
Instructions
sent to
Ormond.

To prevent a step so undesirable in his own interests Charles
was prepared to descend to the lowest depths of intrigue. Ormond was to recommend the Scots to listen to the English Parliament, and to refuse to be bound by the cessation. As soon
as a breach of the peace had been committed by the Scots, he
was to invite the Irish to lay hold of that occasion and to fall
upon them, promising them, if he saw fit to do so, that Charles
would, in that case, take their further demands into favourable

consideration. On the other hand, if Monro persisted in a reso
lution to transfer his army to England, he was to be 'attempted
by money or gifts.' The Scottish colonists, too, were to be
warned that Monro's desertion of Ireland would lead to their
extirpation. If, in spite of all, Monro actually embarked, the
Irish were to 'be incited to fall upon the inhabiting Scots, as
the best means to draw back the auxiliaries in case the inhabiting Scots have not entirely submitted themselves to the cessation.' There would not be much difficulty in persuading the
Irish to a course so agreeable to their own interests, if they were
put 'in hope to get the lands.' Nor was this all. After Monro's
troops were fairly gone, the Irish were to be told that they could
'in no ways so much recommend themselves to the King nor
obtain for themselves such conditions as by following of them
and falling upon them.'[1]

After this it is hardly necessary to ask why Charles's whole
career ended in failure. The simplicity of aim which is the
one common feature of the designs of the successful heroes and
the successful villains of the world was wholly wanting to him.
If the Parliamentary leaders had no knowledge of the details of
his intrigues, they had no difficulty in divining their general
tendency. Even the belief, widely prevalent in England, that
Irish native troops had been sent over was not much, if at all,
in advance of Charles's intentions. On November 10 Digby

Nov. 10.
Irish to
come over. informed Ormond that the King was now ready to
accept a proposal made by Lord Taaffe to bring over
2,000 Irish, conceiving that he shall not only be ad-
vantaged by their presence in the affairs of England, but also
in the affairs of Ireland by their absence. "It is therefore,"
added Digby, "his Majesty's pleasure that your lordship give all
possible furtherance to the coming over of as many of the principal Irish as can be engaged, leaving the kingdom strong enough
against the Scots."[2]

It is not unlikely that some inkling of Ormond's instructions reached the Parliamentary leaders through the lips of

[1] Instructions sent by Sir G. Hamilton, October 19. *Carte MSS.* vii.
fol. 188.

[2] Digby to Ormond, November 10. Carte's *Ormond*, v. 503.

Holland.[1] At all events, it was at this time that the Houses took a step which, purely formal as it was, served as an indi-

Nov. 11.
The use of the new Great Seal authorised.

cation that they no longer intended to keep terms with the King. On November 11, by authorising the use of the new Great Seal, they laid claim to possess the highest symbol of sovereignty, and on the 30th it was actually entrusted to six Commissioners named by themselves.[2]

Stern as was the resolution of the Houses, their anxiety must have been great. Newcastle's failure at Hull had given

The southern armies on the defensive.

them a breathing time, but it had hardly given them more. Essex remained immovable at St. Albans, and Skippon at Newport Pagnell. Waller, more active than Essex, was the favourite of all who believed that greater energy would produce more successful

Nov. 4.
The South-Eastern Association.

results. On November 4 he was placed at the head of a new South-Eastern Association, comprising the counties of Kent, Surrey, Sussex, and Hampshire.[3] What supplies could be procured were hurried forward to his

Nov. 7.
Waller attacks Basing House.

headquarters, and on the 7th he set out to besiege Basing House—Loyalty House, as its owner loved to call it—the fortified mansion of the Catholic Marquis of Winchester, now garrisoned by a party of London Royalists. Basing House commanded the road to the West through Salisbury, as Donnington Castle, now garrisoned for the King, commanded the more northern road to the West through Newbury.

Nov. 12.
Mutinous spirit of his troops

Waller's first attack upon Basing House was frustrated by a storm of wind and rain. His second attempt came to nothing from a cause far more

Nov. 14.
Desertion of the Londoners.

ominous of disaster. His troops had long remained unpaid, and a mutinous spirit was easily aroused amongst them. On the 12th a Westminster regiment refused to obey orders, and two days later the London trained bands, bidden to advance to the assault, shouted

---

[1] This is hinted at in a newsletter of November $\frac{15}{25}$. *Arch. des. Aff. Étrangères*, xlix. fol. 333.

[2] *L. J.* vi. 305, 18.   [3] *Ibid.* vi. 294.

" Home ! home ! " and deserted in a body. It was impossible
to continue the siege under such conditions, and Waller was
compelled to return to shelter at Farnham.[1]

The desertion of the Londoners was the more serious as it
was evident that the King's troops from Ireland would take the
field before the Scots were ready to cross the border. Hopton,
bringing with him the regiments from Munster, was already on

Nov. 18.
Troops
from Ire-
land at
Mostyn.

the move ; and on November 18 a force 2,500
strong, the first detachment of the Leinster troops,[2]
had landed at Mostyn, to defend Chester and its
neighbourhood against Sir William Brereton and Sir
Thomas Middleton, who had lately been making vigorous
progress in Flintshire. Byron, too, was already on his way
northwards with a force of 1,300 men to join the recently
landed soldiers, and to take the command of the united
army.[3]

The knowledge that they would have to prepare under
such circumstances for a winter campaign in Hampshire and
Cheshire was most unwelcome to the leaders at Westminster.
To add to their perplexity, they learnt that even the friendly
authorities of the City were dissatisfied with their financial

Nov. 28.
The City
asks that
its troops
may be
called home.

arrangements. On the 28th the Sheriffs of London,
accompanied by a deputation from the Aldermen,
appeared at the bar of the Commons. They bluntly
asked that the three London regiments serving under
Essex might be called home. As to those under Waller, if a
considerable sum of money were provided for them, ' they
would use their best arguments unto them for their stay for a
longer time with him.'

[1] *The Parliament Scout.* E. 76, 8. *The True Informer.* E. 76, 10.
The Scottish Dove. E. 76, 26. D'Ewes's Diary. *Harl. MSS.* 165, fol.
211b.

[2] See p. 247.

[3] *Certain Informations.* E. 67, 6. *The Kingdom's Weekly Intelligencer.* E. 67, 10. *The Weekly Account.* E. 67, 16. The King to
Rupert, November 11. *Warburton,* ii. 329. Ernely to Ormond,
November 19. *Carte MSS.* vii. fol. 533. Trevor to Ormond, November
21. Carte's *Ormond,* v. 520. Yonge's Diary. *Add. MSS.* 18,779,
fol. 22.

Experience was, in fact, teaching the Parliamentary chiefs
that the trained-band system, admirably adapted as it was for
Inadequacy   the suppression of passing tumults, was entirely un-
of the
trained-band   suited for a prolonged war.   The very Londoners,
system.   whose conduct at Newbury had roused the admiration of their opponents, shrank from the continuous abandonment of their duties as civilians.   The Commons were not
slow to perceive that the remedy lay in the encouragement of
the system of standing armies, raised for permanent military
service, and attached to the standards by the regularity of their
pay.   That system already existed, and it had only been the
stress of danger which had led to its being supplemented by
Dec. 4.   the temporary expedient of an appeal to local forces.
Vote on the   On December 4 the Commons voted that the army
strength of
Essex's   of Essex should consist of 10,000 foot and 4,000
army.   horse, and on the 7th they fixed its monthly pay at
30,404*l.*, to be raised partly out of the assessments and partly
out of the excise.[1]

It was a good beginning, if only it could be carried out in
practice.   Parliament would be all the stronger if its forces
were reduced in numbers but rendered more efficient by the
regularity of their pay.   Yet the financial burdens already
undertaken were so enormous as to render the prospect of
such a solution well nigh desperate, and many a month was to
pass away before the principle now enounced was finally to be
adopted in fact.

For the present, at least, time was not allowed for any
transformation of Waller's army.   During the greater part of
Hopton in   November Hopton had been hanging about Win-
Hampshire.   chester and Alton.   He, too, had his difficulties, of
a kind somewhat similar to those with which Waller was beset.
His brave Cornishmen were no longer with him.   His army
The soldiers   was mainly composed of undisciplined levies, and
from Ire-   the presence of the four or five hundred veterans who
land.   had recently arrived from Ireland could hardly be
counted as an advantage.   They were 'bold, hardy men, and

---

[1] Yonge's Diary. *Add. MSS.* 18,779, fol. 21. D'Ewes's Diary.
Harl. MSS. 165, fol. 233b.

excellently officered, but the common men were mutinous, and shrewdly infected with the rebellious humour of England, being brought over merely by the virtue and loyalty of their officers, and large promises which there was then but small means to perform.'[1] Not long before they had broken out into open mutiny when they had been sent to take part in the siege of Wardour Castle, and had been brought away by Hopton in the hope that they would do their duty if they were overawed by more loyal regiments. The King's plan of bringing soldiers from Ireland did not seem likely to meet with success. Their presence irritated the Parliamentarians, whilst they were themselves too strongly Protestant to have much heart in the royal cause.

Hopton was further embarrassed by the want of confidence reposed in him at headquarters. His own wish had been to secure his rear before advancing, by the capture of the fortresses held by Parliament in Wilts and Dorset, whilst the King, anxious to take up his old plan of an advance into Sussex and Kent, had, without any reference to him, authorised Sir William Ogle to surprise Winchester, and, when Ogle had accomplished this feat, had ordered his reluctant commander to move forward into Hampshire to Ogle's support.[2]

Hopton
ill-treated.

Hopton's nature was too loyal to revolt against the treatment to which he had been subjected. Eagerly striving to carry out the plan imposed on him by Charles, he ordered Sir Edward Ford, the King's High Sheriff of Sussex, to collect a force upon which he could depend and to seize Arundel. These instructions were carried out. The town was occupied on December 6, and on the 9th the castle surrendered to Hopton himself.

Dec. 6.
Arundel
seized.

Dec. 9.
The castle
surrendered.

----

[1] Narrative of Hopton's campaign. *Clarendon MSS.* 1738b.

[2] Compare the narrative cited in the last note with Ogle's account of his own proceedings in *Add. MSS.* 27,402, fol. 86. Ogle was created Viscount Ogle in the Irish Peerage in 1645. This date is given as 1615, by a misprint in Lascelles' *Liber Munerum.* In the catalogue of the *Add. MSS.* in the British Museum the account given by this Ogle is incorrectly attributed to the Marquis of Newcastle, whose second title was Baron Ogle.

The capture of Arundel marked the high tide of Royalist success which had begun to swell at Stratton. It was soon to be discovered that the forces of which Charles could dispose were insufficient to support so daring a strategy. Hopton's little army was scattered over a tract of country too wide for safety in the presence of so able a tactician as Waller. On the early morning of the 13th the Parliamentary general fell upon Lord Crawford's quarters at Alton. Crawford escaped with the greater part of his horse, but his foot surrendered after a short resistance. Of near upon a thousand prisoners five hundred took the Covenant and transferred their services to Parliament. The newsmongers at London had their laugh when they heard that Waller had recaptured a cask of sack which he had courteously presented to Crawford a few days before. It was of greater importance that the Westminster regiment, which had refused to advance at Basing, showed no signs of flinching at Alton.[1]

Dec. 13. The surprise at Alton.

The loss of Arundel, in fact, had roused London and the southern counties from their apathy. Two fresh regiments of City trained bands had been despatched to take the place of those which had deserted their commander, and 600 horse were sent by Essex to complete Waller's force. If the majority of the gentry of Kent and Sussex were on the side of the King, the middle classes did not share their opinions, and even those who under ordinary circumstances would have wished to remain neutral had no desire to see their own district the seat of a desolating war. Hopton, fearing a repetition of the surprise of Alton, abandoned Petersfield, and thus broke the line of communication between Winchester and Arundel. Waller was now at liberty to move. On December 20 he sat down before Arundel. The surrender of the castle on January 6 definitely placed a limit to the Royalist invasion of the South.

Waller rein orced.

Dec. 20. Waller at Arundel.

1644. Jan. 6. Surrender of Arundel Castle.

---

[1] *The Parliament Scout.* E. 79, 19. *A narration of the great victory.* E. 79, 22. *The Kingdom's Weekly Intelligencer.* E. 79, 24.

CHAPTER XIII.

PRESBYTERIANS AND INDEPENDENTS.

LONG before the tidings of Waller's success reached London the statesman whose unflagging confidence during the darkest

1643.
Nov. 8.
Pym Master of the Ordnance.

hours of adversity had made success possible was beyond the reach of joy or sorrow. On November 8 the Houses had conferred upon Pym the Mastership of the Ordnance, entrusting to him, as to one of whose fidelity no doubts could be entertained, the care of the store of arms in the Tower.[1] He had been ailing for some

Sickness

months, and though at one time he seemed to be recovering, the improvement was not of long continuance. In the early days of December, as he lay on his sick bed, he told his sorrowing friends that to him life or death was indifferent : —'if he lived, he would do what service he could ; if he died, he should go to that God whom he had served, and who would carry on His work by some others.' Pym's disease was an internal abscess, and on the evening of

Dec. 8. and death of Pym.
Dec. 15. His funeral.

December 8 he died.[2] On the 15th Lords and Commons, accompanied by the Assembly of Divines, followed to its grave in the Chapel of Henry VII. the body of their uncrowned leader. By an unprecedented step the Commons voted 10,000*l.* for the payment of the debts of the man who, abandoning himself to the service of the State, had impoverished his own family.

"I beseech you," said Stephen Marshall in his funeral

[1] *C.J.* iii. 303. *L.J.* vi. 297.
[2] *A narrative of the death and disease of John Pym.* E. 79, 27. *Sermon* by Stephen Marshall. E. 80, 1.

sermon before the assembled Houses, "let not any of you have one sad thought touching him ; nor, secondly, would I have you mourn out of any such apprehension as the enemies have, and for which they rejoice, as if our cause were not good, or we should lose it for want of hands to carry it on. No, beloved, this cause must prosper ; and although we were all dead, our armies overthrown, and even our Parliaments dissolved, this cause must prevail."

"The greatest liberty of our kingdom," Pym had once said, "is religion." [1] In this characteristic utterance he gave

Pym's character and work. the key to his life's work. Above all existing law, above all popular rights, he placed religion. For him, however, religion did not stand in opposition to the world and the things of the world. He never thought of deserting work amongst his fellow-men to devote himself to the salvation of his own soul. Divine laws, apprehended by the individual conscience, were to be applied to the government of society, and these laws were, in his mind, very closely connected with the existing laws of England. The nature of the struggle against Charles and Laud led him to look to Parliament as a fitting instrument of government wherewith to replace the failing authority of the King, though he never idealised Parliament quite as much as Eliot had done. Unlike Eliot, he lived long enough to see the principles which he cherished rejected by one House of Parliament, and supported only by a minority in the other, who, through the desertion of a large number of their fellow-members, were able to pose as a majority. His situation was one to test the strongest brain— one, it may fairly be said, from the difficulties of which no single brain was capable of discovering a way of escape. If Pym had been a mere Parliamentarian, wishing to substitute the sovereignty of the many for the sovereignty of one, his work would have been, intellectually at least, comparatively easy. His difficulties arose from his recognition that more than the form of government was at stake, and from his belief that religion—or, in other words, Puritanism—must be upheld

[1] *A short view of the life and actions of . . . John Pym.* E. 68, 13.

if the nation were to live, even against the will of the nation itself.

In Pym's days the modern system of party government was beyond reach, as neither the constitutional habit nor the assured liberty of speech and writing, which is essential to the maintenance of that habit, was in existence. What Pym did was to attempt to replace the monarchical organisation by an organisation resting on voluntary association. In 1621 his first recorded Parliamentary utterance asked for 'an oath of association' to secure Englishmen against the Catholics at home, 'and that those who should refuse the same should not hold any office in the commonwealth.' This proposal, which grew out of the Association of 1584, was the germ of the Protestation of 1641, and of the Parliamentary Covenant of 1643, if not of the Solemn League and Covenant itself.

He is a precursor of party government.

Out of the idea of mutual association in defence of a principle, as better than mutual association in defence of a person, party government would eventually grow. Its time was not yet come. Not only did the new system then, as ever, find itself scouted by those who clung to older forms, but all healthy political development was made impossible by the King. In that adherence to narrow legality tempered by a mixture of force and intrigue, which was Charles's ideal of statesmanship, Pym at once recognised a disturbing element to be cast out at all hazards, even if its existence necessitated an appeal to the arbitrament of the sword.

Under the stress of this danger Pym threw away one half of his creed in order to preserve intact the other and the nobler half. It is true that the religion of Falkland and of Jeremy Taylor was as elevated as that of Winthrop and Baxter, but the pressing question of the day was not whether one belief could subsist side by side with the other, but whether one was to be imposed on the other by the aid of army plots and Irish cessations. Before this danger Puritanism stiffened itself for the conflict, and it found its leader in Pym. There was to be no counting of heads—no trust in old constitutional forms. If the Lords would not join the Commons, the

Commons would save the State without them. If the Commons hesitated, the shouts of the citizens must awaken them to their duty.

When the danger passed away Pym's services would be forgotten, or would be counted as crimes. As long as Charles lived services such as his could not be dispensed with. Honourable combination with men of good-will to the cause which they reverenced was Pym's defence against the shifty politics of Charles. The power of a resolute and devoted minority was to be opposed to the weakness of a distracted majority, and until that majority should obtain the coherence which alone could make it strong, the fewer in number were certain to prevail.

Whatever differences of opinion there may be with regard to Pym's aims, there can be none as to the spirit in which he pursued them. In his personal dealings with men of his own party there was no assumption of superiority, no contemptuous disregard for those who differed from him. It is hard from such record of the Parliamentary debates as remains to us to recognise him as a leader at all. He worked by influence, not by eloquence ; and his influence was founded on his power of distinguishing the important points of a complicated situation from those which were comparatively unimportant. Hence his anxiety to gain allies by any concession of which circumstances would admit. During the crisis of July and August he had succeeded in reconciling Essex to his duty to the Parliamentary cause. In accepting the Covenant he had striven to give it as wide an interpretation as possible. Those who speak of him as the leader of the Presbyterian party mistake the nature of the man. He was neither Episcopalian nor Presbyterian by conviction. He regarded forms of church government as of very secondary importance. In the last speech which he is known to have uttered in Parliament,[1] he based his acceptance of the abolition of Episcopacy solely on the strength which that abolition would give to those who were fighting against Charles. The one thing which he asked for the Church was

[1] See p. 233.

that it should be sincerely Protestant. All else was but a matter of expediency.

It may be that Pym was happy in the opportunity of his death. New issues were opening before the nation, with respect to which his judgment was likely to be at fault. His own greatness was, unlike that of Strafford, the greatness of one who embraces much to which he can give no definite form. The whole future constitution of England was in his mind, but it was there in a fluid state, incapable as yet of being reduced into practical shape. King and Lords and Commons were there, with the Commons to give the decisive word. The right of appeal from the House of Commons to outside opinion was there, and due submission to the majesty of the law was there as well. Party discipline and combination filled no small place in his plans. All these things floated before him as the wreaths of smoke which poured from the opened casket in the Arabian tale. The time would come when the coiling vapours would take shape in that settlement of the Revolution of 1688, which was one day to give repose to England.

When Pym died there was sorrow and regret, but there was no wail of despair. The Parliamentary party was not likely to perish with him, and as long as Charles lived and reigned it would in some form or other continue to exist.

To meet Pym with an ecclesiastical policy broader and nobler than any that had yet been enunciated was beyond Charles's power, but he could hardly fail to perceive the strength which his adversaries derived from the mere name of Parliament. That strength he was now resolved to have upon his own side. On December 22 he summoned all the members of either House who had left Westminster already, or were willing to leave it on promise of pardon, to meet on January 22 in Parliament at Oxford. Forgetful of his own transactions with the Irish, he was prepared to stand forth as the champion of English nationality, and to call on the loyal Houses to express their indignation at the invitation given to the Scots to invade England.

Dec. 22.
Charles summons Parliament to meet at Oxford.

That the meeting of a partisan Parliament at Oxford should lead to a good understanding with the partisan Parliament at Westminster was most improbable. Charles's only real chance lay in the enunciation of a broader and more attractive policy, which would rally to his side, not indeed his opponents in the field and in the senate, but the nation as a whole. Neither himself nor his advisers were capable of devising such a policy. The military party, headed by Rupert, urged him to finish the war by victory, not by negotiation. Digby, the mercurial Secretary of State, had favoured the transportation of the Irish army to England, and he was equally ready to break the strength of his adversaries by winning over to his side either classes or individuals to whom he had anything to offer. Statesmanship became in Digby's hands a mere policy of intrigue.

A broader policy needed.

By this time parties were more thoroughly divided by their religious proclivities than they had been some months before, and the conduct of the Hothams and of Sir Alexander Carew was not likely to find imitators. Captain Backhouse, who had been invited to betray Gloucester to the King, met guile with guile, and pretended to enter into the plot in order that he might lure his adversaries to their destruction. The nobler Colonel Hutchinson, to whom 10,000*l.* and a peerage was offered in the handwriting of Newcastle himself, as the purchase-money of the betrayal of Nottingham, scornfully rejected the temptation.[1]

Attempts to gain Nottingham and Gloucester.

Digby had a larger net to throw than might suffice for the gaining possession of a fortress or a town. For some months a movement had been gathering head at Westminster which he hoped to turn to the profit of his master.

The evident wish of the great majority of the divines in the Assembly to impose Presbyterianism upon the nation had met with unlooked-for opposition. The old Separatists, Anabaptists, Antinomians, and the like, had indeed found no place in a body chosen by the two Houses, but there were a few members to whom the public voice, in

Opposition in the Westminster Assembly.

[1] *A true relation of a wicked plot,* in *Bibl. Gloucestr.* vol. ii. *A discovery of the treacherous attempt.* E. 79, 30.

spite of their own disclaimer, persisted in giving the name of Independents.[1] Five of the most notable of these, Thomas

The five dissenting brethren. Goodwin, Nye, Simpson, Bridge, and Boroughs, were University men who had been driven from England at the time of the Laudian persecution, and who had recently come back to England after occupying ministerial positions at Rotterdam or Arnheim. Though concurring in the main with the Separatist ideas on church government, they had refused to follow them in denouncing the Church of England as apostate, and they fancied that they had hit upon a ·wise middle course between the loose independency of the Separatists and the iron discipline of the Presbyterians. They

Modified Independency. held that no congregation ought to be subjected to coercive jurisdiction outside itself, though they allowed to each congregation the right of remonstrating against the proceedings of any other, and even, if it saw fit so to do, of refusing to hold communion with it. The theory adopted by the five dissenting brethren, as they came to be called in the Assembly, was only one of many which were floating about at a time when the existing church organisation was thrown into the crucible. Its importance lay in the fact that it was vigorously defended by men of ability and culture, and was by them cleared from the harsh and uncharitable judgments which gave reasonable offence in the mouths of many of the older Separatists. It was only indirectly, by weakening the clerical organisation and by strengthening the authority of the laity, whose influence was more likely to prevail in separate congregations than in the larger Presbyterian assemblies, that it appealed to the deeply seated English suspicion of clerical rule.

That suspicion had been recently invigorated by the imposition of the Covenant and the calling in of the Scots.

Reaction against the Covenant. The last achievement of Pym's statesmanship, which had made more bitter the bitterness of Oxford, and had made it possible for Charles once more to gather a Parliament around him, was driving the more resolute Puritans in an opposite direction. Men who had struck out

[1] See p. 229.

for themselves some new theological system, and who had lost all sense of proportion in the intentness of their gaze upon one biblical doctrine or the other, made common cause with men who, like the dissenting brethren, accepted the received theology of the day, but who objected to the imposition even of their own beliefs by an external clerical authority.

The Independency of the Civil War was the joint product of these two factors. The former derived its strength from the lower classes in the towns, from the yeomanry in the country, and more especially from those soldiers in the army who had come forth from amongst the yeomanry at Cromwell's bidding, and who, inspired with all the vigour which a self-chosen belief brings with it, were beginning to be known amongst themselves as the godly party. Amongst these men the Covenant was regarded as a mark of bondage. Cromwell himself had deferred his adhesion to it as long as it was possible to do so, and in London many of the more fiery spirits prepared a petition to Parliament, in which they denounced the tyranny of Presbyterianism, and declared that if the Covenant were enforced they would induce the soldiers of their way of thinking to lay down their arms. It was only at the urgent entreaty of Nye that the petition was suppressed by those who had drawn it up.[1]

The new Independency.

Proposed petition against the Covenant.

Nye, it may be supposed, acted as the mouthpiece of the Assembly Independents, who still cherished a hope that the Assembly would render the government to be established in the Church sufficiently elastic to accommodate those who were disinclined to place their necks under the Presbyterian yoke. The tone of the Assembly when, on October 17, the discussion on the re-organisation of church government was opened, was such as to make them hopeful. If there were any who thought that a body of English clergymen would accept the Scottish system without discussion, they were speedily undeceived. Point after point was argued with pertinacious minuteness. The spirit of the Assembly was thoroughly in

The Independents of the Assembly.

The Assembly discusses church government.

[1] Ogle to Bristol, October 17. *A secret negotiation*, 1. *Camd. Misc.* vol. viii.

accordance with Vane's amendment. Its members cared much less about the example of the best reformed Churches than about the authoritative doctrine of the Word of God. What that doctrine was it was not easy to discover. Efforts were made to construe writings which bristled with metaphor and allusion as if they were Acts of Parliament. Yet, after all, no man, and especially no assembly of men, is guided by logic alone. The example of the vigour of the Scottish Church weighed in the balance more heavily than its authority. When, after some weeks' debate, the first steps were taken in favour of the Presbyterian system, it became evident that the organisation of the Church of Scotland would, as far as the Westminster Assembly could prevail, be adopted in England as well.

Presbyterianism favoured by it.

The burden of what opposition there was fell upon the five dissenting brethren. It is unnecessary to recite the details of the struggle. It is enough to remember the difference of principle which lay behind each petty contention. The Presbyterian ideal was an official Church with the right of enforcing discipline on recalcitrant members, and resting on the general support of Puritan Englishmen. The Independent ideal was the abolition of coercive discipline over congregations in which the lay element would obtain, by the very fact of its direct incidence, a preponderating influence.

Opposition of the Independents.

Outside the doors of the Assembly feeling was likely to be divided. If the Independents had on their side the English dislike of clerical rule, they had against them the English dislike of strange opinions. From such opinions they were themselves entirely free. They had no wish to re-baptise infants, to declaim against the sinfulness of regarding the moral law, or to deny the divinity of the Saviour. Nevertheless, they had to share in the unpopularity of those who did. Many a sober Englishman who had rebelled against the tyranny of Laud refused to allow doctrines to be openly preached which appeared to sap the very foundations of morality as well as of religion. The question of Presbyterianism or Independency would be thrust

Public opinion.

into the background, and the question of toleration or no toleration would take its place.

It was no wonder therefore that the Assembly Independents should feel their relations with the members of the sects to be somewhat uncertain. The successful intervention of Nye to stop the presentation of the petition against the Covenant is sufficient evidence that the two wings of the party had been forced into accord by the common dread lest the Scots should impose Presbyterianism by force of arms. The same dread led to negotiations of an unexpected kind. The old Peace-party was still strong in the City, and its leaders were startled to find that they had now a common ground with those whom they had long regarded as their bitterest enemies. An intermediary was found in a certain Thomas Ogle, who had been connected with the plots of Sir Nicholas Crisp,[1] and who, on some charge, the nature of which is now unknown, had been lying in various prisons for nearly seven months.

The Independents and the Peace-party.

The result of the communications thus opened between the sects and the Royalists of the Peace-party was a resolution to appeal to Charles for a settlement which it seemed hopeless to expect from a Parliament which had called in the Scots. The terms agreed to were to be forwarded by Ogle to Bristol, the least bigoted of Charles's influential adherents. The letter which Ogle wrote to accompany these proposals was dated on October 17, the day on which the Assembly entered upon its debate on church government, but it was not sent off till November 24, and the delay of more than five weeks may conjecturally be attributed to the desire of some of its promoters to avoid an appeal to the King till the course of the Assembly had been clearly indicated.

Oct. 17.
A negotiation with the King proposed.

Nov. 24.
Terms offered.

The propositions forwarded to Bristol asked that Episcopal government might be retained, though the whole of the existing Episcopate was to be deprived of office. Their successors were to be such as 'through their unblameable lives and doctrine have interest in the people's affection.' Visitors were

[1] See p. 111.

to be appointed to abolish obnoxious ceremonies, justice was to be done to those who had suffered in past times, and the trial of delinquents was to be conducted either by a known law or in full and free Parliament. The breach between King and Parliament was to be repaired, and Charles was to admit to audience some persons selected by the thousands in London who wished to be eased of the burdens laid on them by the Bishops.[1]

A popular Episcopacy with toleration for those who declined to submit to the Episcopal system was the burden of Gist of the these proposals. In the main it was the settlement proposals. of 1688 anticipated. No special blame is due to Charles for rejecting an offer which would have been equally rejected by the great majority of his opponents. Where he went wrong was that, instead of accepting or rejecting so important an overture on its own merits, he allowed himself to be entangled by it in an intrigue, the discovery of which inflicted a severe blow on the royal cause. The Plot for the Parliamentary garrison of Aylesbury had long been a betrayal of thorn in the side of the King's commanders, and Aylesbury. when Ogle intimated that an officer of the garrison, Colonel Mozley, was prepared to betray Aylesbury, as a proof of the serious intentions of the negotiators, Charles's interest was at once aroused. He was also told that Devenish, the keeper of the prison in which Ogle was, would connive at his prisoner's escape, in order that he might come to Oxford to explain the whole matter in person.

Already Ogle's plot was being met by a counter-plot. Both Mozley and Devenish had communicated their know- The plot ledge to the Committee of Safety, and the letters betrayed. which passed between the conspirators and Oxford were duly laid, either in the original or in copy, before that body. In this way the Committee learned that on December 7 a bill of exchange for 100*l.* had been sent to Ogle, together with a safe conduct for three persons to come to Oxford to carry on the negotiations. Three or four days later

---

[1] Ogle to Bristol, October 17. Propositions sent by Ogle. *A secret negotiation*, 1, 8. *Camd. Misc.* vol. viii.

Mozley was in London, ostensibly to ask for money for the garrison of Aylesbury, but mainly, it would seem, to arrange with the Parliamentary leaders the mode in which Charles's plot was to be met. Early in January Ogle was allowed to escape, and appeared at Oxford, where he urged the acceptance of the propositions of the Independents, without the faintest suspicion that every step taken by him was duly noted at Westminster. On January 5 Devenish wrote to Bristol, telling him that Ogle before leaving London had held a conversation with Nye and Goodwin, and had found them very reticent in consequence of the want of an answer from the King to assure them ' what they may trust to.' Without a definite understanding with Charles they could not engage themselves ; 'for if they have nothing to move them by way of allurement, and that all shall be left to their jealousy and fear of the Scotch and Presbytery, it may prevail with them perhaps to retire, but not apply themselves to the King without some reasonable invitations, which these very fears and jealousies may make way for the embracement of.'[1]

margin note: 1644. January Ogle at Oxford.

margin note: Nye and Goodwin draw back.

Though it is far from certain that these words were spoken by Nye and Goodwin, there is at least a strong probability that they express the feelings which they entertained towards the King. Charles had shown great haste to get possession of Aylesbury, but no eagerness whatever to adopt a policy of wise toleration. Bristol was, no doubt, more accessible to large ideas than his master, but his language was far too vague to attract men whose hearts were set on solving a great spiritual problem. "You go," he had written to Mozley, "upon a good ground, and such a one as must unite all honest Englishmen, although in other things of different minds, which is not to be overrun by an invasion of the Scots, who, if they should prevail, will tyrannise both over our estates and consciences."[2]

margin note: 1643. Dec. 19. Bristol's letter to Mozley.

[1] *A secret negotiation*, 10–27. *Camd. Misc.* vol. viii.

[2] Bristol to Mozley, December 19. *A secret negotiation*, 25. *Camd. Misc.* vol. viii.

Not only was the acceptance of the Independent scheme by Charles extremely uncertain, but in the last weeks of the year the Independents in the Assembly were able to entertain hopes of obtaining from that body all that they could reasonably desire. It is possible that the three members of the Committee of Safety who, on December 11, learned the secret of the negotiations with the King, intimated to the Presbyterians in the Assembly that it would be dangerous to push the Independents to the wall. Even if this was not the case, it was evident that it was no time to divide the Parliamentary party, when Pym was no longer there to lead them, and when Towcester and Arundel were both occupied by Royalist garrisons. Even Baillie, who had recently arrived to attend the meetings of the Assembly as a Scottish Commissioner, and who hated the very idea of toleration with a perfect hatred, was convinced that for a time at least the Independents must be conciliated. "With them," he naïvely wrote on December 7, "we purpose not to meddle in haste, till it please God to advance our army, which we expect will much assist our arguments."[1] Other reasons too there were for yielding something. No strong Presbyterian party was yet formed amongst the laity, and it was perhaps hardly possible to form one till Independency came to be associated with military aggression. In the meanwhile greater dangers than were to be feared from the Assembly Independents were impending. "In the time of this anarchy," complained Baillie, about December 14, "the divisions of people weekly does much increase. The Independent party grows, but the Anabaptists more, and the Antinomians most. As yet a Presbytery to this people is conceived a strange monster."[2] Before long it was a matter of general knowledge that some negotiations had been opened between the Independents and the King. "I know," wrote Baillie on January 1, "they have offers from the Court of all they require."[3]

The conciliatory feeling generated by this condition of affairs found expression in a declaration issued on December 23 in the

Marginal note: Hopes of the Independents from the Assembly.

---

[1] *Baillie,* ii. 111.   [2] *Ibid.* ii. 117.   [3] *Ibid.* ii. 133.

name of the Assembly.[1] Though, as far as its title went, it
was a warning against the gathering of new congregations, the

Dec. 23.
Declaration
by the
Assembly.

Assembly in point of fact offered to 'concur to preserve
whatever should appear to be the rights of particular
congregations, according to the Word ; and to bear
with such whose consciences cannot in all things conform to
the public rule, as far as the Word of God would have them
borne withal.' To this declaration were appended the
signatures of such decided Presbyterians as Twiss and Marshall,
Herle and Palmer, and the five dissenting brethren were fairly
justified in believing that more was to be obtained from
the Assembly than they had any reason to expect from
Charles.

Yet, either because the five distrusted the majority of the
Assembly, or because they wished to bring before the know-

1644.
Jan. 1 (?)
The Apo-
logetical
Narration.

ledge of the public their real wishes, they published
about the beginning of the new year a statement of
their views. From the Apologetical Narration, as
they termed it, it appeared that they were not in
agreement with the authors of the propositions sent to Charles
in asking for liberty to form separate congregations uncon-
nected with the principal Church of the nation. What they
asked was that no ecclesiastical assembly should exercise any
coercive jurisdiction at all. Such coercive jurisdiction as might
be necessary was to be exercised directly by the State.[2]

The Apologetical Narration was therefore rather an appeal
against clericalism than a complete vindication of liberty of
conscience. Its authors were not long in assuring themselves
what they had strongly suspected already, that nothing was to

Jan. 6.
Offers from
Oxford.

be expected from Charles. On January 6, Ogle
urged Nye to hasten to Oxford, where he would 'be
admitted his Majesty's chaplain, and highly preferred
upon the conclusion.' On the 9th Bristol sent a

Jan. 9.

warm exhortation to rise against the tyranny of the
Scots, and a vague assurance that the Independents should be

---

[1] *Certain considerations to dissuade men from further gathering of
Churche:.* E. 79, 16.

[2] *The Apologetical Narration.* E. 80, 7.

satisfied in such a way as to content all discreet persons.[1] The want of precision in Bristol's overtures, coupled with the appeal to the lowest motives contained in Ogle's offers, was in itself calculated to warn Nye and his fellows off the track, even if their knowledge of the plot for the betrayal of Aylesbury had not made them shy before. Still more untrustworthy must Charles have appeared to them when they learned that he was engaged in yet another intrigue, of which the threads were kept distinct from those in which he was attempting to involve themselves.

Some time before Ogle opened communications with the King, Colonel Reade, the officer who had been tortured in

1643.
December.
Reade and
Brooke's
plot.

Dublin,[2] and who had long been a prisoner in the Tower, had made his escape to Oxford, and had entertained Charles with tales of the good-will of the Londoners. Himself a Catholic, he urged the King to open a correspondence with Sir Basil Brooke, a Catholic who in Charles's palmy days had risen to favour under Portland's protection, and who, in the time of trouble, had negotiated with the Catholics for their support to the throne. Brooke agreed to do his utmost to win over the City to Charles's cause. He was the more hopeful, as in the end of 1643 there was a widespread dissatisfaction with the absorption of the trained bands in distant military enterprises, and with the ruinous effects of the prolongation of the war upon trade. Brooke's main instruments were Violet, a Royalist goldsmith, who had been in prison for refusing to pay his share of the Parliamentary taxation, and Riley, a scout-master, who would be able to bring him into communication with the disaffected militiamen. Charles was sanguine enough to imagine that if he addressed a letter to the Lord Mayor and Aldermen assuring them of his constancy in religion, they would at once break with the Parliament and declare for peace.

The scheme was favoured by the Queen and the Duchess of Buckingham, and on December 26 the letter was despatched. As so often happened with Charles's compromising despatches,

---

[1] *A secret negotiation*, 27, 31. *Camd. Misc.* vol. viii.

[2] See p. 112.

it fell into the hands of the Committee of Safety. Even if the scheme had been more promising than it was, it was incredibly foolhardy to entrust its execution to a handful of schemers, of whom the principal were Catholics. The letter itself contained no hint at that liberty of conscience which was the corner-stone of the negotiation with the Independents, and it therefore led surely to the conclusion which most men had reached already, that Charles was ready to make himself all things to all men, with no intention of fulfilling any one of his promises, and with the absolute impossibility of fulfilling all.[1]

The plot discovered.

Ogle's plot was not yet ripe for discussion in the House of Commons, if the time was ever to arrive. The attempt on Aylesbury had not yet been made, and it was undesirable to compromise the Independents by revealing all that had taken place. The denunciation of Brooke's plot was admirably suited for a rallying cry. On January 6 the Commons were informed of their danger. The irritation was the greater as with the intercepted letter had been seized a copy of the King's proclamation, summoning Parliament to Oxford. On the 8th the Lords not only showed that they shared in the angry feeling of the Commons, but gave signs of an intention to proceed with the Queen's impeachment.[2]

Ogle's plot not revealed.

1644. Jan. 6. Brooke's plot denounced.

Two days later the Houses were reminded that, concurrently with the intrigues which had recently been brought to light in England and Ireland, there was an outer network of diplomacy, the object of which was to rouse foreign Powers to afford moral or material assistance to the King in his war with his own subjects. One danger indeed was now happily averted. A war had broken out between Denmark and Sweden, and the Danish troops which were to have been purchased by the cession of Orkney and Shetland, as Charles had continued to suggest,[3]

1643. War between Denmark and Sweden.

---

[1] *A cunning plot.* E. 29, 3. . *L.J.* vi. 370.

[2] *L.J.* vi. 369. *Clarendon's Life,* iii. 38.

[3] Fridericia, *Danmarks ydre politiske historie,* 1635–45, p. 316.

would now be needed at home. As, however, the chance of
Danish help diminished, Charles and the Queen had turned their
eyes upon France, where those who were now in authority might possibly be more ready to sympathise with
a king and queen in distress than Richelieu had been.

A change
of Govern-
ment in
France.

Louis XIII. had died in May, and in the minority of his
successor, Louis XIV., his widow, Anne of Austria, exercised
the sovereignty as regent. Though she was utterly
devoid of the political spirit, she could rouse herself
at times when her authority was assailed, and her
maternal instinct hindered her from carrying out, now that
she was in power, the schemes in favour of Spain
to which she had lent too ready an ear as a neglected
wife. Mazarin, who, with a fine sense of the limits
which separate the possible and the impossible, was already
carrying out with success the anti-Spanish policy of the Iron
Cardinal, won her respect alike by his skill in baffling political
intrigues and by the fame which accrued to her by victories in
the field. So firmly, indeed, did she cling to the minister, that
a not very probable rumour asserted that respect before long
warmed into a tenderer feeling, consecrated by the bond of a
secret marriage.[1] The first days of the new reign were
brightened by the tidings that the young Duke of Enghien,
neglecting the advice of older warriors, had dashed
to pieces at Rocroi that Spanish infantry which for
more than a century had given to Spain military
predominance in Europe. Enghien followed up the blow in
August by the capture of Thionville. The Spanish frontier
definitely receded before the French armies.

May 4.
14
Death of
Louis XIII.

Anne of
Austria and
Mazarin.

May 9.
19
Battle of
Rocroi.

The protection of France was now indeed worth having,
and it was with no slight satisfaction that Charles heard that a
French ambassador was on his way to mediate a
peace in England—a peace the terms of which, as
might easily be concluded, would be very different
from those which he had rejected at Oxford. When, early in
October, Harcourt, who was entrusted with this mission

October.
Harcourt's
mission.

---

[1] Cheruel, *Hist. de France pendant la minorité de Louis XIV.* ii. 136.

arrived in London, he was welcomed by crowds weary of the
war with shouts of "God bless the prince who brings us
peace!"[1] The Parliamentary leaders were less
enthusiastic. They seized on Walter Montague, who
accompanied the ambassador, and shut him up in
the Tower, as being liable as a priest of English birth to
English law ; and upon the ground that Harcourt refused to
acknowledge the Houses as the Parliament of England they
refused him the audience which he demanded.[2]

W. Montague imprisoned.

In November, therefore, Harcourt betook himself to Oxford.
What passed there was veiled in secrecy, and when, early in
January, a letter of Digby's was intercepted, in which
it was stated that Harcourt's mission had failed as
completely at Oxford as it had failed at Westminster,
because Charles had refused to acknowledge the
Houses as a Parliament, there must have been a feeling of
relief amongst all who regarded a French mediation with
suspicion.

1644.
Jan. 6.
Harcourt's mission said to have failed.

On January 10 the Houses learnt that they had congratu-
lated themselves too soon. Another intercepted letter—this
time from Lord Goring, the King's ambassador in
Paris—told another tale. Harcourt had been discussing a proposal for a league between Charles and
the Queen Regent of France, and if the league had
not been concluded it had been because Charles
had overreached himself by demanding too much and offering
too little. Mazarin, however, had assured Goring that if
Harcourt's mediation failed he was ready to serve their
Majesties to the utmost in arms or money, and though diplomatic assurances might not go very far, Goring at least believed
that a loan of money would be easily attainable, as well as an
actual declaration of the enmity of France against the Parliaments of England and Scotland. Goring, too, had succeeded
in obtaining large sums of money for the Queen's jewels, which

Jan. 10.
Goring's letter.

Harcourt's real object.

[1] Harcourt to Mazarin, October ²⁄₁₃. *Arch. des Aff. Étrangères,* xlix.
fol. 333. Greçy to Brienne, October ¹²⁄₂₂. *Harl. MSS.* 4,551, fol. 175.
[2] *L.J.* vi. 302, 308.

he had pawned, and was sending a considerable store of arms to England.[1]

Before Goring's letter was read in the Commons an appeal had been made by the Houses, not to the Lord Mayor and Aldermen, but to the more popular assembly of the Common Hall. The disclosure of Brooke's plot was received with the greatest indignation. On the 13th the Sheriffs and the Aldermen, probably knowing that some at least of their number were regarded with suspicion, invited the two Houses, together with the Scots Commissioners and the Assembly of Divines, to a banquet, to be given as a manifestation of the City's resolution to maintain its union with the bodies invited in spite of Charles's efforts to divide them.[2]

Jan. 8.
The Houses
appeal to
the City.

The banquet was given on the 18th in Merchant Taylors' Hall. In a preliminary sermon Stephen Marshall urged the necessity of union. He drew special attention to the unprincipled combinations of their adversaries. "You shall see them," he said, "sending into France, offering offensive and defensive leagues. What infinite endeavours are used! what sort of men is not attempted—what profession soever they be of—be they Jesuits, be they friars, be they priests, be they professors, be they such as they call Puritans."[3] Only a few of Marshall's hearers would recognise the meaning of the last allusion, but the general bearing of the passage would be in accordance with the feeling of all. If it is too much to say that the vast audience was as united as it professed to be, at least it was far more united than could have been possible a month before, and for this Charles was mainly responsible.

Jan. 18.
The City
banquet.

As might have been expected, the fact that Catholics had been largely employed in the recent plot was thrust into the foreground. When the procession swept along from the sermon to the feast, light was set to a pile of 'pictures and Popish trinkets' heaped up on the spot where Cheapside Cross had formerly stood. The

Th: bonfire
in Cheap-
side.

---

[1] Goring to the Queen, January $\frac{5}{15}$. *L.J.* vi. 375.

[2] *L.J.* vi. 378. [3] *A sacred panegyric.* E. 30, 2.

bonfire delighted the multitude. Inside the hall, as soon as the banquet was over, Dr. Burgess called upon all present to sing the eighty-fifth Psalm, the psalm of joy in the Divine forgiveness, of the union of mercy and peace, of truth and righteousness.[1]

In that song Cromwell and Warwick joined with Manchester and Essex. One day divisions might spring up between them, but for the present their hearts were united. No offer made by Charles had a chance of being taken seriously ; yet so little intelligence had Charles that the effect of the discovery of his intrigue with the City was simply to throw him back on his intrigue with the Independents. If any man had succeeded to the authority of Pym it was the younger Vane. In his advocacy of the most trenchant measures against the royal power, and in his conviction of the uselessness of negotiation, Vane's sentiments were even more decided than those of Pym ; but he had given proofs whilst he sojourned in America of his devotion to the new principle—still imperfectly understood even by many of its champions—of liberty of conscience. Through Lord Lovelace Charles now assured Vane of his readiness to grant that liberty.

Charles offers liberty of conscience to Vane.

Vane can never for one moment have supposed that Charles's mind had been suddenly illuminated. The befitting reply would have been to request Charles, as Philip of Spain had requested him at Madrid, to put his offers in practice before using them as a weapon of diplomacy. Instead of answering thus, Vane, himself not unversed in diplomatic art, affected to believe Charles to be in earnest, probably in the hope of discovering the secrets of the enemy. The negotiation was not long-lived, as its existence was soon discovered by Essex, who took offence at the initiation of a secret understanding without reference to himself. Incidentally the affair nearly led to a quarrel between the two Houses. The Lords were not only inclined to support Essex as a peer, but they were specially offended with Vane, as having thrown obstacles in the way of Holland's restoration to his seat in Parliament.[2]

[1] *A secret negotiation*, x. *Camd. Soc.* vol. viii.
[2] *Arti-Aulicus.* E 31. 17. *Baillie*, ii. 135.

One hope remained to Charles. If he could not divide his enemies, he might yet, through Mozley's treason, make himself master of Aylesbury. Anxious to strike the blow before his Oxford Parliament assembled on the 22nd, he sent out a force under Rupert himself to effect the surprise on the night of the 21st, in spite of the deep snow which covered the fields. To increase the number of troops at his disposal he withdrew his garrison from Towcester. The inclemency of the weather indeed saved him from a grave disaster. The forces which Essex, acting in concert with Mozley, was preparing to throw between the assailants and Oxford were prevented by the depth of the snow from stirring; but the mere refusal of Mozley to open the gates accomplished nearly all that Essex had desired. That night the long frost broke up, and gusts of warm wind turning the snow into slush made it hard for the weary soldiers to make good their footing, whilst the brooks which on the day before they had crossed with ease were now swollen into torrents. Some four hundred perished in the retreat, and Rupert, furious at the rebuff, was about to hang Ogle as a traitor, when Digby interfered to save him.

Jan. 21. The attempt on Aylesbury.

Jan. 26. The plot made known to Parliament.

On the 26th the main circumstances of the plot were made known to the Houses, but care was taken not to print evidence which might raise suspicion against the leading Independents.[1]

[1] *C.J.* iii. 378. Warburton (ii. 361) bases his account of the thaw on Rupert's Diary; but, as he knew nothing of Ogle's plot, his account of the attempt on Aylesbury is very unsatisfactory.

CHAPTER XIV

LIBERTY OF CONSCIENCE.

CHARLES's clumsy efforts to divide his opponents had only re
sulted in knitting them more closely together. Success never

1644.
Religious
liberty not
yet a pro-
blem for
practical
statesmen. attends those who play with great ideas for selfish
purposes ; and seldom indeed did Charles show any
sign of doing more than this. The idea of liberty of
conscience was as yet too new to be adopted by any of
those practical statesmen who had to rest upon that
general public opinion into which it had not yet insinuated itself ;
and though it is true that during the next few years special causes
brought it prominently before the thoughts of Englishmen,
there was no evidence of permanency in that early growth,
and it was not till a generation had passed away that it rooted
itself firmly in the soil. Yet already the pioneers were at work,
each cutting his way aloof from the other through the dense
thicket of the prejudice of centuries.

Neither of the two great parties into which England was
divided can claim the final victory as entirely their own. The

Two
tendencies
working for
liberty. sons of the Renaissance, who had been temporarily
merged in the Cavalier party, prepared the way for
Locke and the ' Letters on Toleration.' The sons of
the Protestant Reformation, temporarily merged in the Parliamentary party, prepared the way for Milton and the 'Areo-
pagitica.' Of the former the best representatives were Fuller
and Chillingworth, of the latter Roger Williams.

Of the larger-minded men who were working for liberty,
the most comprehensive in his genius was Thomas Fuller.
To a place amongst logical reasoners he makes no claim, but

the abounding wit which rested on his instinctive recognition of resemblances where no one else would have thought of

Thomas Fuller. looking for them was mentally connected with his still more abounding charity, ever finding points of sympathy in the midst of discord. His burly frame, his broad countenance beaming with good-nature, betokened a man with whom it was impossible to quarrel. The sharpest and most unjust criticism never drew from him an angry word. No one ever formed warmer or more enduring friendships, and before he died he counted amongst his friends, in addition to Cavaliers who had followed Charles in his adversity, at least one of that stern band which had sentenced their king to death. Such a career might have been that of a time-server, but a time-server Fuller never was. His warmth of heart and the roominess of his mind embraced every man of good-will, and fixed upon whatever of purity or nobleness might be in him as the bee fixes on the honey.

Fuller was a nephew of Davenant, the Calvinist Bishop of Salisbury, and as a member of the Convocation which passed

1640.
Fuller in Convocation; the new canons after the dissolution of the Short Parliament, he had opposed the system of Laud without siding with the stricter Puritans. In 1641 he sat in

1641.
in Williams's Committee; the sub-committee which strove, under the chairmanship of Williams, to prepare a scheme which might restore harmony to the Church. The Chapel of the

and at the Savoy. Savoy, whenever he preached as chaplain, was filled to overflowing with an enthusiastic and intelligent audience. If it was impossible for him to keep entirely aloof from the strife of the day, it was equally impossible for him to speak a word with any other object than to allay its bitterness.

During the first winter of the war Fuller made it evident that he had thrown in his lot with the Peace-party led by Holles and Maynard.[1] His first published sermon, preached on

---

[1] The materials for the early part of Fuller's history have been carefully worked up by Mr. J. E. Bailey in his admirable *Life of Fuller.* Mr. Bailey, however, writing at a time when the proceedings of the Peace-party were almost entirely veiled in MS., makes Fuller, in my opinion, too directly a Royalist at this period of his life. The language

December 28, 1642, is instinct with the sentiments to which these men were giving utterance in the House of Commons.

1642.
Fuller and the Peace-party.

Knowing that the peace propositions of the Lords had been accepted by the Lower House on the 26th,[1] he took for his text, " Blessed are the peacemakers." During the past weeks the cry of " No peace without truth ! " had been ringing through the streets. In answer,

Dec. 28.
Fuller's plea for peace.

Fuller avowed his conviction that during the two years which preceded the war England had possessed the truth in all essential points. The sword could not discern between error and falsehood. It had 'two edges, but never an eye.' In a fair discussion by a synod of divines, and in the ultimate arbitration of supreme authority, lay the only path of safety. "Think not," he added, defying the prejudices of his hearers as well as their opinions, " that the King's army is like Sodom, not ten righteous men in it, and the other army like Sion, consisting all of saints." [2]

Three months later, when, on March 27, 1643, Fuller preached at Westminster, his royalism was more pronounced.

March 27.
His roy-alism.

The negotiations at Oxford, though trembling in the balance, were not as yet wholly broken off, and the preacher, no longer content with a vague reference to the decision of the supreme authority, boldly exhorted his audience to rely on the promise of the King, and assured them that they would have no peace till the King brought it with him.[3]

A few days after this sermon was delivered the hopes of the Peace-party were dashed to the ground by Charles's exorbitant pretensions. Waller's plot was followed by the imposition of the Parliamentary Covenant, and this Covenant was taken by Fuller with certain reservations publicly stated. Then came the Royalist victories in the West, bringing renewed vigour to the friends of peace. On July 26 Fuller preached the most

used by Fuller about ' truth and peace' seems to me to bring him rather into connection with the middle party.

[1] See p. 81.
[2] *A Fast Sermon.* E. 56, 16.
[3] *A sermon preached at Westminster, on the 27th of March.*

noteworthy of his sermons, the sermon on Reformation;[1] a sermon in which he lifted up a standard round which all

July 26.
His sermon on Reformation.

who wished to find a tenable position between the narrowness of Laud and the narrowness of the Presbyterians of the new Assembly might safely rally. What the Whigs afterwards were in the political world, Fuller was at this time in the ecclesiastical world. All times, he urged, were times of reformation, of continual progress, in which old errors were swept away and new truths discovered. After urging that the supreme authority, whatever that might be, was alone to be trusted with the power of reforming the Church, he called on all his hearers to fulfil their own duty of reforming themselves. After this prelude he struck at the heart of the controversy. Beginning with a plea for the maintenance of historical continuity, he told his hearers plainly ' that a perfect reformation of any Church in this world may be desired, but not hoped for.' " Let Xenophon's Cyrus," he cried, "be king in Plato's commonwealth, and bachelors' wives breed maids' children in More's Utopia, whilst roses grow in their gardens without prickles, as St. Basil held they did before the fall of Adam. These fancies are pleasing and plausible, but the performance thereof unfeasible ; and so is the perfect reformation of a Church in this world difficult to be prescribed, and impossible to be practised. For besides that Satan will do his best, or rather his worst, to undo it, man in this life is not capable of such perfection. . . . I speak not to dishearten men from endeavouring a perfect reformation, but to keep them from being disheartened when they see the same cannot be exactly observed." Those who in the nineteenth century read these words of wisdom may almost fancy themselves in the presence of Burke denouncing Rousseau.

Fuller's growing royalism was but the result of his antagonism to the makers of systems, and as the makers of systems had

His flight to Oxford.

it all their own way at Westminster, his position soon became untenable. He was ordered to take the Parliamentary Covenant without reservations. He replied by

---

[1] *A sermon on Reformation.* E. 63. 3. See Bailey's *Life of Fuller,* p. 258, as corrected at p. 721.

flight to Oxford.   The later Solemn League and Covenant did
not even come into his hands.[1]

Fuller was no more at ease at Oxford than he had been in
London.   He was far too outspoken to avoid giving offence.

He urges the King to make peace.

In a sermon preached before the King he spoke of
'the blessings of an accommodation,' and pressed his
hearers to remember that the distractions of the kingdom 'could not be better allayed than by a fair condescension
in matters of Church reformation'   He was happier when, towards the end of the year, he left Oxford, and followed Hopton
into the field as chaplain of his army.[2]

"As for any transcendent extraordinary miraculous light,
peculiarly conferred on our times, the worst I wish the opinion

Fuller and the Puritans.

is this—that it were true."   In these words Fuller
flung down the gauntlet to the Puritan clergy.   He
had anticipated the sentiment of a later poet :

> 'Our little systems have their day ;
>   They have their day and cease to be.
>   They are but broken lights of Thee,
>   And Thou, O Lord, art more than they.'

From the Presbyterians who crowded the benches in the
Jerusalem Chamber, to the lay preacher who was the oracle of
an obscure Separatist congregation, there were few Puritans
who did not believe that there was some special plan of doctrine, or some special form of Church government appointed
by Heaven itself, and certain, if only it could obtain its due
recognition, to work out the moral and spiritual regeneration
of mankind.   Fuller's reluctance to abandon himself to sectional aims thrust him into a royalism which was, in many ways,
uncongenial to him.   It is indeed as a thinker rather than as a
Royalist that Fuller is to be judged.   He, and not the Puritans,
stood on the true line of national progress, though it must also
be acknowledged that without the Puritan that progress would
have been impossible, and that the enthusiast, the idealist, and
even the fanatic, has more part in shaping the destinies of his
country than the wise forecast of the solitary thinker, who
knows that life has many sides, but who fails to impress upon

---

[1] Fuller's *Church History* (ed. Brewer), vi. 267.
[2] Life prefixed to the *Church History*, i. xiv.

his contemporaries the conclusions of a mind with which they are in little sympathy.

Like Fuller, Chillingworth, in his hatred of dogmatism, had been driven to take part with the King. At Oxford he had learned that there were other sins as great as those of violence and rebellion. "Seeing," he declared in a sermon preached before the Court, "publicans and sinners on the one side, against scribes and pharisees on the other; on the one side hypocrisy, on the other profaneness; no honesty nor justice on the one side, and very little piety on the other; on the one side horrible oaths, curses, and blasphemies, on the other pestilent lies, calumnies, and perjury; when I see among them the pretence of reformation, if not the desire, pursued by anti-Christian, Mahometan, devilish means, and among us little or no zeal for reformation of what is indeed amiss, little or no care to remove the cause of God's anger towards us, by just, lawful, and Christian means; I profess that I cannot without trembling consider what is likely to be the event of these distractions." [1] "How few," he said in another place, "of our ladies and gentlewomen do or will understand that a voluptuous life is damnable and prohibited unto them!" [2] The men too came in for their share of blame: "They that maintain the King's righteous cause with the hazard of their lives and fortunes, but by their oaths and curses, by their drunkenness and debauchery, by their irreligion and profaneness, fight more powerfully against their party than by all other means they do or can fight for it, are not, I fear, very well acquainted with any part of the Bible." The London newspapers had hardly worse charges to bring than this.

Chilling-worth at Oxford.

His sermon on publicans and pharisees.

After such a sermon Oxford was no place for Chillingworth. He, like Fuller, took refuge with Hopton, the stout soldier, the lover of peace, the enemy of all license and irregularity of life. Being with him when he took possession of Arundel, Chillingworth was left behind stricken

Chilling-worth at Arundel.

---

[1] *Chillingworth's Works* (ed. 1838), iii. 14. The sermon is supposed to have been preached on October 13, but the exact date is uncertain. See Des Maizeaux, *Life of Chillingworth*, 283. [2] *Works*, iii. 9.

down by sickness in the bitter cold of a winter remarkable for the severity of its long frost. With the soldiers in the castle during its siege by Waller the great logician's relations were not happy. They resented his talk about Roman engineering, and fancied him a spy set over them by

1644. Jan. 9. Is a prisoner and falls into Cheynell's hands.

the Queen. When the castle surrendered Chillingworth was too ill to be removed to London. One of the ministers of the Assembly, Francis Cheynell, obtained permission from Waller to take the sick man with him to Chichester, where he tended him with all possible solicitude till he died.[1]

If Cheynell was tender-hearted he was also a controversialist. He had already, in a book published in May 1643, charged Chillingworth with Socinianism ;[2] and the charge, which was also brought against Hales and Falkland, was to be understood as implying not that he denied the divinity of the Saviour, but that he held doctrines which exalted human reason above faith and revelation. Sheer compassion for the sufferer joined with theological vanity in urging Cheynell to rescue the sick man from the pit of destruction into which he had fallen.

To Cheynell's arguments on the right of Parliament to make war against the King Chillingworth replied soberly. The soldiers in the Parliamentary army behaved like Christians, whereas there was 'little of God or godliness' amongst the King's soldiers. There were some arguments which made for the Parliament, but after all Parliaments were not infallible, and certainly war was 'not the way of Jesus Christ.' In speaking of public affairs, Chillingworth, ill as he was, was still at his ease. To more personal enquiries he answered little or nothing. When Cheynell asked 'whether he conceived that a man living and dying a Turk, Papist, or Socinian could be saved,' he answered that he did not absolve them and would not condemn them.' It was probably not mere bodily weakness which led Chillingworth to shrink from disputation. The minds of the two men were moving in different planes of thought, and Chillingworth at least could see well enough that

---

[1] He was still alive on January 23.

[2] *The rise, growth, and danger of Socinianism.* E. 103, 14.

controversy was useless. He pleaded for charitable dealing on the ground that he had ever been a charitable man. "Sir," replied his interrogator sharply, "it has been confessed that you have been excessive with your charity."

The well-intentioned torment grew worse and worse. The dying man was pestered with demands for the acknowledgment of the covenant of grace. A religious officer of the garrison implored Chillingworth to satisfy the world by a declaration of his religion. The wearying interrogations took no hold on him to whom they were addressed. He had declared his mind in his book, and he would say no more. Death at last, probably on January 30,[1] gave him the peace which his kind questioners would not give him on earth.

1644.
Jan. 30. (?)
Death of
Chilling-
worth.

Controversy pursued Chillingworth to the grave. There was a warm dispute between his friends who wished to inter him with honour in the chancel of the Cathedral and his enemies who wished to give him the burial of a dog. A middle course was ultimately adopted. It was thought fittest to permit his burial in the cloisters 'amongst the old shavelings, monks, and priests, of whom he had so good an opinion all his life. . . . Free liberty was granted to all the malignants of the City to attend the herse.' When the mourning followers reached the grave they were startled by the apparition of Cheynell carrying in his hands *The Religion of Protestants.* Chillingworth, he said, had once been a Papist, and he had not died 'of that faith or religion which is established by law in England.' "He hath," continued Cheynell, coming closer to the point, "left that fantasy which he called his religion upon record in his subtle book. He was not ashamed to print and publish this destructive tenet, 'that there is no necessity of Church or Scripture to make men faithful men,' in the 100th page of that unhappy book, and therefore I refuse to bury him myself; yet let his friends and followers who have attended his herse to this Golgotha know that they are permitted, out of mere humanity, to bury their dead out of our sight. If they please to undertake the burial of his corpse, I

His funeral.

[1] Des Maizeaux, *Life of Chillingworth,* 346.

shall undertake to bury his errors which are published in this so much admired but unworthy book ; and happy would it be for this kingdom if this book and all its fellows could be so buried that they might never rise more, unless it were to a confutation ; and happy would it have been for the author if he had repented of those errors, that they might never rise for his condemnation ; happy, thrice happy will he be if his works do not follow him, if they never rise with him nor against him."

Then, suiting the action to the words, Cheynell cast the hated volume into the open grave. "Get thee gone," he cried, "thou accursed book, which hast seduced so many precious souls ; get thee gone, thou corrupt, rotten book, earth to earth and dust to dust ; get thee gone into the place of rottenness, that thou mayest rot with the author and see corruption."

"Let the dead bury their dead," were the closing words of this remarkable address, "but go thou and preach the kingdom of God." Turning upon his heel, Cheynell ascended the pulpit to warn those who were willing to listen against the errors of him whose work he had bitterly condemned. He little knew that if his own name was not utterly to perish among men, it would be owing to connection with the scholar whom he sentenced to forgetfulness. In all probability the copy of *The Religion of Protestants* which he flung into the grave was picked out by one or other of the mourners almost as soon as his back was turned, and was long cherished as a memorial of the departed worthy.[1]

In modern times no words have been too hard to fling at the bigot who harassed a dying man with importunate questionings. The opinion which justifies a lawyer in troubling one sick unto death with questions about the disposition of his worldly property no longer justifies a clergyman in troubling him about his theological opinions. It might perhaps have been remembered in Cheynell's favour that he pronounced no positive sentence of damnation upon the heretic, and that at least in political matters his question, "Do you believe that tyranny is God's ordinance?" went more to the root of the matter, was more reasonable in short, than all

Nature of the controversy.

[1] Cheynell's *Chillingworthi Novissima.* E. 36, 7.

Chillingworth's appeals to the Biblical texts which he quoted in condemnation of rebellion. Still more might it be remembered that Cheynell was not contending for the mere chips of orthodoxy. He saw, and rightly saw, that the contention between him and Chillingworth was one beside which the mere struggle of the Civil War shrinks into insignificance. He who wrote 'that there is no necessity of Church and Scripture to make men faithful men' had lodged an appeal to human reason. Dimly in the distant future Cheynell descried, behind the bed of Chillingworth, the shadowy forms of Voltaire and the Commune of Paris.

Neither the sympathetic charity of Fuller nor the intellectual unrest of Chillingworth could occupy the whole ground needed to carry to victory the banner of religious liberty. Fuller and Chillingworth alike stood in opposition to the men of definite opinions and absolute convictions who fancied that the secret of Divine truth was attainable by themselves. Such they thought, as Marcus Aurelius thought of the Christians of old, were arrogantly lost in their own self-conceit, and were the authors of a discord which marred the harmony which all wise men sought to realise. Yet without these despised sectarians no complete solution of the problem was possible. Not only was it impossible to create a Church so comprehensive as to embrace all opinions, but it needed the stirring energy, the robustness of faith which is generated by definiteness of aim, to enable men to shoulder their way through a crowd careless or contemptuous of all who separate themselves from their fellows by their views of the spiritual world.

Incompleteness of the views of Fuller and Chillingworth.

The more peculiar each man's belief was the more need he felt for defence against persecution, and the more, if his sympathies were wide and his intelligence acute, he sought to erect his own necessity into a system which should protect others as well as himself. Hence the doctrine of the incapacity of the State to meddle in spiritual affairs, which was grasped by the early Separatists, and was handed down by Robinson to the Pilgrim Fathers. The settlers of Massachusetts, more numerous and exposed to greater

Views of the Separatists.

danger from colonists hostile to their principles than their neighbours at Plymouth, had abandoned to some extent the full doctrine of Robinson, and had not only made church-membership a condition of citizenship, but had exercised the right of expelling from their community men whose principles appeared

1641. to them to be dangerous. Even Mrs. Catherine
Mrs. Chidley's plea for toleration. Chidley, a female Separatist preacher, who in 1641 wrote ably in defence of her own sect, and who argued that kings are not to bear rule over the conscience, did not care to face the question of religious liberty as a whole.[1]

What the Separatists were to other Christians in the public estimation the Baptists, or Anabaptists, as they were then called, The Baptists. were to the Separatists. They still bore the burden of the misdeeds of the Anabaptists of Münster, whose name they shared, though they repudiated their vices. In the ordinary language of the day they were classed with Antinomians, who, theoretically or practically, held that their faith enabled them to wallow in sin without evil consequences to themselves.

Exposed as they were to contempt and persecution, the Baptists early rallied to the doctrine of a complete separation Separation between Church and State. In 1612 or 1613 an between Church and State. English Baptist congregation at Amsterdam declared its belief that "The magistrate is not to meddle with religion or matters of conscience, nor compel men to this or that form of religion, because Christ is the king and lawgiver of the Church and conscience."[2] This idea firmly took root

---

[1] *The Justification of the Independents' Churches*, by Catherine Chidley. E. 174. 7. At p. 44, in answer to the *reductio ad absurdum*, that if Separatists are tolerated Jews and Anabaptists must also be tolerated, she merely says, "For my part I speak for myself, and I suppose that they may say as much for themselves."

[2] Professor Masson, whose services in tracing out the growth of tolerationist principles it is impossible to exaggerate, is mistaken in supposing these words to occur in a confession of faith reprinted in Underhill's *Tracts on Liberty of Conscience* They are to be found in a confession appended to a tract by Piggott, which is printed from a unique copy as an appendix to Chapter vi. of Barclay s *Inner Life of the Religious Societies of the Commonwealth.*

amongst the Baptists, and found expression from time to time
in petitions and pamphlets, which were far more thorough in
their claim that liberty of conscience was the right of all men
than those put forward by the ordinary Separatists.

If the full doctrine of liberty was a natural result of extreme
exclusiveness and singularity, where was it more likely to be

1635.
Roger
Williams
in Massa-
chusetts.
found than in the mouth of Roger Williams, who, if
he was one of the most combative of reasoners, was
also one of the gentlest of men? There was
certainly no want of exclusiveness in him when he
flaunted his criticism in the faces of the pious and self-satisfied
New Englanders, reproving them as being devoid of the graces
of separation, because, having left their homes beyond the ocean,
in order that they might separate from a worldly Church, they
allowed those of their members who visited England to listen
to a sermon in a parish church, without bringing them under
ecclesiastical censures on their return. Nor was there any want
of singularity in his assertion—a serious offence in New England in the days in which Charles and Laud were at the height
of their power—that the patent on which the government of
Massachusetts rested was null and void, on the ground that the
King had no right to give away land which was the property

Williams at
Providence.
of the Indians.[1] Having been banished from Massachusetts as one who had run a-tilt against the settled
notions of the community, Williams removed to a spot which
he named Providence, where he laid the foundations of a State
the lands of which he had first taken care to purchase from the
natives, and in which the man who had known what it was to
battle unsupported for his solitary opinion announced that, as
far as legal and material penalties were concerned, absolute
liberty of conscience was to prevail.

Few except persons unlikely to be tolerated in more settled
communities could be expected to avail themselves of the open-

1639.
He becomes
a Baptist.
ing thus provided for the more extreme sectaries.
Williams himself became a Baptist not long after the
foundation of the colony at Providence, but three
or four months after his baptism he convinced himself that

[1] On this part of Williams's career see Dexter's *As to Roger Williams.*

perfection was not to be found even amongst the Baptists. He went out into the spiritual wilderness professing himself to be

Leaves the Baptists and becomes a Seeker. a Seeker, looking for a revival of apostolic power which might enfold him in the arms of that everlasting truth which he had sought in vain to find amongst men.[1]

Standing absolutely alone, Williams was of necessity a pleader for liberty of conscience. Before long he found an opportunity of upholding his principles on a more resounding stage than the New World had as yet to offer. The basis of

1641. Conflict in Providence. political right in Providence was placed on a voluntary compact between the settlers, but in 1641 a quarrel arose amongst them which made it necessary

1643. Williams in England. to seek elsewhere than in their own discordant wills for the means of maintaining peace. In 1643 Williams sailed for England to obtain from a pious Parliament the authority which he needed.[2]

The Houses were quite ready to take the colonies into their hands. On November 2, 1643, a Parliamentary ordinance

Nov. 2. Colonial Commissioners. appointed the Earl of Warwick and others to be Commissioners with power over the colonies.[3] On March 14, 1644, those Commissioners granted a charter to the inhabitants of Providence.[4]

During the winter Williams had found congenial occupation. On the one hand he travelled in search of fuel for the dis-

1644. March 14. A Parliamentary charter for Providence. tressed Londoners, whose supply of coals had been cut off by the Royalist occupation of Newcastle. On the other hand he thought out his great defence of religious liberty,[5] which was published in the following

February. Williams on liberty of conscience. July under the title of *The Bloody Tenent of Persecution.* The main principles of that more famous work were, however, embodied by him earlier in the year in a reply to a letter written by John Cotton, of

---

[1] Knowles's *Memoir of Roger Williams.*

[2] *Knowles*, 182.   [3] *L.J.* vi. 291.   [4] *Knowles*, App. E.

[5] *The Bloody Tenent yet more bloody.* E. 661, 6, p. 38. The time of the preparation of the book is fixed by the mention of the lack of coals, as the Sunderland coalfields were opened by the Scots in the spring.

Boston.[1] Williams in this reply reproved Cotton for holding
'that body-killing, soul-killing, and State-killing doctrine of not
permitting but persecuting all other consciences and ways of
worship but his own in the civil State, and so consequently in
the whole world, if the power of empire thereof were in his
hand.'[2] "Spiritual offences," said Williams again, "are only
liable to a spiritual censure."[3]

Williams, in his preface to *The Bloody Tenent*, quoted
Williams quotes Vane. with approbation the words of one who can hardly
have been other than the younger Vane, who was
already learning

> 'to know
> Both spiritual power and civil, what each means,
> What severs each.'

"Mine own ears," wrote Williams, "were glad and late witnesses of an heavenly speech of one of the most eminent of that
High Assembly of Parliament, . . . 'Why should the labours
of any be suppressed, if sober, though never so different? We
now profess to seek God, we desire to see light.'"

Between all these seekers after liberty there were points of
contact, but there were also points of variance. Fuller and
Chillingworth, charitable from a sense of the fallibility of human
reason and of the imperfection of human effort, longed for
peace through mutual concession, and through the acknowledgment of each man's right within certain very wide limits freely
to speak his own opinion. They stood on the King's side
because they feared the dogmatism of the Puritans and the
tyranny of the Covenant. Williams indeed, as one who was
but a stranger in the land of his birth, stood aloof from the controversies which agitated Englishmen ; but Vane at all times,
and even the Independents of the Assembly, at least after their
short dream of obtaining toleration from Charles was at an end,
were the bitterest opponents of all peace with the Royalists, of
any sort of compromise which would base the Church upon
anything but a strictly Puritan foundation.

[1] *Mr. Cotton's letter . . . examined and answered.* E. 31, 16. Thomason's note of the date of publication is February 5.

[2] *Ibid.* p. 6.   [3] *Ibid.* side note, p. 10.

Something was wanted to fill up the deficiencies of either
side.   Men like Fuller and Chillingworth had to learn that with-

Need of
more
complete
teaching.

out liberty of sectarian association the edifice of intellectual toleration which they would fain have reared
would echo with the shouts of the persecutor and the
cries of the oppressed.   Men like Williams and Vane had to
learn that liberty stood in need of a wide and more rational
culture than theirs.   That such a lesson should be really learned
by the many for years to come was absolutely impossible, and
that any single person should conceive the idea of teaching it
might well seem to be so improbable as to be all but impossible.

Nevertheless, the all-but-impossible was achieved by Henry
Robinson, the author of a tract, which, published in March

March.
A tract on
liberty of
conscience.

1644, four months before the appearance of *The
Bloody Tenent*, serves as a high-water mark of the
controversy on religious liberty in the seventeenth
century.   In *Liberty of Conscience, or the sole means to obtain*

Its political
advice.

peace and truth, the writer begins by suggesting
means for putting an end to the war which was
devastating the land.   He recommends the disbandment of
the armies and the demolition of the fortresses.   He recommends Parliament to abandon its intolerable demand for the
punishment of delinquents, and the King to forego the fulness
of his claims.   He thinks that if the habit of mutual consultation
were brought back, reconciliation would follow.   Mutual consultation, however, is only possible on one condition.   " Because,"

Its advice
that reli-
gious liberty
be the first
condition of
peace.

says the author, " I am verily persuaded that one great
reason which moved God to permit these kingdoms
to be thus divided and engaged in a civil war was the
general obstinacy and averseness of most men of all
ranks and qualities in each nation to tolerate and bear with
tender consciences and different opinions of their brethren,
unless they were thereunto so far necessitated that without it
there must inevitably ensue on both sides a total ruin and destruction ; . . . in this respect, as also in that I cannot think
that God suffered so much bloodshed either to establish the
King's prerogative or the privilege of Parliament only, but that

He hath yet a far greater work of His own to bring about, I humbly conceive that liberty of conscience may deservedly require to be first treated on, what and how far forth it may and ought to be permitted ; which being thoroughly debated and agreed on by both sides as the first article to be forthwith ratified by the three estates in Parliament, all the rest will doubtless follow more willingly and sweetly."

One exception only he makes to this sweeping demand. The worship of Catholics is to be prohibited as idolatrous, though they are to be freed from all fines and other penal consequences of their refusal to join in the worship of their countrymen. Beyond this there is to be no limitation to the complete establishment of liberty.

Suggested treatment of the Catholics.

Those who made this demand were neither lukewarm nor irreligious. They asked to be allowed ' to enjoy that religion which they have examined and found the true one, and not be subject to a change so often as the civil State or those of the highest court shall please to vary.' To the usual objection that the toleration of separate congregations would lead to confusion he has a peremptory answer. " I crave leave to ask," he writes, " if it be not a far greater confusion both before God and man, and of more dangerous consequence to the State and their own souls, for a thousand men and women of ten several religions or opinions to assemble together every Sunday [1] in a parish church for fear of imprisonment, fines, banishment, and worse, or else that the same thousand men and women, being permitted freely, may meet in a peaceable manner at ten several places, according to their respective differing opinions and religion ?" How little profit there was in outward conformity was shown by the enforced subscription of the Covenant. " Scarce one man in a hundred throughout all London but hath subscribed to it. I find notwithstanding by discourse that the greatest part of the people are little weaned from the present service-book, and wish better to Episcopacy a little reformed, rather than

Religious liberty does not create confusion.

---

[1] This is one of the many passages which show that the writer was not a Puritan of the strictest sort. If he had been, he would have written ' Lord's Day ' or ' Sabbath.'

Presbyterial or any other church government whatsoever; but for such as hold with Independency, how their stomachs can thoroughly digest the Covenant I cannot any ways imagine."

Still higher is the strain when the author rises to the great argument on which Milton was so soon to place the stamp of his resounding eloquence. "It is true," he says, "that if liberty be given for men to teach what they will, there will appear more false teachers than ever; yet it were better that many false doctrines were published, especially with a good intention and out of weakness only, than that one sound truth should be forcibly smothered or wilfully concealed, and by the incongruities and absurdities which accompany erroneous and unsound doctrines the truth appears still more glorious, and wins others to the love thereof." At last we reach the conclusion. "My humblest desires beg leave to prostrate themselves in meekness and most submissive manner unto the three estates in Parliament,[1] that all former Acts which countenance persecution for matters of religion may be repealed, and liberty of conscience, which is the greatest liberty the Gospel brings, restored; lest whilst the prevailing party of Protestants in England think it lawful to force other Protestants, because less in number and differing from them in opinion, to change religion, God in His justice permit Papists to do the like with Protestants in Ireland, as well for their sins as their own, to the further desolation of both kingdoms."[2]

False doctrine not the worst evil.

Danger of retaliation.

The word had at last been spoken which alone could heal the disorders of the times. Yet no evidence exists that any one at that day thought Robinson's arguments even worthy of

---

[1] In an earlier passage the writer says 'that it cannot be for the good of King and people that the three estates in Parliament, though arms were quite laid down, should stand severally on their negative voices.' The three estates must mean King, Lords, and Commons, an error which was being widely adopted since the breach with the King.

[2] E. 39, 1. Thomason's date of publication is March 24. The authorship of the pamphlet, which appeared anonymously, was correctly assigned to Robinson by Mr. Firth in the *Historical Review* for October 1894, p. 715. Robinson was a London merchant who wrote many controversial works.

a reply. In our own day they have remained neglected and unread.[1] There is a glory due to writers whose works have been so far in advance of the times as to be suppressed and burnt ;[2] but a greater glory is due to one whose work was so far in advance that no one considered it to be worth the trouble of burning.

[1] Its name occurs in the catalogue appended to Mr. Dexter's *Early Congregationalism*, and Mr. Underhill mentions it in the preface to his reprint of *The Bloody Tenent*, but he speaks of it in so slight a way that I doubt whether he had read it. Professor Masson, who seems to have known of every other pamphlet on the subject of toleration, does not even allude to it.

[2] On August 9, 1644, the House of Commons ordered the burning of Williams's books. *C.J.* iii. 584. *Liberty of Conscience* is, however, mentioned as one of four dangerous books in a sermon preached on September 25 by Seaman. E. 16, 23.

CHAPTER XV.

THE COMMITTEE OF BOTH KINGDOMS.

ALL the current of events was setting against peace. On January 19 the first regiments of the Scottish army crossed the

1644.
Jan. 19.
The Scots
cross the
Tweed.

Tweed, and the Royalists of Northumberland after a short hesitation withdrew to Newcastle, where the Marquis of Newcastle soon arrived to put himself at their head.[1]   In Cheshire, in the last weeks of 1643,

1643.
December.
Byron in
Cheshire.

Byron had made considerable progress against Brereton with the help of the English soldiers newly landed from Ireland.   One act of his indeed had roused that exasperation which is usually so dangerous to the

Dec. 26.
The mas-
sacre in
Barthomley
Church.

offender.   On December 26 he butchered to a man a detachment of Brereton's men who had taken refuge in the steeple of Barthomley Church, and who refused to surrender at the first summons.   " I put them all to the sword," he wrote triumphantly to Newcastle, " which I find to be the best way to proceed with these kind of people, for mercy to them is cruelty."   Unluckily for Byron, the letter in which this was written fell into the enemy's hands.[2]

Newcastle, fully occupied with resistance to the Scots, could send no help to Byron.   By the recapture of Gainsborough, which took place on December 20,[3] Sir Thomas Fairfax had

Dec. 29.
Fairfax sets
out to help
Brereton.

been liberated to bring help to Brereton.   On December 29 he set out.   His men were ragged and unpaid, and though he did what he could to relieve their wants out of his own purse, he had hard work to put them

[1] *The Scots army advanced.* E. 30, 16.   *The Scottish Dove.* E. 32, 12.
L.J. vi. 400.

[2] *Merc. Civicus.* E. 30, 7.   [3] *The Parliament Scout.* E. 79, 23.

in a condition to march. In the clothing towns of Yorkshire he was joined by many of his old soldiers, and he drew other reinforcements from Lancashire. Having effected a juncture with Brereton, he made for Nantwich, the only town in Cheshire which had not yet been lost to the Parliamentary cause

On January 25[1] the combined forces fell on Byron's besieging army. The thaw which a few days before had been

Jan. 25.
The battle of
Nantwich.

so disastrous to Rupert on his retreat from Aylesbury had flooded the Weaver, a stream which divided the forces of the Royalists, and Fairfax hoped to beat them in detail before they were able to unite. The ground, however, on which he himself had to advance was cut up with hedges, and his progress was so slow that the enemy had time to bring together his scattered forces. After some sharp fighting a sally of the garrison threw the Royalists into confusion. Two of the regiments from Ireland broke and fled. The officers retreated into Acton Church, and were forced to surrender. The victory was complete, and 72 officers and 1,500 privates fell into the hands of the conquerors.[2] Amongst the former was Colonel Monk, who had been arrested by Ormond's directions immediately upon his landing at Bristol, as one who could not safely be trusted, but had begged his release from Rupert, and had been allowed to take service under Byron.

The defeat of the troops from Ireland must have been hard

Conduct of
the troops
from
Ireland.

for Charles to bear. It was harder for him to know that it had been caused by a want of interest in his cause. Eight hundred of the prisoners took the Covenant and enrolled themselves under Fairfax.

"Truly, my Lord," wrote Byron to Ormond, "the enemy is grown so strong upon their late success, that without a larger

Byron calls
for the Irish.

supply we shall be able to do little good ; and I wish they were rather Irish than English, for the English we have already are very mutinous, and being for the

[1] Various dates are given in contemporary pamphlets. I follow Sir R. Byron, who was present at the battle.

[2] Fairfax to Essex, January 29. *Rushw.* v. 303. Sir R. Byron to Ormond, January 31. Carte's *Orig. Letters*, i. 40. Fairfax's *Short Memorial* in *Somers' Tracts*, v. 387.

most part this-countrymen, are so poisoned by the ill-affected people here, that they grow very cold in this service; and since the rebels here call in the Scots, I know no reason why the King should make any scruple of calling in the Irish, or the Turks if they would serve him." " I must renew my suit," he

Feb. 6.

wrote a week later, " concerning the sending over of a considerable number of Irish natives with as much speed as may be ; the English—excepting such as are gentlemen—not being to be trusted in this war." [1]

The mere talk of sending for native Irish was doing more to damage Charles's cause than the arrival of whole regiments could have done to support it. In London the weekly press played on the popular imagination. Fairfax had captured after the battle 120 Irish women, the wives or followers of the soldiers. One of the newspapers discovered that these women were armed with knives more than half a yard long, and it is likely enough that women who followed camps might sometimes need a good blade for purposes of self-defence. It was said, however, that there was a hook at the end of each knife, which was thus 'made not only to stab, but tear the flesh from the very bones.' Therefore the wretches were 'to be put to the sword, or tied back to back and cast into the sea." [2] Fairfax was more merciful than the scribblers in London, and allowed the poor women to return to their homes.[3]

Irish women taken.

The London newspapers did but echo the sentiments of their readers. "This victory," said one of their writers, "so successfully obtained, doth eminently confirm that general observation concerning the unsuccessfulness of his Majesty's forces since the coming over of the Irish, since which time his Majesty hath lost more of the English cavaliers than there have been Irish come over. Besides he hath lost the affections and assistance of most of his English subjects which were formerly addicted to neutrality.

Feb. 3.
A newspaper comment.

[1] Byron to Ormond, January 30 and February 6. Carte's *Orig. Letters*, i. 36. *Carte MSS.* ix. fol. 123.

[2] *The True Informer.* E. 31, 10. *Certain Informations.* E. 33, 10.

[3] *Merc. Veridicus.* E. 33, 23.

We may see how justly God doth avenge the blood of the innocent Protestants in Ireland, who are made a prey to the rebels and murdered in divers places by the occasion of the absence of those who should have defended them, but have now like vipers returned to eat out the bowels of their own mother." [1]

If these were the feelings evoked by the mere transportation from Ireland of English troops, what would have been the passionate detestation which would have stormed round Charles's head if he had succeeded in carrying Byron's wishes into effect, and had landed an army of Irish Catholic Celts on English soil ! Yet if he did not do this it was certainly not for want of will. Even at the time when he was coquetting with Vane and the Independents, he was giving a favourable ear to a scheme which, if it had succeeded in its entirety, would not only have made peace with his opponents hopeless, but would have cost him the hearts of at least half of his own followers.

English feeling against the Irish.

Nevertheless, unless Charles could set himself to conciliate reasonable men of both parties, hardly any policy was open to him except to appeal to every passion which he could enlist on his behalf, hoping that when he had trampled down his enemies he would be able through some fortunate chance to curb the heterogeneous elements which he had aroused. Mischievous as such a policy was, it was pressed on him by a little knot of men, to whom, as his manner was, he gave ear from time to time.

A dangerous policy.

The soul of this party, if party it can be called, was Montrose. For many months he had been urging Charles to vigorous action in the north, but his advice had fallen on closed ears. The approaching invasion of the Scots gave him the opportunity which he needed. Every Scotsman who had been on friendly terms with the invaders, or had been lukewarm in resisting them, was now regarded at Oxford as a public enemy. In November, Lothian, who had lately returned from a mission to France on which Charles had sent him, was cast into prison in Bristol Castle, upon his refusal to swear that he would

1643. Montrose at Oxford.

November. Imprisonment of Lothian.

[1] *The True Informer.* E. 31, 10.

never bear arms against the King.[1] On December 16 Hamilton and his brother Lanark, arriving at Oxford from Scotland, were

1644.
January.
charged with connivance with the Scottish Presbyterians in their resistance. Lanark succeeded in making his escape, but Hamilton was sent into close confinement in Pendennis Castle.[2]

Montrose, backed by Nithsdale and Aboyne, was all the while imploring Charles to return to the plan which he had re-

Montrose's
Scottish
scheme.
fused to adopt in the preceding spring. He himself, if only he could be fortified by a royal commission, would rally all loyal Scotland to the King, and would fall upon the rear of the invading Scots. Antrim, who was again at liberty, might bring over 2,000 Irish Celts to attack Argyle in his own country. His own part of the scheme would not be difficult. If Newcastle would lend him a small body of horse, he could easily make his way across the Lowlands to those lands beyond the Tay where his own estates lay, and where the great house of Gordon, represented at Oxford by Aboyne, was the bitter enemy of the Covenanting rulers of Scotland. If a party of German horse could also be borrowed from the King of Denmark, so much the better.[3]

Amongst the Oxford Royalists both Montrose and Antrim passed as mere adventurers. Digby, however, gave their scheme

Digby supports it.
Jan. 20.
Charles's
instructions
to Antrim.
a good word. It was probably in his hands that it grew beyond the limits of a merely Scottish enterprise. On January 20 Charles instructed Antrim—a man who had never performed a successful action in his life—to go to Ireland and to negotiate with the confederate

[1] *Ancram and Lothian correspondence*, lxviii. 155. *Baillie*, ii. 155.

[2] *Burnet*, 251–269.

[3] *Wishart*, 23. I see no reason to believe that Montrose had as yet thought of raising the Highlanders. Wishart's narrative points the other way. He says Montrose purposed to go '*in intima Regni*' (*Wishart*, ed. 1648, p. 61). Later on (p. 84) he says that some emissaries of Montrose penetrated '*in intima Scotiæ*,' and reported that the '*aditus, arces, urbes*' were occupied by the Covenanters. These were neither *arces* nor *urbes* in the Highlands. Wishart gives 10,000 as the number of the men to be sent with Antrim. This appears from the correspondence in the *Carte MSS.* to be wrong and is evidently transferred from the number planned to be sent to England

Catholics, not only for the 2,000 men needed for the expedition
to the Highlands, but to ask them for that complete army of
10,000, which had been offered in 1643 for service in England,[1]
together with the necessary arms and ammunition and the ships
required to bring them across the sea.   He was also to do his
best to bribe Monro to abandon his masters by the offer of
a pension of 2,000*l.* a year and a Scottish earldom.[2]   On

Feb. 1.   February 1 Montrose received a commission as Lieu-
His commis- tenant-General to Prince Maurice, who had been
sion to
Montrose.   named Captain-General of all the King's forces in
Scotland, probably in order to make it easier to obtain the
obedience of the proud Scottish nobles.[3]

Charles's difficulties would begin when, if ever, the time
arrived for putting in execution this marvellous plan.   Two days

Jan. 22.   after he signed his instructions to Antrim those
The Oxford   members of the two Houses who had obeyed his
Parliament.
             mandate appeared before him in Christchurch Hall.
He was not likely even to allude to the overtures which he had
just been making to the Irish.   In his opening speech he threw
stress on the Scottish invasion, and called on all loyal subjects

The King's   to join with him in repelling the strangers who had
opening   dared to set foot on English ground.[4]   "The King,"
speech.
             according to a London newspaper, "was bitter against
the Scots.   He had reason, for the Scots are irreconcilable to
the Irish rebels."   What were the sentiments of Charles's
audience we have no means of knowing ; Oxford shrouded its
discussions behind a veil of darkness.   In London it was

Alleged op   believed that Culpepper not only moved that propo-
position of   sitions of peace might be sent to Westminster, but
Culpepper.
             that a Bill 'against Papists.' should be prepared, and
that those who had been declared traitors to his Majesty before
the war began—that is to say, amongst others, Jermyn and Digby
—might be delivered up as delinquents.[5]   It is not probable
that such words were openly spoken, but there can be little

[1] See p. 123.   [2] Instructions to Antrim, Jan. 20.   *Clar. S.P.* ii. 165.
[2] Commission, February 1.   *Hist. MSS. Rep.* ii. 172.
[4] The King's speech.   *Rushw.* v. 560.
[5] *The Kingdom's Weekly Intelligencer.*   E. 30, 19.

doubt that at the time they represented the sentiments of many of the Royalist country gentlemen. And it was even now the policy of Hyde and Nicholas, and of the sterner adherents of the King's cause. Yet it is hardly to be wondered at that amidst the miseries of war Culpepper and others should have defended the scheme afterwards adopted by Shaftesbury, of granting concessions to the Puritans and refusing them to the Catholics. Between the two policies Charles drifted aimlessly. By temperament he was inclined to the first, whilst his interest, real or imaginary, drew him from time to time to take measures which would seem to involve the adoption of the second.

Of all this the records of the Oxford Parliament tell us nothing. On January 26 both Houses joined in a declaration that the Scots had broken the pacification of 1642, and must therefore be treated as invaders.[1] On the following day they despatched a letter to Essex, entreating his assistance in bringing about a peace on the ground of the King's readiness ' to receive advice for the preservation of the religion, laws, and safety of the Kingdom.'[2] The letter was signed by forty-four lords—amongst them the Prince of Wales and Prince Rupert, who had recently been created Duke of Cumberland—and by 118 members of the House of Commons. If the names of those who were unavoidably absent had been added, Charles would have had on his side an array of 82 Peers and 175 Commoners. He had therefore on his side the great majority of the Peers and about a third of the Lower House. Such a body would have been highly effective if Charles had been able to use it for conciliatory legislation, which might have rallied the lukewarm to his cause. As a medium of negotiation with the members at Westminster it was worse than useless. Its claim to be a Parliament at once raised the question whether the Westminster Parliament was a Parliament at all. When therefore Essex received, under cover from Forth, the letter of the Oxford Houses, he

Jan. 26.
Protest against the Scots.

Jan. 27.
The Houses write to Essex.

Composition of the Oxford Parliament.

Its mediation hopeless.

---

[1] Votes at Oxford, January 26. *Rushw.* v. 564.

[2] The Houses at Oxford to Essex, January 27. *Ibid.* v. 566.

declined to present it to those to whom it was addressed, sending in return a copy of the Covenant and a declaration by the Parliament at Westminster. In this declaration pardon was offered to all who would return to their duty and take the Covenant, though even in this case their estates were to be assessed for the relief of the public burdens.[1]

Jan. 30. Answer of Essex.

The first to take advantage of the overture was Sir Edward Dering, who, as he declared, was driven from Oxford by the King's refusal to dismiss Catholic officers.[2] He died not long afterwards in straitened circumstances, before his assessment was completed and his estate restored.[3] From that time a stream of converts began to flow from Oxford to London, as in the year before a similar stream flowed from London to Oxford. If the deserters were not numerous as yet, it must be remembered that it is hard for men when sides are once taken in a civil war to abandon their comrades, and it may fairly be argued that for every one who left the King at this crisis of his fortunes there were at least ten who were dissatisfied with his conduct. Charles's attempt to come to terms with the Irish Catholics was a more powerful dissolvent on the one side than the introduction of a Scottish army was likely to prove on the other.

Sir E. Dering's submission.

The Parliamentary leaders, on their part, were more than ever disposed to draw a clear line of demarcation between those who were Puritans and those who were not. If there was to be liberty of conscience at all, they were unanimous in thinking that it must not be granted to the supporters of the Book of Common Prayer. On February 5 an ordinance appeared directing that the Covenant should be taken by every Englishman over the age of eighteen, and though no specific penalty was mentioned, the names of all who refused to obey were to be certified to Parliament.[4] Some days

Feb. 5. The Covenant to be universally imposed.

---

[1] Declaration, January 30. Husband's *Collections*, 417.

[2] *The Kingdom's Weekly Intelligencer.* E. 31, 21.

[3] The sequestration was ordered to be taken off after his death. Order of August 22, 1644 (*C.J.* iii. 603). The Royalists said that Dering had left Oxford because the King would not make him Dean of Canterbury. See *Proceedings in Kent* (Camd. Soc.). [4] *L.J.* vi. 411.

before, on January 22, Manchester had been empowered by
ordinance to purify the University of Cambridge and
the associated counties generally, by ejecting all
members of the University and all holders of bene-
fices in the neighbouring counties who refused the
Covenant.[1]

The agony of Cambridge had been long drawn out. Ever
since Cromwell had frustrated the attempt made early in the
struggle to convey college plate to the King, heads
of Houses and learned doctors had dragged on a
precarious existence in their ancient haunts. In the first
months of the war three of the Heads of Houses had been
dragged up to London and flung into prison. Those who remained in the University were subjected to rude and unman-
nerly treatment. On a cold night in March 1643—Good
Friday was maliciously selected for the purpose—the Vice-
Chancellor and other chief personages in the University,
having refused to contribute to the Parliamentary taxation,
were kept till midnight in the public schools without food or
firing. The University preacher, proposing to preach, according to custom, a Latin sermon before the opening of term, was
set upon by the soldiers, and was glad to escape without suffering personal violence. The Book of Common Prayer was torn
to pieces in St. Mary's, in the presence of Lord Grey of Wark
and of Cromwell. Colleges were converted into barracks or
prisons, the dinners swept off the hall tables, and prized collections of ancient coins carried off for sale at their metallic
value. Only partisans indeed were likely to complain that
college timber was used, avenues of trees cut down, and
bridges destroyed, for the purpose of fortifying the town against
the enemy; but in those days a man was counted a partisan
who complained that a Parliamentary commissioner busied
himself with smashing the painted glass in the college chapels,
that Cromwell ordered the wood carvings in St. Mary's to be

[1] William Dowsing has left a curious journal, which was printed in
1786, of his proceedings in visiting the churches in Suffolk, where he
pulled down crosses and pictures, and tore up brasses on which were the
words *Orate pro animâ*, &c.

broken up,[1] or that Crawford was welcomed to Cambridge with a review of troops held in King's College Chapel.

The time was now come for a more sweeping change. For some weeks Manchester's chaplains, Good and Ash, were busily engaged in weighing the demerits of the members of the several foundations. All who were judged guilty of opposing the proceedings of Parliament—and the refusal of the Covenant was held to be a sure test of such opposition—were to be summarily ejected. In the end twelve Heads of Houses and 181 Fellows or persons officially attached to the colleges were sent adrift to shift for themselves. The more energetic of them gained a livelihood by teaching in schools ; others sought protection in the households of the Royalist gentry as long as the Royalist gentry had anything to offer. At Queens' College there was a clear sweep. Not a single member of the old foundation was left. The places of the ejected Heads and Fellows were filled with approved Puritans.[2]

The ejections.

The excluded Fellows were treated as Puritans had been treated before, and as Catholics had been treated earlier still. As long as the State is allowed to decide what religion is to be taught, it must begin by laying a heavy hand on the school and the college. Laud had understood this, and his Puritan successors were bettering his teaching. Their labour would be in vain. In the world of intellect was a current making for liberty, and amongst the very men imposed on Cambridge as the guardians of Calvinistic verity were some who, like Whichcot and Tuckney, were to shine forth as champions of intellectual freedom.

Logical as was the policy of those who bore sway at Westminster, it was only by an energetic prosecution of the war that it could be carried into effect. For some time it was evident that a firmer hand was needed at the helm. The strife between Essex and Waller might at any

Need of a Government.

---

[1] According to the author of *Querela Cantabrigiensis*, 17, this structure ' had not one jot of imagery or statue work about it.'

[2] *Ibid.* Fuller's *Hist. of the University of Cambridge*, sect. viii. 37.

moment burst again into a flame, and similar disputes might easily arise whenever military commanders claimed powers independent of one another. At this very time Parliament was engaged in an attempt to soothe the angry feelings with which Lord Willoughby of Parham regarded his supersession by Manchester in Lincolnshire, for which, as he alleged, no sufficient authority had been given by the Houses. The inferior officers took part with their respective commanders, and on January 22 Cromwell, in his place in the House of Commons, not only charged Willoughby with dereliction of duty in abandoning Gainsborough and Lincoln in the summer, but with encouraging 'loose and profane commanders,' one of whom had even directed a warrant to a constable directing him to bring young women to him for the worst of purposes.[1] Sir Christopher Wray, a Lincolnshire gentleman, warmly defended Willoughby, and three of Wray's sons inflicted a good cudgelling on one of Manchester's officers. Willoughby himself challenged Manchester to single combat.[2] The quarrel was with some difficulty appeased, and Willoughby was induced to return to his duty for a time,[3] in subordination to Manchester.

Ill-feeling between Manchester and Willoughby of Parham.

Jan. 22. Cromwell's attack on Willoughby.

On January 30, whilst this unseemly dispute was at its height, a motion was made by Crew in the House of Commons for the appointment of a small Committee of two or three members to treat with four Scottish Commissioners, whose speedy arrival was expected, in order to 'keep unity and prevent discontents between them and us,'[4] and to report to Parliament the conclusions to which they might come.

Jan. 30. Motion for a Committee to treat with the Scots.

The leadership of the war party—so far as weight or character and influence could give leadership—was now vested in Vane and St. John, and for Vane and St. John the ordinance which was drawn up to give effect to Crew's proposal did not go far enough. They at once

Scheme of Vane and St. John.

---

[1] D'Ewes's Diary. *Harl. MSS.* 165, fol. 280b.

[2] *L.J.* vi. 404. *C.J.* iii. 387.

[3] He took part in the operations against Newark.

[4] Yonge's Diary. *Add. MSS.* 18,779, fol. 57.

prepared another ordinance for the appointment of a permanent Committee of seven Peers and fourteen Commoners to
join with the Scotch Commissioners, not merely with the view
of reporting their opinions to the Houses, but 'for the better
managing the affairs of both nations in the common cause.'
What was contemplated was to supersede the existing Committee of Safety by a body which would be less absolutely
dependent on Parliament. Thinking apparently that their
chief difficulty would be with the Peers, they persuaded Say[1] to

Feb. 1.
The ordi-
nance pro-
posed by
them
adopted by
the Lords.

move it on February 1 in the Upper House. Either
Say took a favourable opportunity when his own
friends were in a majority or the Lords were in an
inattentive mood. They at once accepted the
ordinance, and, as far as in them lay, empowered the
new Committee[2] 'to order and direct whatsoever doth or may
concern the managing of the war . . . and whatsoever may
concern the peace of his Majesty's dominions.'[3]

In the Commons the new scheme met with violent opposition from the Peace-party, partly as having originated in the

Feb. 7.
A new ordi-
nance in the
Commons.

other House, but far more as threatening to establish
an executive Government which might ultimately
set aside the authority of Parliament itself. The
first objection was met by the introduction of a new ordinance,
in which the names were entered by a direct vote of the
Commons. On the other hand Vane and St. John yielded in
details. They inserted a provision that the Committee in treat-
ing with the Scots should only propound what they might
'receive in charge from both Houses,' and were 'to report
the results to both Houses.' With respect to military
operations they stood firm. The new Committee was to
'advise, consult, order, and direct concerning the carrying on
and managing of the war.' It was to be trusted with negotiations entered on with foreign States. On the other hand it was

[1] His name is given in *Merc. Aulicus* (E. 35, 27), and it is probably
correct.

[2] *L.J.* vi. 405. *C.J.* iii. 384. D'Ewes's Diary. *Harl. MSS.* 166, fol. 64.

[3] *C.J.* iii. 504. This particular ordinance was ultimately adopted by
the Commons under peculiar circumstances on May 22.

to have nothing to do with any cessation of arms or treaty of peace with the King without the express order of Parliament.[1]

When the new ordinance reached the Upper House the Peers opened their eyes to the effect which it would have upon

Feb. 8.
The Lords' amendments.

themselves. To the Lords, weak in number and reputation, the appointment of the new Committee, to the importance of which they had been blind a few days before, appeared now to be a far heavier blow than it could be to the Commons. They would no longer be consulted as heretofore on every matter of military detail, and they could no longer hope that their wishes would be indirectly taken account of. They fought hard on every point on which it was possible to resist, struggling longest on the clause which em-

Feb. 16.
The Lords give way;

powered the Committee to order and direct all military matters. On February 16 they gave way, and the Committee of Both Kingdoms, as it was styled came into existence for a limited period of three months, under the conditions insisted on by the majority of the Commons.[2]

" Craven Lords ! " was D'Ewes's cyphered exclamation entered in his diary, as he announced the result of the conflict.[3]

Feb. 24.
but refuse to allow the new Committee to take an oath of secrecy.

On a point subsequently raised the Peers held out with more success. They objected to the imposition on the Committee of an oath of secrecy, on the ground that every member of either House had a right to know all that concerned the affairs of the State,[4] and for a time at least the Commons, who had favoured the suggestion, gave way before the objection.

The Committee thus brought into existence numbered amongst its members Essex and Warwick, Manchester and

Composition of the Committee.

Northumberland, Waller, St. John, Cromwell, Hazlerigg, and the two Vanes, besides the Scottish members, Loudoun, Maitland, Johnston of Warriston, and Barclay. Its influence on the conduct of the war could not

---

[1] Compare the Commons' ordinance at *C.J.* iii. 392, with the previous one of the Lords at *C.J.* iii. 504. See also Yonge's Diary, *Add. MSS.* 18,779, fol. 59; Whitacre's Diary, *Add. MSS.* 31,116, fol. 113 ; D'Ewes's Diary, *Harl. MSS.* 166, fol. 9.   [2] *L.J.* vi. 418-430.

[3] D'Ewes's Diary. *Harl. MSS.* 166, fol. 14.   [4] *L.J.* vi. 440.

fail to be considerable. To the constitutional historian the ordinance by which it was appointed is important as containing not only the first germ of a political union between England and Scotland, but also the first germ of the modern Cabinet

Germ of the Cabinet system. system. As far as the English members of the Committee were concerned, it was a body composed of members of both Houses, exercising general executive powers under responsibility to Parliament, and not merely, like the old Committee of Safety, a mere channel to convey information to Parliament and to take its orders. Though it was not, like a modern Cabinet, composed of persons of only one shade of political opinion, the opinion that the war ought to be carried on with vigour was decidedly preponderant in it. The opposition of the Lords to the oath of secrecy may be paralleled with the insertion into the Act of Settlement in 1701 of the clause which bound Privy Councillors to append their signatures to their advice.

That the Committee thus instituted could never be more than an interesting experiment was the natural result of the fact

Negotiation talked of. that the Parliament from which it sprung had no claim to be regarded as a national body. Both at Westminster and at Oxford the war spirit was predominant. Yet at Oxford there was at least a show of anxiety to treat. Charles was always honestly desirous of putting an end to the war, if only he was not expected to abandon any of his claims. Early in February an embassy from the States-General, offering

Feb. 19. Fresh overtures from Oxford. to mediate, was courteously received by him.[1] On the 19th a letter was despatched by Forth to Essex asking for a safe conduct for messengers charged with overtures of peace. On the reply of Essex that the request

March 3. The King's letter. must be addressed to Parliament, the King himself wrote a letter to the Houses, styling them 'The Lords and Commons of Parliament assembled at Westminster,' and proposing, 'by the advice of the Lords and Commons of Parliament assembled at Oxford, that Commissioners might meet to discover a way to peace, and

---

[1] The Ambassador to the States-General, February $\frac{15}{25}$. *Add. MSS.* 17,677 R. fol. 216. *The Parliamentary Scout.* E. 38, 18.

especially to consider how 'all the members of both Houses' might 'securely meet in a full and free convention of Parliament.'

The formal difficulty which Charles had attempted to evade had not been evaded. On March 9 the Houses at Westminster

March 9. *Its rejection.* refused to treat on the basis of an acknowledgment that their rivals at Oxford were in any sense members of

March 12. *The Oxford Parliament declares the members of the Westminster Parliament traitors.* Parliament. On March 12 the Oxford Parliament took up the challenge, and declared the members of the Houses sitting at Westminster, together with their abettors, as well as all persons who had taken part in the introduction into England of the invading Scots, to be guilty of treason.[1] There had never

been much expectation among the Royalists that the proposal to negotiate would be accepted. One of Rupert's correspondents kept him informed of what was passing. "Not," he added, "that I dream of success, but because I would have their shame perfect."[2] In fact the overtures failed, not merely on the formal ground alleged, but because the intellectual basis of peace had not been discovered.

At Oxford, Parliament turned its attention to preparations for war. Early in February it authorised Charles to issue

Privy Seal loans. *Excise.* Privy Seals for a loan of 100,000*l.*,[3] and it subsequently granted an excise, in imitation of the excise ordinance at Westminster.[4]

Finance was arrayed against finance. That more money would be brought into the treasury at Westminster than into

Comparison between Royal and Parliamentary finance. the Treasury at Oxford could hardly be doubted, but the outgoings at Westminster were far larger than the outgoings at Oxford. The King had no navy to support and no Scottish army to subsidise. The enormous burden of the expenses, which fell heavily on the counties subject to Parliament, made all men anxious for peace, though they might differ as to the best mode of obtaining it. The more thoroughgoing Puritans looked hopefully for a re-

---

[1] *Rushw.* v. 565.
[2] Trevor to Rupert, February 24. *Add. MSS.* 18,981, fol. 60.
[3] *Rushw.* v. 580.   [4] *Clarendon,* vii. 396.

construction of the army, and it was rather on the forces now gathering under Manchester than upon those commanded by Essex that their eyes were fixed. There at least the idea which had emanated from Cromwell of an army animated by the strongest Puritanism seemed likely to be carried out. Manchester's troops, it was said by a London newspaper, would be 15,000 strong. "Neither," continued the writer, " is his army so formidable in number as exact in discipline ; and that they might be all of one mind in religion as of resolution in the field, with a severe eye he hath looked into the manners of all those who are his officers, and cashiered those whom he found to be in any way irregular in their lives or disaffected to the cause. This brave army is our violets and primroses, the first-fruits of the spring, which the Parliament sends forth this year for the growth of our religion and the reimplanting of this kingdom in the garden of peace and truth." [1]

Composition of Manchester's army.

With this opinion on the true mode of aiming at peace and truth, so different from that of the tract on liberty of conscience, Cromwell fully sympathised. Utterly intolerant of the worship and doctrine which found favour at Oxford, his one aim was not to conciliate the foes of Puritanism, but to crush them. To him the Book of Common Prayer contained but the weak and beggarly elements of an outworn creed. On January 10 he had appeared in Ely Cathedral to order a clergyman who persisted in using the 'choir service' to desist from so 'unedifying and offensive' a practice. The clergyman refused. Cromwell, who was Governor of the Isle of Ely, went out, fetched some soldiers, and returned. "Leave off your fooling and come down," was the peremptory order, and the Ely congregation was driven out in much the same way as the Long Parliament was driven out nine years later. [2]

Cromwell intolerant of the Prayer Book.

Jan. 10. Cromwell in Ely Cathedral.

For a 'choir service' Cromwell had no tolerance. It was sheer Popery, and as such to be suppressed with a strong hand. Inefficiency or faint-heartedness in that work of repression was

---

[1] *The Weekly Account.* E. 35, 23.
[2] Walker's *Sufferings of the Clergy*, Part II. p. 23.

the one unpardonable crime in his eyes. With that masterful temper which marks the ruler of men, he had shouldered aside Lord Willoughby as he was afterwards to shoulder aside men far more conspicuous. The one characteristic which attracted him was zeal in the Puritan cause, and he had too keen an eye, too much real earnestness himself, to be satisfied with any merely hypocritical semblance of zeal. For the nice questions which divided Puritanism he cared nothing. He was profoundly indifferent as to forms of church government, as long as these forms were not used to restrain the zealot, nor did he ever interest himself in those disputations about nice points of doctrine in which his comrades delighted. Yet, if he turned aside from their arguments, he was in full sympathy with the arguers, because the practical instinct, which placed him intellectually above them, was combined with an enthusiasm, sometimes kindling into fanaticism, which drew him to all enthusiasts. Thus it was that in him and around him sprung up a new doctrine of toleration, which may be termed a fighting doctrine of toleration. Without the broad intellectual sympathy which made Fuller and Chillingworth tolerant, and not having been personally exposed to the scorn and persecution which made Roger Williams tolerant, he conceived service to the Puritan cause to be the measure of toleration, just as Charles conceived service to the Royalist cause to be the measure of that liberty to tender consciences which he was perpetually announcing. The difference between the two men was that, whilst Charles's doctrine never went farther than his lips, Cromwell's rooted itself in his heart.

Becomes tolerant for fighting purposes.

It was probably a growing feeling of dissatisfaction with the principles of the Presbyterians in the Assembly which led Cromwell to defer so long his adhesion to the Covenant. During a great part of January he was at Westminster, but the Covenant remained unsigned by him. It was not till February 5, the day on which the ordinance enforcing the Covenant was issued,[1] that he registered his formal acceptance of it, doubtless placing special emphasis

Feb. 5. Cromwell signs the Covenant.

---

[1] *C.J.* iii. 389.

on Vane's saving words, 'according to the Word of God.'
Something, too, may be due to the fact that he had just
Appointed
Lieutenant-
General. been appointed Lieutenant-General in Manchester's
army—a post which he would not be permitted to
hold unless he signed the Covenant.[1]   With the
Covenant in its denunciation of the Church of the Royalists
March. Cromwell was in full sympathy.   Since his appointment he had been actively engaged in the country
round Newport Pagnell, under orders to secure the safe arrival
at Warwick of a supply of ammunition on its way to Gloucester,
March 4. which town was by this time again in distress.[2]   On
Hillesden
House
taken. March 4 he captured Hillesden House, an advanced
post of the Oxford Royalists.[3]   On the 10th he
was at Cambridge, where he found one Lieutenant Packer,
who had been sent there under arrest by Crawford from
Buckingham.

Laurence Crawford was a Scotchman who had served
under Ormond in Ireland, and who had made his escape to
Major-
General
Crawford. England when called on to take an oath expressive
of detestation of the Covenant, and to bear arms
against his own countrymen in Ulster.[4]   His military
knowledge and his proved fidelity to Puritanism had gained
him access to the Parliamentary leaders, and he had recently
received the appointment of Major-General in Manchester's
army.   His Puritanism, however, was of the narrow Scottish
type, and having discovered that Packer was an Anabaptist, he
had sent him to Manchester to be examined.   Manchester,
however, was either absent from Cambridge or otherwise

[1] We do not know the exact date of Cromwell's appointment, but
Crawford's commission as Major-General amongst the *State Papers* is
dated February 1, and it seems probable that Cromwell's commission was
issued on the same day, or, at all events, not long before or after.

[2] This has given rise to an unfounded supposition, which was adopted
by Carlyle, that Cromwell conveyed the ammunition to Gloucester itself.
See *The Scottish Dove*. E. 34, 3.

[3] Luke to Essex, March 6. List of the prisoners. *Egerton MSS.*
785, fol. 5b, 8b.

[4] Crawford to Ormond, November 26. Vaughan to Ormond, November
28, 1643. *Carte MSS.* vii. fol. 606, 623.

engaged, and Cromwell sent Packer back to Buckingham with a letter to the Major-General.

"Surely," wrote Cromwell, "you are not well-advised thus to turn off one so faithful to the cause, and so able to serve you as this man is." It was said that Packer was an Anabaptist. "Admit he be, shall that render him incapable to serve the public? . . . Sir, the State in choosing men to serve it, takes no notice of their opinions; if they be willing faithfully to serve it—that satisfies. I advised you formerly to bear with men of different minds from yourself. If you had done it when I advised you to it, you would not have had so many stumbling-blocks in your way. Take heed of being sharp, or too easily sharpened by others, against those to whom you can object little but that they square not with you in every opinion concerning matters of religion."[1]

How to get the best soldiers was the problem which made Cromwell tolerant, and tolerance built upon so material a foundation would to the end have something in it narrower than Chillingworth's craving for the full light of truth. Cromwell, with all his massive strength, remained always the practical man, asking not so much what the thing is as how it can be done.

Manchester's army was not yet what Fairfax's afterwards became in the main—an army of Sectaries; but under Cromwell's protection the Sectaries were strong within it. Like the followers of the Laudian reaction, the Sectaries gathered strength from the decline of sympathy with Calvinism which set in early in the seventeenth century. To cultivated, scholarly minds dislike of Calvin's discipline showed itself in a craving for somewhat of intellectual liberty, and for a form of worship which had nothing to jar upon their sensitive perceptions. To the sturdy peasant or artisan, whose sole literature was the Bible, and whose earnest but narrow vision was hampered by no traditional interpretations, it was easy to pick out passages which lent themselves to well-nigh any interpretation whatever. Yet it was not the variety of opinion, however marked, which was the special characteristic of these enthusiasts. It was rather their aim at that ideal perfection which Fuller

Character of the Sectaries.

[1] *Carlyle,* Letter XX.

had wisely declared could never be attained by any earthly Church. The nickname of Donatists—taken from those African Christians of the fourth century who refused Church fellowship to all who had shown the slightest weakness in the days of persecution—with which Fuller had attempted to brand them was not wholly undeserved. Separatists existed because they were resolved to draw round themselves a fence of orthodoxy and holiness which would keep them apart even from men of ordinary honesty and righteousness whose spiritual attainments were, as they believed, inferior to their own. Baptists existed because there were those who could not conceive that anything short of the strong heartfelt conviction of the adult could make him a fit subject of the ordinance which was the sign of the Christian profession, whilst Roger Williams tore himself asunder from the Baptists because the ideal which he followed was too high and glorious to be realised even by those who, in the fulness of their years of discretion, had set themselves to live a purer and more divine life than that which seemed possible to the New England Separatists.

In the normal condition of society the enthusiast and the man of common sense plays each his appointed part. Unless, on the one hand, there are those who attempt to shape their lives and the lives of others by a standard which never can be realised, and which does not perhaps deserve to be exclusively realised, stagnation will set in. Unless, on the other hand, there are those who apply to such efforts the criticism either of practical sense or of the cultivated intellect, the world will become the prey of chimeras. In 1644, however, the condition of society was anything but normal. The uncultured enthusiasts suddenly found men to discipline and train them who could give them the cohesion which they needed. For a time, but only for a time, they would carry all before them ; they would strive to mould the nation, of which they became the masters, after their own likeness. It would be all in vain. The cold tenacious resistance of use and wont would be too much for them. The Church of England, with its historic memories and its literary culture, was not about to transform itself into a congeries of Separatist congregations, any more than the well-worn social structure of the realm was about to transform itself into an ideal democracy 'fearing God and hating covetousness.'

Yet if the sword of Marston Moor and Naseby was to drop from the hands of a disconcerted soldiery on Blackheath, it was not in vain that such as these bled and suffered. Salvation for a people does not lie in that reverence for authority or in that distrust of ignorant energy which marked the Royalists, nor yet in that respect for the predominance of theological learning which was the mark of the Presbyterian. It lies in those who, however much they may wander from the path, are ready to offer up their lives for that which appears to them to be the highest spiritual good for themselves and for the world.

The time for peace was not yet. The men after Cromwell's heart were no lovers of war, but they had come to believe that such peace as they would have must be reached through victory, and not through negotiation. They had their own sorrows, and they knew well what desolation was spreading over England. Scarcely was the ink dry on Cromwell's letter to Crawford, when he learned that his eldest surviving son, the

Death of Cromwell's son. Oliver who had fought at Edgehill, was dying of small-pox in the garrison at Newport Pagnell. The young soldier was, as one who seems to have known him testified, 'a civil young gentleman, and the joy of his father.'[1] Such sorrows fell thickly in those years. Cromwell had a tender heart, but he turned away from the mourner's part, leaving the dead to bury their dead, and—so he seems to have read the text—to fight for the kingdom of God.

[1] *The Parliament Scout*, March 15-22. E. 38, 18. The passage has a genuine ring about it, and I am quite incredulous about the story told in the *Squire Papers*, that Cromwell's son was killed in a fight at Knaresborough just before Marston Moor. Of all the numerous letters and pamphlets, including the official despatches of the Committee of Both Kingdoms, which treat of the Marston Moor campaign, not one mentions such a fight; and it is hard to see how it could have taken place without notice being taken of it. On the other hand, I have learnt from Mr. Ottley, the Vicar of Newport Pagnell, that the name of Oliver Cromwell does not occur in the register of burials, though I hardly think, unless the registers were kept with unusual care, that the fact is of much importance.

CHAPTER XVI.

NEWARK, CHERITON, AND SELBY.

WHILST the weapon was being forged which was ultimately to bring ruin to Charles's cause the Royalist commanders were

1644. Course of the war in the North.

not inactive. It required no great clearness of vision to discern the danger which overhung the North, or the necessity of striving to the uttermost to recover the ground which had been lost at Nantwich. Newcastle, fearing to be crushed between the Scots and the Fairfaxes,

Jan. 28. Newcastle calls for help.

had loudly called for help. Though the younger Fairfax was still detained in Cheshire, his military hold upon the clothing towns of Yorkshire was complete. The West Riding, wrote Newcastle, was in the hands of Sir Thomas, and the East Riding in the hands of his father. Manchester would soon be bringing his new army into Yorkshire. To oppose these combined forces he was himself able to muster no more than 5,000 foot and 3,000 ill-armed horse. All other enterprises in the North must be laid aside in order to destroy the Scots. "If your Majesty," he wrote

Feb. 16.

on February 16, "beat the Scots, your game is absolutely won. . . . For Lancashire and Cheshire, if you should think fit, they should lie fallow for a while." [1]

Newcastle may well have been anxious. By this time not

Parliamentary successes in Yorkshire.

only had Lord Fairfax become completely master of the East Riding, but he had been able to despatch Sir William Constable to overrun the North Riding. To capture Scarborough was beyond Constable's power, but he had secured Whitby without difficulty. Newcastle, leaving a

[1] Newcastle to Rupert, January 28. Lucas to ——, February 2. Newcastle to the King, February 16. *Warburton*, ii. 368, 370, 384.

strong garrison to defend the town from which he derived his title, had taken the field. His force, however, was but a small one, and he had never shown signs of that strategical skill which sometimes makes up for deficiency of numbers. His military adviser, Lord Eythin, was a methodical commander from the school of the Thirty Years' War.

Wherever it was felt that the services of a methodical commander were insufficient, the cry was raised for Rupert.

Feb. 6.
Rupert sets out for the North.

Rupert was already on the way. Some troops he took with him, but an army adequate to the work before him was still to be collected. The title of President of Wales had lately been conferred on him, and Wales was always a good recruiting ground. On the 21st he was at Shrewsbury, and before long, gathering men around him as best he could, he made his way to Chester.[1] He was

March.
Lathom House.

there met by applications for help from all quarters The Earl of Derby pleaded hard with him to hasten to the assistance of his Countess, who had bidden defiance from behind the walls of Lathom House to all the efforts of the Lancashire Parliamentarians.[2] Rupert thought that Lathom House could hold out without relief for some time to come, and he had more important matters to consider than a lady's distress. Meldrum and Willoughby were besieging Newark, and if Newark fell all possibility of cutting in two the hostile line which now stretched from north to south would be for ever at an end.

An order from the King decided Rupert's choice. On March 13 he started for Newark.[3] Picking up scattered de-

March 13.
Rupert sets out for Newark.

tachments from every Royalist garrison he passed, he found himself on the 20th[4] at Bingham, some twelve miles south-west of the fortress which he was hastening to relieve. At two on the morning of the 21st he was again in the saddle. Sweeping round Newark, he reached

---

[1] Dugdale's *Diary*. Intelligence from Shrewsbury. *Egerton MSS.* 785, fol. 126b.   [2] Derby to Rupert, March 7. *Warburton*, ii. 382.

[3] Robert Byron to Ormond, March 14. *Carte MSS.* ix. fol. 534.

[4] On the 19th according to the Royalist narrative, but this is evidently a mistake.

the Beacon Hill with his advanced guard of horse between eight and nine, the rest of his little army with the artillery being still two miles behind.   Rupert's sole notion of tactics was to charge the enemy, and this time he could have found no better.   The bulk of Sir John Meldrum's army had abandoned the siege works, and were crowded round the shell of a house known as the Spittle,[1] which had been burnt in the siege of 1643, and which lay by the river's side outside the gate of the town.   Immediately in front of Rupert, at the foot of a gentle slope, was a body of horse.   Perceiving signs of wavering amongst them, he gave the word to charge.   There was a short resistance, and then victory and a chase.   The arrival of Rupert's infantry and a sally from the garrison of the town rendered Meldrum's position hopeless, especially as the men whom he had placed to secure his retreat by guarding the bridge over the Trent deserted their post and fled to Nottingham.   On the following morning Meldrum capitulated.   His troops were to march away, but his siege artillery, together with three or four thousand muskets and a large number of pikes and pistols, were to remain in the hands of the victors.[2]

*March 21.
The relief
of Newark.*

*March 22.
Meldrum
capitulates.*

Congratulations poured in upon Rupert from all sides. Yet the result of this brilliant achievement was barely more than negative.   At the head of a coherent army Rupert would doubtless have hewn his way into the heart of the Eastern Association, and would either have made all co-operation between Manchester and the Scots impossible, or would have perished in the attempt.   Rupert's troops, however, were for the most part derived from scattered garrisons, and could not be spared for many days.   He had indeed gained arms for his new levies, and in Charles's armies arms were always harder to come by than men.   Gainsborough, too, was dismantled and abandoned by the Parliamentary garrison,

*Results of
the victory.*

[1] It is near the place where 'the King's sconce' is marked on a map of the siege of 1646 in the Museum Library.   See Thoroton's *Hist. of Nottinghamshire*, i. 390.

[2] *His Highness Prince Rupert's raising of the siege of Newark.* E. 38, 10.   *A brief relation of the siege of Newark.* E. 39, 8.

and Lincoln, Sleaford, and Crowland were rapidly overpowered. Yet what was the gain of a few scattered posts without an army to support them? Before long Rupert had returned the greater part of his force to the garrisons from which they had been taken, and was once more in Wales levying contributions, by means of which he hoped to raise an army which he might permanently attach to his person.[1]

Rupert's diversion at Newark made Newcastle again clamorous for aid. He had found himself unable to maintain
Newcastle
and the
Scots.
his ground against the Scots in the neighbourhood of Sunderland, and, leaving them to complete their preparations for the siege of Newcastle, had fallen back on Durham. The number of his enemies was ever on the increase. "They say," he wrote to Rupert, "Sir Thomas
March 29.
Newcastle
urges
Rupert to
help him.
Fairfax is coming into Yorkshire for certain, which will much disturb his Majesty's affairs here. Could your Highness march this way, it would, I hope, put a final end to our troubles ; but I dare not urge this, but I leave it to your Highness's great wisdom." "I thought," he added plaintively in a postscript, "my Lord Byron would have followed him close. Your Highness's presence would dissolve him." [2]

Not the will but the power was wanting to Rupert. The sense of being overmatched was growing on the Royalists. If Rupert's presence in the North brought hope to the King's struggling partisans in Yorkshire and Lancashire, it was regarded with despair in the South. Scarcely had he reached
April 3.
Rupert
recalled.
Wales when a despatch arrived summoning him in hot haste to Oxford, and although the order
April 4.
The order
counter-
manded.
was countermanded on the following day,[3] that it should have been given at all was a sure sign how far the King's fortunes had ebbed since the days of Adwalton Moor and Roundway Down. Charles had indeed

---

[1] *The Weekly Account.* E. 40, 16. Porter to Rupert, April 1. Sir R. Byron to Rupert, April. *Add. MSS.* 18,981, fol. 119, 120. Proclamation, March 29. *Warburton,* ii. 401.

[2] Newcastle to Rupert, March 29. *Warburton,* ii. 400.

[3] Digby to Rupert, April 3, April 4. *Add. MSS.* 18,981, fol. 126, 130.

suffered a defeat in Hampshire which was only less than a serious disaster.

In the last week in February the Parliamentary commanders of the Southern forces had held serious consultations in London. The plan of the campaign laid down combined an attack on the King's position at Oxford, which was to be entrusted to Essex, and an effort to reconquer the West, which was to be made by Waller. As far as it is possible to judge by events, the latter prospect was altogether premature, but there was always a temptation on both sides to go beyond military exigencies in the acquisition of territory, as every square mile of ground gained added something to the financial resources of one side and deducted it from the other. This time, however, the members of the council of war fixed their immediate hopes on a plan which, if it had been conceived by Charles, they would have stigmatised as treachery, but which, as coming from themselves, they doubtless regarded as a mere stratagem of war.

The Parliamentary plan of campaign in the South.

Basing House was in the custody of Lord Charles Paulet, the brother of the Marquis of Winchester, and it was believed in London that Lord Charles was prepared to betray his trust.[1] Amongst those who took part in the council of war was Sir Richard Grenvile, a younger brother of Sir Bevil. A selfish and unprincipled man, he had gone through the evil schooling of the Irish War, and, falling into the hands of the Parliamentarians upon his landing at Liverpool, he had declared himself willing to embrace their cause. His military experience gained him the appointment of Lieutenant-General of Waller's horse and admission to the councils of the Parliamentary generals. He was not a man to feel at home in an atmosphere of Puritanism, and on March 3 he fled to Oxford,

Proposal to betray Basing House.

Sir Richard Grenvile.

---

[1] Nicholas to Ormond, March 5. Carte's *Ormond*, vi. 46. *The Weekly Account.* E. 35, 23. According to Agostini's despatch of $\frac{\text{March 22}}{\text{April 1}}$, there were also plans for treacherous designs in Reading and Oxford 'anzi contro la stessa persona del Rè.' As this is not hinted at anywhere else, it is probably a mere rumour.

carrying with him the secret of Paulet's treachery and of the
plan of campaign for the coming season.[1]   Grenvile's name
was attached with every injurious epithet[2] to a gallows in
London, whilst at Oxford he was regarded as a pattern of
loyalty.   Paulet was arrested and sent before a court-martial.
Eventually, however, he received a pardon from the King,
who, as may be conjectured, was unwilling to send the brother
of so staunch a supporter as the Marquis of Winchester to an
ignominious death.[3]

The time when either side could hope to effect its purpose
by treachery had passed away.   Open warfare alone could
decide the quarrel.   Early in March the hearts of
the Oxford Royalists were gladdened by the arrival
of a long string of carts laden with arms for 10,000
men, the result of Lord Goring's bargaining in France.[4]   Yet
even this store was insufficient.   "The King," wrote one of
Ormond's correspondents, "wants arms and money abomi-
nably."[5]   It was thought possible, however, to keep Hopton
in the field at the head of eight or ten thousand men.   It was
now more important than ever to occupy the attention of
the Parliamentary commanders in the South, as Gloucester
was again in distress, and a recent attempt to revictual it from
Warwick had signally failed.[6]

With the force thus equipped Hopton advanced to

*March.
A convoy
of arms.*

---

[1] "Sir R. Grenvile came hither yesternight and brought with him
Waller's commission of Lieutenant-General of the Horse unto him.   He
brought with him some thirty horse, but that which is most valuable in
the puritan is that he hath brought with him all the new MS. of the
councils at London which were held this last week for all this summer
service."   Trevor to Rupert, March 8.   Mr. Firth's *Rupert Transcripts.*

[2] Skellum Grenvile is the name by which he is now known in the
parliamentary newspapers : Skellum, I suppose, being equivalent to
'Schelm.'

[3] Nicholas to Forth, May 7.   *S.P. Dom.* di. 108.

[4] Intelligence from Oxford, March 8.   *Egerton MSS.* 785, fol. 122b.
Agostini to the Doge.   *Venetian Transcripts, R.O.*

[5] Trevor to Ormond, March 9.   Carte's *Ormond,* vi. 57.

[6] Walker's *Historical Discourses,* 7.   Agostini to the Doge, $\frac{\text{March 22}}{\text{April 1}}$.
Venetian Transcripts, R.O.

Winchester. Waller, having been joined by some 4,000 horse
Hopton and
Waller. and dragoons under Balfour, was able to dispose of
an army slightly more numerous than that which
was opposed to him. On March 25 he was at West Meon,
where he could guard the road from Winchester to Petersfield.[1]
It was here that he received the news of Rupert's success
at Newark, with a recommendation from the Committee of
Both Kingdoms not to venture rashly upon an engagement.[2]
Hopton's army, on the other hand, was in good spirits. The
Earl of Forth himself, having brought a reinforcement of
2,000 men, remained to give Hopton the encouragement of
Forth in
command
of the
Royalists. his personal assistance in the manœuvres which
were about to open. There had been much
straining of courtesy between the two commanders,
each insisting that the other should give orders to the troops.
In the end Hopton's urgency prevailed, and Forth, who was
suffering from a severe fit of the gout, was induced to occupy
a position which would require all the energy of a general
in robust health.

Ill as he was, Forth's skill as a strategist did not fail him.
On the 27th he made for Alresford, and occupied the town
March 27.
Forth
occupies
Alresford. before Waller, perceiving too late the importance of
the post, was able to reach it. At Alresford the
Royalists commanded the road to London, whilst
Waller was compelled to halt at Hinton Ampner, between
Cheriton and Bramdean, where the clear stream of the Itchen
rises from the chalk. In this situation he could only put himself in communication with his base of operations either by a
decisive victory or by a dangerously circuitous march. Once
more, as at Newbury, the strategical advantage lay with the
March 28.
Waller
pushed
back. Royalist commander. It seemed as if the tactical
advantage was to be on his side as well. During
the 28th Forth and Hopton, having established
themselves on the crest of the hill which separates Alresford

---

[1] *The True Informer.* E. 39, 24.

[2] The Committee of B. K. to Waller and Balfour, March 24. *Com. Letter Book.*

from Cheriton, succeeded in pushing their outposts over the
top, to the tongue of high ground which rises from the north
bank of the Itchen, about a hundred feet lower than the crest

POSITION OF THE ARMIES ON THE MORNING OF THE BATTLE OF CHERITON.

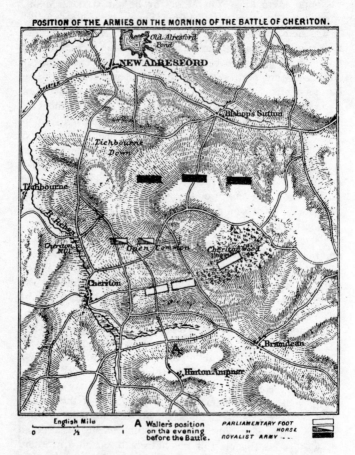

itself.   From this point Waller's army could be descried in a
field near Hinton Ampner, on the south side of the Itchen,
surrounded by a thick hedge and supported by artillery ranged
on the slope behind.   Leaving Sir George Lisle with a small

detachment to guard the lower eminence, Forth and Hopton occupied in force the height behind.[1]

Waller's officers were dispirited with the result of such fighting as there had been. They now knew that in consequence of Rupert's success at Newark no help from Essex or Manchester[2] was to be expected. A council of war decided to retreat, and in the dark hours of the night Lisle learnt from the sound of rolling wheels that it had already commenced.[3] If, however, the retreat was begun, it was soon countermanded. Whatever military prudence might dictate, the advice of the council of war was hateful to the sturdy Puritanism which made much possible to man by believing all things to be possible to God. "Surely," said Captain Birch to Hazlerigg, "we fear whether that were God's cause we have in hand ; for did we assuredly believe it, when He calls us to fight with His enemies we should not run from them ; for man's extremity is God's opportunity."[4] As officer in charge of the outposts, Birch took care, by keeping his men in contact with the enemy, to make it difficult for the army to draw back. Time was gained,

March 29.
Battle of
Cheriton.
and at break of day Waller, who probably repented of the pusillanimous decision of the preceding evening, took advantage of a thick mist which filled the valley to throw a considerable force into Cheriton Wood on the higher ground in front of his right wing. Some two hours after dawn Lisle, finding himself outflanked, fel back from his advanced position, leaving the ridge to be occupied by Waller.[5]

---

[1] Account of Hopton's manœuvres. *Clarendon MSS.* 1,738 (6).

[2] The Com. of B. K. to Waller and Balfour, March 26. *Com. Letter Book.*

[3] *Clarendon MSS.* 1,738 (6).

[4] *Military Memoir of Col. Birch* (Camd. Soc.), 19.

[5] Hopton's own account of these early manœuvres, *Clarendon MSS.* 1,738 (6), is by far the best, but even this is not clear in all points. "The enemy," he says, referring to the morning of the day before the battle, "had taken their quarters in a low field adjoining to Lady Stukely's house"—i.e. at Hinton Ampner—"not a mile and a half from our army, so as there was but a little hill and a little vale between us." This 'little hill' is the ridge on which Waller was subsequently posted, and the

The occupation of Cheriton Wood was not the only act by which Waller vindicated his title to be the best 'shifter and chooser of the ground' amongst the commanders of his day.[1] Between him and the Royalist army lay a depression, shallow by the wood on his right, but broadening out into a wide and comparatively deep valley opposite his centre and left. At the bottom was an open common, whilst the ridges on both sides were covered by enclosed fields. Waller's quick eye saw how to utilise the accidents of the locality, and, abandoning the usual practice of drawing up cavalry on the wings, placed his horse on the common in front of the foot, in order that it might be ready to attack the enemy's cavalry if it poured in disorder out of the lane which offered its only means of access to the open ground.[2]

vale the dip in which most of the fighting took place. "The hill they endeavoured to keep because it covered them from us, and gave them the advantage of looking into us. We disputed that ground that day with little parties and loose skirmishes, but towards the evening we got the top of the hill and the view of the enemy's quarters." Then, after describing how Lisle was left behind with 1,000 foot and 500 horse in a little wood, which has long since disappeared—unless, indeed, it is a corner of Cheriton Wood that is meant—and how the bulk of the army retreated to the higher ridge behind, Hopton says that Lisle, ' being so near as he heard them span and drive their waggons, conceived they were drawing off.' On this Forth made preparations for pursuit. At daybreak Hopton went to Lisle's post to see what was going on. "The morning," he continues, "was very misty, so as he could not make a clear discovery till the sun was near two hours up, and then he found that the enemy was not drawing off, but that they had, in the dark of the night, possessed themselves of a high woody ground that was on the right hand of their own quarters, and placed men and cannon in it that commanded the hill where Sir G. Lisle was ; of this he presently advertised the Earl of Brentford," i.e. Forth, who was subsequently raised to that title. There is no direct evidence of Lisle's retreat, but it would almost necessarily follow, and all the accounts of the battle itself which have reached us imply that Waller occupied the ridge which Lisle had been placed to guard. I have to thank Mr. Stratton, of Chilcombe, for kindly accompanying me over the field, and pointing out the sites traditionally connected with the battle.

[1] See p. 169.

[2] It is this position which is represented in the map at p. 322. There is no local tradition of any ground known as the Common, but the fencing in the valley has the appearance of being comparatively new, and I was

In spite of his gout Forth had come out from Alresford to take the command of the Royalists. He had entrusted the left wing to Hopton, who, as soon as he saw the advantage which had been gained by Waller, ordered Colonel Appleyard to clear Cheriton Wood. After a sharp struggle, Appleyard effected his object, and Hopton would gladly have pushed the success home by a charge with both horse and foot along the ridge on which the bulk of Waller's army lay, especially as it was giving signs of being shaken by its failure to hold the wood. Forth, however, always a cautious tactician, shrank from the risk involved in Hopton's proposal. It would be better, he thought, to allow the enemy the choice between an attack at a disadvantage and a retreat, which, as the Royalists were in possession of his line of communication with London, could hardly fail to end in disaster. If Waller's army were ruined, not only would Kent and Sussex lie open to the invaders, but Manchester and Essex would perforce be summoned to the rescue, leaving Rupert time to complete his preparations for the defence of the North against the Scots.

Such were the chances which hung upon the fortunes of the day. In the Royalist armies generals might scheme aright, but victory or defeat depended on the ill-considered zeal of some high-spirited officer, too untamed to allow military discipline to stand in his way when he was burning to strike a gallant blow at the rebels he despised. This time it was young Sir Henry Bard who, in defiance of orders, galloped down the hill into the fatal valley at the head of his regiment. Unsupported for a time, he was soon surrounded and his followers annihilated ; but his movement had made it impossible for Forth to persist in his Fabian tactics, and Sir Edward Stawell was despatched to the succour of the impetuous Paladin, too late to be of service to his comrades. For a full half-hour Stawell fought on. He succeeded in driving back the enemy's horse on the common ; but he flung himself in vain upon the Parliamentary artillery drawn up behind the hedges on the

told that the land had been enclosed in the last generation. Even if it was not spoken of in Cheriton at the time of the battle as the Common, it was open enough for a Royalist officer to call it by that name.

hillside beyond. His troopers were driven back in utter rout,
and he was himself left as a wounded prisoner in the enemy's
hands.

If Stawell was defeated it was not because he was left
entirely without support. Other cavalry regiments had been
ordered down, but the lane which led to the open ground was
so narrow that the reinforcements arrived slowly, and as soon
as the Parliamentary horse was again in full possession of the
common it could fall upon each regiment as it entered and
overpower it before help came.[1] Never, by the confession of
friend and foe, had the Cavaliers fought so vigorously as they
did under these adverse circumstances,[2] and if cowardice was
shown at all on their side it was only by the soldiers of the
Queen's Regiment, which was composed mainly of Frenchmen,
who were without spirit for a fight in which their national
sympathies were not engaged. For three hours the gallant
English gentlemen struggled in vain to win the common. Yet,
if they could not gain the open ground, their foot lining the
hedges on the northern slope made it impossible for Waller
to push his advantage home. At last Hazlerigg spied a gap
between the enemy's horse and foot. Thrusting his troopers
into the unoccupied space, he gained a position which decided
the battle. Sullenly the Royalists drew back, leaving their
best and bravest, amongst them Lord John Stuart, one of
Lennox's gallant brothers, and Sir John Smith, who had
snatched the standard from the secretary at Edgehill, dead or
dying on the ground.

Forth's spirit rose with adversity. The skill which he had

---

[1] Slingsby's narrative. *Clarendon MSS.* 1,738 (7).

[2] Clarendon's assertion to the contrary is no doubt founded on the
behaviour of the Queen's Regiment, and, as far as the English regiments
were concerned, cannot stand in the face of the statements made by
those who were present. Slingsby, on the one side, writes, "I am confident our horse did perform more gallant charges that day than hath been
known in any one battle this war," and Hazlerigg, on the other, reported
to the House of Commons (Yonge's Diary, *Add. MSS.* 18,779, fol. 87)
that 'their horse, being very good, gave many charges, and maintained
their charges on both sides three hours.'

displayed in the manœuvres which preceded the battle was

The retreat
of the
Royalists.
not wanting to him in the conduct of the retreat·
Showing to the enemy a firm front which checked
all efforts to improve the victory, he pushed on in
the direction of Winchester. Then, suddenly turning to the
right, the defeated army made its way to Basing House, whence
the way to Reading lay open before it.[1]

In London the news of Waller's victory, coming as it did
upon the heels of the ill tidings from Newark, was received

The recep-
tion of the
news in
London,
with enthusiastic joy. At Oxford every effort was
made to extenuate the defeat. Forth, it was alleged,
had retreated in good order and had lost no guns.

and at
Oxford.
It was quite true ; but for all that the defeat at
Cheriton was no ordinary repulse. Not only had

Importance
of the
victory.
it put an end for ever to that scheme for the invasion
of Kent and Sussex which, from the very beginning
of the war, had played such a part in the Royalist strategy,
but it set free the armies of Essex and Manchester for offensive
operations. Morally, the effect of the battle was even more
decisive. It now appeared that no strategical skill, no splendid
chivalry, could compensate for the inherent indiscipline of the
Royalist gentry. At Newbury it had been possible to throw
the blame on the failure of ammunition. No such excuse
could be pleaded at Cheriton.

Waller's success at Cheriton came opportunely to strengthen
the hands of the War-party at Westminster. That party, led

Its effect
on parties
at West-
minster.
now by Vane and St. John, were thoroughly convinced that victory alone could lead to a peace which
would give them satisfaction. For some weeks they
had been struggling with difficulty against the widely diffused
craving for peace, which was the natural result of the hardships
and miseries of war. Those hardships and miseries were not
confined to the scenes of actual strife, and members of the
House of Commons whose rents remained unpaid found it

---

[1] Account of Hopton's manœuvres, *Clar. MSS.* 1,738 (6). Slingsby's
narrative. *Ibid.* 1,738 (7). Hazlerigg's report in Yonge's Diary. *Add.
MSS.* 18,779, fol. 87. *Britannicæ Virtutis Imago.* E. 53, 10.

difficult to obtain purchasers for land which was to be sold either to pay off an incumbrance, or to find a portion for a daughter, and had therefore every reason to feel sympathy with sufferers more hardly bestead than themselves. It was under the influence of this feeling that the Scotch Commissioners had

*March 9.
Germ of the idea of the King's dethronement.*

been able to modify the reply which on March 9 had been sent to Charles's offer to negotiate. As originally framed the letter had contained a clause fixing a time for the King's return to Parliament, failing which means were to be taken to provide for the government of the country without him. The clause was withdrawn, but it contained the germ of an idea which, as long as Charles lived, would never be lost sight of.

So trenchant a solution of existing difficulties was not likely to be widely accepted. Yet Charles was doing his best to make

Foreign intrigues.

its acceptance possible, not so much by his military efforts as by the successive blows which his foreign intrigues were striking at what remained of the intimate relationship between King and people. In the winter he had been detected in attempting to overpower his subjects by the aid of France. When a company of Dutch ambassadors arrived in

*Jan. 12.
Dutch ambassadors arrive.*

January to offer mediation, the leaders of the War-party must have been much worse informed than they usually were if they had not cause for suspecting that the new mediation was intended to be as favourable to the Court as that of Harcourt had been.

In point of fact, Charles had long been angling for effectual aid from the Prince of Orange and the States-General. The bait which he had to offer was the hand of the youthful Prince

*1643.
Proposed marriage of the Prince of Wales.*

of Wales, which Frederick Henry, and still more his ambitious wife, coveted for their daughter. Something had been said about the matter when Henrietta Maria was at the Hague in the spring of 1643, but when she met her husband in the summer after the victories of Adwalton Moor and Roundway Down, events appeared to have taken so favourable a turn in England that foreign aid might be dispensed with. A letter written by Jermyn two days after the battle of Newbury shows that Charles did not then think fit to take up the scheme, though he did not wish to cut off all expectation of success.[1]   The growing strength of the Parliamentary armies during the winter, together with his disappointment of any immediate results from Harcourt's mission, probably turned Charles's thoughts once more towards a Dutch

1644.
Feb. 12.
Hopes held
out.

alliance.   At all events, on February the 12th, when the ambassadors from the States had been some weeks in London, Jermyn wrote that the King and Queen were more favourable to the marriage than the Prince of Orange had supposed, and that they only wished to be sure that their affairs would be advanced by its means.[2]

On the ambassadors and their proposals the Parliamentary leaders, though probably not in possession of the key of the enigma, not unnaturally looked with suspicion.   When the Dutchmen demanded an audience of the Houses they found

March 14.
Dutch
mediation
offered.

every diplomatic obstacle thrown in their way.   At last, on March 14, they contrived to intimate to the Lords that they were ready, with the full approbation of the King, to tender their good offices to put an end to the war.[3] So hard was it, in the existing state of feeling, to meet any proposal tending to peace with a direct negative, that Vane and his friends preferred to get the negotiation—if negotiation there was to be—into their own hands.   Under their influence

March 15.
Proposal of
the War-
party in the
Commons.

the Commons voted that the Committee of Both Kingdoms should be entrusted with the preparation of the terms to be laid before the King.[4]   The Lords, longing for peace, and being well aware that nothing

March 20.
Proposal of
the Lords.

acceptable to Charles would be offered by the existing Committee, proposed the appointment of a new joint Committee, to be specially entrusted with the negotiation, on which they hoped to secure a preponderance of men who shared their views.   The real motives of either House would

---

[1] Jermyn to Heenvliet, $\frac{\text{Sept. 22 and 23}}{\text{Oct. 2 and 3}}$, 1643.   *Groen van Prinsterer,* Ser. 2, iv. 92, 94.

[2] [Jermyn] to [Heenvliet], Feb. $\frac{12}{22}$.   *Ibid.* 98.

[3] The Dutch ambassadors to the States-General, March $\frac{15}{25}$.   *Add. MSS.* 17,677 R, fol. 246.   *L.J.* vi. 419.

[4] *C.J.* iii. 428.   D'Ewes's Diary.   *Harl. MSS.* 166. fol. 33.

hardly bear exposure to the public view, and for some time
arguments of a practical or constitutional nature were made to
do duty in the controversy which arose between the Houses.
On March 30, Vane had such difficulty in carrying a majority
with him on what appeared to be a mere question of procedure,
that the numbers were equally divided, and he only gained his
point by the Speaker's casting vote.[1]

The news from Cheriton, which reached Westminster on
April 1, did much to strengthen Vane's shattered position.

April.
Waller's
successes.

Day after day fresh messengers brought tidings of
Waller's continued prosperity. Within ten days
after the battle he had occupied Winchester, though
the castle still held out, had overrun Andover, Salisbury, and
Christchurch, and was threatening to advance into Dorsetshire.

The news from Hampshire had very nearly led Charles to
a resolution which would hardly have failed to prove disastrous.

The Queen
intends to
remove from
Oxford.

The Queen was once more near the time of her
delivery, and was impatient to take refuge in a place
of safety far from the tumult of war, perhaps too to
escape from the bitter tongues which found occupation in
defaming her at Oxford. In her choice of quarters she hesitated for a time between Bristol and Chester. From the
former it would be easier to escape to France ; from the latter
the passage was open to Ireland,[2] where the Confederate
Catholics assured her of a hospitable reception, as well as of a
revenue of 4,000l. a month. Her decision for the time at least
was in favour of Chester. Yet how to reach Chester now that
the Roundheads were triumphant, save under Rupert's guidance,

April 3.
Rupert
summoned
to escort
her.

she hardly knew, and on April 3 Digby, by Charles's
orders, summoned Rupert to leave his preparations
for the defence of the North to escort the terrified
Queen.[3] Yet even Charles's uxorious fondness
could not persist in a course so ruinous, and the order given
on the 3rd was recalled on the 4th.[4]

[1] *L.J.* vi. 472, 482, 483, 491.   *C.J.* iii. 442.
[2] Trevor to Ormond, March 9, April 13.   Carte's *Ormond*, vi. 57, 87.
[3] Digby to Rupert, April 3.   *Add. MSS.* 18,981, fol. 126.
[4] Digby to Rupert, April 4.   *Add. MSS.* 18,981, fol. 130.   See p. 375.

The Queen had been the more anxious to place herself under Rupert's care as she knew that her husband had not

Charles resolves to take the field.

a man to spare for her protection. Charles had already announced his intention of taking the field in person, and Marlborough was selected as the place where his standard was to be set up for the new campaign.

April 10. He leaves Oxford.

On April 10 he left Oxford, and on the following day reviewed his army, 10,000 strong, near Aldbourne, on the open ground which had been the scene of the skirmish preceding the battle of Newbury. On the 12th he returned to Oxford to await the development of

Proceedings of the Oxford Parliament.

the plans of the enemy, and to bring to a close the session of his Oxford Parliament. That Parliament had taken its duty too seriously to give complete satisfaction at Court. It had raised objections to official proceedings, had overhauled accounts and suggested economies.

April 15. Its address to the King.

In an address presented to the King on the 15th it manifested both its undoubted loyalty and its entire incapacity for the higher work of statesmanship. In words which did no more than echo the vague sentiments which were so dear to Charles's heart, it begged him to repeat once more his assurances of protection to the Protestant religion, his promise to convoke a national synod to establish the peace of the Church, and to recommend it, whenever the time came for it to meet, to have 'a care for the ease of tender consciences,' whatever that might mean. A single example of actual toleration accorded to some one particular tender conscience would have been worth more than the most solemn engagement to recommend toleration in the distant future. Charles was, moreover, asked to assure his subjects that he

April 16. The Oxford Parliament prorogued.

had no thought of abandoning the use of Parliaments in the future, and that the exactions authorised in time of war should not be followed as a prece-

April 17. The Queen leaves Oxford.

dent in time of peace. To all this Charles replied most graciously, and on the 16th he prorogued Parliament to October 8.[1] On the 17th the Queen set out, not for Chester, but for Exeter. France, not Ireland,

[1] *Rushw.* v. 597.

was in case of necessity to be the place of her retreat. The farewell which she now took of her husband proved to be the last.

If Charles decided that his wife was not to take refuge in Ireland, it was probably because he knew that his relations

Charles's
relations
with Ire-
land.

with Ireland were far more unpopular amongst his own supporters than was to be gathered from the courtly expressions of the address which had just been presented to him. He had not hitherto reaped much advantage even from the English troops which he had been enabled to bring over in consequence of the Irish cessation. One body of those troops had thrown down their arms at Nantwich. Another body had shared in the defeat at Cheriton. It was but a poor compensation for the obloquy which had fallen on him that a third body of about 2,000 men was now engaged in the siege of Wem, and might possibly be made available to swell the numbers of that army which Rupert was still engaged in raising.

Charles's larger scheme of enlisting the Irish Catholics on his own side was even less likely to prove a success than his scheme for transporting the English army from Ireland. On

Feb. 23.
Antrim at
Kilkenny.

February 23 Antrim arrived at Kilkenny. He was instructed to urge upon the Supreme Council the advantage which it would be to them if, without waiting for concessions from Charles, they at once despatched to his aid the 10,000 Irish Celts whom they had offered him a year before,[1] and if they added 2,000 more to serve under Antrim himself in the Scottish Highlands, and a supply of muskets and gunpowder for Rupert. The reply of the Supreme Council was not encouraging. They had no muskets or powder to spare, and if they took under consideration the proposed employment of 2,000 men in the Highlands, it would be only on the understanding that the port at which the men were to embark should be entrusted to their own keeping, thus giving them a footing on that part of the coast which looks towards Scotland, and from which they had hitherto been excluded. As for the 10,000 men for England, they must wait to see

[1] See p. 123.

what the King would do for them before they did anything
for the King.[1]

The Supreme Council was the less likely to consent to
Antrim's unreasonable demand as there was some probability
Distress of   that before long it would be master of all Ireland.
the Scottish   In February the Scottish army in Ulster, half-starved
army in
Ulster.   in spite of the promises of the Parliament at Westminster, was making active preparations to return to its native
country, and the three English regiments which still held
Belfast and the neighbouring towns for the King were, from
sheer distress, on the verge of mutiny.[2]   Charles was doing his
The Presi-   best to weaken his own position in Munster. Lord
dency of   Inchiquin, a descendant of the house of O'Brien,
Munster
asked for   whose Protestantism had kept him firm in his loyalty
by Inchi-
quin,   to the English Crown, and who had commanded
troops with credit in the war in the South, arrived at Oxford in
February to ask for the vacant Presidency of Munster. All
who knew Ireland thought him eminently qualified for the
but given to post. Charles, however, had a year and a half before
Portland.   promised it to Portland at the request of Lennox,
and though it would have been easy enough to make Portland
understand that in such times private engagements must give
way before public necessities, Charles insisted on keeping his
promise, though Portland had never been in Ireland in his
life, and had never shown that he possessed the qualities of a
soldier. Inchiquin went back to Ireland a disappointed man,
ready to use against the King the sword which might have been
drawn in his cause.[1]

If Charles was in danger of losing ground in Munster, his
hope of gaining strength in Ulster was speedily quenched.
Early in March Sir Frederick Hamilton brought assurances
from Scotland that the wants of the Northern army should be

---

[1] D. O'Neill to Ormond, Feb. 24 ; D. O'Neill to Digby, March 2 ;
Ormond to Digby, March 13. Carte's *Ormond*, vi. 42, 43, 60.

[2] The Colonels in the North to Ormond, Feb. 5, 20, 21. *Carte MSS.*
ix. fol. 104, 256, 273.

[3] Digby to Ormond, Feb. 8 ; Inchiquin to Ormond, Feb. 10 ; Trevor
to Ormond, Feb. 19. Carte's *Ormond*, vi. 30, 35, 37.

relieved, and before long the English Parliament, terrified at the risk which they would incur if the Scots withdrew from Ireland, made good the promises of Hamilton. All thought of returning to Scotland was at an end.[1]

Charles had still to confront the Agents whom the Supreme Council had despatched to Oxford to lay its grievances before

The Irish Agents at Oxford.

March 29. Their demands.

him, with a view to the conclusion of a permanent peace. Amongst other demands there were two of pre-eminent importance. The Agents asked for complete liberty for the Roman Catholic Church in Ireland and for the complete independence of the Irish Parliament. In order to ensure the permanence of the new arrangement, official posts were to be fairly divided among his Majesty's subjects of both religions, and an Act was to be passed authorising the levy of trained bands as in England—that is to say, the creation of an army preponderatingly Celtic in origin, and Roman Catholic in religion. Only if these requests were granted were the 10,000 Celts, for whom Charles was anxiously waiting, to be despatched to his aid. "We know not," wrote Lord Muskerry, the principal personage among the Irish Agents, "how it may be hoped that the nation may subsist in the condition of free subjects if our desires be not granted."[2]

Charles had now to listen to another tale. The Irish Catholic Agents had been followed to Oxford by agents appointed by

Demands of the Irish Protestants.

the little group of Irish Protestants who had remained faithful to the King. Their demands, presented on April 18, were still more uncompromising than those of their opponents. Protestantism was to be established and Popery suppressed. The existing Parliament at Dublin, from which all Catholics had been expelled, was to be recognised as alone legitimate. The Confederate Catholics were to be deprived of all authority, and the arms and fortresses in their possession were to be taken from them. As soon as they were

[1] The Colonels in the North to Ormond, March 12. *Carte MSS.* ix. fol. 493.

[2] Demands of the Irish Agents, March 29. Gilbert's *Hist. of the Irish Confed.* They were again presented with some modifications on April 2. Carte's *Ormond*, vi. 75.

disarmed they were at their own expense to restore the estates of Protestants to the condition in which they had been before the war. Poyning's law was to be maintained and a Protestant army kept on foot. No one who refused to take the oaths of allegiance and supremacy was to sit in the House of Commons.[1]

Between the two programmes no compromise was possible. On the one side was the harshest and most brutal assertion of

Compromise impossible. Protestant ascendency, and of the right of the alien minority to enslave the children of the soil. On the other was a scheme fairer in appearance, fairer, as far as we can now judge, in intentions, but leading inevitably to a situation in which the Protestants would have been at the mercy of their adversaries, and that too in days when the line of religious demarcation rose up as an impenetrable wall of separation between the professors of antagonistic creeds. Even Charles, eager as he was to secure the 10,000 Celts, could not blind himself to the fact that he was asked to place his own co-religionists in the hands of a Catholic Parliament and a Catholic army, and what he felt hesitatingly and uncertainly was felt with passionate

Feeling at Oxford. energy by the mass of his supporters. Their scornful rejection of the Irish demands is to be read between the lines of the vague address on the subject of religion which was presented by the Oxford Parliament on the 15th,[2] and it was the comprehension of this which directed the Queen's steps to Exeter and not to Chester on the 17th.

Charles might hesitate long before giving a final answer which would cut off all hopes of further military assistance from Ireland, but his hope of entering on the new campaign with a

Charles's hopes from Ireland disappointed. reinforcement of 10,000 Irishmen was none the less signally baffled. A disappointment as great as Charles's awaited Montrose. Antrim, indeed, who continued to be treated with all courtesy at Kilkenny, had been enrolled as a member of the Supreme Council, and had been decorated with a high command in the Catholic army, but as yet there were no signs of any intention to provide him with the 2,000

[1] Propositions of the Protestant Agents, April 18. Gilbert's *Hist. of the Irish Confed.* iii. 143.

[2] See p. 331.

men he required for his expedition to the Highlands. Mont-

Montrose
Lieutenant-
General in
Scotland. rose, who on February 13 had been appointed the King's Lieutenant-General in Scotland—this time the name of Maurice was omitted from the commission [1]

March 4.
Montrose
at York. —had hastened to York to urge Newcastle to supply him with the means of making his way into Scotland, whether Antrim effected a diversion in the Western Highlands or not. Newcastle, who had all the Scottish army to face, and who could ill spare a single man, gave him 100 men mounted on worn-out horses and two small pieces of ordnance. Picking up a small force of horse and 800 foot in Cumberland and Westmoreland, he crossed the border on April 14, and occupied

April 14.
He invades
Scotland, Dumfries, in the hope that the nobles would rise against Presbyterian tyranny. Either the nobles distrusted Montrose or were cowed by the energy of the Committee of Estates. The local forces rose against him, and

and returns
to England. his only course was to retreat hastily to England. Huntly, who about the same time raised the banner of revolt at Aberdeen, was without difficulty suppressed by Argyle.[2] On May 6 Montrose was created a marquis,

May 6.
Montrose a
Marquis. a title which had no doubt been promised to him before he left England.

There was too little coherence in Charles's schemes to bring success within his reach. The chief result of them was to create an ineradicable distrust of his character, and to bring down upon the unhappy Irish, whose fate in those times was not the one least deserving of sympathy, the inextinguishable hatred of all English Puritans and of most English Protestants. There can be no

Irish
soldiers in
England. doubt that some Irish soldiers were mingled with those of English birth who had been shipped from Ireland.[3] In London it was believed that the native Irish had already flocked over in thousands, and had robbed and mur-

---

[1] Commission, Feb. 13. *Hist. MSS. Com. Rep.* ii. 172. See p. 351.

[2] *Wishart*, 30. Macbrayre to Spottiswood, March 15. Napier's *Memorials of Montrose*, ii. 389. *Spalding*, ii. 332. *Merc. Aulicus.* E. 39, 2.

[3] On March 8 Ormond says that he is sending over five good companies of Irish and English. Ormond to Digby, March 8. Carte's *Ormond*, vi. 51.

dered with an inhuman cruelty surpassing even that of the ideal
debauched Cavalier of the London press. Every Irishman was
regarded as beyond the courtesies of honourable warfare, and
when Captain Swanley, who kept guard off the coast of Pembrokeshire, captured a vessel laden with troops from Ireland, he
first offered the Covenant to the Englishmen among them, and

Irish
drowned by
Swanley.

then tied the Irish back to back and flung them into
the sea to drown. Not a voice was raised in Parliament or in the City in reprobation of this barbarous
cruelty.[1]

The Parliamentary armies were making head on every side.
With Swanley's help Pembrokeshire was recovered and the

Pembroke-
shire re-
covered.

neighbouring counties threatened.[2] On April 6 Crowland was recovered, and a limit placed to the incur-
sions of the garrison of Newark. Before long still more
exhilarating tidings reached Westminster from the North. Sir
Thomas Fairfax had left Lancashire, and, driving the Royalists
out of the West Riding on his way, had joined his father before

April 11.
Selby taken.

Selby. On April 11 Selby was stormed, and more
than 3,000 prisoners fell into the hands of the victorious generals. The effect on the Marquis of Newcastle was
instantaneous. The danger in his rear drew him back from
confronting the Scots at Durham. On the 18th he shut him-

April 18.
Newcastle
at York.

self up in York with 5,000 horse and 6,000 foot.
The Scots followed promptly, and on the 20th they
effected a junction with the Fairfaxes at Tadcaster.
After due consultation the three generals applied themselves to
prepare for the siege of York. If help did not speedily arrive
the King's cause would be ruined in the North.[3]

---

[1] *The Kingdom's Weekly Intelligencer.* E. 46, 4.

[2] *A true relation of the routing of his Majesty's forces.* E. 42, 13.
A true relation of the proceedings of Captain Langhorn. E. 42, 19.

[3] *The Kingdom's Weekly Intelligencer.* E. 44, 1. The Com. of B. K.
to Manchester, April 27. *Com. Letter Book. Rushw.* v. 620.

CHAPTER XVII.

THE PARTING OF ESSEX AND WALLER.

THE Parliamentary chiefs had reason to look with hopefulness to the campaign which was about to open. Waller's victory at

1644.
Prospects
of the
campaign. Cheriton and Fairfax's victory at Selby had more than counterbalanced Rupert's achievement in relieving Newark. On April 6 orders were given to Essex and Manchester to rendezvous at Aylesbury on the 19th,[1] and there was every reason to suppose that their combined forces would be more than a match for the inferior numbers of which the King was able to dispose. Waller's army would thus be left free to push on towards the West.

Yet even before a single regiment was on the march signs were not wanting of the existence of the causes which ultimately

Causes of
failure in
the Parlia-
mentary
armies. frustrated all these hopes, and showed that the Parliamentary armies in the South were wanting in that unity of purpose and in that resolute determination without which numerical superiority is vain.

Distrust of
Essex. Essex was the first to discover that he was distrusted by the men who bore sway in the Committee of Both Kingdoms. His relations with the Peace-party in the House of Lords were too close not to excite suspicion in those who believed that any attempt to open negotiations with Charles would be disastrous to their cause, and who therefore feared lest he might use his military position to impose a ruinous peace, as he had been tempted to use it after the defeats of Adwalton Moor and Roundway Down. That in this they did

---

[1] The Com. of B. K. to Manchester, April 6. *Com. Letter Book.*

him grievous wrong there can be no doubt whatever. Not
His con-
stancy. only was he chained by a stern sense of duty to the
exigencies of generalship, but his religion lay on the
Puritan side of the party-wall which separated the contending
forces. He now believed as sincerely as Cromwell that the
peace for which he longed was only to be attained through the
gate of victory,[1] though it might reasonably be doubted whether
his was the arm to achieve the needful end.

On April 8 Essex presented to the Lords a pathetic and
dignified remonstrance. The delay in furnishing him with an
April 8.
His remon-
strance to
the Lords. army, he said, had cost the country much, and might
have cost it more. "Newark," he pleaded, "is not
taken, Lincolnshire is lost, Gloucester is unsupplied,
and the last week"—the week of Cheriton Fight—"there was
but a step between us and death, and—what is worse—
slavery."

"For my part," continued the suspected commander, "as I
first engaged myself in this cause and undertook this service
with an honest and single heart, without any particular end of
my own, but merely to serve my country and defend religion
and liberty, in which cause both Houses of Parliament and the
good party of the whole kingdom have solemnly protested to
live and die with me, which hath kept up my spirits all this
while, and would not suffer me to lay down my commission
notwithstanding all my discouragements . . . so I shall be
ready still to prosecute it with the utmost of my endeavours,
and desire no longer to live than I shall be faithful in it ; and
though you have been pleased to reduce my army to 7,000
foot and 3,000 horse, when my Lord of Manchester is allowed
an army of 14,000 and receives 34,000*l.* a month for the pay of
it—since it is done by you I submit, and with them or a lesser

---

[1] "The Committee of Both Kingdoms . . . have presented their
opinions . . . that it is requisite that the Parliament draw all their
forces together, and put it suddenly to a day, and fight with the King's
forces, or pursue them if they refuse ; and further declare that my Lord
General did deliver it as his opinion that there was no way so likely as
this to put an end to our miseries." *The Kingdom's Weekly Intelligencer.*
E. 42, 4.

number, if it be your pleasures, I will, as I have several times already, adventure my life for the service of this cause." [1]

Essex concluded by recommending a fresh appeal to the City. The simple and manly tone of his complaint was sure to go straight to the hearts of Englishmen, and on the 13th

April 13. The City offers men and money.

the City answered his appeal by a resolution to raise a considerable loan upon the usual security of the estates of Papists and delinquents, and to send out three regiments of trained bands to the rendezvous at Aylesbury, whilst three more were to be held in readiness to follow if their services were required. [2]

Yet, admirably as the cause of the Parliament was served by the devotion of the City, the very necessity of appealing to it pointed to a danger even greater than that which would result from the mutual jealousy of the commanders. To draw

Danger of reliance on local forces.

upon local resources was to rely upon help which, by the very nature of the case, could not be permanently rendered. The local officials, zealous when war approached their own borders, would grow cool when the thunderstorm had drifted away. The local troops, whose daily toil was interrupted and whose means of livelihood were threatened by long service in the field, would soon cry for a speedy return to their homes. As it had been after Newbury, so it would be again till the discovery was made that victory was only to be attained by a trained and disciplined army, which had cast off all local ties and was commanded by officers bound to one another by the strictest military subordination.

Already, when the City took its resolution, there had been fresh evidence of the instability of local forces. Waller's

Waller's retreat.

victorious advance had come to an end because his City regiments had insisted upon returning home. Finding himself with numbers too reduced to enable him to make head against the enemy on the borders of Dorsetshire,

April 12. He takes up a position at Farnham.

he drew back to his old quarters at Farnham, as if Cheriton had never been fought. Taking advantage of his enforced retreat, a Royalist party made

[1] *L.J.* vi. 505.
[2] *Six speeches spoken in the Guildhall.* E. 42, 18.

a dash at Wareham, captured the place, and threatened Poole. The City authorities indeed announced that two regiments were already on the way to take the place of their returning comrades, and that a third would soon follow, but the mischief which had been done was only too likely to be done again at some equally unseasonable moment.[1]

On the day on which the City's offer of its trained bands was made, the controversy between the Lords and Commons

April 13. Proposal of the Lords about a negotiation.

on the matter of the negotiations took a new shape. The Peers saw that to insist upon their refusal to entrust the proposed negotiation with Charles to the Committee of Both Kingdoms was equivalent, in the face of the opposition of the other House, to an abandonment of the negotiation itself. They therefore gave way on the point on which they had long been obstinate[2] and sent down an ordinance authorising the Committee to treat, but directing it to present its terms of peace not later than the 17th, in order that an attempt to open negotiations might be made before the armies took the field on the 19th.[3] The majority of the Commons, hoping that a victory might precede the negotiation, altered the date to the 26th, and this amendment was accepted by the Lords, who knew that, if they rejected it, there would be no negotiation at all.[4]

There was still a delay in bringing the quarrel to decision in the field. Ample as were the resources of the South-East

Delay in opening the campaign.

of England, they were all too little to support the armies of Essex and Waller and Manchester, as well as those of Leven and Monro. Parliament was always behindhand with its payments, and the recruiting of the new armies, even with free recourse to the press-system, proceeded but slowly. The 19th, appointed for the rendezvous at Aylesbury, arrived, but Essex was not ready to stir.[5]

---

[1] *C.J.* iii. 458. The Com. of B. K. to Waller and Balfour, April 13. The Com. of B. K. to Waller, April 14. The Com. of B. K. to the Commanders of the City regiments, April 14. *Com. Letter Book.*

[2] See p. 329.   [3] *L.J.* vi. 514.

[4] *C.J.* iii. 460. *L.J.* vi. 520.

[5] Agostini to the Doge, April $\frac{19}{29}$. *Venetian Transcripts, R.O.* The

Manchester, indeed, had an army equipped for a campaign, but his first duty was to the Eastern Association, and that duty required him to watch Rupert's movements as long as Lincoln remained in the hands of the Royalists.

Hoping more from war than from negotiation, the Committee of Both Kingdoms delayed its appointed task as long as

April 29.
The peace
propositions
of the
Committee.

was decently possible, and when at last, on April 29, it produced its propositions, they were such as were only compatible with a virtual capitulation of the Royalist party.

Weak as the Peace-party was, it had never appeared to greater disadvantage than now. Counter-policy to propose it

The Peace-
party has
no counter-
policy.

had absolutely none. The King's vague and uncertain note of consideration for tender consciences seemed statesmanship itself by the side of the silence of Holles and Maynard, of Salisbury and Pembroke. The conflict between the two Houses, which blazed up again as soon as the Committee's proposals were presented, turned upon purely

Disputes
between
the Houses
on the seats
of returned
members;

secondary points. There was a long wrangle over the wish of the Lords to re-admit to their seats the members of both Houses who had returned from Oxford, in which the Commons, whose negative voice was conclusive, took the stricter view, no doubt in order to prevent the reinforcement of the Peace-party in the Lords by Bedford and Holland, Clare and Conway, who with others had been dropping in and tendering their submission from time to time. Another subject of dispute was the wish of the Commons to give to Manchester the authority of an indepen-

on Man-
chester's
command;

dent command, whilst the Lords were anxious to keep him in subordination to Essex.[1] Still more

on the re-
appoint-
ment of the
Committee
of Both
Kingdoms.

desperate was the struggle over the reappointment of the Committee of Both Kingdoms, the three months for which it had been established expiring in May. The Commons insisted upon a simple

Dutch ambassadors to the States-General, May $\frac{3}{13}$. *Add. MSS.* **17,677** R, fol. 289.

[1] The details will be found spread over the journals of the two Houses in April and May.

renewal of the powers of the existing Committee, whilst the Lords, doubtless with the intention of giving a larger representation to the Peace-party, wished to increase its numbers. Day after day the Lords sent down amendments to the ordinance proposed by the Commons. Day after day the Commons threw out the amendments of the Lords. Before an agreement could be effected, the Committee reached its term, and for some days at a most critical moment there was no central authority except a discordant Parliament to direct the movements of the armies in the field.

A deadlock such as this had in some way or other to be brought to an end. The way in which the object was attained

May 22
The Committee reappointed.

was characteristic of the leadership of Vane and St. John,[1] as opposed to that of Pym.

An old ordinance revived.

On February 1, when the proposal to appoint a governing Committee was first mooted, the Lords had been surprised into passing an ordinance for its creation, in which they conferred upon the new body for an unlimited time powers so vast as to rouse a warm resistance in the House of Commons.[2] This 'omnipotent ordinance,' as it was then called, had never been rejected by the Lower House, but had simply been laid aside. It was now taken up and passed by the Commons. As the Lords had already sent it down, it was unnecessary to ask them to vote on it again. It therefore became law, as far as anything could become law without the royal assent, and the baffled Lords, circumvented

May 24.
The Committee again sets to work.

by a trick, had to look on without the possibility of giving effect to their dissatisfaction, when the old Committee met on May 24 to continue its work.[3]

All this while Charles had been doing his best to strengthen his main army. It was indeed a matter of serious consideration

The siege of Lyme.

to him that, since the middle of March, Prince Maurice, at the head of a force 6,000 strong, had

---

[1] D'Ewes ascribes the plan to them. *Harl. MSS.* 166, fol. 64b.

[2] See p. 305.

[3] *C.J.* iii. 503. *L.J.* vi. 564. Whitacre's Diary. *Add. MSS.* 31,116, fol. 145b. D'Ewes's Diary. *Harl. MSS.* 166, fol. 64b. *Day Book of the Com. of B. K.*, May 24.

been engaged in an attempt to beat down the stubborn spirits
of the men of Lyme. In vain storming parties had been led
again and again against the fortifications hastily thrown up.
Yet Maurice could not bear to leave his task unaccomplished,
even to bring succour to his uncle in his hour of danger.[1] By

Vavasour
recalled.

recalling Sir William Vavasour, who was posted in the
neighbourhood of Gloucester, with the greater part of
the troops under his command, Charles was indeed able to raise
the numbers of his main army to about 10,000 ; but the price
which he paid for this reinforcement was the completion by

Relief of
Gloucester.

the Parliamentarians of the work of supplying
Gloucester with ammunition, which had been to
some extent successful before Vavasour's recall, but which
Mynn, who was left in charge of the small force remaining in

Charles
summons
Rupert.

the Severn Valley, was entirely unable to hinder.[2]
So hopeless did the situation appear to Charles, that
he once more summoned Rupert to his side. Rupert,
knowing the supreme importance of the relief of York, despatched Byron to plead against his uncle's resolution. Before
Byron's urgency Charles gave way, and announced that he
would for the present be content if Rupert would send to
Worcester a body of 2,000 foot and a regiment of horse, and
if he would himself abstain from engaging so far 'in northern
designs' as to be unable to join the army near Oxford in the
first week in June. Rupert could ill spare a single man, and
he was most unwilling to abandon his march to the help of

April 25.
Rupert at
Oxford.

Newcastle on which his heart was set. On April 25
he was himself at Oxford, entreating that his army,
brought together with the greatest difficulty, might
be suffered to remain intact.[3]

Before Rupert had been long at Oxford the news of the
gathering of the Parliamentary armies round York [4] sharpened

---

[1] Relation concerning the siege of Lyme. *Clarendon MSS.* 1,738 (8).

[2] Corbet, *Mil. Gov.* of Gloucester, 90. *Bibl. Glocestr.*

[3] The King to Rupert, April 20, 22. Mr. Firth's *Rupert Transcripts.*
Byron to Ormond, April 29. *Carte MSS.* x. fol. 464. Dugdale's *Diary.*

[4] Commissioners at Newark to Rupert, April 24. Mr. Firth's *Rupert
Transcripts.*

his eagerness to march to the relief of the threatened city. For ten days he strove to impart his own unwavering courage to the irresolute King. If Chatles, he argued, would keep _{His military} strong garrisons in Reading, Wallingford, Abingdon, _{advice.} and Banbury, manœuvring round Oxford with a strong body of horse, it would be as impossible for the combined armies of the Parliament to master so extensive a position as it would be for them to push on, leaving the fortresses unassailed in their rear. Prince Maurice, with some reinforcement of cavalry, would thus be at liberty to beat down what resistance still hampered his movements in the West, whilst Rupert would have a free hand to make himself master of the _{May 5.} North.[1] When, on May 5, Rupert left Oxford he _{Rupert leaves} had every reason to believe that his plan of campaign _{Oxford.} had been adopted.

The next day Rupert's plan was, at least in part, abandoned. Forth, perhaps wisely, thought that the position recommended _{May 6.} by Rupert was too extensive, and had already sug- _{Forth's plan} gested that the fortifications of Reading should _{adopted.} be demolished.[2] There was the more reason why Charles should contract his efforts, as his military inferiority was being brought home to him in every direction. Barnstaple _{Massey's} had revolted in January, and now Massey was _{successes.} taking one post after another in the neighbourhood _{May 6.} of Gloucester, whilst Maurice had not yet succeeded _{Lincoln} in reducing Lyme. On May 6 Manchester stormed _{taken by} _{Manchester.} the Close of Lincoln. The whole county fell speedily into their hands. A bridge was swiftly thrown over the Trent at Gainsborough, and Manchester, to whom orders had been given to proceed to the North, instead of effecting a junction with Essex at Aylesbury, as had been originally intended, _{Manchester} carried the army of the Eastern Association into _{moves to-} Yorkshire, to take part with Leven and the Fairfaxes _{wards York.} in the momentous siege of York. Already Newcastle had made every preparation to hold out as long as possible,

---

[1] *Clarendon,* viii. 26.
[2] Nicholas to Forth, May 12. *S. P. Dom.* di. 121.

sending away the greater part of his cavalry, as Fairfax had done at Hull, before the investment was completed.[1]

On May 18 the demolition of the fortifications of Reading was finished, and its garrison of 2,500 men was rendered avail-

May 18.
Reading dismantled;

May 19. and occupied by Essex and Waller.

able for service in the field.[2] On the following day Essex and Waller, to whom the conduct of the campaign against the King was entrusted now that Manchester had been despatched elsewhere, met for consultation in the town which had just been abandoned by Charles.[3] There was no lack of courtesy apparent on either side, but it did not bode well for the harmonious co-operation of the two Parliamentary Generals that it was arranged between them that the two armies should operate separately.

In the royal camp there was every token of despondency There had even been a talk of sending the Prince of Wales

Despondency in Charles's camp.

into Cornwall as a measure of precaution.[4] The ever-present apprehension of coming danger did much to prolong the discussion between the King and the representatives of the Irish Catholics. The prospect of seeing 10,000 Irish soldiers landing in England was very

Feeling at Oxford about the Irish offers.

tempting to Charles, but on the other hand it was terribly unpopular among his own supporters. "Although," wrote Digby to Ormond, "the Irish Agents should be moderate and reasonable, it is so nice and dangerous a business, that it will hardly be in the King's power at present to give them, with any approbation of his Council any such conditions as wise men can accept and answer to those that trusted them. The danger of scandal for his Majesty to grant them almost anything more than private promises, which I conceive he will also be chary to do, is likely to be much improved by the wild and extravagant propositions of those that call themselves the Protestant Agents. The truth of the

---

[1] *A particular relation.* E. 47, 8. *The Kingdom's Weekly Intelligencer.* E. 47, 19.

[2] Walker, *Hist. Disc.* 13. [3] *Merc. Civ.* E. 49, 12.

[4] Elyot to Rupert, May 21. Digby to Rupert, May 26. Lennox to Rupert, May 26. *Add. MSS.* 18,981, fol. 180, 182, 184.

case is this : Everybody that is faithful to the King's interests apprehends the necessity of a peace,[1] both for the preservation of the Protestants in Ireland and the support of our affairs here ; but everybody also is seeking, as the ape did, to pull the chestnuts out of the fire with the puppy's foot, and to cast off the counsel of granting the Irish anything at all to his neighbour ; which is the reason why I do not wonder at all that in none of your letters I have ever received any opinion from you concerning this matter. Only in one thing I shall presume to provoke your advice, and that is how you think it may agree with his Majesty's interests there and the safety of the Protestant subjects' condition ? For, to tell you freely my apprehension, I do not think the matter likely to proceed to further terms of accommodation than so ; not but that everybody desires a better settlement in relation to Ireland, but everybody is restrained in counsel by apprehensions of the ill effects which any concession of the Irish Catholics at this time may have upon the affections of the people here." [2]

When such sentiments as these prevailed—and necessarily prevailed—at Oxford, the acceptance of the Irish terms was

May 22.
The negotiation with the Irish turned over to Ormond.

impossible for Charles. Yet he was unable to look the fact fairly in the face, and, hoping that time would bring a remedy, he contented himself with asking for a renewal of the cessation, turning over the negotiation for peace to the patient, much-enduring Ormond, in the vain hope that that loyal servant would in some way find a solution which would reconcile incompatible

May 23.

claims. The Irish agents were dismissed from Oxford with every appearance of favour.[3] They seem to have been assured that in case of an agreement Ormond would be directed to combine with the Confederate Catholics in military operations against the Scots.[4]

[1] I.e. a peace in Ireland.

[2] Digby to Ormond, May 9. Carte's *Ormond*, vi. 114.

[3] Dugdale's *Diary*. Percival to Ormond, May 23. Radcliffe to Ormond, June 11. Carte's *Ormond*, vi. 129, 146. Digby to Ormond, July 7. *Carte MSS.* xi. fol. 379.

[4] Ormond to Digby, July 17. Carte's *Ormond*, vi. 163.

Charles appears to have been thoroughly convinced that without extraneous aid he could not make head against his enemies, and he could not be brought to understand that extraneous aid might do him more harm than good. On

May 30.
The Dutch
marriage
treaty
taken up.

Goffe's
mission.

May 30, a week after the dismissal of the Irish Agents, a letter written from Exeter by the Queen to the Prince of Orange announced that the treaty for the marriage of the Prince of Wales was at last to be seriously taken up. The letter was carried by Dr. Goffe, who had been chaplain of Lord Goring's regiment in the Dutch service, and in that capacity had done much to forward the use of the Book of Common Prayer by the English soldiers in the Netherlands.[1] He was now sent as a negotiator, on the ground that a personage of higher rank might raise suspicion.

His instructions were more than usually indicative of Charles's ignorance of the ways of men. The Prince was to

His in-
structions.

be informed that the proposed marriage was to form a link between England, France, and the Dutch Republic. The three nations were, therefore, to enter into an offensive and defensive alliance. Frederick Henry, if France should so desire, was to go to war with the Emperor, and to give general military assistance to France. He was also—and this was the clause which alone possessed direct interest for Charles—to furnish fifteen or twenty ships of war for two months, and a sufficient number of other vessels to bring over to England 4,000 French foot and 2,000 French horse. Mazarin, it was true, had hitherto made no promise to allow Charles the benefit of this little army, still less to advance the money to pay it. If, then, the French Court should prove obdurate, Frederick Henry was at once to give up the French alliance and to make a truce with Spain. He was also to send over to England the English regiments in his service, to agree upon the sum due as an acknowledgment of the wrongdoing of the Dutch in the massacre of Amboyna, and to pay his daughter's portion in ready money.[2]

---

[1] *Hist. of Engl.* 1603–1642, vii. 316.

[2] Jermyn to the Prince of Orange, May 30. Henrietta Maria to the

Even Charles, it is probable, never proposed anything more fatuous than the suggestion that the Dutch should make terms with Spain. It is difficult to understand how any sane man could have supposed that an old warrior like the Prince of Orange, who had three months before renewed the treaties which bound him to France, and who was now preparing to join the French with a Dutch fleet in laying siege to Gravelines, should have been willing—or should have been able if he had been willing—to fling up one alliance and to adopt another merely for the pleasure of seeing his daughter married to the Prince of Wales. As might have been expected, the Prince replied that he should be glad to see a good understanding arrived at between England and France, but that he would have nothing to do with Spain.[1]

A foolish suggestion.

Long before this answer reached England it had been necessary for Charles to consider how he might defend himself if foreign aid failed him. In his Council the notion of offering battle was only suggested to be rejected, and on May 25 Abingdon was abandoned. On the 26th it was occupied by Essex, whilst Waller pushed on in the direction of Wantage, to gain, if possible, a passage over the Thames above Oxford, and so to cut off Charles from the West.[2]

June 14.
Answer of the Prince of Orange.

May 25.
Abingdon abandoned;

May 26.
and occupied by Essex.

Charles's hold upon the West was already loosening. On the 24th Malmesbury surrendered to Massey, and on the 26th, the day on which Essex entered Abingdon, Charles despatched Hopton to Bristol, that he might at least preserve the great Western port from falling into Parliamentary hands. Maurice was still occupied with the siege of Lyme, and Rupert was only just starting for the relief of York.

May 24.
Massey takes Malmesbury.

On the 27th a council of war met at Oxford. Scouting the

Prince of Orange, May 30 (?). Instructions for Goffe. *Groen van Prinsterer*, Ser. 2, iv. 99, 100, 101.

[1] Reply of the Prince of Orange to Goffe, June $\frac{14}{24}$. *Groen van Prinsterer*, Ser. 2, iv.

[2] Walker, *Hist. Disc.* 14.

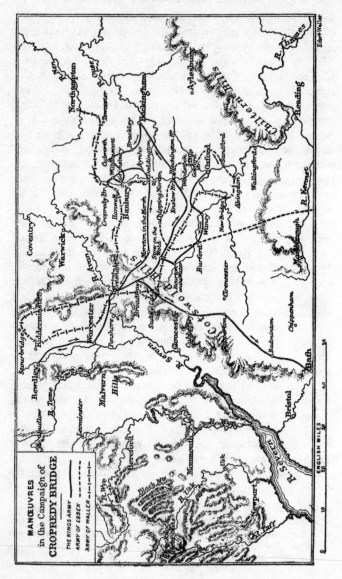

MANŒUVRES
in the Campaign of
CROPREDY BRIDGE

THE KINGS ARMY ——————
ARMY OF ESSEX – – – – –
ARMY OF WALLER –·–·–·–·

ENGLISH MILES

notion of fighting under present circumstances, it recom-

mended that, if Essex and Waller combined to attack Oxford, Charles should post himself in such a position as to keep the communications of the city open, at least on one side. If they separated, the Royal army was strong enough to fall upon each of them alternately with every prospect of success.[1] The plan was rather a modification of Rupert's scheme than an original conception. Rupert had proposed that Charles, with all his force, should guard a large circle of fortifications round Oxford, whilst he was himself set free to strike at the enemy at a distance. According to the new plan a small force only would be left at Oxford, whilst Charles, with at least a part of his army, would be as free as Rupert. It is probable that the modification was due to Forth. At least his creation as Earl of Brentford in the English peerage on the very day on which the council of war was held goes far to show that his influence was at this time in the ascendant.

Whoever was the author of the plan, it marks a change in Charles's strategy corresponding with the change in his military

position which resulted from the entrance of the Scots. In the campaign of 1643 he had hoped to outflank and to crush the enemy by the weight of superior numbers. In 1644 he knew his forces to be numerically inferior, and he fell back upon the idea of compensating for that inferiority by rapidity of movement from his central position at Oxford.

It is not sufficient for a general to form a good plan. It is also necessary for his success that his opponents should commit blunders, and Charles had not long to wait to see the blunder on which he had counted committed before his eyes.

On the 28th Essex crossed the Thames at Sandford, and took up his quarters at Islip, leaving Waller to operate independently on the Berkshire side. The separation of the two armies was not yet complete, but there was an evident tendency to separate.

---

[1] Advice of the council of war. *Add. MSS.* 18,981, fol. 185.

During three days Essex strove in vain to seize the bridges over the Cherwell at Gosford and Enslow. On June 2 the

Essex
on the
Cherwell.

Dutch ambassadors, who, in despair of obtaining a hearing at Westminster for their proposal to mediate,

June 2.
Dutch
mediation
offered.

had recently arrived at Oxford, waited upon Essex to urge him to open direct negotiations with Charles. Anxious for peace as he was, Essex was too loyal to his employers to respond to the overture, and he told the ambassadors plainly that if they wanted to treat they must apply elsewhere.[1]

It seemed at last likely that military events would take a decisive turn. On the very day on which the ambassadors

Waller
destroys
Abingdon
Cross,

were pleading with Essex, Waller, who had signalised his occupation of Abingdon by hewing down with Puritanic fervour the stately market-cross adorned

and seizes
Newbridge.

with images of saints and kings, forced a passage over the river at Newbridge, some miles above

Charles
escapes
capture.

Oxford. Charles himself, who was that evening at Woodstock, was in imminent danger of being captured. In such a crisis timid counsels were not wanting. Would it not be the best course, suggested someone, to surrender on conditions? "I may be found in the hands of the Earl of Essex," was the King's reply, "but I shall be dead first."[2]

In all haste Charles withdrew to Oxford, but there at least it was impossible to remain. If his whole army were blocked up in the city, a single fortnight would suffice to starve it out.

June 3.
He leaves
Oxford.

On the morning of the 3rd, by a feigned attack on Abingdon, he drew Waller to its defence, and then, turning sharply back to Oxford, he rode out as soon as it was dark at the head of some 3,000 horse and 2,500 foot.

June 4.
Massey
takes
Tewkes-
bury.

On the afternoon of the 4th he was at Burford, and a second night march brought him to Bourton-on-the-Water. There had been some thought of making for Bristol, but when Charles arrived at Evesham he

---

[1] The Dutch ambassadors to the States-General, June $\frac{7}{17}$. *Add. MSS.* 17.677 R. fol. 321.   [2] *Clarendon*, viii. 47.

learned that Tewkesbury had surrendered to Massey; that Denbigh, who for some months had been holding his own at the head of a small force in Shropshire and Staffordshire, was advancing southwards; and that Essex and Waller were on the march. To make for Bristol would be to hazard a battle, and a battle was the very thing which Charles most wished for the present to avoid. He therefore pushed on for Worcester,

June 6.
Charles at
Worcester.

where he took up his quarters on the 6th. The prospect before him was not a bright one. "When I have told your Highness this," wrote Digby to

June 8.
Digby's
account
of the
situation.

Rupert, after recounting the incidents of the march, "and that Essex comes upon us one way, Waller likely to go about us on the Welsh side by Gloucester, that Massey and the Lord Denbigh towards Kidderminster, both with considerable forces; and when to all this I shall add the uncertainty of your brother's succeeding before Lyme, and that Oxford is scarcely victualled for a month, and for aught we know blocked up in a manner by the enemy's horse, your Highness will easily frame to yourself an image of our condition."

Charles had intended to make a stand at Worcester, but on the 9th Sudeley Castle surrendered to Waller, and on the

June 12.
Charles
retires to
Bewdley.

12th orders were given for a retreat to Bewdley.[1] If only the King's enemies had been under a single commander, it would have been almost impossible for him to escape destruction. Deliverance came to him because neither of the Parliamentary commanders was ready

June 6.
Council of
war at
Stow-on-
the-Wold.

to take orders from the other. On June 6 a council of war was held at Stow-on-the-Wold, at which both Essex and Waller were present. It might have been thought that a council held under these circumstances would have recognised that the one paramount obligation of the Parliamentary commanders was to crush the King. As a matter of fact, its attention was directed to the relief of Lyme. It was the decided opinion of the council that if Lyme was to be relieved, it was on Essex rather than upon Waller that the

---

[1] Digby to Rupert, June 8. *Warburton*, ii. 417. Walker's *Hist. Disc.* 15. Symonds' *Diary*, 8.

task ought to devolve. Not only was Essex farther from the King and nearer Lyme than Waller, but his army was more homogeneous, as being composed of men enlisted for general service, whilst that of Waller was mainly composed of men who had been furnished by the Association of Kent, Sussex, and Surrey, and who were therefore likely to be unwilling to be long absent from their homes.

In truth this extraordinary diversion of half the army from its proper work was but part of a preconceived plan. It was no mere relief of an heroic but unimportant garrison which was contemplated. Essex, always prone to fall under the influence of those around him, had fallen under the influence of Lord Robartes and the gentlemen of Devon and Cornwall. He fancied that if, after relieving Lyme, he pushed on into the West, he should not only occupy a province which Waller had long regarded as his own, but should, by cutting off one main source of Charles's supplies, do more to bring the war to an end than if he had defeated the King in a pitched battle.[1]

Essex designs to march into the West.

It is evident that Essex altogether underestimated Charles's resources. Waller, he thought, had no more to do than to drive the King before him, and then to turn back to the dull work of besieging Oxford. Waller, at least, knew better than this. The chase after the King's person appeared to him to be an endless task, yet one which, endless as it was, must necessarily be faced. As long as Charles was at large there would be no end to the war, 'for, break his army never so often, his person will raise another.'[2]

Waller's opinion.

To the members of the Committee of Both Kingdoms the announcement of the impending division of the armies was an unpleasant surprise. Vague and uncertain as their language had been, they had intended that Essex should employ the bulk of his army in

June 12. Dissatisfaction of the Committee of Both Kingdoms.

---

[1] Robartes and others to Lenthall, May 28. Printed without a date in *L.J.* vi. 16; the date is supplied from D'Ewes's Diary. *Harl. MSS.* 166, fol. 86.

[2] Essex to the Com. of B. K., June 6; Waller and Hazlerigg to the Com. of B. K., June 7. *Com. Letter Book.*

besieging Oxford, and, having received the approbation of
Essex ordered to return. the Commons, they sent off a letter to the self-willed
commander, in which they directed him, after de-
spatching a sufficient force to relieve Lyme, to hasten back
towards Oxford with the remainder of his army.[1]

The Peers stood by Essex, and called on the Committee
to inform their House what instructions had been sent to the
June 13. Objection of the Lords. General. The Committee had grown accustomed
to treat the mutilated House of Lords with contempt,
and replied with a refusal to give information except
at the demand of both Houses. The insult was the greater,
as the Commons had already been taken into council. The
Lords were, however, powerless, and could do no more than
direct that both their own question and the Committee's
answer should be deleted from their journals, so that no
evidence of their helplessness might remain on record.[2]

It was easier for the Committee to set the Peers at naught
than to impose their will upon a General in command of an
June 14. Essex refuses to obey the Committee. army. Their letter overtook Essex on June 12 at
Blandford, where he was well on his way towards
Lyme. He replied that he was carrying out their
orders to relieve Lyme in the only manner in which
it was possible for him to do so, and he further asserted that
he had their approval in devoting himself, after Lyme had been
relieved, to the reconquest of the West. Having thus put
upon ambiguous passages in former letters [3] an interpretation
which served his purpose, he proceeded to enlarge on Waller's
unfitness for the task of overrunning the West. His rival, he

[1] Com. of B. K. to Essex, June 12. *Com. Letter Book. C.J.* iii. 528.

[2] *L.J.* vi. 590, 591. *C.J.* iii. 529.

[3] "The Committee are clearly of opinion that it is necessary to send
presently such a strength as may relieve Lyme ; which will not only preserve that town, that deserves so well, but be a means to prevent the levies
of men and money now raising by a new association in those parts, and to
recover the whole West."—Com. of B. K. to Essex, May 30. *Com.
Letter Book.* This does not seem to imply more than that the relief of
Lyme would be a step to the recovery of the West at some future time.
A letter from the Houses on June 10, however, seems to approve of the
forward march. *L.J.* vi. 588.

alleged, after disposing of the King, would be in a good position for turning back to undertake the siege of Oxford with the assistance of the reinforcements which might reasonably be expected to join him. "Pardon me," continued the aggrieved commander, "if I make bold to order and direct my own Major-General,[1] for in truth I do not see how Sir William Waller can take care of all the countries along the seaside from Dover to St. Michael's Mount. If you think fit to set him at liberty and confine me, be pleased to make him General and me the Major-General [2] of some brigade, that my soldiers may have free quarter, free plunder, and contributions besides, as his have without control. Finally, that army which hath the greatest strength of foot will be most able, by God's blessing, to reduce the West, and I believe that I have the most resolute foot in Christendom. Take heed how you disaffect them, for if you lose them either by commanding me [3] to be still or putting them upon ordinary services which are below them, you will repent too late, and I too soon. If you encourage me to advance further into the West, I hope in a reasonable time to relieve Lyme and distress Weymouth ; but if you call back Sir William Waller from pursuing the King and stop me in my march to the West, we are like to lose the benefit of both armies this summer, because we are put upon cross services, which lie far out of our way, and are denied the benefit of those fair opportunities which God hath put into our hands. Consider what I have said, and if by following your advice the West be not reduced, Hopton's army be re-cruited, and Lyme lost, let not the blame be laid upon your lordships' innocent though suspected servant, ESSEX." [4]

Essex would soon have to make up his mind whither he would betake himself. Lyme was still untaken. On May 23

Progress of the siege of Lyme.
Warwick had arrived off the little port with a few ships, in which he had conveyed supplies to the besieged. His presence encouraged them, although he was absolutely powerless against the army of the enemy

---

[1] "Major" in the MS.   [2] Also "Major" in the MS.

[3] 'One' in MS.

[4] Essex to the Com. of B K., June 14. *Com. Letter Book.*

which was lying on the lower slopes of the hills. Behind the
slender line of fortification, over which an active man could
without difficulty leap, the townsmen held sturdily out ; all the
more resolutely as amongst the scanty military garrison was the
Colonel Blake who was afterwards the indomitable Admiral of
the Commonwealth and Protectorate.[1] After every effort to
storm the place had failed, Maurice had recourse to one
desperate expedient. He poured a shower of red-hot iron
upon the town in the hope of lighting up a conflagration
which would render defence impossible. Maurice was, however, disappointed, and the fires which he raised were ex-
tinguished almost as soon as they were kindled. Lyme was
at last delivered by the approach of Essex. At two o'clock in
the early morning of the 15th the Royalist army
drew off. The townsmen, sallying forth on the
following day, gazed with admiration at the solidity
of the works of the besiegers. One characteristic act of cruelty
sullied the whiteness of their triumph. An Irish woman, left
behind by Inchiquin's Munster regiment, 'was slain and pulled
almost to pieces by the women of Lyme.'[2]

June 15.
The siege
abandoned.

The relief of Lyme was quickly followed by the occupation
of Weymouth. Having achieved these two objects,
Essex deliberately resolved to push forward into
the West. "If," he wrote to the Houses, "after all my sad

Weymouth
occupied.

---

[1] The details of Blake's early career given in the usual biographies are
possibly more or less untrustworthy. Professor Laughton, who repeats them
in his article in the *Dict. of National Biography*, acknowledges that they
are founded on a ' mendacious chap-book.' The story, however, as has
been pointed out by a writer in the *Saturday Review*, of Blake's holding
out in a fort outside Bristol after Fiennes had surrendered the place, is
corroborated by Prynne's statement that Fiennes ' left Captain Blake and
Captain Husbands in Brandon Hill and Prior Hill forts behind him.' *A
true and full relation of the . . . trial . . . of N. Fiennes.* E. 255,
16, p. 45. Blake, however, does not appear to have been assaulted, so
that he did not on this occasion display any special heroism.

[2] *A letter from the Earl of Warwick.* E. 51, 9. *A full relation of
the whole siege of Lyme.* E. 51, 15. *Journal of the siege*, Roberts' *Hist.
and Antiquities of Lyme*, 82. Blake was in Lyme, but was not the
governor, as is sometimes stated. See *Roberts*, 89.

consultations, faithful endeavours, and, by God's blessing,
happy success, you shall call me back as one that
is not fit to be trusted any further in a business
of such high concernment, I will come and sit in
Parliament as not knowing any military employment worthy of
my presence in any associated county, which is wholly committed to the care and trust of some inferior commander." [1]

*Essex per-
sists in
going to
the West.*

Essex here appears at his worst.   There are no signs in
any of his letters that his mind embraced the campaign as a
whole.   He had reasons to give, which were at least
worthy of consideration, why, if he could possess
himself of the West, the royal cause would receive a
heavy blow by the loss of the contributions of those regions ;
but he never asked whether, as things stood elsewhere, he was
capable of possessing himself of the West.   It was, in fact, his
own incapacity to act as a commander-in-chief which almost
justified the Houses and their Committee in refusing to treat
him as such.   Their mode of dealing with the difficulty was
indeed as fatal as his own.   Though Essex and Manchester,
Cromwell and Waller, were all members of the Committee of
Both Kingdoms, it was seldom that any of them were able
to take part in its deliberations.   Its acting members were
civilians, and civilians are necessarily incapable of wisely
directing the movements of armies.   Their own instructions to
Essex had been vague and uncertain, and in distrust of the
General they had divided his authority amongst officers
nominally under his command, whilst they did not venture to
remove him from his post, inefficient as he was, because he
had a large following amongst the officers, and because he
was regarded with affection by that numerous body in the two
Houses which hoped against hope that he would one day
declare himself on the side of peace.   On June 25
the Commons gave way before the persistence of the
General, and directed that Essex should be informed
that he was at liberty to pursue his westward march. [2]

*Defects of
Essex as a
commander.*

*June 25.
Essex
ordered to
the West.*

---

[1] Essex to the Houses of Parliament. *L.J.* vi. 602. The letter is not
dated, but was probably written either on the 17th or 18th.

[2] *C.J.* iii. 542.

It was only gradually that the Parliamentary commanders would learn that neither the besieging of towns nor the occupation of territory would end the war so long as the enemy was unbeaten in the field. The Royalist commanders had already

June 13.
Council of
war at
Bewdley.

discerned the truth, and, when once the separation of Essex and Waller was known, the only question agitated amongst them was whether the King should march northwards to assist Rupert in beating Manchester and the Scots, or should carry out his original plan of falling alternately upon Essex and Waller. Local considerations, derived from the positions of the armies, decided Charles in favour of

June 14.
Charles
resolves to
return to
Oxford.

the latter plan, and on June 14 he made up his mind, though personally inclined to despondency, to hurry back to Oxford in order to collect reinforcements which would enable him to fight Waller with advantage.[1]

The Royal army was better horsed than that of Waller, and could easily outmarch its opponents. On June 21 it

June 21.
Charles at
Woodstock.

reached Woodstock, where, after a junction with such troops as could be spared from Oxford, it numbered 5,500 foot and 4,000 horse, the cavalry being more than six times as numerous as was usual in other armies of the time.[2] That evening Charles pushed on for

He reaches
Buckingham.

Buckingham. Waller was toiling heavily after him, and the way seemed open to any enterprise. At a council of war held on the 22nd, some advised that

June 22
A council
of war.

the plan of marching into the North should again be taken up, whilst others recommended an attack on the Eastern Association, which would draw back Manchester's army from the siege of York. A third party talked of a swoop upon undefended London, and for a time this last plan commended itself to Charles's mind. As usual, however, he

Charles
loses time.

had many to consult, and he lost time in sending Digby and Culpepper to Oxford to learn the opinion which prevailed there. When the answer came it was too late

---

[1] Walker's *Hist. Discourses*, 24.

[2] *Ibid.* 28. Symonds (*Diary*, 18) gives the King's numbers as rather greater.

for him to act. Waller was close at his heels, and without fighting it was impossible to shake him off.[1]

Great was the alarm in London when it was known that the King was at Buckingham. Everything possible was done

June 23.
Preparations in London.

to send help to Waller. Major-General Browne, who, as the Royalists were never tired of reminding

Major-General Browne.

him, had formerly been a woodmonger, had for some time been slowly gathering a force which, in conjunction with that of Waller, was intended to conduct that siege of Oxford which Essex had refused to undertake. As a soldier, Browne had done good service in the winter campaign in Hampshire and Sussex, and had contributed largely to the victory of Cheriton. On the 23rd he

A force to march under him.

was ordered to march to protect the country between London and the Royal army. Yet the force under his command was far too scanty to be of much service, and the Committees of Herts, Essex, Suffolk, and Norfolk were urged to send their trained bands to assist him in guarding the threatened districts. In this way it was calculated that Browne would have about 3,000 men under his orders. There was, however, not a single horseman amongst them, and, in those days, it was impossible for infantry to march safely without a convoy of horse over the open country beyond St. Albans. To overcome this difficulty Colonel Norton, who commanded a body of cavalry attached to a Hampshire force, then occupied in besieging Basing House, was instructed to place himself temporarily at Browne's disposal.[2]

All the faults which characterised Waller's army reappeared in a far more glaring manner in that of Browne. His little

Browne's difficulties.

force would be composed of troops derived from six different sources, each distinct body regarding the others with a jealous eye, and each depending for its pay upon a separate local Committee, which might at any time see fit to recall its own men to service nearer home. Nor was the

[1] Walker's *Hist. Discourses*, 29.

[2] *Day Book of the Com. of B. K.*, June 23, 24.   Com. of B. K. to the Com. of Herts, June 23.   *Com. Letter Book.*

military instinct likely to be strong in men immersed in the ordinary avocations of life, and called away to undertake a hard service for which they had neither special aptitude nor special training.

In spite of the risk he was running, Browne set out on his mission. On the 25th he was at Barnet. On the following

June 25.
Browne at
Barnet.

day he reviewed his three London regiments, which numbered in all no more than 500 men. When he reached St. Albans he found the Hertfordshire Committee hard to move. Who, they asked, was to pay their soldiers? In any case, they added, trained bands were not bound to overstep the limits of their county. On the 28th Browne, finding that he could make no impression on the Committee, took the matter into his own hands, and issued warrants ordering the men of Herts and Essex to meet him at Dunstable. In the face of his resolution the Committees of the two counties submitted. In a day or two he found himself at the head of about 4,000 men, a larger number than he had himself expected. The City regiments now amounted to 1,000, and three Essex and two Hertfordshire regiments made up the remainder of the force. From Suffolk and Norfolk not a single man had yet arrived.[1]

It might have gone hard with Browne if the King had been in a condition to attack him. Fortunately for his raw troops, Waller had hurried back to his aid, and Charles had faced about to meet his old antagonist. During the whole of

June 28.
Manœu-
vres of
Waller and
Brentford.

the 28th the King, with Brentford at his side, was manœuvring round Banbury for an opportunity to fight Waller with advantage; but Waller's tried skill availed him here, and on the following morning the

June 29.

Royal army turned off towards Daventry in the hope of enticing Waller to leave the strong position which he had taken up.[2]

As Charles marched northwards on the eastern side of the Cherwell, Waller marched in the same direction on the

---

[1] Browne to the Com. of B. K., June 25, 27, 28; Hazlerigg to the Com. of B. K., July 1. *Com. Letter Book.*

[2] Walker's *Hist. Discourses*, 30.

western. Waller was anxious to fight if he could do it with
advantage to himself. "This day," he had written on the
morning of the 28th, when the two armies first faced one
another at Banbury, " in all likelihood will prove a deciding
day ; the Lord prosper His own cause for His great name's
sake." On the 29th he was full of hope that the time was

Battle of
Cropredy
Bridge. come. Seizing Cropredy Bridge, he watched the
enemy marching past. Suddenly Charles's vanguard
and main force hastened their steps on the news
that a Parliamentary force of 300 horse was in front, and might
be cut off before Waller could come to the rescue. Charles,
however, had omitted to inform his rearguard of his intentions,
and there was soon a considerable space between that part of
his army and the rest. Waller at once seized the opportunity.
Sending Lieutenant-General Middleton, the Scotch officer who,
with Montrose, had forced the Bridge of Dee, across a ford
about a mile lower down the river, he himself pushed over
Cropredy Bridge to cut off the loiterers. For a while everything went well with him, and the King's rearguard was almost
reduced to the necessity of surrender. In the meanwhile,
however, the main body of the Royalists had hastened back to
the relief of their comrades, and a sudden charge made by the
Earl of Cleveland, and supported by Lord Bernard Stewart,
changed the fortune of the day. Middleton was routed, and
ultimately, after a second onslaught, in which Wilmot took
part with Cleveland, Waller's park of artillery was captured.
The Parliamentary General drew back to his own side of the
little river, and though he firmly held the bridge the Royalists
succeeded in crossing at the ford. By this time the bulk of
Waller's army was drawn up on a rising ground above the

Charles
offers to
treat. western side of the valley, and Charles lost hope of
making much impression upon it. With that strange
belief in the readiness of his opponents to accept his
terms, if only he could be allowed to state them in their
hearing, which never left him, he sent a trumpeter to Waller
asking him to receive a message of peace. Waller, like Essex
before Oxford, answered that he had no power to treat.[1]

[1] *Walker*, 31–33. Symonds' *Diary*, 22.

Once more Charles had thrown away a great opportunity by hesitation in the execution of a well-laid plan. Yet so superior was the composition of his army to that of Waller, and so hopelessly were the councils of the Parliamentary Generals in the South divided, that, unless disastrous news arrived from the North, the Royal army could hardly fail to get the upper hand in the regions in which Charles himself was fighting.

CHAPTER XVIII.

MARSTON MOOR.

FOR more than six weeks before the fight at Cropredy Bridge Rupert had been hewing his way through foemen, with the deliverance of York ever in view. Yet when, on May 16, he set out from Shrewsbury, it was not towards York that the tramp of his horsemen was directed. He had to seek recruits for his not too numerous army, and the deliverance of Lathom House, bringing with it the restoration of the authority of the Earl of Derby in Lancashire, was the likeliest means of effecting that object. Nor could the enterprise itself fail to touch the heart of a commander far less chivalrous than Rupert. For three months the Countess had held out, as Lady Blanche Arundel had held out at Wardour Castle, and as Lady Harley had held out at Brampton Bryan. The worthy daughter of the House of La Tremouille had flung defiance at Fairfax fresh from the victory of Nantwich. " Though a woman and a stranger," she replied to his summons, " divorced from my friends and robbed of my estate, I am ready to receive your utmost violence, trusting in God for protection and deliverance." To Rigby, the Puritan lawyer, who succeeded to the command of the besiegers when Fairfax was called away to Yorkshire, she replied in haughtier terms. " Tell that insolent rebel," she answered, after musket and cannon had been doing their worst, " he shall neither have persons, goods, nor house. When our strength and provision is spent, we shall find a fire more merciful than Rigby." Lady Derby was not yet at that extremity. She sent out a party, which seized and carried off in triumph a huge mortar which

marginal notes:

1644.
May 16.
Rupert leaves Shrewsbury.

The siege of Lathom House.

had worked the greatest mischief. The puzzled besiegers drew
back and changed the siege into a blockade. The news that
Rupert was on the way struck them with alarm. Covering

THE CAMPAIGN OF MARSTON MOOR.

their fears with bravado, they once more summoned the
Countess to submit to the mercy of Parliament. As the
messenger was reading the summons the lady broke in with a
correction, telling him that he should have said 'the cruelty of

Parliament.' "No," answered the man, "the mercy of Parliament." "The mercies of the wicked are cruel," said the Countess, with a quiet smile.[1]

Rupert was indeed on the way. On the 25th he seized on Stockport, and delivered the place over to plunder. Avoiding

May 25.
Stockport
plundered.

Manchester, in which was a strong Parliamentary garrison, he made for Bolton, where he fell upon Rigby and the force which had been drawn hastily

May 28.
Bolton
stormed.

off from before Lathom House. On the 28th, with Lord Derby riding by his side, he stormed the town. Sixteen hundred of the enemy were cut down on the spot, and seven hundred carried off as prisoners. The massacre was, as

The stan-
dards sent
to Lathom
House.

usual, followed by a sack of the houses of inoffensive citizens. Rupert at once despatched a messenger to Lathom to present to the Countess of Derby the twenty-two standards which had lately waved over the heads of her besiegers.[2]

Rupert was bent upon greater things than the relief of a single castle. York must be relieved, and the whole balance

Rupert's
designs.

of the war redressed in the North. On June 1 Goring joined him with 5,000 horse and 800 foot,

June 1.
Goring
joins him.

the former including the force which had been dismissed from York when the siege began. Recruits,

Recruits
pour in.

too, came trooping in. Though Lancashire was a stronghold of the Puritans, it was also a stronghold of the Catholics, and Lord Derby's tenants, whatever their religion might be, were eager to take service under the Prince.

June 5.
Rupert at
Wigan.

When Rupert rode into Wigan the streets were strewn 'with rushes, flowers, and boughs.'

The army which Rupert needed for the succour of York was thus at last brought together ; but he had one task to perform before he was ready to set out on his main enterprise. Liverpool was held by a Parliamentary garrison, and Liverpool was the gate through which Irish reinforcements

---

[1] *A Journal of the siege of Lathom House.*

[2] "The goods of the town were the soldiers' reward." Proceedings of the army. *Carte MSS.* x. fol. 664. *A Journal of the siege of Lathom House.*

could reach Lancashire. On the 7th Rupert turned upon the

June 7.
Rupert
attacks
Liverpool. little port. Its mud walls were stoutly manned, and on the 10th the assailants were repulsed. Yet a long resistance was felt to be hopeless, and at midnight the greater part of the garrison took ship and sailed away. About 400 men were left behind, and most of these were butchered by the Royalists when they entered on the

June 11.
The place
taken. following morning. The town was, as usual, plundered. "Whatever," says the brief journal of the expedition, " was desiderable was the soldiers' right for their hard service." [1]

Rupert's track had been marked more than was customary in that sad war by blood and desolation. No wonder alarm was felt both at Westminster and in the leaguer before York

June 3.
Vane sent
to York. at his conquering progress. On June 3 the Committee of Both Kingdoms despatched Vane to urge the Generals of the armies before York to send Manchester and Fairfax into Lancashire to nip the mischief in the bud.[2] The Generals, however, would not hear of the proposal. They were ready, they said, to throw out cavalry to guard the approaches to York, but they refused to abandon

The siege
of York to
be pursued. the siege. If Rupert appeared in the neighbourhood of York whilst the city was still untaken, they would leave their works to give him battle. "Wherein," they added, " if it please God to give us victory, all Lancashire and Yorkshire will fall to us." [3] Nothing that could be urged had the slightest effect in shaking this resolu-

June 10.
The Gene-
rals persist
in their
resolution. tion. On the 10th, when rumours had reached York that the King himself was on his way to the North, a long consultation was held; but the Generals persisted in their refusal to raise the siege, and Vane himself was convinced that the Generals were in the right.[4]

---

[1] Proceedings of the army. *Carte MSS.* x. fol. 664. Meldrum to Lord Fairfax, May 28. *S. P. Dom.* di. 144.

[2] Vane's instructions. *Com. Day Book.* Com. of B. K. to Manchester, June 3. *Com. Letter Book.*

[3] Leven, Fairfax, and Manchester to the Com. of B. K., June 5. *Com. Letter Book.*

[4] Vane to the Com. of B. K., June 11. *Com. Letter Book.*

That Vane should have been sent in person on a mission which would have been better entrusted to a soldier raises a suspicion that more was intended than meets the eye. In truth, Vane came from London to York, not to instruct Leven, Fairfax, and Manchester how to carry on war, but to urge them to make some provision for the government of England which would exclude Charles from all authority. Vane and his immediate followers had come to the conclusion that no settlement satisfactory to the Puritans was attainable with Charles on the throne. The attempt made by them in March to procure a recognition of this doctrine had failed through the resistance of the Scottish Commissioners,[1] and that resistance was still stubborn. Vane, however, appears to have imagined that an idea which had shocked politicians might be accepted by practical soldiers. In this, however, he was bitterly disappointed. Not one of the three Generals would listen to so startling a proposal as the actual or virtual deposition of the King. In this resolution Leven and the Scots seem to have taken the lead, whilst, though no actual evidence exists on the subject, it is in the highest degree probable that Cromwell was won over to Vane's side, and that his quarrel with the Scots and with Manchester, as the supporter of the Scots, dates from these discussions outside the walls of York.[2]

Vane's secret mission.

Proposed deposition of Charles.

It is rejected by the three Generals.

---

[1] See p. 328.

[2] Agostini in his despatch of June $\frac{7}{17}$ (*Ven. Transcripts, R.O.*) says that the true end of his mission was 'di persuader i Capi di quell' armata ad accordare la depositione del Re, sperando come si desidera e spera da una gran parte d'Inglesi, resti prigionere, o esca dal Regno, à che si mostrano renitenti questi Deputati Scocesi, che sono nel Consiglio, escusandosi non esservi espresso punto così importante et ardito nelle loro commissioni.' On $\frac{June\ 21}{July\ 1}$ Agostini further states that Vane, finding opposition in the camp before York, had gone on in the greatest secrecy to Scotland to get a more favourable answer. On $\frac{Aug.29}{Sept.\ 8}$ Sabran, the new French Resident (*R.O. Transcripts*) writes that Holland had called on him two days before, and had told him : 'Que le S^r. Vanne, le fils, lequel fut envoyé vers les Generaux d'armée du Nord, Anglois et Escossois pour sçavoir leur intention et advis pour une solide paix, voyant que tous les Generaulx inclinoient

The controversy as to the possibility of making peace with Charles which had long been smouldering in Parliament had Nature of thus been transferred to the camp. All subsequent the dispute. experience, indeed, went to show that Vane and Cromwell were in the right in coming to the conclusion that it was impossible to expect any reasonable security for the maintenance of Puritanism if Charles were re-established on the throne. Yet the very horror with which men of ordinary capacity, like Manchester and the elder Fairfax, regarded any meddling with the occupancy of the throne might have served as a warning of the enormous difficulties in the way of those who should attempt permanently to settle the government on a

à porter le Roy de la Grande Bretagne par leurs soumissions à traitter, et avec des conditions néantmoins qui assurassent la liberté et les priviléges, il fust si hardy que de dire que le Parlement et le peuple ne pouvait trouver sureté avec sa Majesté Britannique, ny les siens, que les choses estoient passées trop avant, et qu'il falloit s'attirer toute la puissance pour plus de seureté et changer la forme du gouvernement, que c'estoit le desir du peuple. Sur quoy les trois Generaux, Manchester, Fairfax—i.e. 'Lord Fairfax'—et Lesler, se levèrent et dirent que jamais ils ne consentiront à cela, ny se laissoient porter à cette pensée, qu'il falloit un Roy, et s'il estoit possible, se remettre avec cestuy-cy avec bonnes conditions et seuretez, que l'on a bien connu que le sentiment dudit Vannes, le fils, estoit celuy de ceux qui veulent renverser l'Estat, lesquels se sentans criminels, veulent s'appuyer du peuple, mais qu'ayant esté descouvert, tous les grands et les principaux de la seconde Chambre y repugnent autant qu'ils peuvent, et portent insensiblement ceulx mesmes qui sont de ce sentiment de n'en estre plus, mais qu'ils n'ont osé resister aux articles concertez, encores que si contraires à la Royauté, de peur d'estre soupçonnez.'

Towards the end Sabran appears to slip off from what the Generals were reported to have said to what Holland said. The earlier part, however, coincides fairly with Agostini's statement. The evidence is in itself not conclusive, as it may have been derived from one of those circumstantial stories which usually float about when party feeling runs high. What is strongly in favour of its substantial truth is that it fits in admirably with all else that is known. It explains the tone of Cromwell's letter written to Walton after Marston Moor, as well as his dislike of the Scots, which now becomes noticeable. It explains, too, how it was that Manchester, who for some time was under Cromwell's influence, came to pass under that of Crawford. That Vane proposed to transfer the crown to the Prince of Wales is said in a letter from Sabran to Mazarin. *Arch. des Aff. Étr.* li. fol. 106.

revolutionary basis. The England of that day could neither be governed by Charles I. nor without a king, and the dread which was entertained of any attempt to dispense with Charles was in reality the expression of a widely felt belief that security for property and life would disappear with the overthrow of the throne. Vane and Cromwell were right in their judgment of Charles, but Manchester and Fairfax had a firmer hold on the possibilities of that future which would arise as soon as Charles was in his coffin.

For the present, however, the business of the Generals was to take York ; not to settle how England was to be governed.

June 13.
Newcastle
offers to
treat.
On the 13th Newcastle offered to treat for the surrender of the city. His demand for permission to march out with bag and baggage, and for security that the clergy should be allowed to carry on ' the altar service ' in the cathedral, having been promptly rejected, the besiegers were further encouraged by the capture of messengers sent out to inform Rupert that York could only hold out for six days longer.[1]

It was the object of the Parliamentary commanders to enter York, if possible, before the six days elapsed. For some time a mine had been in progress which was expected to effect a practicable breach. Its explosion had been entrusted to Crawford, the Scottish Major-General of Manchester's army, who, three months before, had come into collision with Cromwell. Anxious in his vanity to secure the credit of the capture of the city, Crawford fired the mine on the 17th without giving notice either to Leven or Fairfax. Manchester's troops, having been warned, gallantly rushed at the breach, but they were promptly overpowered and driven out, in consequence of the enforced failure of the other two commanders to second them by assaults on the sides of the fortifications opposite to their respective quarters.

June 17.
Failure of
a mine.

A delay of some days was thus secured by the garrison. Rupert might surely be expected to hasten to its succour ; and if he had needed a spur, he would have found it in a letter

[1] *The Kingdom's Weekly Intelligencer.* E. 51, 10.

written to him by his uncle before that march from Bewdley
June 14. to Oxford which led to the fight at Cropredy Bridge.
The King's "Now," wrote Charles, "I must give you the true
letter to
Rupert. state of my affairs, which, if their condition be such
as enforces me to give you more peremptory commands
than I would willingly do, you must not take it ill. If
York be lost I shall esteem my crown little less, unless supported
by your sudden march to me, and a miraculous conquest in
the South, before the effects of the Northern power can be
found here ; but if York be relieved, and you beat the rebels'
armies of both kingdoms which were before it, then, but other
ways not, I may possibly make a shift upon the defensive to
spin out time until you come to assist me ; wherefore I command and conjure you, by the duty and affection which I know
you bear me, that, all new enterprises laid aside, you immediately
march according to your first intention, with all your force, to
the relief of York ; but if that be either lost or have freed
themselves from the besiegers, or that for want of powder you
cannot undertake that work, that you immediately march with
your whole strength directly to Worcester, to assist me and my
army, without which, or your having relieved York by beating
the Scots, all the successes you can afterwards have most in-
fallibly will be useless to me." [1]

Whatever may have been the precise meaning of these
painfully involved sentences, there could be no doubt what
Rupert in- interpretation would be put upon them by Rupert.
terprets it "Before God," said Culpepper to Charles when
as a com-
mand to he heard that the letter had been sent, "you are
fight. undone, for upon this peremptory order he will
fight whatever comes on't." [2]

Since the failure of the mine the besiegers of York had
been looking anxiously for Rupert's coming. The six days
York holds which Newcastle declared to be the utmost duration
out. of his resistance passed away, and there were no
signs of surrender. At last the three Generals learnt that

[1] The King to Rupert, June 14. Forster's *British Statesmen*, vi.
129.
[2] *Warburton*, ii. 438.

Rupert had completed his preparations and was actually on
the move. On the 28th tidings arrived that he had
crossed the range of hills which divides Yorkshire
from Lancashire. On the 30th it was known that
he had reached Knaresborough,[1] and was therefore about
twelve miles from York. The Generals had already summoned
Denbigh and Meldrum to their aid, but neither Denbigh nor
Meldrum would be at Wakefield before July 3, and unless
reinforcements arrived it would be ruinous to be caught between
Rupert's army and Newcastle's garrison, as Meldrum had been
caught in March at Newark, and as Waller in the preceding
summer had been caught at Devizes. On the
morning of July 1, therefore, the whole besieging
force marched off towards Marston Moor, on the
road to Knaresborough, hoping to bar the way to York. Its
leaders had learnt the lesson that it was useless to besiege a
fortified town with an enemy unbeaten in the field.[2]

*June 28.
The coming
of Rupert.*

*July 1.
The siege
broken up.*

The tactics of the Parliamentary Generals were simple—
too simple to baulk Rupert of his design. Sweeping round to
the left by Boroughbridge, and crossing the Swale
at Thornton Bridge, he wheeled sharply to the right,
and, driving off a guard placed by Manchester over the
bridge of boats which had been thrown over the Ouse at the
commencement of the siege, crossed that river into a place of
safety. Halting for the night outside York, on its northern
side, he sent orders to Newcastle to come out and meet him
on the following morning.

*Rupert's
manœuvres.*

While Newcastle was pondering over this message the
Parliamentary Generals were holding serious debate on Marston Moor. York was lost, and the
turn of the Eastern Association would come next.
To defend those trusty counties the army fell back
on the morning of the 2nd in the direction of Tadcaster

*Resolution
of the Par-
liamentary
comman-
ders.*

---

[1] There is not a single hint of any fighting here, a fact that should
be borne in mind by those who maintain the authenticity of the *Squire
Papers.*

[2] Stockdale to Rushworth, July 5, in D'Ewes's Diary. *Harl. MSS.*
166, fol. 87b.

and Cawood.[1] The infantry had almost reached Tadcaster

July 2.
The retreat
to Tadcas-
caster.
when a message arrived from Fairfax, who, with David Leslie and Cromwell, was still guarding with horse the long ridge which slopes down to Marston Moor, to tell them that Rupert's cavalry was gathering in front of them, and that a conflict was imminent. If Rupert meant to fight and not to manœuvre, there was no reason why he should not

The return
to Marston
Moor.
be gratified. The Parliamentary infantry was hurried back, and by two in the afternoon had established itself amidst the rye which waved on the summit of the ridge. Some attempt was made by a party of Royalists, probably under Lord Byron,[2] to win ground on the extreme left of the Parliamentary ground at Tockwith, but the attempt was repulsed and the assailants driven back upon the moor.[3]

The Royalists, on their part, had been slow to gather to the field. Rupert was burning for the fight, but Newcastle, always unadventurous, and vexed at Rupert's appointment to be his

---

[1] Stockdale to Rushworth, July 5, in D'Ewes's Diary. *Harl. MSS.* 166, fol. 87b. Slingsby's *Diary*, 112.

[2] Byron is said in the so-called Rupert's Diary to have begun the actual battle. As this is not countenanced by any other authority, it is not unlikely that he really took part in this preliminary skirmish. The account given in the text receives further corroboration from ' News sent from Mr. Ogden,' copied for me by General Wrottesley from Lord Wrottesley's MSS. after my narrative had been printed. "They," the Parliamentarians, writes Ogden, " set on the Prince towards night, when they were least looked for."

[3] *A full relation.* E. 54, 19. This is always quoted as Captain Stewart's, simply because his name occurs in large letters on the title-page as that of the officer who brought the trophies of the battle to Westminster. The author was, I think, Lord Eglinton, and I shall quote the pamphlet as his. Baillie, in writing to Eglinton (ii. 210) says : " After Captain Stewart came up, and also your Lordship's large letter to Sir John Seaton, I was much comforted." At p. 209 he speaks of the coming of Lindsay's letters. " Then," he adds, " we sent abroad our printed relations, and could lift up our face." The printed letter can hardly be Lindsay's, as he would not speak of his own bravery in such complimentary terms as those employed in it, and it appears to be written by someone on the left part of the right wing. Eglinton answers to this description, as he was in command of the only cavalry regiment attached to Fairfax's army which kept its ground.

superior officer, was by no means so ardent.   His men, too,
had broken into mutiny, crying aloud for pay.   When the two

Meeting of
Rupert and
Newcastle. Generals met, Rupert was already on the march.
"My Lord," said the Prince, as soon as the first
compliments had been exchanged, "I hope we shall
have a glorious day."   Newcastle replied that it would be
better not to fight at all.   The enemies' commanders were on
bad terms with one another, and their army would break up
before long.   Reinforcements under Clavering were already
on their way from the North.   It may be that Newcastle was
wounded by Rupert's abrupt manner, but there was nothing in
the military antecedents of the courtly Marquis to lead Rupert
to treat him with respect.   He had frittered away great opportunities before, and he seemed bent on frittering them away
again.   The fiery young Prince cut him short by announcing
that he had a letter from the King 'with a positive and absolute command to fight the enemy.'   Before this announcement Newcastle withdrew all objections.   "Happen what
will," he said to his friends, who told him it was unworthy of
him to be commanded by Rupert, "I will not shun to fight,
for I have no other ambition but to live and die a loyal subject
to his Majesty."[1]

No doubt the King's letter was not so plain of interpretation as Rupert asserted, but it does not follow that Rupert
was obviously in the wrong in calling for a battle.   He had
never yet met the horsemen whom he had not scattered, and,
as the events of that evening were to prove, if he had personally
been as successful on Marston Moor as he had been on every
field stricken since the war began, the victory would have been
won along the whole line, and there can be no serious doubt
that that victory would have given to Charles once more an
undisputed throne.   As for Newcastle's projected war of
manœuvre, it was at least as likely to turn against him as in his
favour.

All through the summer afternoon, with rain-showers

---

[1] *Lives of the Duke and Duchess of Newcastle*, by the Duchess (ed.
Firth), 76.   Compare *Clarendon MSS.* 1,805.   Rupert evidently never
entered York.   See Slingsby's *Diary*, 112.

falling heavily at times, the two armies faced one another ; the Parliamentary soldiers on the summit or slope of the long hill

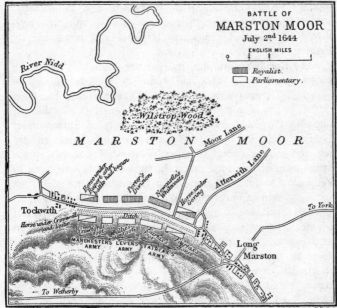

BATTLE OF
MARSTON MOOR
July 2nd 1644

ENGLISH MILES

▨ *Royalist.*
▢ *Parliamentary.*

F. S. Weller, F.R.G.S.

considerably outnumbering their opponents,[1] and being dis-
Arrangement of the Parliamentary army. tinguished by white handkerchiefs or white pieces of paper in their caps. Baillie, who was, under Leven, at the head of the Scottish infantry, held the centre of the line. On his right were the Fairfaxes, Sir Thomas commanding, under his father, his own horse on the extreme right, a reserve of Scottish cavalry being posted behind

[1] "The enemy's number was far above the Prince's, having in the front 1,200 more than he." News sent from Mr. Ogden, *Wrottesley MSS.* This is in accordance with other statements. Colonel Ross in reviewing the first edition of this work in the *Hist. Rev.* for April 1890, calculated the numbers as 17,000 or 18,000 for the Royalist army, and 26,000 or 27,000 for the Parliamentarian.

his own regiments, whilst there was also a reserve of Scottish infantry behind those led by Lord Fairfax in person. On the left was Manchester's army of the Eastern Association, the infantry being commanded by Crawford, and the cavalry, supported by some Scottish dragoons and by three regiments of Scottish horse under David Leslie, being led by Cromwell.[1]

The Royalist centre was under the command of Eythin, the professional soldier who had come to England from the German wars as General King, and who had long been the military adviser of Newcastle. On the left, opposite the Fairfaxes, was a strong body of horse, under Goring, whilst Rupert himself sent his own and other cavalry regiments to the right. Whether he intended to take his place at the head of this force when the time of battle arrived, or to keep aloof to fulfil the duties of a Commander-in-Chief must remain uncertain. With a soldier's instinct Rupert had singled out Cromwell as the one soldier worthy of his steel. " Is Cromwell there ? " he is reported to have asked of a prisoner. " And will they fight ? " continued Rupert as soon as he was informed of his presence. " If they will, they shall have fighting enough." Rupert bade the prisoner return to his own people to bear this message. " If it please God," was Cromwell's answer when he heard it, " so shall he." [2]

The Royalist army.

Rupert and Cromwell.

It was weary waiting amidst the rye, but Leven did not judge it prudent to attack. A long ditch ran along the edge where the moor skirted the hill, and that ditch was occupied by Rupert's musketeers. About four in the afternoon Eythin brought up some 3,000 of Newcastle's foot. The cautious veteran was struck with surprise at the rashness of the Prince. The Royalist line was drawn up close to the enemy, with only the long ditch between, which neither side had as yet ventured to cross, but which was unlikely to prove an insuperable obstacle to a dashing commander. Rupert, heedless of the fault which he had committed, gaily

Altercation between Rupert and Eythin.

---

[1] Fairfax's *Short memorial* ; Ash's *Intelligence.* E. 2, 1.

[2] *The Parliament Scout,* 5, 20.

asked Eythin how he liked the marshalling of his army, pointing to a paper on which he had sketched the position of the
troops. " By God, sir," answered Eythin, " it is very fine in
the paper, but there is no such thing in the field ! " Rupert, so
far as can be gathered from the fragmentary information which
has reached us, contemplated an attack upon the enemy as
soon as Eythin arrived. The old soldier would not hear of
beginning a battle so late in the day, and found fault with
Rupert for placing his men so near the enemy. "They may
be drawn," said Rupert, with unwonted meekness, "to a further
distance." " No, sir," replied Eythin, " it is too late." Risky
as his position was, Rupert did not seem to understand his
danger. " We will charge them," he said to Newcastle, " to-
morrow morning ! " It was now between six and seven, and
Rupert, calling for provisions, dismounted and began to eat his
supper at some little distance in the rear. A large number of
his followers did the like. Newcastle strolled towards his
coach to solace himself with a pipe. Before he had time to
take a whiff the battle had begun.[1]

It may well be that the Parliamentarians on the hill marked
these signs of unpreparedness. In an instant horse and foot
Beginning of dashed forward, the horsemen of the Eastern Asso-
the battle. ciation leading the way over the ditch.[2] Rupert
had neither the advantage of being the first to charge nor
a defensible position to fall back upon. In a moment he
had recovered his vigour so far as recovery was possible and
flew at Cromwell's horse. His first regiment was beaten and

[1] Account of the movements of the Northern armies. *Clar. MSS.*
1,805. Memorials touching the battle of York. *Id.* 1,764. The conversation given above is a combination from the two sources. I have
adopted the view that Rupert had been originally for fighting at once, and
that he was dissuaded by Eythin, not only because the narrative from
which I gather it is the more explicit of the two, but because it is in con-
sonance with Rupert's character and position. Rupert would have been a
madman to draw up at the edge of the ditch if he did not mean to fight,
but it was only too like his carelessness that, when he was once there, he
should omit to take precautions against surprise.

[2] For the story of the battle having been begun by Byron, see p. 373,
Note 2.

driven back, but the charge was well supported. Cromwell was slightly wounded in the neck, and for an instant his whole force recoiled.[1] The reserves under David Leslie hastened up and loosened Rupert's hold. Cromwell and Leslie forced their way steadily onwards, pushing Rupert's hitherto unconquered cavalry before them, and at last scattering them 'like a little dust.'

Shock of
Rupert and
Cromwell.

In the centre the Parliamentarians were hardly less successful. In front of Crawford, who, as Major-General, commanded Manchester's foot, the ditch had been filled up, and the Royalists opposed to him had drawn aside towards their own left to avoid the unsheltered position. There was therefore a gap between the right of their foot and the left of Rupert's horse. Into this gap Crawford dashed, and then, wheeling sharply round, threw himself on the flank of the Royalist infantry. Its hold upon the ditch was loosened, and Baillie with his Scots poured over it to attack them in front. Yet, pushed back as the main Royalist battle was, it did not break into flight as Rupert had fled before Cromwell, and under a dark pall of smoke, lighted up where the guns flashed and roared, the wild work of slaughter had bestrewed the moor with the dying and the dead.[2]

Partial
success of
Crawford
and Baillie.

Whilst the Scottish foot were struggling thus manfully, a great disaster had happened on the Parliamentary right, where

---

[1] Cromwell's Scoutmaster Watson says nothing of this check. Ash is equally reticent ; Stockdale, however, puts it plainly (D'Ewes's Diary, *Harl. MSS.* 166, 87b). ' The Earl of Manchester's horse in the left hand battle first routing one regiment or body of horse of the enemy's . . . yet after a little time the Earl of Manchester's horse were repulsed by fresh supplies of the enemy's, and forced to retreat in some disorder.' This comes from an English source. Leslie's flank charge is mentioned by Eglinton (E. 54, 19). Putting these together we can account for the ridiculous story told by Crawford of Skeldon to Baillie, that Cromwell retired, ' so that he was not so much as present at the service, but his troopers were led on by David Leslie.' Hepburn of Humbie, too, says that Rupert's charge so humbled Cromwell's men, ' that if David Leslie had not supported them they had fled.' On Cromwell's wound, see Bowles's *Manifest Truths*, E. 341, 1, p. 30. There was probably a slight check resulting from Cromwell's being momentarily incapacitated.

[2] Eglinton's *Full relation.* E. 54, 19.

the Yorkshire men were fighting under the two Fairfaxes.

Fairfax
defeated.

On that side the moor was covered with furze, and the enemy was only to be reached by way of a narrow lane, which ran at right angles with the positions of the two armies. The passage was the more difficult as a ditch ran on one side of the lane and a hedge on the other, and both hedge and ditch were already lined by the musketeers of the Royalist army. In that part of the field, too, fought New castle's Whitecoats, the chosen regiment which had been raised on the edge of the Northern moors, and which had clothed itself in a uniform of undyed cloth, vowing to dye it red in the blood of the enemy.[1]

Whilst Lord Fairfax was struggling with difficulty through the lane, his son, picking his way as well as he could farther to the right amongst the furze, charged Goring's horse. Sir Thomas, indeed, with his immediate followers, broke through, but the main body of his cavalry was utterly routed. Dashing back upon the Yorkshire infantry on their flank, the frightened horsemen trod them down or scattered them irretrievably. One Scottish regiment of horse under Lord Eglinton alone maintained its steadiness, whilst the Scottish foot, placed in reserve behind Lord Fairfax, shared in the general ruin. The hillside and the roads which led to Tadcaster were choked by the flying rout. The sabres of Goring's horse had full work among the fugitives, till the victors wheeled round to betake themselves, not to the attack of the enemy's regiments which remained unbroken, but to the tempting plunder of the baggage. As the runaways swept past Tadcaster in panting confusion, exultant Royalists sped on the news of victory, and bells rang and bonfires blazed at Oxford and wherever Charles's name was held in honour.[2]

On the field it seemed as if the news so prematurely

Resistance
of the
Scottish
infantry.

believed would be justified by the event. Not all of Goring's cavalry had followed him in the charge and in the pursuit, and enough remained behind, under Sir Charles Lucas, to join their comrades on foot in

[1] *Lives of the Duke and Duchess of Newcastle* (ed. Firth), 157.
[2] Eglinton's *Full relation.* E. 54, 19. Fairfax's *Short memorial.*

pressing hard upon the Scottish infantry in the centre. Taken in front and flank, the hardy Scots were exposed to a trial the most severe which on that day befell any part of the Parliamentary army. Twice they repelled attack, but each time their ranks were thinned. Whole regiments broke and fled. Old Leven toiled in vain to restore order. "Although," he cried out to the fugitives, "you run from your enemies, yet leave not your General." It was all to no purpose, and at last the veteran, believing that all was lost, set spurs to his horse, galloping for dear life's sake to Wetherby, and through Wetherby, as some reports averred, even to Leeds. Yet, though Leven fled, his subordinate, Baillie, kept the field. Under him fought the regiment of Lord Lindsay, and that which bore the name of Lord Maitland, but which was under the command of Lieutenant-Colonel Pitscottie, whilst a third in reserve under Lumsdaine moved up in support and maintained the unequal fight. A third attack was repulsed, and some ground was even gained. Yet so desperate a struggle could not last much longer. Unless help came the three heroic regiments which maintained the honour of the Scottish name would be swept away.[1]

The needed help was already at hand. The younger Fairfax, staggering from the effect of a wound on his face, had flung away the white handkerchief which would expose him to death

[1] Eglinton passes over the flight of the greater part of the Scottish foot. After describing how his countrymen repulsed two attacks, he says that 'Lieutenant-General Baillie and General Major Lumsdaine . . . perceiving the greatest weight of the battle to lie sore upon the Earl of Lindsay's and Lord Maitland's regiment, sent up a reserve for their assistance, after which the enemies' horse, having made a third assault upon them, had almost put them to some disorder, but that the Earl of Lindsay and Lieutenant-Colonel Pitscottie . . . behaved themselves so gallantly, that they quickly made the enemies' horse to retreat, killed Sir Charles Lucas's horse, took him prisoner, and gained ground upon the foot.' Afterwards we are told that Cromwell and David Leslie came up ' and met with the enemies' horse, being retreated upon the repulse they had from the Scottish foot.' For Leven's flight, however, we are not dependent merely on English authorities. Spalding (ii. 383) tells us of it, and adds that ' none of our Scottish army bade except three regiments, one under the Earl of Lindsay, another under Sir David Leslie, and the third under Colonel Lumsdaine, who fought it out stoutly.

or capture from the stragglers in the rear of the Royalist army, and groped his way behind the fight to the spot where Cromwell was already halting his victorious horsemen, and peering through the smoke to discern, if possible, how the battle was going elsewhere. As at Gainsborough, Cromwell had kept his men well in hand ; and Crawford, too, had preserved unbroken the ranks of the infantry of the Eastern Association. Learning the tale of misfortune from the lips of Fairfax, he took his measures promptly. Sending a party to follow up Rupert's flying squadrons, and leaving David Leslie to deal with the Whitecoats, whilst Crawford supported Baillie, he betook himself to the lane's end through which Fairfax had emerged. Fronting south-

Defeat of
Goring by
Cromwell. wards, as Goring's horse had fronted at the beginning of the battle, he caught the disordered Royalist cavalry on their way back from pursuit and plunder. The disadvantage of the ground, the narrow way through the lane, the furze bushes on either side, told heavily against the confused mass of horsemen, and Goring's Cavaliers were hurled back into hopeless ruin by the serried ranks of the Puritan troopers.

In the centre David Leslie had flown at the Whitecoats. That faithful band retreated into an enclosure, resolved, like

Destruction
of the
Whitecoats. the King's Red Regiment at Edgehill, to die where they stood. They had their wish. Scarcely one of their number left the field alive. On the other side, Baillie and Crawford advanced steadily against the remainder of the Royalist infantry, and when Cromwell and David Leslie, having accomplished each his own immediate task, came up to aid, all resistance was at an end.[1]

---

[1] Ash's *Intelligence.* E. 2, 1. Watson's *Relation.* E 2, 14. Eglinton's *Full relation.* E. 54, 19. Stockdale to Rushworth in D'Ewes's Diary. *Harl. MSS.* 166, fol. 87b. The story told to Holles (*Memoirs,* 15) by Crawford about Cromwell's supposed cowardice clearly refers to the interval between the defeat of Rupert and the attack on Goring. Crawford was too busy in attacking the Royalist foot at the beginning of the battle to be with Cromwell at the time of the first charge. Besides, he dates his accusation as relating to a time ' when the whole army at Marston Moor was in a fair possibility to be utterly routed, and a great part of it running.' It is quite possible that the story had some sort of foundation. When Cromwell faced round he may well have halted for a time to see what

The Parliamentary victory was complete. Four thousand Royalists had been slain. Colours enough, as a contemporary
A complete victory. publication expressed it, 'to make surplices for all the cathedrals in England, were they white,'[1] had fallen into the hands of the victors. What was more to the purpose, the great force to which they had been opposed had ceased to exist as an army. The mutual jealousies of the Royalist commanders were inflamed too highly to bear the strain of defeat. Rupert threw the blame on the sluggishness of Newcastle, and Newcastle threw the blame on the rashness of Rupert. The courtly Marquis, who was more at home in a riding-school
July 3. Newcastle's flight. than on a field of battle, had yet borne himself bravely in the fight. When the fight was over he thought more of himself than of his master's cause. Abandoning all hope, like a fair-weather warrior as he was, on the day after the battle he rode off to Scarborough, to ship himself for a secure retreat on the Continent. With him were Eythin and a crowd of dissatisfied officers, who thought it no shame to desert their King. "I will not endure the laughter of the Court," was the only explanation of his misconduct which Newcastle chose to give.[2]

Rupert was made of sterner stuff. Collecting about 6,000 horse who still remained together, he rode out of the gates of
Rupert leaves York. York, not to fly, but to retrieve, if it were yet possible, the great disaster. With no relieving army in
July 16. Surrender of York. the field York was plainly untenable, and on July 16 the garrison left in it, under Sir Thomas Glenham, surrendered to the conquerors of Marston Moor.[3] A few isolated fortresses would still have to be besieged and captured, but the defeat of Rupert virtually placed the whole of the North at the mercy of the Parliamentary Generals.

was going on amidst the smoke, and Crawford might choose to fancy that his inaction proceeded from cowardice.

[1] *A true relation.* E. 54, 7.

[2] *Lives of the Duke and Duchess of Newcastle* (ed. Firth), 78. Extract from the so-called diary of Rupert. *Warburton*, ii. 468.

[3] *Rushw.* iv. 640.

Spottiswoode & Co. Ltd., Printers, Colchester, London and Eton.